NEW EMERGING ECONOMIES AND THEIR CULTURE

NEW EMERGING ECONOMIES AND THEIR CULTURE

JANEZ PRAŠNIKAR
AND
ANDREJA CIRMAN
EDITORS

Nova Science Publishers, Inc.
New York

For permission to use material from this book please contact us:
Telephone 631-231-7269; Fax 631-231-8175
Web Site: http://www.novapublishers.com

NOTICE TO THE READER

The Publisher has taken reasonable care in the preparation of this book, but makes no expressed or implied warranty of any kind and assumes no responsibility for any errors or omissions. No liability is assumed for incidental or consequential damages in connection with or arising out of information contained in this book. The Publisher shall not be liable for any special, consequential, or exemplary damages resulting, in whole or in part, from the readers' use of, or reliance upon, this material.

Independent verification should be sought for any data, advice or recommendations contained in this book. In addition, no responsibility is assumed by the publisher for any injury and/or damage to persons or property arising from any methods, products, instructions, ideas or otherwise contained in this publication.

This publication is designed to provide accurate and authoritative information with regard to the subject matter covered herein. It is sold with the clear understanding that the Publisher is not engaged in rendering legal or any other professional services. If legal or any other expert assistance is required, the services of a competent person should be sought. FROM A DECLARATION OF PARTICIPANTS JOINTLY ADOPTED BY A COMMITTEE OF THE AMERICAN BAR ASSOCIATION AND A COMMITTEE OF PUBLISHERS.

LIBRARY OF CONGRESS CATALOGING-IN-PUBLICATION DATA
New emerging economies and their culture / Janez Prasnikar and Andreja Cirman (editors).
   p. cm.
Includes index.
ISBN-13: 978-1-60021-754-8 (hardcover)
ISBN-10: 1-60021-754-0 (hardcover)
1. International business enterprises--Developing countries. 2. Globalization--Economic aspects--Developing countries. 3. Corporations--Developing countries. 4. Corporate culture--Cross-cultural studies. 5. Developing countries--Foreign economic relations. I. Prašnikar, Janez. II. Cirman, Andreja.
HD2932.N49   2007
338.8'881724--dc22   2007017810

Published by Nova Science Publishers, Inc. ✦ New York

CONTENTS

PREFACE

With globalization our world has become smaller and geographical distances much less important. Economic integration and interdependences among countries are increasing. Competition between businesses substitutes for competition between supply chains, which tend to be increasingly global. Focusing on core businesses, elimination of non-core activities and various partnerships are basic mechanisms for increasing allocative efficiency and cost efficiency of business. Managing risk in the supply chain is the crucial factor of its success.

The process of globalization poses many challenges to the contemporary business world. Although the process has its roots in the economics sphere, globalization also has important political effects. At the same time, growing global networks have raised the issue of the role of cultural diversity. Where in this new world order is there a place for the societies regarded as "peripheral" in the recent past? Would China, Russia and Turkey, because of their size, growth dynamics, geopolitical position, specialized competences and disposal of limited resources, change the present globalization processes? What is the position of small countries in South-Eastern Europe? Could cultural entropy be a reason that globalization processes diverge from outlined directions?

The aforementioned questions are addressed in the book *New Emerging Economies and Their Culture*, edited by Janez Prašnikar and Andreja Cirman. The book is divided into six parts. The introductory paper outlines basic features of the globalization process and presents challenges for the business world. The first part of the book deals with some globalization dilemmas. The authors discuss the impact of globalization on emerging business models, balance in global society, and the problem of international security. The role of culture as a potentially integrating or disintegrating force in globalization processes and the framework for studying culture in business models is described in the second part of the book. Presented methodologies for measuring national and organizational culture are used to assess Slovenian national culture, to compare cultural profiles of young managers from emerging economies of South-Eastern Europe and Russia, and to illustrate the link between the organizational culture and managerial control in three international acquisition cases. The next four parts of the book are dedicated to specific emerging economies: Turkey, South-Eastern Europe, Russia, and China. Each part gives a macroeconomic and political outline of the economy as well as the cultural characteristics, underlined by the implications on specific case studies of Slovenian companies facing cultural and organizational diversity of the discussed economy.

Globalization has changed the political and economic picture of the contemporary wrold. This book addresses the questions of globalization, international trade, microeconomics and new business models and comparative economic systems. The author discusses the integration of cultural and strategic fit in the development of competitive advantages of firms. The role of corporative and national culture on the efficiency of international companies is analyzed. A special contribution of the book is that it offers tools for the research of the international alliances with the companies in most important developing countries.

Janez Prašnikar and Andreja Cirman

ACKNOWLEDGEMENTS

This is our third consecutive book published by Nova Science Publishers, Inc., giving further proof of the publisher's trust in our work. We would like to thank them for their trust. Most of the articles in the book have come to being within the Research Center of the Faculty of Economics, University of Ljubljana, and its Institute for South-Eastern Europe. The majority of papers were presented at the seventh Portorož Business Conference, which took place in November 2005. This annual conference, organized jointly by the Faculty of Economics in Ljubljana and the daily newspaper, *Finance*, has become strongly established in the region of Central and South-Eastern Europe. This book proves that not only business but also academic research has become global. Many researchers from various countries contributed their papers and the cooperation with the authors was excellent. The same goes for cooperation with Rebeka Koncilja, Marjana Dremelj, Suzana Gerželj, Jurij Giacommeli, Andreja Saich, Eva Jelnikar, Tatjana Pogačnik, Tanja Rajkovič, and staff of *Finance*. Our acknowledgements also go to students of the full-time Master of Science in Business Administration program at the Faculty of Economics, who contributed to the success of the conference and to the creation of this book. And finally, we are very grateful to our families for their understanding and support.

Janez Prašnikar and Andreja Cirman
Ljubljana, April 2006

LIST OF CONTRIBUTORS

Andreja Cirman is Assistant Professor at the Faculty of Economics, University of Ljubljana.

Vlado Dimovski is Professor at the Faculty of Economics, University of Ljubljana.

Janez Drnovšek is the President of the Republic of Slovenia.

Tony Fang is Assistant Professor at Stockholm University School of Business.

Güliz Ger is Professor at the Faculty of Business Administration, Bilkent University, Ankara.

Sergei Guriev is Professor at the New Economic School, Moscow. He is Research Fellow at the Centre for Economic Policy Research, London, and at the William Davidson Institute at the University of Michigan.

Marijana Jazbec is the CEO of the Centre for Management Development and Training at the Faculty of Economics, University of Ljubljana.

Paul R. Kleindorfer is Professor at The Wharton School of Business at the University of Pennsylvania.

Robert Kaše is Teaching Assistant at the Faculty of Economics, University of Ljubljana.

Ljubica Knežević Cvelbar is Teaching Assistant at the Faculty of Economics, University of Ljubljana.

Črt Kostevc is Teaching Assistant at the Faculty of Economics, University of Ljubljana.

Aleksander Kuljaj is Manager in Kolektor, d.d. Idrija.

Monika Lisjak is Teaching Assistant at the Faculty of Economics, University of Ljubljana.

Maja Makovec Brenčič is Assistant Professor at the Faculty of Economics, University of Ljubljana.

Mojmir Mrak is Professor at the Faculty of Economics, University of Ljubljana.

Bilin Neyapti is Assistant Professor at the Department of Economics; Bilkent University, Ankara.

Marko Pahor is Assistant Professor at the Faculty of Economics, University of Ljubljana.

Janez Prašnikar is Professor at the Faculty of Economics, University of Ljubljana. He is Research Fellow at the Centre for Economic Policy Research, London, and at the William Davidson Institute at the University of Michigan.

Darja Peljhan is Teaching Assistant at the Faculty of Economics, University of Ljubljana.

Stanislav Pirogov is Professor at MIRBIS, Moscow Business School.

Tjaša Redek is Teaching Assistant at the Faculty of Economics, University of Ljubljana.

Adrijana Rejc Buhovac is Assistant Professor at the Faculty of Economics, University of Ljubljana.

Özlem Sandikci is Assistant Professor at the Faculty of Business Administration, Bilkent University, Ankara.

Sergeja Slapničar is Assistant Professor at the Faculty of Economics, University of Ljubljana.

Miha Škerlavaj is Teaching Assistant at the Faculty of Economics, University of Ljubljana.

Mateja Štembergar is Manager in Kolektor, d.d., Idrija.

Metka Tekavčič is Associate Professor at the Faculty of Economics, University of Ljubljana.

Svetlana Tvogorova is Lecturer at MIRBIS, Moscow Business School.

Danilo Türk is Professor at Law Faculty, University of Ljubljana and former UN Assistant Secretary-General for Political Affairs.

Milica Uvalić is Professor at the Department of Economics, Faculty of Political Sciences, University of Perugia.

Hugo Zagoršek is Assistant Professor at the Faculty of Economics, University of Ljubljana.

Nada Zupan is Associate Professor at the Faculty of Economics, University of Ljubljana.

PART I: SOME GLOBALISATION DILEMMAS

In: New Emerging Economies and Their Culture
Editors: J. Prašnikar, A. Cirman, pp. 3-21

ISBN: 978-1-60021-754-8
© 2007 Nova Science Publishers, Inc.

Chapter 1

GLOBAL ECONOMY AND CULTURAL DIVERSITY

Janez Prašnikar and Andreja Cirman

INTRODUCTION

Globalization has, despite the diversity of its processes, become the reality of the modern world. It is an abstract concept and does not have a uniform definition. Lubbers and Koorevaar (2000) define it quite broadly. It is a process in which geographic distances become a factor of diminishing importance in the establishment and maintenance of cross-border economic, political and socio-cultural relationships. This process reaches such intensity that relations change fundamentally, and people become aware of that change. The potential internationalization of relationships and establishment of mutual dependencies creates many opportunities but also causes fear, resistance and triggers various actions and reactions.

Globalization is not just a recent phenomenon. Trade and financial flows have been occurring between rural and city markets and financial centers since early times. The difference between globalization in the past and the one we talk about today is the extent of the interactions and their movement to the supranational level. And it is the latter that differentiates globalization from internationalization. Globalization is not only about the increase in the extent and the frequency of international interactions, it refers to the process of the dismantling of national borders. Global standards are established, enabling the individuals, groups, companies and international organizations to operate in a new way (Kimura, 2003). The dependencies within those global networks have become so great and interaction among them so dense that they form a sphere unto themselves and are more or less independent of the local configuration in which they operate (Lubbers and Koorevaar, 2000).

The process itself therefore poses numerous challenges for the business world on both the macro- and micro-level. At the country level, questions arise regarding the stability of political relationships, international safety and various forms and levels of an individual country's involvement in global economic flows. But at the same time, significant changes also appear at the corporate level.

FORCES BEHIND GLOBALIZATION

Knowing the forces that guide and direct the whole process is important for understanding globalization. The most important one is certainly technological innovation, particularly in information and communication technology, which has enabled an increased flow of information. The effects of globalization include the shift from industrial capitalism towards post-industrial conception of economic relationships (Lubbers and Koorevaar, 2000) and in the decreased importance of agriculture in less developed economies on the account of industry. Communication and information technologies have facilitated a faster and higher quality exchange of information and has, by lowering transaction costs, decreased distances in the economic meaning of the word.

Economic globalization based on its dominant neoliberal ideology strongly interacts with technological globalization (Lubbers and Koorevaar, 2000; Glyn, 2004). Economic globalization, with its market orientation, has led towards the liberalization of trade, investment and migration, deregulation of economies, privatization of the public sector and growth of the private sector. Liberalization of trade has reduced trade barriers and therefore opened opportunities for companies to enter foreign markets more easily, and simultaneously extended the level of competition. In the 1980s and 1990s, the IMF and the US Treasury tried to push capital market liberalization around the world (Stiglitz, 2004). Globalization in the financial sphere has proceeded at an even faster pace than in trade and production. It has created a variety of new investment opportunities and improved the access to financial markets; however, it has also contributed to the emergence of the financial crises that we have witnessed in Asia, Russia, Argentina and some other countries (Gatignon and Kimberly, 2004). So far, the mobility of people has been the least impacted by globalization but there is a positive trend in this area as well. On the company level, the increased mobility has important implications for human resources decisions and affects the diffusion of products, ideas and culture (Gatignon and Kimberly, 2004). Expansion of international trade and higher mobility of people at the global level can be at least partially explained by a decrease in transportation costs. On the company level, increased transport capacities and technological advancement have facilitated global consolidation with various forms of proprietary and contractual cooperation in complex global supply chains.

THE EXTENT AND CHALLENGES OF GLOBALIZATION AT THE MACRO LEVEL

The most obvious effect of globalization as a consequence of deepening the influence of market forces is in increased international economic integration (Glyn, 2004). Its main vehicles are the growth of international trade, increased flows of foreign direct investments (FDI), increased flows of financial capital (portfolio and banking), and increased international migrations.

a) International Trade

Globalization is primarily marked by an exceptional increase in international trade which manifests itself in a growing share of exports in the world gross domestic product and thus an increased share of economic activity exposed to international competition. In 2004, world exports of goods reached USD 9,123 billion (World Development Report 2006). Between 2001 and 2004, the level of international trade increased on average by 5.4% annually (OECD Main Economic Indicators, 2005). Among developed countries the share of international trade in total output (the sum of exports and imports of goods relative to GDP) rose from 32.3% in 1990 to 41.6% in 2004. Among low- and middle-income countries this share in the same period increased from 33.5% to 59.2% (World Development Indicators 2005; World Development Report 2006). Technology based electronic sales reached USD 2,293 billion in 2002. For the year 2006, this is expected to be USD 12,837 billion, 93.3% coming from developed countries.

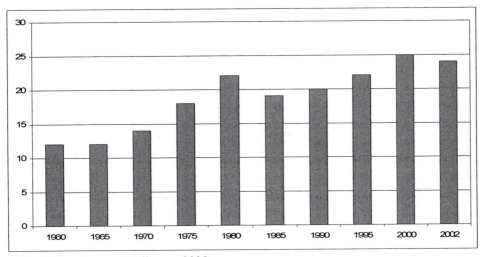

Source: World Development Indicators 2005.

Figure 1.1. World Exports as a Percentage of World GDP (Current Prices and Exchange Rates).

b) Foreign Direct Investment

Over the past few decades, the inflows of foreign direct investments (FDI) increased markedly and reached a peak in 2000 with USD 1,400 billion. Due to the slowdown of global economic activity and political crises, their extent decreased in the following years and in 2003 it reached USD 560 billion (World Investment Report 2004, 2004), 65.5% of which was directed towards developed economies. In the sectoral composition the share of services in FDI is substantially higher compared to international trade, characterized by a prevalent share of industry. In the 1990s about one half of outward FDI was in the services sectors. Therefore, FDI can reach into the parts of economic structure in individual countries that do not face direct competition from imports (Glyn, 2004).

Table 1.1. Foreign Direct Investment 1992—2003 (in% of Gross Domestic Investments)

	World		Developed countries	USA	EU	Developing countries
	1992–1997	1998–2003	1998–2003	1998–2003	1998–2003	1998–2003
Inward	5.2	12.7	12.6	9.1	23.8	12.5
Outward	5.5	12.0	14.8	7.7	30.1	3.7

Source: World Investment Report 2004.

c) Capital Market Flows

Intensified economic integration at the global level is also evident from the expansion of international financial flows. Investors, especially in developed countries, have increasingly diversified their portfolio by including foreign financial assets (debt and equity instruments) while borrowers increasingly turn to sources of funds on foreign financial markets along with domestic ones. Obersfeld and Taylor (2002) show on a larger sample of countries that the total value of stock of foreign assets increased from 36% of GDP in 1980 to 71% of GDP in 1995, and foreign liabilities increased from 30% to 79%. When compared to FDI and international trade, capital flows are characterized by much higher volatility and have also been restricted to a narrower range of emerging market countries. Globalization of capital markets gives countries access to new sources of capital driving economic growth. However, the volatility of such flows increases the risk of financial and currency crises (Obersfeld and Taylor, 2002; Buckley, 2002).

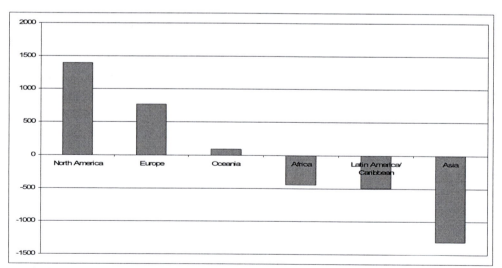

Source: Global Policy Forum, 2005.

Figure 1.2. Average Annual Net Flow of Migrants in 1995–2000 (in thousands).

d) International Labor Migrations

International labor migrations are certainly the least intensive aspect of global economic integration, however, their importance is increasing (Figure 1.2). The future of this trend is also supported by the fact the population of industrial countries is getting older, while the workforce of developing countries, with a young and active population, is growing faster compared to the labor demand on domestic markets. Developed countries answer the migration pressures by tightening controls against most unskilled migrants, together with attempts to attract certain skilled ones (Glyn, 2004).

EXTENT AND CHALLENGES OF GLOBALIZATION AT THE CORPORATE LEVEL

Due to progressing globalization trends in the last few decades, globalization is no longer confined to companies in industries such as electronics, pharmaceuticals, the automotive industry and branded consumer goods. While at the national level discussions about the benefits, negative impacts and approaches toward globalization continue, for most midsize to large companies globalization is no longer a discretionary option but a strategic imperative (Gupta and Westney, 2003). Similar to the macro level, globalization at the corporate level is also a double-edged sword. On one hand, a company integrated in global economic activity can take advantages of a larger market potential, scale- and location-based cost efficiencies and exposure to new product and process ideas. On the other hand, globalization exposes firms to numerous strategic and organizational challenges arising from increased diversity, complexity and uncertainty (Gupta and Westney, ibid).

Globalization at the corporate level is not only the presence on foreign markets but also the development of global strategies. The latter is based on a core business strategy being a source of firm's sustainable competitive advantage. The usual path to a global strategy includes internationalization of the core business strategy through international expansion of activities and through adaptation and integration of international strategy across countries (Picture 1.1).

The implementation of global strategy requires cross-border networks that are denser, more widely dispersed, more complex, and more differentiated compared to those in the past (Gupta and Westney, ibid). Competition between businesses substitutes for competition between supply chains, which tend to be increasingly global. Global strategies are based upon the interplay between competitive advantages of companies and the comparative advantages of individual countries (Kogut, 2003). The key to developing global strategy is therefore in identifying and focusing on the activities within the value chain that give the company its distinct competitive advantage and exploiting the differences in comparative advantages between geographic locations to enhance that advantage.

As a consequence of globalization, increased focus on the core business (strategic alignment), outsourcing and formation of various forms of cooperation among companies, the number of participants needed to produce a product or service for the end consumer has drastically increased. Paul Kleindorfer in his article, "Implications of Globalization and Sustainability for Emerging Business Models" (in this book), states that, in general, from the

1980s, global value chains have been substantially changed by approaches such as Just-in-Time Manufacturing (JIT), optimized logistics between producers and distributors, including the implementation of Efficient Customer Response–ECR) and improved Customer Relationship Management (CRM).

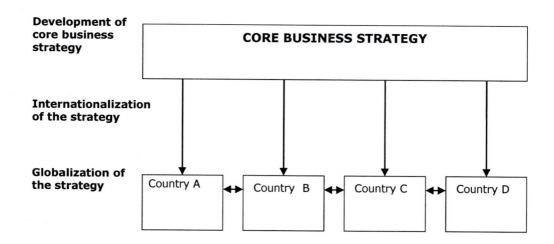

Source: Yip, 2003.

Picture 1.1. Total Global Strategy.

These changes in the architecture of the supply chains at corporate level have led to a shift towards Lean Enterprises and Lean Consumption. According to Kleindorfer, new business models are often web-centric, not firm-centric and the key efficiency concern is not transformation efficiency but interaction efficiency, where the interactions of interest encompass global supply chains and empowered consumer groups. New markets and new forms of contracting are supporting outsourcing, unbundling, contract manufacturing and a variety of other forms of extended value chains. Today the key factor of success in supply chain management is in striking the right balance between product availability, cost, and asset management, and in the management of inherent risks. However, it must also enable a logical connection between the well-being of the firm in relation to the global value chain in which it is embedded, and it must allow many different stakeholders to understand the narrow economic value proposition supporting the firm's profitability as well as the broader implications of the firm's activities for sustainability.

WE LIVE IN A DIVERSIFIED WORLD

The last issue is a very important one. Although globalization has touched all parts of the world, the biggest effects of the process are felt in a relatively small number of countries of high and middle income class while the majority of countries are only partly involved in global forces. Integration through international trade, capital market flows and communication network is most intense among high income members of the OECD. Close behind are former transition countries of Central and Eastern Europe and the countries of East Asia that are steadily converging towards the per capita income levels of the industrialized countries. In Latin America only a handful of countries have gradually started to open their economies while the remaining middle income and developing countries lag behind with the income gap between them and the most prosperous countries constantly increasing (Yusuf, 2004). Janez Drnovšek, President of the Republic of Slovenia, in his contribution to this book, "Towards More Balance in the Global Society", elaborates on the negative consequences of globalization. Above all, we are faced with poverty threatening a large part of the world. Climate change, terrorism and other forms of violence, and the steady movement of migrants from poor countries are also important world issues. Drnovšek stands for solutions that have to be found on a global scale and with Europe taking bigger commitment in those processes. One solution might be the establishment of a globalization fund earmarked for the restructuring of industries facing destruction due to globalization, and for the creation of new, quality jobs. In the framework of international organizations, European countries and the United States should likewise stand for developing countries to gradually raise their labor standards in order to reduce the existing high pressure for migration. And what can the companies do? They should take their part of the responsibility for sustainable development, since this is indispensable if they want to stay in business.

Danilo Türk, a former UN Assistant Secretary-General for Political Affairs in his contribution, "Challenges to International Security Today – An Overview", offers an interesting perspective on security conditions in the global world. In his opinion the current conditions could be characterized by: 1) a relatively high level of strategic stability, despite existing uneven distribution of power among major players; 2) decreased number of armed conflicts around the world and their confinement to local areas; 3) changed nature of threats to international peace with major threats being poverty, armed conflicts between countries and within them, nuclear, radiological, chemical and biological weapons, terrorism and transnational organized crime. He supports the establishment of the polycentric world and similar as Haass (2005) builds on co-optism, cooperation among major sources of power instead of competition, as mechanisms of international integration. However, this is a long-term project. In the short term, the world will have to find ways to solve the nuclear problem and the problem of terrorism. Türk claims that the nuclear issue calls for a partial transfer of the responsibility of states with legally permissible nuclear programs on the regional level, and for the need to recall the Treaty on Non-Proliferation of Nuclear Weapons dating back to 1968. In order to resolve the second problem, a larger emphasis should be given to the use of preventive strategies, and above all, to start eradicating the roots of the terrorism, such as foreign military occupation and a link between terrorism and internationally organized crime.

Both authors, Drnovšek and Türk, stress that finding solutions to global problems is possible only with strong regional involvement. A justified question is, What should the once "peripheral" countries, the new emerging economies, like Russia, Turkey, China, and also Slovenia do to be successful in the economic sphere? What should their resident companies do and what competences should they develop? One of the options is to enter the already existing supply chains. Above all, this could be facilitated by FDI, especially if they build their competitive advantages on a qualified and cheaper workforce, compared to their competitors. However, new supply chains that are competitive to the existing ones, might be established in cases when certain competitive advantages can be developed due to, for example, knowing more about less developed markets in the emerging economies and therefore lower information asymmetry.[1] But with the development of the market these advantages disappear. Companies that have achieved a cost or benefit advantage, as well as strategic fit, are in a better position. Nevertheless, achieving only the strategic fit is often not enough. A cultural fit is also desired. Strategic and cultural (mis)fits act alongside as well as on each other. The more successful a company is in aligning them, the better the chances for achieving competitive advantages and establishing itself in global competition. A strategic and cultural fit, and how to find balance between them in emerging economies, is a subject of this book. In the next sections we will introduce to the readers the rest of the contributions dealing with cultural issues.

FRAMEWORK FOR STUDYING CULTURE IN BUSINESS MODELS

Studying differences in national cultures arises from Hofstede's study of over 116,000 employees in IBM subsidiaries from around the world in mid 1970s (Hofstede, 1980). Hofstede defined cultural dimensions that can be used to define differences in national cultures (power distance, individualism/collectivism, uncertainty avoidance, masculinity/femininity and short-term/long-term orientation). Several authors later developed their own models of national culture, with some differences in dimensions (Schwartz, 1994; Trompenaars, 1993; GLOBE program/House et al., 2004; and others), triggering substantial competition among them. On the other hand, the question has arisen as to what extent it is possible to define differences in organizational cultures of companies by using differences in national cultures. Hofstede (2001) claims that organizations can influence the two external layers of culture (physical culture and behavioral patterns, rituals, symbols etc.), but can influence people's values and norms to a much lesser extent. Values belong more to people than to companies and therefore the latter mainly "import" them (with the selection and hiring system) and do not create them. According to this concept, to be able to diagnose organizational culture one must develop specific dimensions that measure typical behavior patterns in an organization. On the other hand, researchers from the GLOBE program (House et al., 2004) take the position that identical dimensions can be used to measure both national and organizational culture. In contrast, Trompenaars and Wooliams (2004) developed an integrated typology of organizational culture on the basis of previous typologies and defined four possible types: the Incubator, the Guided Missile, the Eiffel Tower and the Family. As evident, a wide selection of instruments exists for studying organizational culture. Although this is an interesting issue, the discussion on which model for studying culture is more suitable is not a central issue for us. In this book we ask what the managers should do in order to make their decisions more successful. In fact, we take the stance that there are models of studying national and organizational culture that are more suitable to be used in some circumstances when dealing with one set of problems, while some models fit more with other circumstances.

In their contribution, "Culture and Its Influence on Business Performance", Hugo Zagoršek and Mateja Štembergar introduce basic concepts dealt with in this book. The focal

---

[1] For further discussion on this see Prašnikar (ed.), 2005.

point of their study is the cultural fit between a company's organizational culture and its strategy. Since companies operate within certain national borders, national culture to some extent influences the organizational culture. The latter is part of the triangle consisting of organizational culture, strategy, and structure and systems, and defines the competitive position of a firm and its performance. Strong organizational culture usually makes it easier for the company to implement its strategy (Green, 1988). On the other hand, similar organizational cultures among business units in a multi–business firm act as a condition for attaining a strategic fit. According to Besanko et al. (2004), strategic fit is the real source of competitive advantages in multi-business companies. An important contribution to value creation in multi–business firms also comes from greater fit between business units in a portfolio and their corporate parent (Gold, Campbell and Alexander, 1994). Zagoršek and Štembergar explain the importance of cultural due-diligence (the first step of cultural study) and of the assessments of strategic and cultural fits (the second step of the cultural study) for efficient decision making. They describe several methodologies for studying national and organizational culture, in particular the methodology by Trompenaars and Wolliams (2004). The latter includes both dimensions of culture – national and organizational – and since the interaction between them is very intertwined due to the turbulent environment in emerging economies, we will use it several times to study the strategic and cultural fit of companies in emerging market countries.

Marijana Jazbec in "Slovenian National Culture and Cross-Cultural Training" raises the question in what cases there is a need to organize managerial cross-cultural training. Based on a wide body of literature on culture and cross-cultural communication she sets a hypothesis stating that the bigger the differences between national cultures, the greater the need for cross-cultural training. By using Hofstede's Value Survey Module (1994) for measuring differences in national cultures on a relatively large sample of Slovenian managers, she establishes that Slovenian managers can be placed in the same cluster with Dutch and Swedish managers. Therefore the need for cross-cultural training is greater for the countries where a difference between own and a foreign culture is greater. For Slovenian managers this holds in relation to the Asian countries, where cultural differences cause larger communication problems. These problems could also be avoided by doing business in culturally more familiar environment in countries such as Russia and Turkey.

Janez Prašnikar, Marko Pahor and Hugo Zagoršek in their contribution, "Comparison of Cultural Profiles of Young Managers from the Countries of South-Eastern Europe and Russia", present the results of a comparative study of cultural profiles of young managers from certain countries in the territory of the former Yugoslavia (Slovenia, Croatia, Bosnia and Herzegovina, Serbia and Montenegro) and Russia. These are managers who have recently completed their education or are still included in post graduate studies of business sciences and therefore have little or even no work experience. Additionally, they come from transitional countries and perceive new social circumstances similarly, thus forming similar values, beliefs and points of view. On the other hand, they are parts of different national cultures. With the help of Trompenaars' methodology, they found that young managers included in the research are very similar among themselves on many dimensions.[2] Moreover,

---

[2] Prašnikar, Pahor and Svetlik (2006) in the follow-up study show that individualistic behavior prevails among younger and more educated managers, who are more inclined toward an organizational culture that emphasizes non-hierarchical relations and is more task-oriented. See also Nordstrom and Ridderstrale (2001).

in value dimensions of the Slovenian, Croatian, Bosnian, and even Serbian young managers, there are some similarities with certain dimensions of Austrian managers, while young Russian managers depart in a few dimensions. All this underlines the importance of national culture. In general, the methodology proves to be a useful tool for studying cultural profiles of different groups of managers.

In contrast to previous authors, Adriana Rejc Buhovac and Sergeja Slapničar in their study, "Organizational Culture and Managerial Control after an International Acquisition", deal with the question of the control mechanisms' impact on the organizational culture in three international post-mergers (Novartis – Lek, Danfoss – Danfoss Trata, Gorenje Group – Mora Moravia). They use Hofstede's methodology of the taxonomy of a national culture (Hofstede, 1980) and Hofstede's model of organizational practices (Hofstede et al, 1990). Both are built on the supposition that certain national values are so strong that they imbue the organizational culture and influence the development of certain practices, all other things being equal. Moreover, if a parent firm wants to start the process of submerging the organizational culture of a subsidiary into the one of the parent firms, both informal (selection, training, transfer, career path of managers etc.) and formal (reorganization of processes, standardization and formalization of procedures and systems) control mechanisms may be used. Authors' research results do not fully support their construct. A joint characteristic of the three acquired companies is that, after acquisition, they all improved their business results. Personal surveillance, establishing sound foundations for trust, and early replacement of incompatible managers represent the mechanisms that were put in place first to help the convergence of divergent organizational cultures. Among formal mechanisms, reorganization of critical activities and process optimization are vitally important to ensure the payoff on acquisition. However, none of the parent companies has yet attempted to change the existing performance measurement system in the subsidiary extensively.

EXAMPLES OF STRATEGIC AND CULTURAL (MIS)FITS IN SOME EMERGING ECONOMIES

Turkey:Today's Challenge or an Option for the Future

The emerging economies are facing a question on how to position themselves in the global economic flows in order to maximize the benefits from the globalization process. The experience of Turkey (Neyapti, in this book), some countries of South-Eastern Europe (Mrak, in this book; Uvalić, in this book), Russia (Guriev, in this book) and China (Kostevc and Redek, in this book) in developing their globalization potential indicate that macroeconomic stability, financial strength, openness of the economy, transparency, appropriate control and management over the integration process are prerequisites for a higher degree of integration.

The contribution by Bilin Neyapti, "Turkish Economy: A Retrospective Assessment and Recent Developments", presents an excellent economic overview of Turkey in the last few decades, its opening toward the global economy and a good description of the current state of the economy. Several factors make Turkey important for global dynamics. Therefore, special attention is given to it. If Turkey manages to reach economic stability, adequate economic growth and political balance, it will gain necessary credibility and higher negotiating power on its way to international integrations. The overview of the past decades' economic performance namely suggests that Turkey was held back from a sustainable growth path due to both policy mistakes, be it political short-sightedness or simply mismanagement, and structural and institutional constraints. However, Turkey is currently in a relatively optimistic phase of recovery that can set a perfect ground for the realization of longer term opportunities. This involves solidifying the institutional reforms that have been launched since the beginning of the 2000s. In the last part of her contribution the author analyzes Turkey's current economic strengths, weaknesses, opportunities and threats.

Turkey still lacks wider recognition, which is evident also from the lack of knowledge about different segments of the consumer market and their behavior. Ozlem Sandikcu and Guliz Ger in the article "Contemporary Turkish Consumptionscape: Polarity and Plurality", paint an excellent picture of contemporary consumptionscape in Turkey. Their contribution starts with a review of economic and political transformations in the Turkish society based on historical analysis. Based on this, they discuss the current consumption environment in relation to different socio-economic groupings. The immense polarity in income levels and lifestyles, increased aspirations for a high level of consumption, constructed and legitimized to be "normal" and modern across all social classes, and the profound relative deprivation experienced by the poor, set the stage for the contemporary consumptionscape. The authors outline four different consumption practices – Islamist, spectacularist, nationalist, and historical – that have become increasingly visible in recent years. The contemporary Turkish consumptionscape is complex and multi-layered with different adaptations of the modern identity and modern consumption practices existing side by side. In each case, the identity and the consumption that expresses it are simultaneously traditional and modern, as well as local and global.

The next chapter, "Strategic and Cultural Fit Assessment in a Diversified Company: Droga Kolinska Case – Possible Entry into Turkish Market", by Ljubica Knežević Cvelbar and Monika Lisjak, deals with two cultural issues. The first one concerns the organizational culture and strategic and cultural fit of Droga and Kolinska that were recently merged into Droga Kolinska. Both operated in the food processing industry, were of similar size, had an important common owner and had lost a substantial share of advantage due to changes in external environment (Slovenia's accession to the EU). The authors use the GE matrix to analyze the portfolio of strategic business units within the newly established merged company on the two key markets – the markets of Eastern and Western Europe. The results show that the existing portfolio of business units is unbalanced. However, limited opportunities exist for increasing the exploitation of economies of scale and scope between the key brands. This analysis is complemented with the analysis of organizational culture. Due to operating in the same industry, similar size and same national culture, there are no large differences in the organizational culture between both companies. In authors' opinion the key importance for the new company lies in its strategic fit. If the merged company does not attain competitive economic advantages, it will face difficulties, even in the process of integrating organizational cultures. One of the possibilities is expanding the prospective Argeta brand to the Turkish market; however, this presents a second cultural issue due to various aspects of the Turkish consumptionscape, discussed in the previous chapter.

South – Eastern Europe: Is It Converging or Staying the Same?

As has been shown in their recent past (i.e. the break-up of Yugoslavia), cultural differences, despite some similarities, play an important role in the countries of South-Eastern Europe. This makes the question in the title of this chapter very relevant, since the countries of South-Eastern Europe (SEE) are still well behind the Central European transitional countries (CEE). Mojmir Mrak in his contribution, "South-Eastern Europe: Economic Trends and the EU Integration Prospects", shows that SEE countries have now recovered from the recession of 1990. Also, indicators of macroeconomic stability point to the progress made in economic development. For now, the biggest problems are external imbalances and still high unemployment rates in most of the cases. Thus, strong export oriented economic development via intensive structural reforms should be the key to long-term sustainability. The author also assesses the EU integration prospects for the region as a whole and for individual countries involved. Here the situation is less pronounced. While Romania and Bulgaria already joined the EU in 2007, and some countries like Croatia and even Macedonia are on their way to join the EU, the perspectives of others are less clear. As claimed by an independent International Commission on the Balkans (2005), the international community has failed to offer a convincing political perspective to the societies in the region, and the European Commission lags behind in its plans on how to integrate the region in the EU.

A large part of reservations about the smoothness of this process is based on the unsolved problem of Serbia and Montenegro's European integration. Milica Uvalić in her contribution, "Transition in Serbia and Montenegro: From Recurrent Crises Towards EU Integration", presents the brighter side of this process. Since October 2000, when Milošević's regime collapsed, Serbia and Montenegro have recorded very good results in some areas. The economy's growth has been satisfactory and inflation has decreased considerably; however, a fiscal deficit, a persistent high rate of unemployment and an unbalanced external sector indicate the economic recovery is still not sustainable. Although Serbia and Montenegro holds the position of the fastest reformer after 2000, and the economy has considerably opened, there are few areas, such as enterprise governance and restructuring, banking reforms, the development of securities markets and non-bank institutions, and competition policies, that still call for more radical economic reforms. According to Uvalić, they would help Serbia and Montenegro make better use of its competitive advantages such as geographical and geopolitical position, qualified and relatively cheap labor force, and SEE regional market. However, the difficult questions on how the EU should negotiate Serbia and Montenegro's greater integration with the EU remains open. Uvalić considers the idea of finding a way to bring Serbia and Montenegro closer to the EU in its existing structure. But if Montenegro and Kosovo take separate paths, the process might take in her view much longer.

After 2000, the investments of Slovenian companies in Serbia have grown in line with more favorable Serbian economic environment (Prašnikar, Domadenik and Cirman, 2001; Damjan, Polanec and Prašnikar, 2005). Good understanding of the current Serbian environment is despite the political instability a competitive advantage of Slovenian companies. Nada Zupan and Robert Kaše in their study, "Helios Group's Investment in Serbia: A Strategic and Cultural Fit", examine the effects of the Helios Group, which is a significant player in the paints and coatings industry in Central and South-Eastern Europe, on its strategic and cultural fit. By using standard strategic fit analysis they found that there are a lot of potential links between the parent company, Helios, and the acquired companies, although the parent has to be aware of the negative consequences of acquisitions, such as too wide diversification. Helios Group is therefore on a good path to successfully prepare itself for global competition through its continuing investment activity. However, the cultural fit analysis establishes important differences in organizational culture between the selected units (Helios and Color in Slovenia, and Zvezda Helios in Serbia). Some similarities in organizational culture profiles of the parent company and its acquisition in Serbia can be explained by similar positions on the market – in the recent history both companies were successful on their own market. It is also a consequence of the cultural transfer of the parent firm that followed the merger. Zupan and Kaše in their contribution also investigated what values should be developed within the Group in order to create an organizational culture that would support strategies for achieving the strategic goals. By using Trompenaars' methodology, they identify the ideal organizational culture that would fit the strategy of Helios Group, point out differences between the existent and desired organizational culture in individual units, and give some suggestions on how they could be diminished.

Russia: Rebirth of a Giant?

As explained by Sergei Guriev in his chapter, "Russia's Futures", Russian growth has tripled since 1998. This growth has been driven by high oil and metal prices but has eventually trickled down to all industries and all parts of society. Poverty and unemployment have fallen by one third. A new middle class has emerged. Yet, Russia faces a number of major challenges, including a corrupt and inefficient government, and major political risk in regard to the 2008 elections. Besides corruption, the most important challenges are related to its human capital. The education system is deteriorating. Health care is in an even worse shape. The Russian population is both aging and shrinking and a decline in the working-age population will be especially severe after 2007. The only solution to this problem is enhanced internal and external migration, which is difficult to achieve due to undeveloped housing and financial markets and due to inefficient bureaucracy unable to effectively regulate external migration. Given the volatile oil prices, it is hard to make any credible mid-term forecasts. If oil prices remain high, which is likely, one should expect a growth rate of 5–6% up until 2008 when both politics and the economy will encounter a severe stress of a potential political upheaval.

While the economic climate in Russia has improved, Stanislav Pirogov and Svetlana Tvorogova show in their contribution, "Cross Cultural Aspects of Doing Business in Russia", that Russian culture of the transition period (which is closely connected with business culture) is subject to significant modifications. With changes starting already in the time of Gorbachev, the socialist regime collapsed. The secular society's position was taken over by the church and religion. The number of believers has increased significantly. Unlimited flow of information through information networks has introduced people to new, mainly Western values. Consequently, some value dimensions of Russian national culture are changing. Pirogov and Tvorogova show the similarities and differences in dimensions of Russian national culture according to Hofstede's research (2001) and the research of other Russian researchers: Naumov (1996), Latova (2003) and Strukova and Pushnykh (2004). Russian researchers unanimously ascertain a substantially lower power distance, indicating significantly lower tolerance for inequality compared to the time Hofstede's research was carried out. Collectivism and femininity are present also in the results obtained by Russian researchers; however, the preference for risk has been systematically increasing year after year. According to the authors, it is still too early to answer the questions whether Russian national culture is about to integrate with European culture. Public opinion in Russia is still in favor of maintaining national identity and Russian way of development.

Metka Tekavčič, Vlado Dimovski, Darja Peljhan and Miha Škerlavaj in their comprehensive study, "Cultural Fit as a Means of Strategy Implementation: The Case of Trimo Trebnje d.d. and Trimo VSK", present the Slovenian company, Trimo, and its investment in the daughter company, Trimo VSK, in Russia. Due to the nature of its industry – Trimo is a highly technologically competent company with products providing complete solutions to its customers in the area of prefabricated steel buildings, roofs and facades, steel structures and containers – the implementation of such a strategy is also supported by a prevalent organizational culture emphasizing a variety of values and standards, and is focused on the employees.[3] The authors research similarities and differences between the organizational culture of the parent company and the daughter company by using Trompenaars' methodology of dimensions of national and organizational culture. They find relatively similar organizational cultures in both companies, although there are some differences due to the influence of national cultures. However, there are no major differences between the ideal cultures of both companies. That could also be a signal that the parent company has been quite successful at introducing its own organizational culture in the Russian environment. The authors also study dimensions of national culture and organizational culture at departmental level and find interesting results in terms of homogeneity of the cultures of both manufacturing departments. At the managerial level, Slovenian managers are more performance oriented and emphasize strict adherence to standardized rules and procedures, while Russian managers show a higher level of individualism and specificity, which can present a barrier to the implementation and increased usage of teamwork as well as knowledge transfer, both being important Trimo values. In conclusion, the authors provide some practical advices on how Trimo should further adjust its strategic orientation towards continuous improvement and innovations with its culture in both companies.

Doing Business with the Chinese

Among all emerging economies included in this book, China has been, with its level of integration in the global economy and its cultural diversity, the most debated in the last few decades. The forecasts show that this is likely to continue in the future. Thus, how to do business with the Chinese? Where does the distinctness of their culture lie, and how to negotiate with them? In the first contribution on this topic, "Globalization and FDI: The Role of China", Črt Kostevc and Tjaša Redek examine the impact of globalization on China, especially on the increased volume of its trade and foreign direct investment. According to the authors, high economic growth is attributable to the following two factors: 1) capital accumulation (both domestic capital accumulation and foreign capital inflow), and 2) exports

---

[3]See also Zupan and Rejc, 2005.

growth in manufacturing, especially in labor intensive production. Both are related to the export-led model of economic growth. However, with such an important growth of the export, China is experiencing equally impressive growth rates in imports, and is today one the biggest importers of oil, steel, metal and chemicals, as well as, for example, automotive products, due to the huge domestic market. China's short-term economic outlook looks promising, although some internal and external limitations (a weak financial system with badly performing state banks, migration pressures due to regional income disparities, weak development of infrastructure, huge trade dependency, opposition from developed countries due to the growth of Chinese trade, etc.) are getting more and more attention in the discussions concerning Chinese growth. As argued by the authors, to achieve long-term sustainable growth, China would have to focus on factors behind total factor productivity increases, including the development of its own technology and the quality of its human capital.

Due to China's growing importance in the global economy, the knowledge of Chinese business culture and negotiating style of Chinese businesspeople has become obligatory. The question is whether they are possible to foresee or place in a bipolarized framework of national cultures in terms of "either/or" cultural dimensions, such as femininity vs. masculinity, collectivism vs. individualism, which is the prevailing way of thinking in the studies of national cultures. Tony Fang in his contribution, Chinese Business Culture and Negotiating Style, thinks it is not. Chinese cultural dimensions are namely "intrinsically 'both/and', embracing both opposite orientations." Therefore, a Chinese businessperson is at the same time sincere and deceptive negotiator. The Yin Yang principle suggests that there exists neither absolute black nor absolute white. Chinese business culture is held together by three different interrelated driving forces, i.e. the PRC condition, Confucianism, and Chinese stratagems. The PRC condition contains different variables related to the People's Republic of China, such as centralized decision making and bureaucracy. Confucianism is a fundamental philosophical tradition in China. This is a form of moral ethic and a practical philosophy of human relationship and conduct. The Chinese stratagem is a strategic component of Chinese culture and is best described by Tzu's strategic thinking "victory without fighting". In Fang's words, a Chinese negotiator may be understood as a blend of a "Maoist bureaucrat in learning", "Confucian gentleman", and "Sun Tzu-like strategist". In addition, a comprehensive case study of negotiation strategy and tactics in the shipbuilding industry is presented and the most important principles behind negotiations, such as *guanxi* ["relationship"], *xianghu zunzhong* ["mutual respect"], and *xianghu peihe* ["mutual collaboration"] are evaluated.

The choice between a win-win and a win-lose negotiating strategy for Chinese businesspeople primarily depends on whether you have managed to win their confidence and when you have won it. It is an entangled process that could be ruined by a single wrong word or gesture. Businesspeople coming from small countries like Slovenia are not sufficiently aware of this negotiating style, as shown in the contribution, "Chinese Negotiation Style: Slovenian Managers' Perspective" by Aleksander Kuljaj and Maja Makovec Brenčič. One of the reasons for this, as stressed also by Jazbec in this book, is a traditional orientation of Slovenian companies to the markets of the EU, South-Eastern Europe and Russia. Only few companies have gone to China, and those who have, have mainly been forced in that by their customers (automotive producers). Kuljaj and Makovec Brenčič examine some of the principles, described in this book by Fang, from the experience of Slovenian managers. On this basis they emphasize three segments of the Chinese negotiating framework: 1) "guanxi" (importance of connections and acquaintances", 2) "mianzi" (relating to a person's reputation and respect), 3) protocol (the pre-negotiation phase is the most appropriate for building trust). At the same time, Slovenian managers also put emphasis on the role of translators, corruption, initial lack of trust in foreigners, the role of various strategies and negotiating techniques, the problem of copying the technology and sharing information, and almost obligatory additional "post-negotiations" after the contract signing. It is interesting that Slovenian managers ascribed no particular importance to some particularities of the negotiation process identified by other researchers, such as the choice of place for negotiations and insisting on an agreement on general principles before moving to any concrete discussions. However, this might be due to a limited number of managers included in the research. In general, the two researchers have encountered many problems finding qualified research participants. They consider this as an indication that the interest of Slovenian businesspeople for this market is too small relative to its size, and that managers are still not sufficiently prepared to act in a proactive manner.

CONCLUSION

Today there is no doubt that the combination of free trade, technological progress and increased capital mobility has increased the intensity of international competition and the interdependency of national economies to such level that one cannot ignore the impact of events in one part of the world to the global economy. It is also clear that cultural differences play a bigger role as has been considered until now. This is especially true for the turbulent environment in the emerging economies, to which globalization presents an opportunity to actively participate in the global economy.

Globalization changes business models within companies. It requires modified strategic thinking aligned with the new global economic order, and the paradigm of sustainable development. As actors on the global market they build their global strategies on the existing competitive advantages. They have to improve their value chains where they lag behind their competitors. Strategies are dynamic since location advantages are changing with the economic development of individual countries. Taking into account the cultural diversity of the participants is therefore a necessary element in the process of forming a strategic and cultural fit and consequently obtaining competitive advantage.

REFERENCES

Besanko, D., Dranove, D. D., Shanley M., and Schaefer, S. 2004. *"Economics of Strategy."* New York: John Wiley and Sons, Inc.

Buckley, R.P. 2002. "Globalization, Capital Markets and Human Rights." *New England Journal of International and Comparative Law* 8(2). [URL: http://www.nesl.edu/intljournal/vol8no2indx.cfm].

Damjan, J., Polanec S., and Prašnikar, J. 2005. "Export vs. FDI Behavior of Heterogenous Firms in Heterogenous Markets : Evidence from Slovenia." *LICOS Discussion Paper*, 147.

Drnovšek, J. 2007. *"Towards More Balance in the Global Society."* In this volume.

Global Policy Forum. 2005. [URL: http://www.globalpolicy.org/globaliz/charts/mignettable.htm].

Gatignon, H., and Kimberly, R.E. 2004. "Globalization and its Challenges." In Gatignon, H., and Kimberly, R.E. (eds.): *"The INSEAD-Wharton Alliance on Globalizing. Strategies for Building Successful Global Businesses."* Cambridge: Cambridge University Press.

Glyn, A. 2004. "The Assessment: How Far Has Globalization Gone?" *Oxford Review of Economic Policy* 20(1): 1–14.

Goold M., Campbell, A., and Alexander, M. 1994. *"Corporate-Level Strategy: Creating Value in the Multi-Business Company."* New York: John Wiley and Sons, Inc.

Gupta, A. K., and Westney, E. D. 2003. "Introduction." In Gupta, A. K., and Westney, E. D. (eds.): *"Smart Globalization. Designing Global Strategies, Creating Global Networks."* San Francisco: John Wiley and Sons, Inc.

Guriev, S. 2007. *"Russia's Futures."* In this volume.

Green, S. 1988. "Understanding Corporate Culture and its Relation to Strategy." *International Studies of Management and Organizations* 18 (2): 6–28.

Haass, R. 2005: "The Opportunity: America's Moment to Alter History's Course." *Public Affairs.*

Hofstede, G. 1980. *"Culture's Consequences: International Differences in Work-Related Values."* Beverly Hills: Sage.

Hofstede, G. 2001. *"Culture's Consequences: Comparing Values, Behaviors, Institutions and Organizations Across Nations."* Thousand Oaks: Sage.

House, R. J., Hanges, P. J., Javidan, M., Dorfman, P. W., and Gupta, V. *"Culture, Leadership, and Organizations: The GLOBE Study of 62 Societies."* Thousand Oaks: Sage.

Jazbec, M. 2007. *"Slovenian National Culture and Cross-Cultural Training of Managers."* In this volume.

Kimura, H. 2003. "Will Globalization Make Notion of Territorial Sovereignty Obsolete?" In Frančević, V., and Kimura, H. (eds.): *"Globalization, Democratization and Development: European and Japanese Views of Change in South East Europe."* Zagreb: Masmedia.

Kleindorfer, P. R., and Van Wessenhove, L. N. 2004. "Risk Management in Global Supply Chains." In Gatignon, H., and Kimberly, J. (eds.): *"INSEAD-Wharton Alliance on Globalizing. Strategies for Building Successful Global Businesses."* Cambridge: Cambridge University Press.

Kleindorfer, P. 2007. *"Implications of Globalization and Sustainability for Emerging Business Models."* In this volume.

Knežević Cvelbar, L., and Lisjak, M. 2007. *"Strategic and Cultural Fit Assessment in a Diversified Company: Droga Kolinska Case."* In this volume.

Kogut, B. 2003. "Designing Global Startegies: Comparative and Competitive Value-Added Chains." In Gupta, A. K., and Westney, E. D. (eds.): *"Smart Globalization. Designing Global Strategies, Creating Global Networks."* San Francisco: John Wiley and Sons, Inc.

Kostevc, Č., and Redek, T. 2007. *"Globalization and FDI: The Changing Face of the World Economy."* In this volume.

Kozul-Wright, R., and Rayment, P. 2004. "Globalization Reloded: An UNCTAD Perspective." *UNCTAD Disscusion Papers.* Geneva: UNCTAD.

Kuljaj, A., and Makovec-Brenčič, M. 2007. *"Chinese Negotiating Style: Slovenian Managers' Perspective."* In this volume.

Latova, N. V. 2003. "*Rossiyskaya ekonomickeskaya mentalnost: kakoy ona stala v 1990-e gody i kakoy tip rabotnika sformirovalsya v resultate.*" Russian Academy of Sciences, Institute of Sociology.

Lubbers, R., and Koorevaar, J. 2000. "Primary Globalization, Secondary Globalization, and the Sustainable Development Paradigm – Opposing Forces in the 21st Century." In: "*The Creative Society of the 21st Century: Future Studies.*" OECD: 7–24

Mrak, M. 2007. "*South-Eastern Europe: Economic Trends and EU Integration Prospects.*" In this volume.

Naumov, A. N. 1996. "*Hofstede izmerenie Rosii.*" Management: 2.

Neyapti, B. 2007. "*Turkish Economy: A Retrospective Assessment and Recent Developments.*" In this volume.

Nordstrom, K.A., and Ridderstrale, J. 2001. "*Funky Business: Talent makes capital dance.*" (Ta nori posel: ko zaigra talent, kapital pleše). Ljubljana: GV Založba, 2001.

Obstfeld, M., and Taylor, A. M. 2002. "*Globalization and Capital Markets.*" NBER Working Paper No. 8846. Cambridge: National Bureau of Economic Research.

OECD Main Economic Indicators. 2005. [URL: http://www.oecd.org].

Pirogov, S., and Tvorogova, S. 2007. "*Cross Cultural Aspects of Doing Business in Russia.*" In this volume.

Prašnikar, J. (ed.). 2005. "*Medium-Sized Firms and Economic Growth.*" New York: Nova Science Publishers, Inc.

Prašnikar, J., Domadenik, P., and Cirman, A. 2001. "Investment Activities of Slovenian Companies in the Countries of Former Yugoslavia" *Econonomic and Business Review* 3(2): 137–154.

Prašnikar, J., Pahor, M., and Zagoršek, H. 2007. "*A Comparison of Cultural Profiles of Young Managers from the Countries of South-Eastern Europe and Russia.*" In this volume.

Prašnikar, J., Pahor, M., and Vidmar Svetlik, J. 2006. "*The Convergence of Cultures: From Socialism to Capitalism.*" Prepared for the 3rd IEEE International Conference on Management of Innovation and Technology, Singapore, 2006. [URL: www.icmit.net].

Rejc Buhovac, A., and Slapničar, S. 2007. "*Organizational Culture and Managerial Control after an International Acquisition.*" In this volume.

Sandikci, O., and Ger, G. 2007. "*Contemporary Turkish Consumptionscape: Polarity and Plurality.*" In this volume.

Schwartz, S. H. 1994. "Are There Universal Aspects in the Structure and Contents of Human Values?" *Journal of Social Issues* 50: 19–45.

Stiglitz, J. E. 2004. "Capital-Market Liberalization, Globalization, and the IMF." *Oxford Review of Economic Policy* 20(1): 57–71.

Strukova, O. C., and Pushnykh, B. A. 2004. "Delovaja kultura Rusije: Izmerenije po Hofstede." *Menedžement Rosii za rubežom*: 2.

Tekavčič, M., Dimovski, V., Peljhan, D., and Škerlavaj, M. 2007. "*Cultural Fit as a Means of Strategy Implementation: The Case of Trimo Trebnje d.d. and Trimo VSK.*" In this volume.

Trompenaars, F. 1993. "*Riding the Waves of Culture: Understanding Cultural Diversity in Business.*" London: The Economist Books.

Trompenaars, F., and Woolliams, P. 2004. "*Business Across Cultures.*" Chichester: Capstone.

THT Consulting. 2005. Internal materials.

Türk, D. 2007. *"Challenges to International Security Today – An Overview."* In this volume.

Uvalić, M. 2007. *"Transition in Serbia and Montenegro: From Recurrent Crises Towards EU Integration."* In this volume.

World Development Report, 2006. Washington: World Bank, 2005.

World Development Indicators, 2005. Washington: World Bank, 2005.

Yusuf, S. 2004. *"Globalization and the Challenge for Developing Countries"*. Washington: World Bank.

World Investment Report 2004: The Shift Toward Services. New York: United Nations Conference on Trade and Development, United Nations, 2004.

Yip, G. 2003. "Global Strategy... in a World of Nations." In Gupta, A. K., and Westney, E. D. (eds.): *"Smart Globalization. Designing Global Strategies, Creating Global Networks."* San Francisco: John Wiley and Sons, Inc.

Zagoršek, H., and Štembergar, M. 2007. *"Culture and its Influence on Business Performance."* In this volume.

Zupan, N,. and Rejc, A. 2005. "Growing Through the HRM Strategies – Trimo Trebnje." In Prašnikar, J. (ed.): *"Medium-Sized Firms and Economic Growth."* New York: Nova Science Publisher, Inc.

Zupan, N., and Kaše, R. 2007. *"Helios Group's Investment in Serbia: A Strategic and Cultural Fit."* In this volume.

In: New Emerging Economies and Their Culture
Editors: J. Prašnikar, A. Cirman, pp. 23-37

ISBN: 978-1-60021-754-8
© 2007 Nova Science Publishers, Inc.

Chapter 2

IMPLICATIONS OF GLOBALIZATION AND SUSTAINABILITY FOR EMERGING BUSINESS MODELS[1]

Paul R. Kleindorfer

INTRODUCTION

The last two decades have seen immense changes in the forces and institutions that govern economic activity. These include a number of important managerial innovations that began with the quality and time-based revolution of the 1980s. They also encompass the on-going changes associated with the European Union, now with 25 member states, and the changes in liberalization and governance initiated by the World Trade Organization. What all this means for business activity has not yet been fully appreciated, but I would like to advance the notion straightaway that traditional ways of thinking of the company as master of its own destiny is too narrow a perspective for the new world order in which we live. Rather, its success is now tightly linked to its supply chain partners, to technology providers and to new markets and institutions that are the channels through which companies will connect to customers and to the revenue only they can provide. This is as true for companies in China or the United States as it is for companies in Slovenia, as our tightly interconnected world makes all of us partners in the global market place. What I believe is required is rethinking of the fundamental conceptual basis for a company's business model and strategy, a rethinking that encompasses the traditional sources of profit through efficiency and innovation, but that is also oriented towards sustainability of the company. I capture this thought under the banner of the Triple Bottom Line (3BL) movement, also called in some circles the "sustainable management" initiative. The 3BL flag proclaims three P's as essential to the long-run growth and survival of a company: People, the Planet and Profits. To support my basic proposition, I

---

[1] This paper is based in part on Kleindorfer and Van Wassenhove (2004) and Kleindorfer, Singhal and Van Wassenhove (2005). The author gratefully acknowledges Professors Singhal, Van Wassenhove and Jerry Wind for permission to use excerpts of our previous work together and for their continuing input on the themes developed in this paper, while maintaining sole responsibility for any opinions expressed here.

want to first sketch the history of business models and trends of the past 20 years, mostly directed towards improving profits. These trends clearly point to increasing globalization and the need to expand the horizons of traditional business models to encompass the new sources of value, and the concomitant new sources of risk associated with the longer and more complex supply chains delivering this value. I then turn to the issue of the other two P's, People and Planet Earth, to explore how the new profit-based business models can be integrated with 3BL thinking.

As the reader will readily note, the scope of this paper is focused on companies in the manufacturing sector. But it will also become clear that much of the service sector, from energy to logistics to communications to financial services, is deeply involved in the transformation and trends addressed through their supporting roles to the manufacturing sector.

UNDERLYING DRIVERS OF BUSINESS CHANGE FROM 1985 TO 2005

The launching of the European Union in 1992 came at an auspicious time for business innovations, as the 1980s had already underlined the benefits of Total Quality Management (TQM) and Just-in-Time manufacturing (JIT), imported to Europe and North America from Japan, where these philosophies had been refined in the 1960s and 1970s and came to be recognized there as the backbone of the reconstruction of the postwar Japanese economy. TQM and JIT (and its more general descendant "time-based competition") provided both tools and the elements of the management systems needed to integrate them with company strategy. These tools and management systems clearly had their locus of control and methodology directly associated with operations, reflecting their origin in the manufacturing sector.

It was not long before these new approaches and tools were integrated with strategy. Perhaps the most important conceptual driver for this integration was the work of Michael Porter who noted in his classic book on *Competitive Advantage* (Porter, 1985) that cost and revenue drivers of profit should not be understood as mere abstractions derived from the accounting structure. They should rather be identified directly with the Value Chain, as shown in Figure 2.1. For example, quality was not something that merely appeared in the final product, but it should be understood and managed as an attribute of the product that was actually built into it along the Value Chain. By relating profit drivers directly to their associated Value Chain activities, and by further mapping the Value Chain into its constituent sub-processes (such as Inbound Logistics, Production, Outbound Logistics, Sales and Customer Support), Porter gave a huge push to new initiatives to improve profitability. No longer was this to be done by command or by wishful thinking. Rather, fundamental drivers of profitability (on the cost and revenue side) were to be identified at the level of individual processes along the Value Chain and these drivers would then be managed and improved through identified activities in specific parts of the company responsible for the individual processes (from Logistics to Customer Support).

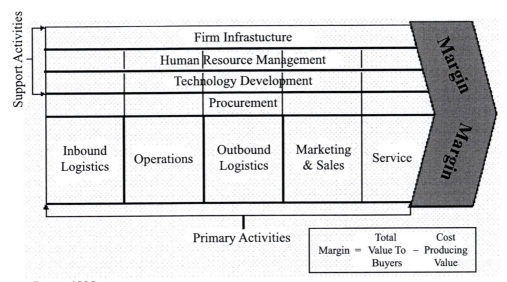

Source: Porter, 1985.

Figure 2.1. Porter Value Chain.

A direct consequence of this new attention to quality and time at the process level was the wave of change that began to take hold in the 1990s under the general heading of Business Process Reengineering (BPR). BPR had been announced in Hammer (1990), and it produced further benefits by applying to other business processes, outside of the Value Chain, the same time-based and waste-minimization efforts that manufacturing had demonstrated earlier in the TQM and JIT revolution. Gradually, this whole evolution came to be captured under the heading of "Process Management". Process management was given further impetus by the core competency movement (Hamel and Prahalad, 1994), which emphasized the importance of competencies, both technology-based and organizational, which a company needed to develop that were profit drivers for the products and services produced by the company and not easily imitable by competitors. The resulting confluence of the core competency movement with the paradigm of process management augured many of the changes that have occurred in the past decade, including unbundling of value chains and outsourcing, and the many contracting and supply chain innovations that have occurred in parallel with these. The relationship between process management and core competency theory is illustrated in Figure 2.2.

At the top of Figure 2.2 is the company mission and strategy process that gives rise to the strategic intent of the company in terms of the products it will produce and the markets in which it will compete. This is translated via core competency theory into those competencies that are required to maintain an advantage in competing against current and potential future products and competitors. But core competencies do not exist as abstractions; they must be translated into the business processes that embody and utilize these competencies. For example, if product design is considered a core competency for a company, it must be embodied in the business processes that deliver this competency. Finally, the key and core processes of the company can be either under the direct (Internal) control of the company itself, in a Joint Venture (JV) or Strategic Alliance (SA) with other companies, or outsourced as part of business process outsourcing and off-shoring (BPOandO). Outsourcing would usually not be undertaken for core processes, central to the survival and profitability of a company, but they very well could be for non-core business processes that exhibit sufficient economies of scale to overcome the transaction costs of contracting and rebundling of outsourced processes.

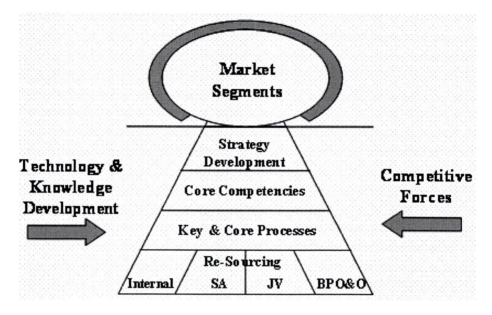

Figure 2.2. Core Competency Theory and Process Management.

As companies began to identify and develop their core competencies, and structure these activities into business processes, they discovered that the key drivers of performance that had been uncovered in the TQM and JIT revolution of the 1980s were precisely the tools and concepts necessary to uncover waste and to improve a wide range of business processes, from clearing the accounting books at the end of a quarter to relocating an executive from one country to another. It was natural that those business processes that encompassed the largest value add for the company, reflected in key metrics like Return on Assets, would become central elements on which corporate strategy and BPR activities focused. For many companies, these key business processes were associated with two fundamental areas, new product and process development and supply chain management, from raw material acquisition to consumption by the final customer. With this realization, another fact soon became clear, namely that these key processes were not company-centered, but rather involved multiple organizations, often globally, in a semi-cooperative activity of improving supply-chain wide performance and splitting the resulting pie amongst supply chain participants.

With the revolution in rationalizing global supply chains, the same process management tools and strategies that had been important to the successful internal redesign of organizations began to be exercised across organizations, from supply chains to new B2B markets. The resulting supply chain rationalization was very evident in post-1992 Europe, where numerous duplicative facilities and organizations that had previously been thought necessary for a company's country-specific operations were rationalized into pan-European supply chains. Company after company went through the progression of first rationalizing/shrinking its supplier base, then incorporating JIT between suppliers and production units, then moving to optimized logistics (including Efficient Consumer Response—ECR) between producers and distributors, then to improved Customer Relationship Management (CRM), and finally to global fulfillment architecture and supply-chain wide risk management, the watchword of today's global supply chain managers. These supply chain-focused trends have inspired similar elaborations at the corporate level, moving from Lean Operations to Lean Enterprises and now to Lean Consumption (see Womack and Jones (2005)). We show these trends and drivers in Figure 2.3 below, based on Kleindorfer and Van Wassenhove (2004). We also show the impact of emerging sustainable supply chains and reverse logistics, to be discussed further below, as encompassing and affecting all aspects of the supply chain in the future.

Starting with Porter's work on the Value Chain, and motivated by the success of the supply chain rationalizations of the 1990s, many of the most successful and innovative companies now formulate their strategies and business models in simple operational terms (Amazon.com, Dell, Li and Fung, Southwest Airlines, Toyota, Zara and many others), such as the JIT fulfillment strategies that are the hallmark of the business model of Dell Computers. Companies have moved from a narrow focus on costs, to an appreciation of the customer (service, willingness-to-pay) and to a closer scrutiny of assets (outsourcing, making fixed costs variable, focusing on core competencies and the costs and value of maintaining them). Logistics and Operations Management became central players in providing both the methods for analyzing and improving the key value drivers at the process level as well as the motive force for measuring and balancing costs, revenues and assets employed through integrated financial metric systems such as EVA = Economic Value Added (Stern and Shiely, 2001).

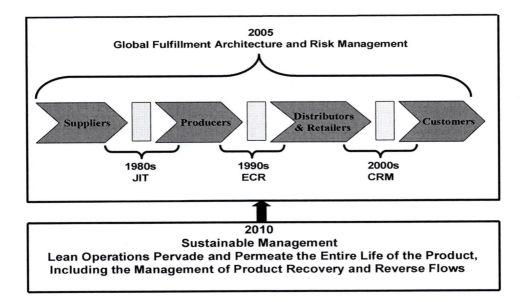

Figure 2.3. Locus of Value Chain Restructuring 1980–2010.

NEW MARKETS AND NEW RISKS[2]

Figure 2.4 illustrates how supply chain variables impact ROA. Traditional supply chain management would only consider costs as reflected by materials and manufacturing overheads, freights and duties, and conventional warehousing costs. With increasing internationalization, companies also started to look at site location for tax purposes and other benefits such as labor cost savings. Increasing risk of supply-demand mismatches led to more attention to inventory-driven costs. The latter are the costs of having the wrong inventories at the wrong time at the wrong place. Finally, Figure 2.4 shows the impact of supply chain management on assets. Decisions about what to keep in house and what to outsource or send offshore influence facility ownership costs and, through supply chain operations, also inventory and many other drivers of ROA.

The modern supply chain challenge is to strike the right balance between product availability, cost, and asset management (Figure 2.5), and there are risks that are inherent in striking this balance. Small inventories in lean supply chains are vulnerable to disruptions in revenue while large inventories (fat supply chains) are vulnerable to high inventory-driven costs (such as obsolescence). The risks from the rise of outsourcing and the pressure on asset base reduction in recent years have not been fully understood. In the expanding European market place and in the process of globalization generally, these complex, lean, and global supply chains are often more vulnerable to major natural and man-made disasters and altered power balances. Managing these risks will therefore become a central problem going forward for companies.

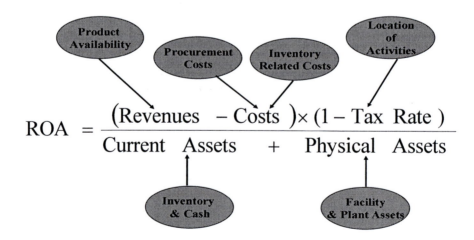

Figure 2.4. The Supply Chain's Impact on ROA.

---

[2]   This section is a very condensed version of Kleindorfer and Van Wassenhove (2004), to which the reader is referred for additional details.

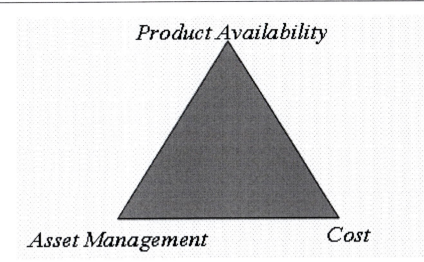

Figure 2.5. The Supply Chain's Balancing Act.

Research on the management of risks arising from global supply chains has generally been studied under two broad headings or categories of risks: supply-demand coordination and supply chain disruptions. Strategies for managing these risks draw upon three general approaches that global companies have typically used to address supply chain risks:

- *Supply chain design:* Design issues include facility location and sizing, product allocation, inventory points and logistics and using contracting innovations to better manage volume and price risk along the supply chain. Redesign activities to decrease cycle times and waste (usually in the form of excess inventory, equipment or facilities) from supply chains have been the chief preoccupation of researchers and practitioners throughout the 1990s. The key risk management question is: What is the appropriate balance between leanness and robustness to disruptions?

- *Contracting:* There has been a revolution in the literature and practice of contracting in supply chains, through both innovations in standard, negotiated contracts between individual buyers and sellers, as well as via B2B and B2C exchanges. Contracting and market instruments have been developed to convey better information on supply and demand, including price discovery and reduction of transactions costs of Buyer-Seller interactions. From a practitioner's point of view, the integrated use of these Internet-based contracting mechanisms, as facilitated by the new exchanges, represents a real opportunity for improved risk management of the supply chain.

- *Risk management systems:* The disciplines for analyzing, quantifying and managing disruption risks also have matured significantly in the past three decades. The field of risk analysis/management in industrial contexts consists of four integrated processes: (i) identifying underlying sources of risk and determining the pathways by which such risks can materialize, (ii) estimating the potential consequences of these risks under various scenarios, and (iii) mitigating these consequences and providing financing for residual risks; (iv) designing appropriate emergency response and crisis management systems.

Technologies such as web-based tools have helped improve coordination and remove information distortions. Effective supply chain contracts have also helped align incentives to mitigate mismatches between supply and demand. These innovative designs have increased transparency and coordination. A classic example of the latter is the collaboration between Wal-Mart and Proctor and Gamble leading to the now widespread practice of Vendor-Managed Inventory. Other innovations included Efficient Consumer Response and systems to support Everyday Low Pricing. Companies also developed modular products and processes to manage product variety and used late product differentiation or postponement to reduce demand-supply mismatches. All of these innovations have increased the efficiency of supply chains and procurement.

Leaner supply chains also increase these risks. Implementation of powerful information systems linked across supply chain partners (web-enabled ERP systems) and efforts to reduce supply chain costs led to smaller inventories and, in general, to leaner supply chains. While these leaner supply chains reduce inventory costs, companies have started to experience some of the negative consequences of leanness when their efficiency-based supply chains were not able to react to changing market demands and led to severe service deterioration. With increasing industry "clockspeed" (Fine, 2000), globalization, decreasing product lifecycles, overcapacity and maturing markets, the efficiency of supply chain management had often become less important than its effectiveness in demand-supply matching. Increasing complexity, more demanding customers, and low margins were increasingly making supply-demand mismatches extremely expensive (lost sales, obsoletes, idle capacity, high inventories), and many of the cost-squeezed lean supply chains were not exactly robust to even moderate environmental changes.

Dynamic supply-demand balancing is just as much about trying to get it right as it is about quickly repairing mistakes. It requires a nimble business process keeping everyone's eye on the ball continuously. Certainly, one of the most important developments in this regard in the past two decades has been the emergence of Internet-based e-Procurement. As the backbone of new B2B markets and exchanges, e-Procurement has advanced the potential of strategic risk management of coordination risks. E-Procurement builds on the developments of several decades in areas such as Material Requirement Planning (MRP), Enterprise Resource Planning (ERP), and supply-chain-wide Collaborative Planning Forecasting and Replenishment (CPFR) Systems. These online markets and exchanges enhance normal procurement and negotiated supply relationships with market-based price discovery and fulfillment. Together with further enhancements likely to follow the adoption of RFID technologies, one can expect supply-wide visibility and dynamic management of supply chains to be fast upon us.

A central feature of B2B and e-Procurement, especially for capital-intensive industries with non-scalable production facilities, is that contracting between buyers and sellers needs to take place well in advance of actual delivery. Failure to do so is a recipe for last-minute confusion and huge excess costs. This has given rise to a general recognition that most of a plant's or service facility's output should be contracted for well in advance. However, there is still a very important role for short-term fine-tuning of capacity and output to contract for, say, the last 10% of a plant's output or a customer's requirements. Doing so requires a conceptual framework, and supporting market instruments, that allows contracting to take place at various points of time, constrained by commitment and delivery options and flexibilities, and mediated by electronic markets where these are feasible. In the resulting integration of spot and contracting markets, contracting serves both the important role of reinforcing price discovery in the spot market as well as the obvious direct role of coordinating capacity commitments with anticipated demand. Together these strategies are the bow wave of a revolution to integrate risk management with supply chain operations, procurement, capacity management, and technology choice.

In addition to the risks of mismatch in supply and demand, disruption is an increasing risk in global supply chains. Disruption risks include: operational risks (equipment malfunctions, unforeseen discontinuities in supply, human-centered issues from strikes to fraud), and risks arising from natural hazards, terrorism, and political instability. Disruption risk has received increasing attention in the last few years. The reason is undoubtedly that, with longer paths and shorter clock speeds, there are more opportunities for disruption and a smaller margin for error if a disruption takes place. Hendricks and Singhal (2005) analyze announced shipping delays and other supply chain disruptions reported in the *Wall Street Journal* during the 1990s and show, based on matched sample comparisons, that companies experiencing such disruptions under-perform their peers significantly in stock performance as well as in operating performance as reflected in costs, sales and profits. As reported in Kleindorfer and Saad (2005), disruptions from accidents in the chemical industry have led to huge economic losses and environmental damages, from the Bhopal and Exxon Valdez disasters to the hundreds of lesser events that continue to occur on a yearly basis. Given these results, and the increasing reliance on cross-country supply chains as exemplified in the EU, it is not surprising that Enterprise Risk Management, including the management of supply chain disruptions, has become a high priority topic for senior management and shareholders.

SUSTAINABLE MANAGEMENT

Even as the new economic order, sketched above, began to unfold, it was recognized that profits and profitability were only one element of longer-term success of companies and the economies within which they operated. This key element needed to be joined to the futures of People, both internal and external to the enterprise, and to the impact of the company on Planet Earth, if the company was to maintain a claim to legitimacy. The new legitimacy was captured in metaphors such as the triple bottom line (3BL), the three P's of People, Profit and Planet, and in the notion that, to ensure its long-run survival and well-being, a company had to maintain both a viable social franchise (the ability to be trusted by its employees, customers, governments and communities in which it operates) as well as a viable economic franchise (the ability to pay from the cash flows it generates for the inputs, including capital, it uses to produces its outputs).

The result is that business models and strategies have been increasingly connected to the sustainability paradigm, and I will use this connection in this paper to speak of "Sustainable Management" (a term that I trace to Lars Bern and The Natural Step approach, as described in Nattrass and Altomare (1999), but which has earlier roots). By this I will mean both the foundations of excellence in execution and Profitability that have characterized the managerial innovations of the past two decades sketched above, as well as the intersection of this with the other two P's of People and the Planet.

The World Commission on Environment and Development (a.k.a. the Brundtland Commission, 1987) defined sustainable development as "development that meets the needs of the present without compromising the ability of future generations to meet their own needs." Criticized by some as murky and even dangerous in its all encompassing scope, the sustainability movement has nonetheless gained considerable traction in national and international circles. The reason is the evident inefficiency of our current products and production processes when it comes to the resources of the planet. This is as true for the industrialized countries as it is for the less industrialized ones, where inefficiency is rampant and provides itself huge opportunities for creating new value (e.g., as argued by Hart (2005) and Prahalad (2004)). To cite but one example of inefficiency, only about one percent of all material that originates at the top of the upstream supply chain for serving the United States remains in use six months after sale of the products containing it (Hawkins, Lovins and Lovins, 1999).

In the face of these growing concerns, there has been strong pressure exerted on business enterprises to measure their impact on the environment and to engage in 3BL reporting that would begin to account for the longer term footprint of the energy and other resources used by these enterprises. The basic activities driving the size of this footprint are the production and transportation of current products, the recycling and remanufacturing and reuse of used products, and the design of new products, so it is quite natural that operations and OM have been fundamental to measuring and reducing this footprint. The basic drivers of this movement are evident in Figure 2.6 below, reproduced from Corbett and Kleindorfer (2001).

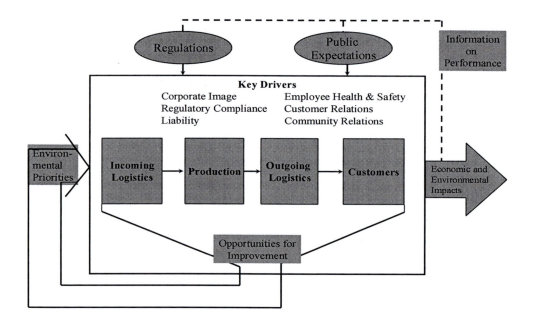

Figure 2.6. Sustainability and the Extended Value Chain.

From Figure 2.6, we see the basic forces shaping the planet/environmental and people side of sustainable management. To begin with the "P = people" side of 3BL, the employees working at an enterprise need to take pride in their work and return to the communities in which they live with a sense that the companies in which they work have operated in a prudent and responsible manner. There are also significant issues of employee health and safety that, if neglected, would give rise both to costly lost-time injuries as well as undermining the loyalty of employees.

On the "P = planet" dimension, alignment with internal employee and market incentives is usually much more difficult than for Profits or People, though community pressures and the threat of liability can be important drivers for improving environmental performance (Snir, 2001). But clearly the more important motivations for companies to improve environmental performance have been public pressure and the regulations put into place in response to this pressure. Companies themselves lobby for regulations (witness the growing number of lobbyists in Brussels!) if they have already developed an environment friendly technology and believe that regulation requiring the technology would give them a competitive advantage.

There has been a significant discussion in the strategy and public policy literature about the ultimate cost and benefits of environmental regulations. Many of the early discussions on the development and implementation of sustainable technologies were debated in terms of trade-offs between sustainability and economic competitiveness. A number of authors challenged this view. Porter (1991) reviewed the debate and argued that the "conflict between environmental protection and economic competitiveness is a false dichotomy based on a narrow view of the sources of prosperity and a static view of competition." Porter argued early on that tough environmental standards can trigger innovation and upgrading of sustainable technologies, noting: "Properly constructed regulatory standards, which aim at outcomes and not methods, will encourage companies to re-engineer their technology. The result in many cases is a process that not only pollutes less, but also lowers costs or improves quality." (Porter, 1991).

Throughout the world the public and its political representatives have been demanding an increased level of performance on environmental, health and safety (EHandS) issues affected by business activity. The question for companies has become not "whether" to commit to a strong EHandS record, but "how" to do so in a manner that is at least cost-effective and perhaps may add long-term value and profits to boot. In the process of facing up to this new reality, companies and entire sectors have discovered that in many instances the early Porter argument, reproduced above, is valid. The early years have been similar to the early quality era when, per Philip Crosby, "Quality is Free" was proclaimed, capturing the idea that if waste and bad quality are sufficiently rampant, then quality improvements pay for themselves. What is required is to add to the performance evaluation for business processes the appropriate metrics and targets for these areas of People and Planet, just the way quality and cost metrics were developed earlier to assure an operational foundation for excellence on the Profit dimension.

A prime reason for enlarging our perspective in our business models to include the other two P's of the 3BL metaphor is simply that this is what will be expected and required of companies going forward. In the short-term, many companies will continue to pursue end-of-pipe approaches (less polluting technologies) and "islands" of sustainable technologies for a particular component or a particular process. But in the long-term, it seems clear that there will have to be a better integration of the entire company (products, processes and operations) and its supply chains with sustainable technologies and operations, including a corporate culture able to internalize sustainability issues. Recently, Stuart Hart has suggested that we might reasonably expect a staged evolution towards sustainable management (see Hart, 2005), moving from a focus on today's activities internal to the firm to an external focus on future possibilities that drive both Profits as well as environmental excellence. Hart proposes the following evolution of increasing awareness and responsiveness to the 3BL challenge:

1. [Internal and Today Strategies] Improving internal operations with continuous process improvements related to sustainability: employee involvement, waste reduction, energy conservation, emission control, and so forth.
2. [External and Today Strategies] Improving extended supply chains: analysis of upstream supply chains to make trade-offs in the choice of materials and processes, closed-loop supply chains for remanufacturing, and safe disposal.
3. [Internal and Tomorrow Strategies] Investments in specific capabilities: recovery of pollution causing chemicals during intermediate stages of manufacturing so that they do not become a part of emissions; development of substitutes for nonrenewable inputs; and redesigning products for lower material content, lower energy consumption in manufacturing, or lower energy consumption in use.
4. [External and Tomorrow Strategies] Development of dynamic core capabilities in products, processes and operations, and supply chains for long-term sustainability and pursuit of a corporate strategy and culture that would facilitate it.

If I am correct in my assessment, we can expect a number of areas that are currently the subject of stage 1 strategies to come further into the light and to proceed through stages 2−4 above, reinforcing the new paradigm of sustainable management. Let me make a few preliminary observations based on recent research.

Corporate Image and Profitability: Mitigating environmental, health and safety (EH&S) impacts of company activities is not only socially responsible behavior; it is good business. Due to the public concern surrounding environmental issues, promoting environmental care can enhance a company's and an industry's image (Chinander, 2001). The adoption of Codes of Responsible Care in the Chemical Industry and the rapid spread of ISO 14000 illustrate this point (Angell, 2001; Corbett and Kirsch, 2001, 2004). Kassinis and Soteriou (2003) find further evidence in the hospitality industry that environmental practices affect profitability by improving customer satisfaction and loyalty.

Synergies between Lean and Green: Better EH&S performance can be an enabler of significant synergies with plant-level productivity efforts (Klassen, 2001; Corbett, 2005), as well as with increased revenues and market share (Delmas, 2001). Achieving these positive results requires management systems and tools that integrate appropriate performance metrics for EH&S with other process metrics, both internal to the company as well as across the supply chain (Bowen et al., 2001). Rothenberg et al. (2001) and King and Lenox (2001) offer empirical examinations of the links between lean manufacturing and green manufacturing, and both find some support that synergies exist here, but their studies also show that harvesting these synergies is by no means simple.

Reverse Logistics, Remanufacturing and Supply Chain Design: Smaller profit margins, shorter product life cycles and increasing environmental concerns are three good reasons why product take-back is a growing preoccupation in business. Small margins in the forward supply chain may easily be offset by the increasing costs of handling product returns, and short life cycles significantly augment the costs of obsolescence. In addition, companies are increasingly expected, or even legally required, to take responsibility for the entire life of their products, including proper recycling and disposal (e.g. the End of Life Vehicle and the Waste Electrical and Electronic Equipment Directives in the EU; see Guide and Van Wassenhove, 2001 for an introduction to reverse logistics). These challenges are increasingly being met and turned into profitable outcomes.

Regulatory Compliance: Regulatory compliance requires companies to track the use of hazardous substances and emissions of pollutants. Because regulatory scrutiny is costly, many companies have begun to commit themselves to go "beyond compliance" (e.g., in the XL and 33/50 programs in the USA and other voluntary programs elsewhere; Rothenberg et al., 2001).

Liability and Negligence: Another factor driving companies to improve their environmental performance is the risk of being held liable, or found negligent, for accidents or environmental damage. This is true even when the company is acting prudently and using state-of-the-art technology. To limit liabilities, many companies implement strict risk reduction mechanisms, with a focus on generally lowering the lower the level of pollution, biocides and toxics (P, B and T) associated with a company's supply chain and products produced (Kleindorfer and Saad, 2005). One aspect of this activity is product stewardship (Snir, 2001), which may be defined loosely as supply-chain wide identification and management of EHandS risks.

Employee Health and Safety: Similar to community concerns, employee health and safety is a key focus of risk reduction and risk communication initiatives (Chinander, 2001). Employee Health and Safety is not limited to company workers or on-site exposures, but includes all parties in the supply chain who may be exposed to a company's product.

Improved Tools and Management Systems for Better Product and Process Design: Achieving sustainable management practices requires integration of EH&S metrics with key business processes, measurement of results and commitment from top management. A number of managerial concepts, tools and systems exist that promote these steps towards sustainable OM practices. For example, life-cycle analysis, gated "Design-for-X" (DfX) screens (where Design for X includes X factors such as Environment, Safety, Disassembly, Recycling, etc.), and Eco-Logistics all promote more sustainable products and supply chains.

In summary, recent research on sustainable management supports the general 3BL hypothesis that "lean and green" seem to be woven from the same cloth of process excellence. Moreover, the growing number of empirical, theoretical and industry-based studies in this area suggest a synergy between management systems and operational excellence that fits well with the evolutionary framework of sustainable management proposed by Hart (2005). If so, then this framework has the power not just to organize our thinking about the history of companies, but also to motivate their futures.

CONCLUDING COMMENT

The world is changing fast, and the emerging economic order now being defined calls for new business models and new thinking about both the economic as well as the social franchises of business. The "new economy" emerging entails unbundled global supply chains, rebundling of these through flexible networks, and continuing pressures to integrate all elements of the 3BL banner: Profits, People and Planet. These changes suggest significant challenges for research and practice in integrating the basic management innovations of the past two decades with a new sense of commitment to sustainable management practices, garnering the profits which these practices have generated and adding to these a sense of pride and ownership by their employees, investors, customers, and surrounding communities in the practices of the company in which they are stakeholders. It is my belief that a long-run commitment to sustainable management principles will be an essential aspect of the new economy. Such a commitment clearly begins with Profits, without which businesses cannot survive, but also encompasses the larger responsibilities of companies to the People and the Planet without which our endeavors are meaningless.

REFERENCES

Angell, L. C. 2001. "Comparing the Environmental and Quality Initiatives of Baldrige Award Winners." *Production and Operations Management* 10(3): 306−326.

Bowen, F. E., Cousins, P. D., Lamming, R.C., and Faruk, A. C. 2001. "The Role of Supply Management Capabilities in Green Supply." *Production and Operation Management* 10(2): 174−189.

Chinander, K. R. 2001. "Aligning Accountability and Awareness for Environmental Performance in Operations." *Production and Operations Management* 10(3): 276−291.

Corbett, C. J. 2005. *"Extending the Horizons: Environmental Excellence as Key to Improving Operations."* Working Paper. Anderson School, UCLA, August.

Corbett, C. J., and Kirsch, D. A. 2001. "International Diffusion of ISO 14000 Certification." *Production and Operation Management* 10(3): 327−342.

Corbett, C. J., and Kirsch, D.A. 2004. "Response to Revisiting ISO 14000 Diffusion: A New "Look" at the Drivers of Certification." *Production and Operation Management* 13(3): 268−271.

Corbett, C. J., and Kleindorfer, P. R. 2001. "Introduction to the Special Issue on Environmental Management and Operations (Part 1: Manufacturing and Eco-Logistics)." *Production and Operations Management* 10(2): 107−111.

Delmas, M. D. 2001. "Stakeholders and Competitive Advantage: The Case of ISO 14001." *Production and Operation Management* 10(3): 343−358.

Fine, C. H. 2000. "Clockspeed-Based Strategies for Supply Chain Design." *Production and Operations Management* 9 (3): 213−221.

Guide, V. D. R. Jr., and Van Wassenhove, L. N. 2001. "Managing Product Returns for Remanufacturing." *Production and Operations Management* 10 (2): 142−155.

Hamel, G., and Prahalad, C. K. 1994. "Competing for the Future: Breakthrough Strategies for Seizing Control of Your Industry and Creating the Markets of Tomorrow." Boston: Harvard Business School Press.

Hammer, M. 1990. "Re-Engineering Work: Don't Automate, Obliterate." *Harvard Business Review*, July−August: 104−112.

Hart, S. L. 2005. "Capitalism at the Crossroads." Philadelphia: Wharton School Publishing Co.

Hawken, P., Lovins, A., and Lovins, L. H. 1999. "Natural Capitalism." Boston: Little Brown and Company.

Hendricks, K. B., and Singhal, V. R. 2005. "An Empirical Analysis of the Effect of Supply Chain Disruptions on Long-Run Stock Price and Equity Risk of the Firm." *Production and Operations Management* 14(1): 35–52.

Kassinis, G. I., and Soteriou, A. C. 2003. "Greening the Service Profit Chain: The Impact of Environmental Management Practices." *Production and Operations Management* 12(3): 386–403.

King, A. A., and Lenox, M. J. 2001. "Lean and Green? An Empirical Examination of the Relationship Between Lean Production and Environmental Performance." *Production and Operations Management* 10(3): 244–256.

Klassen, R. D. 2001. "Plant-Level Environmental Management Orientation: The Influence of Management Views and Plant Characteristics." *Production and Operations Management* 10(3): 257–275.

Kleindorfer, P. R., and Saad, G. H. 2005. "Disruption Risk Management in Supply Chains." *Production and Operations Management* 14(1): 53–68.

Kleindorfer, P. R., Singhal, K., and Van Wassenhove, L. N. 2005. "Sustainable Operations Management." *Production and Operations Management* 14(4): 482-492.

Kleindorfer, P. R., and Van Wassenhove, L. N. 2004. "Risk Management in Global Supply Chains." Chapter 12 in Gatignon, H. and Kimberly, J. (eds.): "The Alliance on Globalization." Cambridge University Press.

Melnyk, S. A., Sroufe, R. P., and Calantone, R. J. 2003. "A Model of Site-Specific Antecedents of ISO 14001 Certification." *Production and Operations Management* 12(3): 369–385.

Nattrass, B., and Altomare, M. 1999. "The Natural Step for Business." Gabriola Island: New Society Publishers. See also [URL: http://www.newsociety.com].

Porter, M. 1985. "Competitive Advantage." New York: Free Press.

Porter, M. 1991. "America's Green Strategy." *Scientific American*, April: 96.

Prahalad, C.K. 2004. "*The Fortune at the Bottom of the Pyramid.*" Philadelphia: Wharton Publishing.

Rothenberg, S., Pil, F. K., and Maxwell, J. 2001. "Lean, Green, and the Quest for Superior Performance." *Production and Operations Management* 10(3): 228–243.

Snir, E. M. 2001. "Liability as a Catalyst for Product Stewardship." *Production and Operations Management* 10(2): 190–206.

Stern, J. M., and Shiely, J. S. 2001. "The EVA Challenge." New York: John Wiley and Sons.

Womack, J. P., and Jones, D. T. 2005. "Lean Consumption." *Harvard Business Review* 83(3): 58–68.

WCED (World Commission on Environment and Development). 1987. "*Our Common Future.*" New York: Oxford University Press.

In: New Emerging Economies and Their Culture
Editors: J. Prašnikar, A. Cirman, pp. 39-43

ISBN: 978-1-60021-754-8
© 2007 Nova Science Publishers, Inc.

Chapter 3

TOWARDS MORE BALANCE IN THE GLOBAL SOCIETY

Janez Drnovšek

Globalization can be classified in any number of ways, as a matter of fact, it has permeated internationally into everything we do. But is globalization balanced? My answer is that it is not. Can market laws or any other autonomous mechanisms lead to balanced globalization? My answer is that they cannot. The situation in the world indicates that global imbalance is increasing at an expanding rate. Mankind as a whole benefits from its rapid development, the development of technologies and communication, but far from uniformly. The gains of globalization are distributed very unevenly throughout the world, and although we do not always seem to mind this or find it a cause for great concern, it is clear that such an imbalance can lead to a situation that will eventually bring any further progress to a halt. We are familiar with some of the primary imbalances in the world: firstly, the severe poverty that afflicts a considerable part of the world and that does not diminish despite the endeavors of the UN and other international institutions; and secondly, the alarming fact that this poverty is on the increase. The promise of the 2000 Millennium Development Goals was to halve extreme poverty; nevertheless, this goal is not being met, even though it is not overly ambitious. The trend, tragically, is moving in the wrong direction.[1]

It is encouraging to see, on the one hand, that new nations are becoming important players on the economic and world scene; China, Brazil and India, to name but a few. On the other hand, however, it is also true that the rapid development of these countries causes extremely large internal imbalances and tensions, social inequities and environmental disequilibrium. Development is not sustainable in these countries – it is not based on the preservation of the environment and on the setting-up of a sustainable, cohesive society in which internal relationships can survive over a longer period. For example, the differences in Communist China, paradoxically, are becoming enormous. We could say that this is capitalism of the most liberal type, causing extreme social splits, stratification and tension. This situation can also be encountered elsewhere in the world.

---

[1] This chapter was written in November 2005.

Another problem or danger that can be seen today when we speak of the world as a whole, is climatic change. All the experts agree that the climate is changing. Some are of the opinion that this is not at all due to the greenhouse gases that we expel into the air, but the majority thinks that it is. But they all concur – and the facts prove it – that the Earth is warming. Sea and air are getting hotter, natural catastrophes are multiplying, and weather phenomena are becoming ever more extreme. Forecasts for the future claim that this trend will continue. These issues require nothing less than the joint, concerted response of mankind. Otherwise, the problems of poverty generated by the environment, which is so sensitive, or terrorism or other forms of violence and the constant pressure of the movement of people, migrants from poor countries, will be transferred to the developed countries of the developed world. These imbalances can only be addressed by a common, united effort and not by haphazard, random economic or other actions without a conscious attempt to alleviate the situation.

This is not the case in today's world. The most developed nations, including the USA, Europe and the European Union, are to a large extent trying to establish an independent system of their own, based on the illusion that in this chaotic world, full of imbalances, they can protect themselves on their own islands of safety and prosperity. Is this possible at all? I think it is not. It is impossible to defend ourselves from all these influences, pressures and imbalances. They appear in different forms. Let us have a look at Europe and the European Union today to see what fears European citizens are faced with. Some of these fears have come to the fore during the public debate on the European Constitutional Treaty in France and the Netherlands: the fear of losing one's job, the fear of immigrants, and increasingly, the fear of natural catastrophes and terrorism. But these are all consequences of imbalanced globalization and mankind's inability to respond to it through concerted action. The pressure exerted by Asian competition, in particular on Europe and the USA, and also by competition based on very low-priced labor, is exceptionally cruel. Consequently, labor-intensive industries in the European Union have practically no possibility of protecting themselves from this pressure, and millions of jobs have already been lost. This competition is not only based on low labor costs, but also on the lack of respect for fundamental labor standards – child labor is very common, for example – and the fundamental social and environmental standards which the European producer is obliged to honor and comply with. This is an economic fact of life in Europe. Maintaining high labor, social and environmental standards makes it almost impossible to compete against other parts of the world where standards are not in force and where labor will always be cheaper, despite technological development.

There are still advantages in the organization that exists in European companies, but how long can this last? These advantages are diminishing, too. It is, therefore, obvious that the developed world and Europe cannot keep up with such competition and continue to respect and maintain its way of life at the same time. This is what workers in France, for example, must have felt when a number of large factories and multinational companies closed down before the referendum on the European constitutional treaty, with tens of thousands of jobs being lost. Neither national nor European politics could come up with answers or instruments to alleviate or overcome this specific fear of European citizens.

What is the way out of such a situation? It is necessary to raise awareness of these issues on a global scale. Awareness needs to be raised not only in citizens and politicians, but also in companies and all institutions and entities where we face these issues in one way or another. Awareness needs to be raised to the fact that we are, ultimately, interdependent and that it is impossible to build development models of the future based on the prosperity of only a part of humanity, while the other part is permanently condemned to living at the poverty line or even worse. We cannot expect that part of humanity to put up with it – sooner or later, the situation will erupt. Ample proof of this was provided last year in France when contained tensions suddenly exploded. It takes no more than a single spark. This can happen elsewhere, too, and may be followed by a second wave. And if this outbreak does not result in change, it is reasonable to expect that it may be followed by a bigger wave of terrorism, which is already in motion but can still gain further momentum. It is pointless to stick one's head in the sand; solutions must be found. They must be found on a global scale, where world organizations, the UN and development and financial institutions are very ineffective now. They are ineffective in solving these issues while they often give the impression that they are there to make us feel better and confident that things are getting done. In truth, not a great deal is happening, and trends show that a better approach will be needed.

Another framework which I would like to talk about is European – the European Union. What can the European Union do here? It should play a bigger role in global processes and carry more weight and influence toward rectifying these imbalances. But Europe is currently facing a crisis. The European Union is at a standstill. After two no-vote referendums in France and the Netherlands, after failing to reach an agreement on the Financial Perspective for 2007–2013, there is a standstill in the European Union. How to go on? The Constitutional Treaty is important because it represents an institutional framework for the future development of the European Union. Not only the future development, already today the number of European Union Member States is too big for the treaties currently in force, e.g. the Nice Treaty and former treaties. Already now, its administration is fairly inefficient. It became generally understood that something had to be done and, therefore, the European Constitutional Treaty was proposed in order to provide a more solid institutional framework and enable the further development of the European Union in a proper manner. However, it has come to a standstill. Two referendums have failed, and politicians seem not to know how to proceed.

I myself see both issues, the European Constitutional Treaty and the Financial Perspective 2007–2013, as mutually related. The Financial Perspective is not just any budget; it is the actual presentation of the priorities and objectives of the European Union. This can be seen through the goals of the Financial Perspective, its budget and what the EU will adopt in the coming seven years. Let us look at the European budget of today and at the one proposed but not adopted in June in Brussels. Almost one half of the funds are still earmarked for the Common Agricultural Policy. Much quoted is the piece of information that each dairy cow in the EU receives a subsidy of two euro a day. And that it is the main priority of the EU. We provide a 100 percent subsidy for agricultural products in the European Union. Agricultural production subsidised in this manner is then used for dumping on the world markets and destroying agriculture in developing countries. It is justifiable to protest here because we are setting up unjust and imbalanced relations in this area.

On the other hand, a relatively small part of European citizens participate in agricultural subsidies, by far the largest item in the European budget. And this part mostly benefits the largest landowners, not so much smaller farmers. In agriculture itself, funds could be allocated differently: more could be earmarked for "bio" production, which would be, I am convinced, of interest to European citizens concerned about their future. Healthier food means a less polluted environment, more for the preservation of rural areas, more for the creation of new jobs, not agricultural jobs in those areas that are in decline. So, reallocation itself could be beneficial. In France, people rejected the Constitutional Treaty in protest. France has always defended the agricultural budget, but how much does the European Union, in which agricultural production is subsidised to such an extent, mean to the vast majority of French citizens? It means nothing; they stand to gain nothing from it. This does not only apply to France, it applies to other EU Member States as well. They cannot provide answers to the problems that are a source of true concern for their citizens.

I am therefore convinced that EU priorities must change if the European Union and the Constitutional Treaty, which we would like to see ratified in all Member States, are to be regarded as needed and meaningful. However, what happened in Brussels in June when the budget was being adopted? First of all, expenditure for the Lisbon Agenda was reduced by forty percent from the sum proposed by the European Commission. The Presiding EU Member State immediately proposed, as a compromise, a forty percent reduction in expenditure for science, technological development, education, encouragement of competitiveness, in short, for everything that had for some years been regarded as the absolute priorities of the European Union. These became the first victim after the budget was set on the table, so that old priorities would remain, so that nothing would change, so that no lobby would be disadvantaged. And who can be enthusiastic about such a budget and an EU that approaches the future in such a way?

It seemed to me that it stood to reason to support the setting-up of a globalization fund, as some term it, in the EU in order to perhaps allocate part of the money released from agricultural subsidies and gained by a parallel elimination of the UK rebate, to this fund. Part would also go to the Lisbon Agenda for science, development and education. The globalization fund could, through its instruments, help those areas and activities that are most affected by the pressure of the competition I have just spoken about: the low-price, low-standard competition in some countries that weighs heavily on Europe. We are losing jobs, and this causes great tension and fear among the citizens of the European Union. If the EU had an instrument to help create new jobs in areas most affected, then it would become much more relevant, even for the French, who would perhaps deliver a yes-vote at a repeat referendum for the Constitutional Treaty. And it could become interesting for many others as well. Such a fund could be justifiable in global terms for as long as widely divergent labor, social and environmental standards exist. Until then, the European Union has a legitimate right to help endangered areas and to try to provide, through whatever instruments, new replacement jobs if current jobs cannot be retained. At the same time, the European Union should exert pressure through world institutions on the countries I have mentioned to gradually start raising their labor, social and environmental standards. I am aware that this is a long process that cannot be realized overnight, but it needs to be set in motion. And this process will lead somewhere: first to the stemming, and then to the gradual decrease of the imbalance existing in the world.

We need to be aware that the ultimate goal is the guarantee of a decent life to everyone; modest, but decent. This must be the ultimate goal: enabling a balanced existence in a world devoid of tensions that can so easily escalate in this way or that, through violence or other forms that can already be seen today. In the framework of the World Trade Organization, the UN, other institutions and development assistance, the European Union could pressure these countries to gradually raise their labor standards. If the situation of workers in these countries improves and if their standards of living increase, the aggressive thrust of migrants trying to enter Europe or the USA will abate. If not, it will continue increasing in the future, and it will not be possible to shield ourselves from it. We can only solve problems where they actually exist, and we need to be aware of them. We need to be aware that we should act over a longer period and be realistic that it cannot be done just by sitting down with the intention of solving it all at once. We can, however, set a direction, a policy, a constant that the European Union could advocate in world relations. This also applies to other issues, such as climate change. Here we shall have to become better organized, and at least respond better to catastrophes when they occur. Better forecasts and responses than recent ones will have to be provided.

The business world can do a great deal on its own. Politicians have to do a great deal, and citizens are already doing a great deal through various non-governmental organizations. Official institutions, though, are often reluctant to change, and something will have to be done there about this. In the business world, the practice of certain multinational companies includes creating and maintaining a sustainable environment, a kind of co-existence with the environment wherever in the world they establish their operations – for example, in Africa. Their experience has shown that this is indispensable if they wish to stay in business. Steps of any kind related to social and environmental aspects are an integral part of their policy. This is the right and only way. Not only socially and politically, but especially in business. Each company must be guaranteed a degree of internal cohesiveness and long-term sustainability of relations, positive, creative and motivating relationships between employees. Wherever personnel are dissatisfied or marginalized, this will reveal itself sooner or later. I recall the words of Peter Drucker, a great guru of the theory of organizations, saying that human relations are of key importance in a company. Motivation is of key importance – much more important than profit – as a driving force of development, a driving force of sustainable relationships and a positive force that can lead us forward.

In: New Emerging Economies and Their Culture
Editors: J. Prašnikar, A. Cirman, pp. 45-53
ISBN: 978-1-60021-754-8
© 2007 Nova Science Publishers, Inc.

Chapter 4

CHALLENGES TO INTERNATIONAL SECURITY TODAY – AN OVERVIEW

Danilo Türk

THE GLOBAL SECURITY LANDSCAPE

Discussions on international security are often influenced by the most acute international problems, usually those with the character of a crisis. However, this is not necessarily the best way to start a discussion. A prior identification of the key features of the general state of international security is necessary – as a platform from which we may proceed to assess sectoral issues such as terrorism or the proliferation of weapons of mass destruction and geographically defined issues such as Kosovo, Iraq or Darfur.

What is, then, the definition of the present global security landscape? Obviously, it would be overly ambitious to offer a single definition. However, it is realistic to identify the key elements which need to be considered in any definition.

Let us start by stating the obvious: We live in a world characterized by a relatively high level of strategic stability. Unlike in the not too distant past, the possibility for a conflagration among the main powers is very low and is likely to stay low. An interesting aspect is that, again, unlike in the recent past, the strategic stability of today is not based on any form of balance of power or balance of terror, but rather on the prevalence of an authentic interest of the major powers to cooperate. In other words, their impulses to compete are, at present, considerably weaker than their needs to cooperate.

This cooperative pattern has emerged in conditions of clear strategic imbalance, which is best described by the fact that the main power of our time, the USA, invests annually more than USD 500 billion in its military force, more than all other major powers - i.e. Russia, China, India, Japan and Europe – combined (the figure does not include US military spending in Iraq and Afghanistan) (Urquhart, 2005). The leading role of the USA is recognized, despite occasional rhetoric to the contrary and despite the fact that its global pre-eminence is not easily translatable into regional prevalence.

The second feature of the contemporary global security landscape is reflected in the fact that the number of armed conflicts around the world has been decreasing for the past ten years and that the positive effect of this should not be overlooked. The High Level Panel on Threats, Challenges and Change established by the UN Secretary-General in 2004 has recognized this and stated that the techniques of organized international community – such as peaceful settlement of disputes, peace-making and peace-keeping contributed to the positive trend witnessed in the past decade (A More Secure World: Our Shared Responsibility, 2004).

About a month ago another relevant study was presented at the UN. A report prepared by Andrew Mack, a former UN official and now professor at the University of British Columbia in Canada concluded that the number of armed conflicts has been reduced by 40% since 1992 and that the number of conflicts with more than 1,000 battle-deaths in a year has been reduced by 80%. Wars are mostly fought not by large mechanized armies but by militias and groups armed with light arms and small weapons (Mack, 2005).

Obviously, this essentially positive trend offers little consolation to victims of today's fighting in Iraq, Darfur, DR Congo or Nepal. However, the international community must appreciate the changing nature of armed conflict in our era and the changing needs resulting from that. The security doctrines, the security systems and the allocation of resources must be adjusted to the new situation. This is a tall order and a task which will require the work of a generation. But it is an urgent one and one has to start thinking about it seriously.

This leads to the third feature: The nature of threats to international peace and security is changing. This has been felt for quite a while now. In early 2003, before the Iraq war, the Secretary-General of the UN started a process aiming at the identification of the main types of threats to peace and security with the objective to offer a platform for a more efficient policy making in the future. He held discreet consultations with the members of the UN Security Council and, after obtaining the necessary support, he established a High Level Panel on Threats, Challenges and Change which – within a year – produced a comprehensive assessment of contemporary threats and proposed policies to address them. There are, according to the Panel, the following five major types of threats to international peace and security today (Report of the High-Level Panel, 2004):

- poverty, infectious diseases and environmental degradation;
- armed conflicts both between states and within states;
- nuclear, radiological, chemical and biological weapons;
- terrorism and
- transnational, organized crime.

The panel offered ideas regarding the necessary policy approaches to each of these major set of threats. They are based on the notion of prevention and suggest the basic elements of strategies to be devised.

The findings and the ideas offered by the Panel are widely shared by policy makers around the world. Let me mention, in passing, that the European Union produced a policy document initiated by its High Representative on Foreign and Security Policy with remarkably similar conclusions. The Secretary-General of the UN summarized the Panel's findings in his own report to the Summit on the occasion of the 60th Anniversary of the UN which took place in September 2005.

These developments are important because they have come a long way towards the crystallization of a common, collective understanding of the threats to international peace and security which is essential for the much needed collective action. Put differently, in the words used by Henry Kissinger (2002), one could say: "It cannot be in either American national interest or the world's interest to develop principles that grant every nation unfettered right to preemption against its own definition of threats to its security"... And what is needed is... "a serious consultation to develop general principles which can be considered being in the general interest." The logical conclusion of this is that a collective definition of threats and collectively developed principles of how these threats are to be addressed also require collective mechanisms of action, which is clearly preferable to individual action.

An agreed definition of threats is an important step in this direction, but it is only the first step. Within the broadly agreed definitions there continues to exist a space for individual interpretations and disagreement which can be overcome only in a permanent dialogue. This is why, more than ever before, the world needs adequate institutions and methodologies which enable discussion, agreement on collective action and collective implementation.

The needed institutional development is neither quick nor straightforward. It resembles a meandering river and is often accompanied by frustrations and disappointment. A good example of this was the failure of 2005 to reach an agreement on the reform of the UN Security Council. It became clear that more discussion and, above all, a more adequate political will among the current permanent members of the Security Council will be needed to develop a model of the Security Council that would be capable of serving the future needs better.

On the other hand, the UN had a degree of success expressed in the agreement to establish the UN Peacebuilding Commission, originally proposed by the High-Level Panel. The Commission which will work under the authority of the Security Council and will deal with post conflict stabilization and reconstruction – with the objective to make peace and stability in post conflict situations irreversible – is likely to come into being in 2006. This creates hope that some of the most important security issues of our time will be more effectively addressed in the future.

THE IMPORTANCE OF POST-CONFLICT PEACE BUILDING

In a world characterized by the decrease of the number of armed conflicts one has to pay attention to post-war problems. Many of these conflicts are not succeeded by durable peace. According to studies by the World Bank, about 50% of the recent armed conflicts have descended back to war. This is a frightening statistic which must resonate also in Slovenia, not far away from Bosnia and Kosovo where post-conflict efforts have not yet produced self-sustaining peace. Further to the east the World is facing the situation in Afghanistan, a country which has endured a generation-long war which devastated Afghan society, destabilized the region and, for a long while, produced a base for terrorism with a global reach. It is clear that situations like this require sustained attention and assistance, including economic assistance. According to the World Bank studies, the need for major economic investment in peace emerges about five years after the ending of the war, at a time when TV cameras are long gone and international attention is difficult to attract.

In the light of this kind of reality it will be very important to devise, through the future UN Peacebuilding Commission, a system of long-term activities. They will require the involvement of international and regional financial institutions as well as that of private companies. Large companies such as Siemens and others have already found their place in post-conflict peace building activities. Many others will have to follow. While the specific modalities of cooperation between intergovernmental and private sectors are not yet defined, this is the time to think strategically and figure out how can the private sector best help in the efforts to stabilize peace.[1] The future institutional development of post conflict peace building will have to include the business sector in new ways.

A POLYCENTRIC WORLD?

The importance of institution building which is clearly present at the global level has also important regional dimensions. Development of regional institutions in Europe, in the Americas, in Africa and in South East and Central Asia has already become a factor of strategic significance. At the institutional level we have seen the regional organizations taking an ever larger share of work for international peace and security although in a number of difficult crises it continues to be necessary to rely on the United Nations. The situations in Kosovo, East Timor and the DR Congo and, more recently, the situations in Lebanon and Bolivia are examples where the unique legitimacy and experience of the UN has become indispensable. However, in most of other regional situations the regional organizations play a leading role.

The institutional evolution in the major regions of the world is underpinned by power. The growing influence of China and Russia in Central Asia has given a great part of relevance to such new institutions in the region as the Shanghai Cooperation Organization which enables its members to enhance their collective action against terrorism, drug trafficking and other security threats. In Africa the creation of the African Union has been complemented by the growing role of such major players as Nigeria and South Africa in the crises in the Congo, in the Sudan and in West Africa. In Latin America where regional cooperation has a long history, the growing influence of Brazil represents a major factor of regional stability.

When put together, these regional trends, together with those in Europe and in South East Asia, offer a picture of a polycentric world, one in which the role of regional actors is growing and is likely to grow further. The capacity in dealing with the security challenges in the regions will grow correspondingly. It appears that the polycentric world offers a possibility of becoming a more secure world, provided that the current level of cooperation among the major powers is maintained and the effectiveness of regional institutions continues to grow.

The vision of a polycentric world should not be confused with the notion of multipolarity, which should be clearly rejected. The future of international security cannot possibly lie in the competition among major powers and the resulting balance of power which is in the core of the idea of multipolarity. Such a course is neither desirable nor realistic. The world has to take

---

[1]   For a discussion of the UN Security Council on the issue of participation of business in the post conflict peace building (with the active participation of a representative of Siemens) see UN. Doc. S/PV.4943, April 15, 2004.

advantage of the fact that the current imbalance of powers has contributed to the spirit of cooperation and that most of the major powers cannot really afford a competition motivated by an aspiration to the global balance of power. The main task now is to ensure that the regional balances of power, in particular those in Asia, take the realities of the regions adequately into account. Cooperation at this level is strongly needed and could, if handled responsibly, create conditions for durable global stability.

The foregoing five points have shown that ours is not the worst of all worlds. That it is not the best we have known since long ago. While the Panglossian hopes are clearly not on the agenda, it is credible to say that improvement of international security is possible, provided that adequate efforts are made. Which among them are essential?

A WAY TOWARDS INTEGRATION

The question of how to take advantage of the current situation of a relatively high level of stability and cooperation and how to translate it to long term improvement is a subject of lively if not comprehensive discussion. One of the recent contributions to this discussion deserves special attention. Richard Haas, former head of policy planning division in the Washington's State Department and current chairman of the Council on Foreign Relations in New York published a book with the ambitious title: "The Opportunity: America's Moment to Alter History's Course". The optimistic title of the book espouses views based on the American military, economic and technological primacy which, according to Haas (2005), "...could turn out to be an era of prolonged peace and prosperity, made possible by American primacy successfully translated into influence and effective international arrangements." However, Haas warns that " ...it could turn out to be an era of gradual decay, an incipient modern Dark Ages, brought on by the loss of control on the part of the United States and the other major powers and characterized by proliferation of weapons of mass destruction, failed states and growing terrorism and instability."

To ensure that the era of prolonged peace and prosperity comes about, the USA should pursue the policy of what Haas calls integration, which would give other powers a substantial stake in the maintenance of order, in fact co-opt them an make them pillars of international society.

These are wise thoughts easy to agree with. They are also not entirely new since the idea of integration has been in the core of President Roosevelt's concept of "four policemen" and the subsequent decision, enshrined in the UN Charter, regarding the five permanent members of the United Nations Security Council. However, the difficulty of implementing the idea of integration in a manner adequate to the changing power relations in the world must not be underestimated. The failure in 2005 to reach an agreement regarding the claim of Brazil, Germany, India and Japan to permanent seats of the UN Security Council is a stark reminder of the difficulties involved. Cooptation suggested by Richard Haas should be a permanent feature, not only an ad hoc, crisis-specific affair, if the prospect of a prolonged era of peace and stability is to succeed. The expansion of the group of permanent members of the UN Security Council will most likely succeed if the present permanent members reach an agreement first. It is realistic to expect that once such an agreement is reached other UN members will follow. A conference resembling the one in Dumbarton Oaks, Washington D.C.

in 1944 which laid down the security architecture of the United Nations, would be required, and the issue should be a matter of importance to the political leaders of the five permanent members of the Security Council.

While the UN clearly needs to be strengthened and reformed, it would be unrealistic to expect a single global organization, no matter how well developed, to be able to cope within the entirety of the issues of global security. The emerging polycentric world requires good management of multiple regional and global organizations, the existing ones and new ones to be developed in the future. The perennial dual issue of legitimacy and effectiveness of the international institutions can be handled only in a setting which accepts plurality of regional and global organizations and other actors capable of making a real contribution.

At the same time, the world, organized in its present form, will have to find ways to solve the most immediate security challenges of our time. Two among them stand out and require urgent attention.

THE NUCLEAR ISSUE

An important challenge which will require a more result-oriented approach is the use of nuclear energy, which is becoming ever more necessary. In this context, the question how to manage the expected heavier reliance on nuclear energy and avoid the danger of proliferation of nuclear and radiological weapons has already become essential.

Today's challenge of nuclear weapons is threefold. The most immediate problem, the one which is on the agenda right now, is posed by states which have legally permissible nuclear programs while they are suspected of pursuing, at the same time, illegal activities aiming at the production of nuclear weapons. The issues of the nuclear programs of Iran and North Korea are high on the international agenda. There is no doubt that the problems posed by these programs require immediate and real solutions. In both cases it would make a great deal of sense to find solutions for regional security issues. The real security needs of Iran and North Korea have to be recognized and collective arrangements for North East Asia and for the Gulf Region have to be devised. Reliance on non-proliferation norms without innovative arrangements addressing regional security concerns is not likely to yield lasting solutions. But even with these solutions the global problem of nuclear proliferation will not be solved.

At present, little attention is paid to a second problem which affects a much larger number of states. Here it is necessary to recall that the Treaty on Non-Proliferation of Nuclear Weapons (NPT) of 1968 very efficiently stopped the process of proliferation at its beginning. Instead of 25 to 50 nuclear states – the figure feared in early 1960s – the world has, 40 years later, only eight nuclear powers, a number which includes the five permanent members of the UN Security Council. In the 1990s a number of states emerging from the defunct Soviet Union as well as the post-apartheid South Africa renounced their ambition to obtain nuclear arms and joined, as non-nuclear states, the Non-Proliferation Treaty, which was made indefinite in 1995. These were major successes but they have not ensured the future of the Non-Proliferation Treaty. Should this important treaty, for whatever reason, unravel and the legal prohibitions of regarding nuclear proliferation wane, one could expect that 40 to 60 states would be able to without difficulty and very quickly build their own nuclear weapons.

In such a scenario the world would very quickly become a very unsafe place. The prospect of such a scenario in Asia is particularly frightening.

The third problem rests with the legitimate nuclear powers themselves. They have reduced their nuclear arsenals but there is still a long way to go. It is very important for them to understand that their progress towards nuclear disarmament in accordance with Article VI of the NPT – a long term objective but also one which calls for constant work on the reduction of nuclear arsenals – will have a major impact on the strengthening of nuclear non-proliferation.

The year 2005 witnessed the failure of two attempts to revive a meaningful discussion on nuclear non-proliferation at the global level – first at the review conference of States Parties to the NPT in spring and, later, at the UN summit in September. This gives rise to serious concern. The paradox is that there is no shortage of good proposals which could ensure progress. Three among them stand out as the most practical: first, the proposal to enlarge the number of states participating in the Proliferation Security Initiative which aims at the suppression of illicit trafficking with nuclear materials; second, to enlarge the number of states parties to the Additional Protocol of the International Atomic Energy Agency which established stricter regimes of control of facilities created for the peaceful use of nuclear energy; and third – perhaps the most important – the proposal for an immediate moratorium on the building of new enrichment or reprocessing facilities for nuclear materials. Such a commitment to the moratorium should be matched with a guarantee of the supply of the fissile materials by the current suppliers at market rates.[2]

The issue of nuclear proliferation requires special attention at this point in time because of its inherent importance for global security and because of its intimate link to the issue of the future energy needs and resources of the world. In all probability the importance of nuclear issues will grow as the prices of oil remain high and the need for additional energy more and more serious. In light of all these considerations one can only agree with the Nobel Committee which in 2005 awarded the Nobel Peace Prize to the International Atomic Energy Agency and its Director-General. IAEA remains the world's best hope for the articulation of solutions needed in the field of nuclear energy and nonproliferation.

THE CHALLENGE OF COUNTERTERRORISM

The problems of nuclear nonproliferation belong to the most serious security problems of our time. In addition, they also demonstrate the importance of preventive strategies, something that also applies to other sectoral security issues such as counterterrorism. Here, the preference for preventive strategies is obvious. Much has been achieved already, especially at the level of information sharing among states and in other forms of cooperation between security services of a wide variety of governments. It might be possible to develop, within a few years, an effective network of prevention.

At the same time, we have to understand two circumstances which affect the limits of efficiency of such a system. First, the terrorist's mind works in its own way, often – seen from our point of view – irrationally. Therefore, one should expect new and surprising forms of terrorist activity.

---

[2]   The Report of the High-Level Panel, 2004, supra, note 2., paragraph 131.

Second, democratic societies must conduct their defense against terrorism with the utmost care for protection of their core values enshrined in the existing codes of human rights. The evolving counterterrorism system will have to conform with the international norms of human rights. Everyone has the right not to be exposed to torture or degrading treatment or punishment and a number of rights defining the concept of fair trial. Freedom from torture and fair trial rights belong to the core values of every democratic society. And even when certain rights – such as the right to freedom of movement – can be limited in the interest of security, this needs to happen in a manner consistent with standards of international human rights law, enshrined in the international treaties on human rights.

In addition to these two essential policy considerations there is yet another layer of the problem which is very seldom discussed. In the recent years there has been far too little progress in attempting to address the root causes of terrorism. Here, the situation is complicated. The root causes are neither well understood nor is there enough international agreement on where to begin. Islamic radicalism, for example, is only an end product of a deeper malaise affecting some – and not all – of the Islamic societies and thus cannot be described as the root cause of all terrorist acts. Emergence of Islamic radicalism in Europe has to do with the larger issues of modernization and identity which emerge in this context. Therefore, they will have to be managed in a long term manner. No quick fixes are likely to succeed.

On the other hand, situations of foreign military occupation have been recognized in recent empirical studies conducted in the USA as a major cause generating terrorist activities, in particular suicide bombings (Pape, 2005). While it has to be stressed that suicide bombing and other terrorist activities are a legally unacceptable and morally repugnant form of combat and have to be clearly condemned, the international community cannot afford to overlook the causal links between terrorism and foreign military occupation. For political reasons it is extremely difficult to even recognize this causal link internationally, let alone agree on the viable policies to deal with this presumably important root cause of terrorism.

The international community may not be able to eradicate all the roots of terrorism. On the other hand, there are clearly discernible social ills which are among the factors contributing to terrorism where more can be done. The networks of internationally organized crime which represent a destabilizing factor per se are often connected with terrorist organizations. They are a significant part of the potential from which terrorist groups draw their financial capacity and firepower. Dismantling networks of arms dealers, drug traffickers and other similar organizations would go a long way to reduce the potential of future expansion of terrorism.

Preventing drug trafficking and related crime in Central Asia is an important priority, directly relevant to combating terrorism. In the Balkans, the institutions of post conflict normalization require an ingredient of prevention of organized crime. The purpose is not only to fight the existing crime organizations but also to prevent creation of possible links with terrorist organizations.

Tasks like this make the counterterrorism agenda complex. Unfortunately there is no easy way out. Terrorism has to be addressed in all of its dimensions if the international community is to succeed.

CONCLUSION

We live in a world which is strategically stable and where large scale wars are unlikely. But for many people the sense of insecurity continues and has new sources. Security today can be undermined by relatively small groups. The danger of a potential explosion of proliferation of nuclear weapons may look distant but real. The threats which might affect our future are not always clearly visible. However, they have to be taken seriously and effective new preventive strategies and forms of international security cooperation have to be devised. All this is doable. An increasingly polycentric international system can yield adequate forms of international cooperation and new institutions necessary to deal with these threats effectively.

REFERENCES

"A More Secure World: Our Shared Responsibility." *Report of the Secretary-General's High-Level Panel on Threats, Challenges and Change*, 2004. UN Publication Sales No. E. 05.I.5. New York: United Nations.

Haas, R. 2005. *"The Opportunity: America's Moment to Alter History's Course."* Public Affairs.

Kissinger, H. 2002. "Consult and Control: Bywords for Battling the New Enemy." *Washington Post*, September 16.

Mack, A. 2005. *"Human Security Report."* Vancouver: University of British Columbia.

Pape, R. A. 2005. "Dying to Win: The Strategic Logic of Suicide Terrorism." New Yoork: Random House.

"Report of the High-Level Panel", UN Publication, 2004

Urquhart, B. 2005. "The New American Century?" *The New York Review of Books* 52(13): 39–42.

PART II: A FRAMEWORK FOR STUDYING CULTURE IN THE BUSINESS MODEL

In: New Emerging Economies and Their Culture
Editors: J. Prašnikar, A. Cirman, pp. 57-71

ISBN: 978-1-60021-754-8
© 2007 Nova Science Publishers, Inc.

Chapter 5

CULTURE AND ITS INFLUENCE ON BUSINESS PERFORMANCE

Hugo Zagoršek and Mateja Štembergar

INTRODUCTION

In a time when we are becoming a part of a global business network, the understanding of culture and its impact on a company's performance is becoming the ultimate challenge for contemporary managers. "In every culture in the world such phenomena as authority, bureaucracy, creativity, good fellowship, verification and accountability are experienced in different ways. That we use the same words to describe them tends to make us unaware that our cultural biases and our accustomed conduct may not be appropriate or shared" (Trompenaars, 1993).

But managers do not need to be in contact with foreigners to experience the power of culture. Organizations have culture as well, often very powerful one. Even though managers all too often fail to pay attention to it, organizational culture often plays an important role in the overall performance of a company. Culture that is aligned with strategy (there is a "cultural fit") represents an important source of competitive advantage. On the other hand, if there is an incompatibility between culture and strategy, the culture may become a major obstacle that obstructs implementation of progressive changes.

This chapter covers three major topics. In the first part we discuss the features of national and organizational culture and their impact on a company's performance. The second part discusses the most relevant typologies that facilitate cultural studies. In the third part we discuss the concept of "cultural fit" – on the level of an individual company as well as on the level of a multi-business company.

CULTURAL STUDIES FRAMEWORK

Culture is not a part of "traditional managerial know-how and skills". It is often misunderstood, particularly due to uncertainty regarding the analysis – how to analyze it and what to do with the results. Picture 5.1 introduces the cultural studies framework, which facilitates the research of the interrelationship between culture and a company's performance.

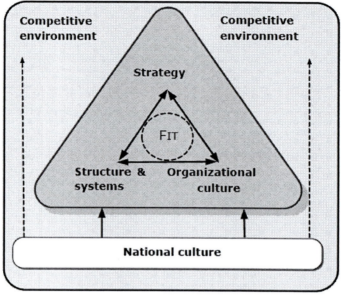

Source: Own work.

Picture 5.1. The Influence of Culture.

National culture is a context in which a company operates. It determines fundamental behavioral patterns, defines mutual relationships and regulates the activity of the people in a certain environment. Moreover, it has an impact on all three essential substructures of the company: strategy, structure and systems, and organizational culture. Even though it is possible that a company to some extent deviates from the prevailing cultural norms, it simply cannot act in opposition to them – there has to be a "cultural fit" between the company and the predominating culture of the environment. National culture has an indirect influence through competitive environment. It determines the nature and behavior of competitors, suppliers, customers, the availability and suitability of substitutes and the behavior of government and other state agencies. Whereas national culture indirectly influences the operation of a company, *organizational culture* represents its constitutive part. Organizational culture is "the essence" of an organization – it is what holds it firmly together. Organizational culture is in close relationship with strategy and structure and systems. Culture to a certain degree defines structure (for example hierarchy), structure in turn impacts culture (an example is formation of cross-functional teams, which should improve interdepartmental communication and establish open organizational culture). Likewise, successful implementation of strategy depends upon suitable culture. Strategy in turn facilitates the shift from existing to desired culture. On the other hand, strategy is *conditional on culture* since the principal participants enter this process with certain presumptions, expectations, ways of thinking and unique understanding of the world around us. If there is a fit between those three key components – strategy, structure and systems, and organizational culture – the the company will outperform. If there is a mismatch among them, the performance might suffer.

NATIONAL AND ORGANIZATIONAL CULTURE

National Culture

National culture is a shared system of meanings that dictates what people pay attention to, how they act, and what they value. It is a set of lenses for seeing and understanding the world (Trompenaars, 1993). Culture is shared among members of one group or society and has an interpretative function for the members of that group. The broadest definition of culture was proposed by Herskovits (1955), where *culture is the human-made part of the environment*. It can be divided into *objective* or *explicit culture*, such as technology, tools, roads and radio, and *subjective culture* such as ideas, meanings, norms, and values (Triandis, 1994; Berry et al., 2002). However, most researchers use the term culture only to denote subjective culture. Hofstede (1980), for example, understands culture as the collective programming of the mind that distinguishes the members of one human group from another. We define culture as a system of beliefs, values, norms, expectations and patterns of behavior common to all members of a society.

National culture is composed of different layers. Each layer lies deeper under the surface, with the invisible core at the center (Hofstede, 2001). The outer layer, which is also the most visible one, represents the *physical culture* (objective culture). This layer consists of objects, artifacts, and products produced by the members of a culture (for example buildings, machines, decorative objects, art, flags, clothes, roads, cities). The second layer consists of behavioral patterns, rituals, symbols and heroes. The first two layers are the reflection of the third layer – norms and practices. The *core layer* of culture rests on some basic assumptions about human existence, the purpose of living, and the most appropriate solutions to some universal problems that all societies face.

Some researchers believe that every culture is unique, non-repeatable and incomprehensible to the outside observers. Culture is not just one of the factors in the business equation, such as technology, strategy, employees' knowledge or market size. Although a good number of researchers agree that culture is a very complex phenomenon specific to a certain group, they still believe that comparison of cultures is possible through cultural dimensions (Box 1).

Box 1

Dimensions of National Culture

Throughout history several models of national culture that rest on empirical data were put forward. All models have a common issue - they try to "break" culture into several fundamental categories (dimensions) that reflect essential social issues that every society faces in the process of regulating human activity. Dimensions are often linear, with two contrary poles.

The fundamental cultural model was developed by Hofstede (1980)[9], who distinguished five elementary cultural dimensions: (1) *power distance, (2) uncertainty avoidance, (3) individualism/collectivism, (4) masculinity/femininity,* and *(5) long versus short term orientation.*

Similarly, Trompenaars (1993) identifies *seven fundamental cultural dimensions* based on which different responses to problems can be interpreted:

1) *Universalism vs. Particularism* is the degree to which universal rules, standards and values are in force. In particularistic societies circumstances are more important than rules.
2) *Individualism vs. Communitarianism* is the extent to which people give priority to an individual over the collective. This dimension is identical to Hofstede's individualism.
3) *Neutral vs. Affective* is the degree to which interactions among people are objective and neutral compared to interactions that are intertwined with emotions.
4) *Specific vs. Diffuse* presents the degree to which personal and professional lives are separated. Specific cultures tend to consistently make a distinction between personal and professional relations. Diffuse cultures on the other hand promote the intertwinement of different types of relationships.
5) *Achievement vs. Ascription* is the degree to which a society values people according to their achievements or according to their status attributed to them by birth, marriage, age, education and social capital.
6) *Attitude to time* reflects the relative importance of the past, present and future in a designated culture. It also defines the mode of time structure. The sequential mode understands time as a sequence of events while the synchronic mode claims that the past, present and future are intertwined in a way that the past and the future shape the present.
7) *Attitude to external environment* is the perception of the natural environment. Mechanistic cultures perceive the environment as a complex machine, which can be observed and directed. On the other side, organic cultures are based on the belief that companies and the environment must coexist.

Organizational Culture

We can claim that culture on the organizational level acts as the "glue" that keeps the company together. It can be defined as (1) the way things are done in an organization; (2) a system of informal and unwritten rules; (3) a system of common values, beliefs, assumptions which direct viewpoints, behavior and customs in the organization; and (4) everything that members of the organization see as a central, permanent and recognizable part of the organization (Trompenaars and Prud'homme, 2004). Organizational culture can consist of a bundle of subcultures formed by different departments, geographical units or groups of people with mutual interests. In a company with a strong organizational culture (e.g. IKEA, 3M, JUB) there is a significant consensus concerning the expected pattern of thinking and behavior. In a company with a weak organizational culture there is a wide variety of different beliefs, values and patterns of behavior, among which none of them stands out in meaning or frequency of appearance.

Organizational culture has a significant effect on organizational performance because it influences the decision-making process, the employment and the organizational response to the environment. Its effects can be positive as well as negative (Table 5.1). Both positive and negative effects are more evident in strong cultures than in the weaker ones. Thus only a strong organizational culture can represent a solid groundwork for competitive advantage in the company. But still, this advantage is not sustainable. If conditions of business substantially change, the culture might become a burden for the company and therefore a competitive disadvantage. This happened to IBM. Throughout its history, IBM had a typical engineering culture, which stirred up high level of pride and affiliation among employees. However, the arrival of personal computers has radically changed the conditions on the market. IBM's focus on big computers, where quality and functionality of the product were not suitable in the environment where smallness, flexibility and low price were more valued. IBM was not able to make a turn because its employees from the top down were caught into outdated ways of thinking. Only when the new top manager came to the company, culture changed.

Culture represents a solid ground for reaching a consensus as it is composed of values, beliefs and symbols that are to a large extent common to all members of the company. With that the *effectiveness of interrelations and communication* between employees can increase. Culture is also a *substitute for supervision*. The more an individual internalizes norms and values of a certain culture, the less formal control is needed. Collins and Porass (1997) in their book *Built to Last* establish that the key difference between average and successful companies included in their research, is a strong culture that performs almost as a cult. A strong culture was found in the most successful companies. It enables empowerment and a higher degree of decentralization compared to the companies that do not possess strong culture. These companies did not need a higher level of formal supervision of their employees or branch offices since strong indoctrination of employees assured that they would work in accordance with a company's norms, values and goals. Culture represents *organizational identity* as well. It is something that differentiates the company and makes it unique. That is why it stirs pride and stimulates employees' motivation.

---

⁹   Among the most cited models are those of Schwartz (1994), Inglehart (1997), Hall (1959) and Kluckhohn and Strodtbeck (1961).

Table 5.1. Effects of Organizational Culture

Positive effects	Negative effects
1 Increases effectiveness of interactions and communication	5 Obstructs changes
2 Conveys the identity	6 Reduces diversity
3 Stimulates commitment	7 Obstructs originality and innovativeness
4 A form of control mechanism/supervises behavior	8 Obstacle at mergers

Source: Own work.

On the other side, organizational culture by its nature *reduces heterogeneity* in the company. When employees share key values, expectations, goals and most adequate behavioral patterns, effectiveness can increase but diversity decreases. The same occurs with originality and new approaches which collide with an invincible obstacle in the form of *old habits and routines*. All of this can result in narrow thinking and comprehension and in *diminished innovativeness*. Affirmed patterns of thinking and behavior can become very hazardous when external environment or business conditions change. Culture can be the major obstacle for change and prevents the enforcement and realization of a new strategy which attempts to confront these changes. Organizational culture is at the same time one of the factors that causes problems in the integration process of two companies in a merger or an acquisition.

ORGANIZATIONAL CULTURE STUDIES FRAMEWORKS

Organizational culture has been explored for various purposes. Within an individual company, organizational culture can be analyzed in the process of strategic planning, as a part of company analysis. An understanding of one's own culture enables better decision-making and more realistic strategy planning. On the level of a multi-business company, we often compare cultures of different business units, companies or businesses. In order to take advantage of synergies and value creation on the level of a multi-business company, the adjustment of organizational cultures between two or more business units represents one of the key conditions. If cultures of various business units differ too much, conflicts and misunderstanding will occur in daily activities. The culture clash will reduce communication, transfer of knowledge and skills and consequently lead to unattained synergies. A similar situation will occur in the integration of two companies, namely in mergers or acquisitions. If two organizational cultures are simply too different, a newly established company will be faced with numerous conflicts and misunderstandings – it will be faced with "a cultural clash" (Weber and Camerer, 2004). In the case of mergers and acquisitions, the organizational culture of both companies need to be explored and the areas characterized by explicit agreements and disagreements need to be identified. The cultural study incorporates three sequential steps:

STEP 1:   Cultural due-diligence.

STEP 2:   Assessment of a fit between culture and strategy and assessment of a cultural fit between business units in the portfolio.

STEP 3:   Formulation of an actual measure that would reduce possible incompatibility.

The focal point of this chapter will be on the first two steps. In organizational culture due-diligence, both quantitative and qualitative approaches can be used. Qualitative approaches, such as semi-structured interviews, focus groups or observation, enable in-depth and rich insight into the specifics of the performance of an individual organization or its unit. However, qualitative approaches do not allow for comparison between different units of organization or between different organizations. They can be unreliable and biased as they depend upon subjective estimation of few employees. Quantitative approaches usually take the form of a survey that includes all employees. Survey questionnaires guarantee the representativeness of answers and facilitate comparisons. Because they are generic in nature, they can overlook the specific characteristics of an individual company. They also do not take into account important information such as stories, myths, legends, rituals and other customs in the organization. The comprehensive understanding of a specific organizational culture largely depends on the suitable combination of both approaches - we get the basic insight through the survey and then upgrade it with interviews with key employees.

Literature offers numerous models, protocols and typologies of organizational culture. They can roughly be divided into two categories. The first category is represented by *classifications of organizational culture*, where based on one or two dimensions authors identify several types of "typical" organizational cultures. Of course, none of the real organizations completely fall into a certain cultural type. Comparison of one's own organizational culture with the ideal type provides managers with an insight into patterns and dynamics of a company's business. The advantage of this typology is in its simplicity, comprehension, graphic representation and immediate comparison of own cultural profile with typical cultural profiles. The disadvantage is that various types of complex information are overlooked due to simplicity. Therefore, decisions based solely on this type of information can be difficult.

The other approach closely follows the tradition of *national culture studies*. Authors empirically or theoretically identify some bipolar dimensions of organizational cultures that represent different solutions to fundamental daily problems of organizational business. They compare different organizations or parts of organizations according to these dimensions. The two basic questions are Which dimensions are the most appropriate for the assessment of organizational culture? and Is it reasonable to assess organizational culture according to the same dimensions that are used in national culture studies?

We briefly present the organizational culture typology developed by Trompenaars and Wooliams (2004) (Box 2). But we should emphasize that there are other typologies that are frequently used in cultural studies. The competing values model (Quinn and Cameroon, 1998), for example, was developed as a result of a quest for factors that influence the organizational performance. The efficiency of the company is defined by two dimensions incorporating opposite values: (1) flexibility and consideration vs. stability and supervision, and (2) external orientation and differentiation vs. internal orientation and integration. These two dimensions classify the efficiency factors into four categories: *clan, adhocracy, hierarchy,* and *market.*

Box 2

Trompenaars and Wooliams Typology

Trompenaars and Wooliams (2004) developed an integrative organizational culture typology that separates between two dimensions: (1) Task or person (strong or weak formalization), (2) Hierarchical or egalitarian (strong or weak centralization). By combining these two dimensions we obtain four possible cultural types presented in Picture 5.2.

Incubator is an organizational culture simultaneously oriented towards equality and individuality. The most explicit attributes of the Incubator are individualization and a low level of formality and centralization. The organizational structure is very loose and supervision is in the form of a collective concern for other members of the organization. This kind of organizational culture is trying to "release" its employees from routine work and motivate them to be creative and innovative.

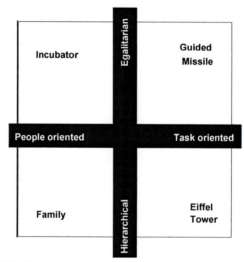

Source: Trompenaars and Wooliams, 2004.

Picture 5.2. Organizational Culture Typology According to Trompenaars and Wooliams (2004).

The organizational culture that Trompenaars denominates as the *Guided Missile* is a task-oriented culture. Achievement of objectives and efficiency are principal values and are far more important than authority, processes and employees. The role of the manager is to successfully manage the team by executing full authority.

The *Eiffel Tower* organizational culture is characterized by a high degree of formalization and centralization. Supervision is executed through a system of rules and is based on rights and obligations defined in advance. Hierarchy and power are of outmost importance. Processes are bureaucratic to the level that they assure accurate, routine and faultless implementation of tasks.

Family is characterized by a high level of centralization and a low level of formalization. Power is concentrated in an autocratic leader who leads the company in a similar way as in the power culture. Employees try to approach the center of power. The hierarchy is very important and is based on power and status. These kinds of organizations are usually family companies. The Family values more *who* the employees are than *what* they do.

CULTURAL FIT

The research of organizational culture allows the identification of the effects that those elements have (or could have) on the performance and effectiveness of the company. It incorporates the assessment of a "cultural fit" between the remaining elements of the company and between business units in a multi-business company. Provided that all constituent parts are adjusted, the sum of the parts exceeds the whole. Otherwise, the company is confronted with a certain degree of incompatibility and mutual exclusion of elements.

The assessment of a cultural fit is implemented on two levels (Picture 5.3):

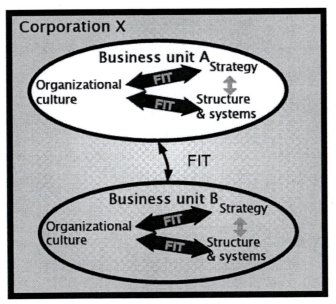

Source: Own work.

Picture 5.3. Cultural Fit in Individual and Multi-Business Company.

The first level examines the existing level of fit *in an individual company*, where the fit between organizational culture on one side and structure and strategy on the other is evaluated. Since all three organizational elements (culture, strategy and structure) represent the groundwork for each company, their compatibility is vital for the successful performance of the company.

The second level deals with the evaluation of a cultural fit *in a multi-business company* (between strategic business units). The assessment of a cultural (and strategic) fit is usually put into practice in mergers and acquisitions, where cultural and strategic due-diligence represent an important step in the pre-integration process. But we should highlight that evaluation of a fit is equally important for multi-business companies that already contain an existing portfolio of business units because a higher level of fit leads towards a higher value at the corporate level.

Cultural Fit in a Single Business Company

Culture by itself is neither good nor bad. Only when it is related to strategy (with preferred objectives and a means of achieving these objectives) can its suitability be properly assessed. For instance, culture that is in favor of risk-taking and a quest for new approaches can represent a competitive advantage in an advertising agency. But the very same culture is completely out of place for employees in a nuclear power station. In the first instance, the agency operates in a dynamic and ever changing environment. Its strategy emphasizes innovativeness and originality as one of the most significant tools for acquiring and retaining demanding clients. Inaccuracies are not fatal since they can merely be reflected on the profitability of the company. A nuclear power station on the other hand operates in a completely different environment denoted by stability, long-term orientation and detachment from daily demands of the market. Effectiveness and security are the key features of strategy. Experimentation and errors are inadmissible as they can result in appalling consequences. To summarize, different cultures are suitable for diverse competitive environments and different strategies.

Studies signify that economic performance is strongly related to a strategically suitable culture (Brown, 1995; Kotter and Hesket, 1992). In other words, companies that succeeded to fine-tune their organizational cultures with the external environment and strategy are on average more successful than companies with a lower level of cultural fit. But this only holds true for *strong* cultures. In the case of weak cultures, there is no correlation between culture and superior performance. Unless strategy is in harmony with the present culture, an enormous amount of energy and effort will be needed in order to overcome and modify established patterns of consideration and behavior (Green, 1988). Instead of adjusting strategy to culture (which is unreasonable) or modifying culture in order to fit the strategy (which is a very exhausting and time consuming process) it is in some cases possible to *overcome the culture* – this means that strategic objectives are attained in a different manner. However, the relationship between strategy and culture can be defined as a two-way process. Just like strategy exerts influence on the formation of organizational culture, the culture in turn influences the strategic decisions (Beach, 1993).

Organizational culture exerts influence on the strategies pursued by a company. Strategic analysis is always to some extent subjective. The decision about the most suitable strategy will for the most part depend upon the type of information selectively chosen by the company, the way this information is interpreted by the managers and also upon the power distribution among different subcultures within the company (Brown, 1995). Thus, organizational culture is the end result of preceding strategies, a factor of present strategies and the definer of future strategies (Williams et al., 1993). The fit between organizational culture and current strategy can significantly contribute to the successful implementation of strategic directions and consequently to the financial performance of the company. If there is a certain degree of incompatibility between culture and strategy, the company has several possibilities: it can alter the strategy, overcome culture or modify culture.

Cultural Fit in a Multi-Business Company

The issue of fit is central to companies that operate in more than one business (Ansoff, 1965). Numerous authors (Goold, Campbell and Alexander, 1994; Lee and Pennings, 1996; Marks, 1999; Thompson and Strickland, 1998; Weber, 1996) claim that there is a direct link between a company's performance and the level of fit between business units within its portfolio. Fit is supposed to be one of the most significant sources of value creation on both the business and corporate level in a multi-business company. The concept of fit is based on the assumption that business units with higher level of fit demonstrate supreme potential to create value (Salter and Weinhold, 1981). When we discuss the fit concept, we generally have in mind two dimensions of fit: (1) *strategic fit* (synergy) and (2) *cultural fit* (Ulijn et al., 2003).[10] Strategic fit represents a potential for attainment of synergistic effects in diverse areas. Cultural fit is on the other hand a prerequisite for realization of these synergies (Picture 5.4).

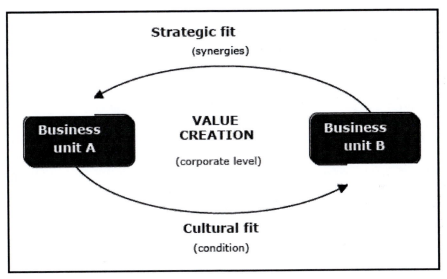

Source: Own work.

Picture 5.4. Strategic and Cultural Fit in a Multi-Business Company.

The strategic fit concept within a portfolio is not a new notion in the theory of strategic management. Ansoff was one of the first who linked fit with the superior performance of multi-business companies. He defines strategic fit (synergy) as compatibility between a multi-business company and a potential fraction of the portfolio (Ansoff, 1965). There are some authors who match up strategic fit with complementarities of business units (Besanko et al., 2004; Lee and Pennings, 1996). This conception of strategic fit highlights organizational processes, which turn out to be so specific for a selected company that we can talk about business models which are nontransferable and are therefore one of the sources of competitive advantage (Besanko et al., 2004). The significance of strategic fit is also

---

[10] We should highlight the fact that strategic and cultural fit are not exclusive components of the fit concept. The contributions that discuss the fit often examine organizational fit, financial fit, operative fit, human fit, managerial fit and competencies fit.

discussed by Porter (1998) who calls attention to management of reciprocal interrelatedness between companies. Without carefully managed interrelationships a multi-business company is little more than a mutual fund. Taking into account that strategic fit for the most part integrates common employment of resources and offers an opportunity for transfer of core capabilities, technological knowledge, managerial know-how, usage of corporate brand name, common distribution channels and financial resources, its benefits exceed standard advantages in companies, which have diversified into related businesses. Although strategic fit within a portfolio received the majority of interest, we have to take into account the level of strategic fit between business units in a portfolio and a corporate parent as well. The assumption behind this category of fit is that a corporate parent needs to develop specific characteristics that facilitate the superior performance of business units. Otherwise the incompatibility between the parent and the portfolio results in value destruction not merely on the business level but also on the corporate level. Goold, Campbell and Alexander (1994) point out that a corporate parent is compelled to create more value than a competitive corporate parent.

Even though the majority of mergers and acquisitions typically start with strategic due-diligence, since strategic fit is a prerequisite for a successful integration process, we need to call attention to the significance of *cultural fit*. The model in Picture 5.4 indicates the relationship between the strategic and cultural fit. Central to the model is the value creation and this value is created as long as the multi-business company administers the accomplishment of the desired level of fit between all business units that constitute the portfolio. If we look at the company from a financial view point, we can notice that strategic fit is one of the main concerns, particularly in terms of financial resource adjustment. But achieving fit on a merely strategic level is not a sufficient condition for improved performance of the company. Strategic fit is highly dependent upon compatibility of different organizational cultures of business units that are a part of the portfolio. We can therefore declare that cultural fit is a necessary condition for the accomplishment of strategic fit. Cultural fit will be less relevant for business units that are a part of a financial holding but very significant for a corporation with related diversification and extremely important during mergers and acquisitions, where complete integration of two business units into a new entity takes place. Cultural differences will be more distinctive in companies originating from diverse countries because they differ in national and organizational culture. Differences in organizational cultures can lead towards misunderstandings, fuel conflicts, cause emotional detachment (employees are no longer concerned with the success of the company and merger process), make a distinction between "us and them" and create an atmosphere of fear and mistrust in a period when it is necessary to create a positive environment and cooperation among employees (Haspeslagh and Jemison, 1991).

We can take a closer look at two companies, Daimler-Benz and Chrysler, which were otherwise aligned on the strategic level but the merger surprisingly turned out to be a failure due to lack of cultural fit and due to the effects of a culture clash on the national and organizational level. The merger had one objective: to establish a new business entity that would take the best from both worlds. Both companies were aware that the success of the integration largely depended on the merger of both cultures. The first obstruction in the integration process appeared to be two different national cultures – German and North American. Germans are known for their formality, planning and following the agenda. Americans, on the other hand, are more relaxed in communication (above all in addressing people and dress code) and sometimes have a tendency to go off on tangents. This was obviously "a marriage of opposites" on the organizational level. Daimler was known for hierarchy, formality and a structured decision making process. At Chrysler, employees worked in cross-functional teams that favored an informal dress code and open communication. Being aware of the cultural problems, Chrysler even organized business culture training. In spite of all that, tensions increased and many managers left the newly established company. The value of the company diminished as well. In short, the level of cultural fit between two companies determines the success of the integration process and a degree up to which benefits arising from strategic fit can be put to profitable use.

CONCLUSION

To summarize, culture has a significant impact on business performance. Companies are on one side confronted with national cultures that represents a broader context and at the same time shape their strategy, structure and systems and organizational culture. Even if companies are inevitably intertwined with their own national culture, they are at the same time also defined by characteristic organizational cultures. For the sake of influence that the culture has on the performance of a company, it is necessary to become aware of one's own culture to surpass cultural differences and diminish cultural incompatibilities. Both theory and practice propose numerous qualitative and quantitative methodologies that facilitate the identification of fundamental characteristics of culture. The results of cultural due-diligence are a significant building block of strategic planning as they allow for more realistic strategy planning and organizational structuring. Nevertheless, the true value of being familiar with one's own culture comes to light in case of mergers and acquisitions when it is necessary to foresee the effect of a cultural clash of two diverse organizational or even national cultures.

The aim of cultural studies is the evaluation of cultural fit, which is in addition to strategic fit one of the major sources of value creation in a multi-business company. Cultural fit does not imply that two cultures need to be identical but they do have to be compatible. Owing to the effects that cultural incompatibility tends to have on performance in a multi-business company and the post-integration process in mergers and acquisitions, the question of reducing the incompatibility is one of the most important issues. Decreased incompatibility is achievable only if managers are well acquainted with their own organizational culture. But since culture is "a living organism" and a human-made component of environment, it is dependent on people who mutually modify it. If we look at a company, we can state that managers are the first who should be aware that every aspect of their activity communicates their fundamental beliefs and values to the employees. If managers want to create a suitable environment, they have to accept and internalize the desired values and perform in accordance with these values. Only then can they anticipate that values and beliefs will not remain clichés on a sheet of paper left somewhere in a drawer but will rather be accepted by employees.

Cultural fit in a multi-business company is bound to coincide with strategic fit. While the strategic fit represents the potential for attainment of strategies on diverse levels, cultural fit represents a necessary condition for realization of synergies. Therefore the desired cultural fit needs to sustain the assurance of strategic fit.

REFERENCES

Ansoff, H. I. 1965. "*Corporate Strategy.*" New York: McGraw Hill.

Beach, L. R. 1993. "*Making the Right Decision: Organizational Culture, Vision, and Planning.*" Englewood Cliffs: Prentice Hall.

Berry, J. W., et al. 2002. "*Cross-Cultural Psychology: Research and Applications.*" Cambridge: Cambridge University Press.

Besanko, D., D., Dranove, Shanley M., and Schaefer S., 2004. "*Economics of Strategy*". New York: John Wiley and Sons.

Brown, A. 1995. "*Organisational Culture.*" London: Pitman.

Collins, J. C., and Porras, J. I. 1997. "*Built to Last: Successful Habits of Visionary Companies.*" New York: Harper Business.

Goold M., Campbell, A., and Alexander, M. 1994. "*Corporate-Level Strategy: Creating Value in the Multi-Business Company.*" New York: John Wiley and Sons Inc.

Green, S. 1988. "Understanding Corporate Culture and its Relation to Strategy." *International Studies of Management and Organizations* 18 (2): 6–28.

Hall, E. T. 1959. "*The Silent Language.*" New York: Doubleday.

Handy, C. B. 1978. "*The Gods of Management.*" London: Penguin.

Harrison, R. 1972. "How to Describe Your Organization." *Harvard Business Review* 50: 1928.

Haspeslagh, P. C., and Jemison, D. B. 1991. "Managing Acquisitions: Creating Value through Corporate Renewal." New York: Free Press.

Herskovits, M. J. 1955. "Cultural Anthropology." New York: Knopf.

Hofstede, G. 1980. "Culture's Consequences: International Differences in Work-Related Values." Beverly Hills: Sage.

Hofstede, G. 2001. "*Culture's Consequences: Comparing Values, Behaviors, Institutions and Organizations Across Nations.*" Thousand Oaks: Sage.

Hofstede, G., et al. 1990. "Measuring Organizational Cultures: A Qualitative and Quantitative Study Across Twenty Cases." *Administrative Science Quarterly* 35: 286–316.

House, R. J., et al. 2004. "*Culture, Leadership, and Organizations: The GLOBE Study of 62 Societies.*" Thousand Oaks: Sage.

Inglehart, R. 1997. "*Modernization and Postmodernization: Cultural, Economic, and Political Change in 43 Societies.*" Princeton: Princeton University Press.

Javidan, M., and House, R. J. 2001. "Cultural Acumen for the Global Manager: Lessons from Project GLOBE." *Organizational Dynamics* 29 (4): 289305.

Kluckhohn, C., and Strodtbeck, F. 1961. "*Variations in Value Orientations.*" Evanston: Row Peterson.

Kotter, J. P., and Heskett, J. L. 1992. "*Corporate Culture and Performance.*" New York: Free Press.

Lee, K., and Pennings, J. M. 1996. "Mergers and Acquisitions: Strategic-Organizational Fit and Outcomes. [URL: www.management.wharton.upenn.edu/pennings/research documents/smjlee11.doc].

Marks, M. L. 1999. "Adding Cultural Fit to Your Diligence Checklist. Mergers and Acquisitions." *The Dealmaker's Journal* 34 (3): 14–20.

Quinn, R. E., and Cameron, K. S. 1998. *"Diagnosing and Changing Organizational Culture: Based on the Competing Values Framework."* Reading: Addison-Wesley.

Salter, M. S., and Weinhold, W. A. 1981. "Choosing Compatible Acquisitions." *Harvard Business Review*: 117–127.

Schwartz, S. H. 1994. "Are There Universal Aspects in the Structure and Contents of Human Values?" *Journal of Social Issues* 50: 19–45.

Thompson, A. A., and Strickland, A. J. 1998. *"Strategic Management: Concepts and Cases."* Boston: Irwin/McGraw-Hill.

Triandis, H. C. 1994. *"Culture and Social Behavior."* New York: McGraw-Hill.

Trompenaars, F. 1993. *"Riding the Waves of Culture: Understanding Cultural Diversity in Business."* London: The Economist Books.

Trompenaars, F., and Prud'homme, P. 2004. *"Managing Change Across Corporate Cultures."* Chichester: Capstone Publishing Ltd.

Trompenaars, F., and Woolliams, P. 2004. *"Business Across Cultures."* Chichester: Capstone Publishing Ltd.

Ulijn, J., et al. 2003. "Culture and its Perception in Strategic Alliances, Does It Affect the Performance? An Exploratory Study into Dutch-German ventures." Eindhoven Centre for Innovation Studies.

Verbeke, W. 2000. "A Revision of Hofstede et al.'s (1990) Organizational Practice Scale." *Journal of Organizational Behavior* 21: 587–602.

Weber, R. A., and Camerer, C. F. 2004. "Cultural Conflict and Merger Failure: An Experimental Approach." *Management Science* 49 (4): 400–415.

Weber, Y. 1996. "Corporate Cultural Fit and Performance in Mergers and Acquisitions." *Human Relations* 49 (9): 1181–1202.

Weber, Y. 2000. *"Measuring Cultural Fit in Mergers and Acquisitions. Handbook of Organizational Culture and Climate."* Thousand Oaks: Sage.

Williams, A., et al. 1993. *"Changing Culture: New Organizational Approaches."* London: Institute of Personnel Management.

In: New Emerging Economies and Their Culture
Editors: J. Prašnikar, A. Cirman, pp. 73-84

ISBN: 978-1-60021-754-8
© 2007 Nova Science Publishers, Inc.

Chapter 6

SLOVENIAN NATIONAL CULTURE AND CROSS-CULTURAL TRAINING

Marijana Jazbec

INTRODUCTION

It took a long time in international business to prevail a belief that the internationalization of companies would create or at least approach the common culture of the world, i.e. Western culture. This would simplify the life of businesspeople. Very quickly, experience has shown that universal solutions do not work and that a dominant culture is no longer untouchable (Adler, 1997; Hofstede, 2001; Deresky, 2002; Jandt, 2004). On one hand, globalization has increased the need for standardization in organizations, systems and procedures; on the other hand it has forced businesspeople to adapt organizations to the local characteristics of a market, legislation, tax regime, social and political system; this is to the national culture (Trompenaars and Turner-Hampden, 2000).

Slovenian international companies are not multinationals. The majority of employees are of Slovenian nationality. In the past they mainly did business with companies from the former Yugoslav republics, Western, Central and Eastern Europe, the USA and Scandinavian countries. Slovenian managers are more or less familiar with the national cultures of these countries, with their values, customs and business practices. An awareness of the importance of different cultures was caused by the globalization of Slovenian companies, especially through business operations with Asian[11] and Muslim countries. Not speaking a local language, an importance of religion in business environment, silence as a part of communication etc. put Slovenian managers in difficult and unfamiliar situations.

---

[11] In Asia there are many countries with different cultures, such as Malaysia, Singapore, Hong Kong, Thailand, South Korea, China, Philippines, Taiwan, India. The common characteristic of "Asian" managers is that they all come from countries with high context in communication, meaning that much remains unsaid and is to be understood by itself. On the contrary the majority of European countries, including Slovenia, have low context communication, which means that all information is explicitly expressed. Therefore the general expression "Asian" has been used in the text.

International companies have developed cross-cultural training in order to improve employees' ability to communicate efficiently in the global business environment and to reduce the cultural shocks of personnel destined for overseas assignments (Hall, 1959; Mead, 1990; Hofstede, 2001; Deresky, 2002; Jandt, 2004). Training programs are based on the experience of former expatriates and differ as regards to the characteristics of a country that a businessperson is going to, tasks he/she will have to do and a person that needs to be trained (Tung, 1981).

LITERATURE OVERVIEW

Culture and Communication

Culture is a collective concept. It is best described with an "onion diagram" with external and internal layers. External layers (symbols, heroes, rituals etc.) are visible, whereas internal layers, such as values, remain hidden and are most resistant to changes. Values are a foundation of any culture (Hofstede, 2001). Each generation to some extent transforms values. Communication among different cultures means that senders and receivers of a message are persons coming from different cultural contexts. The greater the difference between the cultural background of a sender and a receiver, the greater the difference in the meaning connected with words and behavior (Samovar and Porter, 1991).

Managers communicate in order to coordinate activities, spread information, motivate people, negotiate etc. Therefore, it is important that a person who receives a message interprets its meaning in the way a sender expects. But unfortunately this is not always the case. The result of cross-cultural communication is not necessarily the understanding of a message. Everyone behaves differently when interacting with others. People subconsciously decide what they will pay attention to. Selective attention is necessary due to the existing mass of information that they are exposed to. People develop cognitive schemes and processes that enable them to categorize individuals and give meaning to societal connections. Besides cognitive processes, verbal and nonverbal processes are of great importance in cross-cultural communication as well. Language is the basic instrument in verbal processes. Nonverbal processes include messages that arouse first impressions; they can be conscious or subconscious, intentional or unintentional (Canary, Cody and Manusov, 2003).

National Culture

Comparing different cultures is usually done on the national basis. It is presumed that countries are culturally homogenous, meaning that cultural groups correspond to national groups. However, this is as a rule not true.[12] Nowadays nations do not have internal homogeneity. On the contrary, "they are a source of a considerable amount of a common mental programming of their citizens" (Hofstede, 1997). National cultures can be compared

---

[12] National cultures also have different subcultures. They are defined by religion (Northern Ireland), languages (Belgium), education (France) and others.

in several ways. The most common one is investigating differences that derive from value systems (Terpstra, 1978; Schwartz, 1999; Trompenaars and Turner-Hampden, 2000; Hofstede, 2001; Javidan and House, 2001). Value systems influence employees' behavior in their environment. It is necessary to point out that value dimensions belong to a national culture and not to individuals. If two nations differ in a specific value dimension, one cannot logically assume that two members of a nation differ as well.

The most widely used model for measuring differences among cultures was developed by Geert Hofstede. He identified the following five value dimensions of a culture: power distance, individualism/collectivism, uncertainty avoidance, masculinity/femininity, and later, being influenced by Chinese researchers, added the fifth dimension that refers to time orientation, i.e. short-term/long-term orientation.

Communicating in the International Business Environment

In the international business environment a response to a different culture may vary among managers. The most frequent one is ignorance of cultural differences. Managers use the same approach for all countries in which they do business. The other approach, also used very often, is ethnocentrism, which means that managers recognize differences, but only as a source of problems. In such companies an opinion prevails that their way is the best way, which can be described as a sort of a cultural dominance. On the other hand, there is a cultural adaptation in a sense "when in Rome, do as Romans do". Adler suggests cultural synergy as a response to cultural diversity. The synergy approach means that modes of managers and other employees differ, but none of them is superior. Cultural synergy is built upon similarities and links together all differences. This approach presumes that people are not all alike and it is necessary to respect and maintain one's own cultural specifics (Adler, 1997).

International companies operate in various cultural contexts. In order to do business efficiently in a global environment, companies must take into account the following cultural aspects: language, religion, values and attitudes, education, social organization, technology and material culture, the political environment, and the legal environment (Terpstra, 1978).

Cross-Cultural Training

Programs of cross-cultural training were, similar to programs of management training, first developed in the USA, which was a result of their low level of cultural sensitivity (Goodall, 2002). The type of cross-cultural training depends on the type of work. Furthermore, needs for cross-cultural training vary among companies. Executives, for example, usually have far more personal contacts with foreign managers than some professionals in a company. And the more personal the interaction, the greater the need for cross-cultural training. The evidence shows that companies, which pay considerably more attention to a recruitment and training of their employees regarding their work abroad, are far more successful than those who neglect the importance of cross-cultural training (Tung, 1981).

HYPOTHESIS AND EXPLANATION OF THE RESEARCH

Knowledge and skills in cross-cultural communication are not inborn; they can be acquired with appropriate training. With regard to this fact a hypothesis has been set stating that Slovenian managers express a greater need for cross-cultural training the greater the difference between their own and a foreign culture is.

The hypothesis was analyzed with the study that focused on value dimensions of Slovenian managers. Research was conducted with the use of Hofstede's Value Survey Module (1994). A calculation of value dimensions, which are always culturally determined, enabled a comparison with other countries in which Hofstede did similar studies. The questionnaire was sent to 1,760 managers by e-mail. The process of collecting data took place from June 28 until July 5, 2004. The sample was composed of managers who participated in short courses organized by the Center for Management Development and Training of the Faculty of Economics of Ljubljana University (CISEF).

The questionnaire contains six demographic questions and twenty questions related to the key topic. According to Hofstede, the experience showed that answers to the twenty key questions vary a lot among different nations. Based on this fact five groups of questions were formed, each containing four questions. These five groups represent five value dimensions of a national culture. All twenty questions were formed on the basis of a five-degree scale, 1 meaning the most important and 5 standing for not important.

The response rate was 31.9%. We received 454 answered questionnaires by e-mail, 48 by fax and 61 by mail.

EMPIRICAL RESULTS

The Results of the Study of Value Dimensions of Slovenian Managers

Among respondents in the research, 66% were female and 34% were male. The majority of them (69.8%) were between thirty and fifty years old. 80.3% of the respondents had a university degree. With regard to work positions, 88.9% held positions in middle or higher management. They were professionals in various business functions and managers, especially department leaders. 98% of respondents were of Slovenian nationality, 95.1% were Slovenians by birth. Although females with a high degree of education prevailed in the research, the calculation based on the ideal sample (ratio 50:50) shows that males and females do not differ significantly with regard to value dimensions. Indexes express the following value dimensions of Slovenian managers:

a) Power distance between superiors and their subordinates should be small (PDI=27.85). This points out that Slovenian managers are against inequality in society. The largest PDI index in Hofstede's research is 104 and the smallest one is 11. Slovenians expect and express the need for low power distance. They are in favor of cooperation and taking part in decision making in society. Interestingly, the PDI index for Yugoslavia, calculated by Hofstede in 1976, was relatively high (76). The situation was similar in the case of the countries of the former Soviet Union. This can be explained through time distance and by the fact that political leaders acted as gods during the communist period (Hofstede, 2002).

In companies with low power distance, organizations are decentralized; leaders are more available to their subordinates and are less controlling.[13] In cases of a low PDI, subordinates observe and evaluate the privileges and status symbols of their superiors. Still, almost half of respondents think that subordinates are often afraid to express their disagreement. Reasons for that might be a bad experience that subordinates have had with their superiors, as well as the Slovenian introverted nature. Slovenians prefer to say nothing than to offend somebody (Musek, 1994). An organizational structure with two or more superiors does not suit Slovenian managers, who are not in favor of matrix organizations. They are far more confident if there is only one superior and even he/she must be careful using his/her position as a superior. As regards to the fact that Slovenian managers are great individualists, we can point out that they could have difficulties with teamwork (Svetlik, 2000).

When calculating the PDI index separately for males and females, the results show that the latter are more inclined toward higher power distance than males. It seems that businesswomen are rational and disciplined in order to be more efficient. Slovenian women actually have two jobs, the second one starts at home. It suits females that their superiors are males. In general, respondents with more then high school education are less inclined toward high power distance. Mostly they are superiors themselves, they have more knowledge, experience and arguments, have better jobs, are more confident and it is easier for them to establish contacts. Surprisingly, those with a lower level of education follow (up to a university degree). Individuals who favor higher power distance are respondents with university-level education. This could be explained by the fact that there were many professionals in the sample who demanded an appropriate level of discipline to be effective at work.

Top managers of Slovenian international companies are in general dissatisfied with low power distance among superiors and their subordinates. They complain about the lack of responsibility. They claim that the middle-level employees demand many rights but do not take responsibility. In interviews one could get the impression that top managers are well aware of the advantages gained by low power distance. For example: information flow toward subordinates, consultations with subordinates, encouraging participation in discussion about improvements, the importance of self-initiative. They use these advantages. However, when making strategic decisions for which they are fully responsible, they are more inclined toward centralized decision-making and consequently higher power distance.

On the other hand, Slovenian companies do business with Asian countries with a higher degree of inequality, for example South Korea 60, Singapore 74, Hong Kong 68 and Taiwan 58.[14] In companies with a high PDI, subordinates do not miss not participating in leadership. They expect authoritative leadership and strong control. This ensures satisfaction, success and productivity. Subordinates simply expect and take orders.[15] These values originate from Confucius's lessons. It is necessary to obey the hierarchy. The stability of a society is maintained through unequal relations among people.

---

[13] A low level of direct control by leaders is one of important factors that contribute to work satisfaction (Svetlik, 1998).
[14] High power distance can also be found in Latin America and Arab countries.
[15] Inequality in societies with a high PDI starts in a family with a highly respectful attitude towards parents and other adults. Young people must listen to elder people, the latter protect the young ones.

b) Individualism/Collectivism. Thirty years ago Slovenia was a republic within a strong collectivistic country (Yugoslavia's IDV was 27). Today, Slovenian managers are among the top individualists (IDV=107.72). The highest index in Hofstede's research is 91, the lowest one is 6. A market economy supports individualism.[16] Slovenian managers take care of themselves and their nuclear families, value personal time and freedom. Time is of important value. Free time is something that a person shares with those who were chosen by his/herself. A variety of work brings Slovenian managers much satisfaction.

There are many more explanations of Slovenian individualism that go much further in the past. Žižek (1982) states that collectivism forced through the former system was not suited to the personality characteristics and tradition of the Slovenian people. "Ideology of irresponsible egalitarianism and antielitism has been forced. In collectivism there was no room for creativity" (Žižek, 1982). Slovenians are a hardworking nation. There is a lot of envy. One can be better in a way that takes something away from somebody else and not by being more productive than others (Musek, 1994; Trstenjak, 1991).

Slovenian men are bigger individualists than women. Such a result was expected, since males in Slovenia have better opportunities for a successful career, whereas females take care of their families. Regarding the education, IDV indexes show that respondents with higher education are greater individualists. On the contrary, those with a lower level of education express a greater need for social life, have fewer personal challenges and do not consider free time to be so valuable.

Slovenian top managers have a different opinion about individualism and collectivism. Those who are also owners of their firms are in favor of individualism, while the others are not. The latter think of Slovenians as "gardeners", each taking care of him/herself. Slovenians act as individualists where there is a question of rights, and as collectivists when making business decisions. They often develop hardly any synergy with other people because they are self-sufficient. Some top managers argue that this is due to capitalism we live in today. Others confirm that Slovenians have difficulties with teamwork. Leaders would rather spend their time in front of a computer than with people.

The Western concept of individualism that is connected with Christianity is less known to majority of Asian collectivistic countries. Their IDV indexes are low: Taiwan 17, South Korea 18, Singapore 20, and Hong Kong 25. In Asia, the smallest unit of the society is considered to be a family, not its individual member. From birth people are a part of strong communities that protect them for life. It is always about "we". "We" is not voluntary. The dependence on people in a community is practical and psychological. Collectivists avoid disagreements; societal harmony is a prime value. In collectivistic societies one does not trust just anybody; one can trust one of "us". In companies children of employees are employed because this lowers the risk. Superior-subordinate relationships are based on morals. In collectivistic societies trust must be established in the first place. This is the condition for signing the contract. It requires more time than Western managers usually plan for. Personal relations are more important than contracts. Chinese culture is still collectivistic, although individualism is increasing through industrialization and economic development of the country. The latest studies of the value's revitalization in Asian countries prove that family

---

[16]   In the 1992 – 1999 period, a decline from traditional collectivism to individualism is presented in the "Poročilo o človekovem razvoju Slovenije 2000–2001 (Human Development Report, Slovenia 2000–2001)". It points out that due to the exaggerated individualism of a free market there is a necessity for various forms of socially responsible development and that rights of individuals cannot be unlimited.

and respect of elder generations remain the main values (Langguth, 2003; Yin, 2003). In a family there is collectivism, in a company there is individualism. The mixture of collectivism and individualism makes business relations relatively hidden and therefore not well understandable to Slovenian managers.

c) *Masculinity/Femininity.* Feminine values prevail among Slovenian managers (MAS=20.26). This is relatively illogical at first sight. First, the data show that males are more individualistic than females. Second, males dominate in politics and economy, and lastly, countries with a Catholic tradition are more masculine than feminine. The empirical data show the opposite situation. A low MAS index is in accordance with a low PDI index and a high IDV index. Slovenians do not like inequality; they seek good relationships and a quality of life and take care of their families. The highest index in Hofstede's research is 95, the lowest one is 5.

Cooperation with others is an important feminine value. It may appear due to altruistic tendencies or pure selfish interests. Women as managers are good motivators for cooperation. Respect for each individual is important. There are no specific masculine and feminine jobs, although an inclination exists.[17] In companies with highly developed feminine values, good working atmosphere, open communication, quality of life etc. are important. Conflicts are solved through negotiations and compromises. A leader is not a hero but the first among equals.

Furthermore, the domination of feminine values is also confirmed by values of young people in Slovenia. Taking care of people, good relationships, the importance of family and the quality of everyday life are their most important values. "Criteria are changing and the meaning of "wealth" and "poverty" is changing, too. Sometimes young people would rather live with less income and a lower social status, if this brings them a higher quality of life or progress in self-realization" (Ule, 2004).

Masculinity/Femininity is a value dimension, which hardly differs among females and males in Slovenia. The prevalence of feminine values supports uncertainty avoidance and the already stated fact that Slovenians are hardworking people, follow rules, respect time, accuracy and reliability.[18] But they are always a step behind others. The calculation of MAS indices regarding education level shows that those with a lower education level have more feminine values, whereas those with a higher level of education express more masculine values. It appears that highly educated people focus on making great business careers. On the other hand, less educated people prefer and value good relationships.

Slovenian top managers believe that the business world in Slovenia is lead by men, not women. However, businesswomen are respected, especially those who are managers and experts in a financial and accounting sector. Only one of the respondents mentioned that in his company there were more women in high positions than men in similar companies in other European countries.

Asians have difficulties understanding the concept of exclusion of poles – positive/negative or masculine/feminine. The best-known dualism is yin and yang. Yin contains feminine elements (moon, water, nonresistant, dark, soft, passive etc.), whereas yang

---

[17] In Slovenia, it is normal for females to have a successful business career. In Arabic countries females do not have even basic rights.

[18] Typical characteristics of Slovenians are: motherhood, affinity for home, sensitivity and nostalgia, rootedness, tradition, societal focus, suppressed expansion, depression, imperfect male identity, hardworking attitude, and discipline (Žižek, 1982).

stands for masculinity (sun, fire, power, light, solid, active etc.). What is important is that yin and yang supplement each other and not exclude one another. They are inseparable (Fang, 2003).

d) Uncertainty avoidance. Slovenian managers prefer to avoid uncertainty (UAI=71.74). They favor order, laws, procedures, discipline, and rules. The highest UAI index in Hofsetede's research is 112, the lowest one is 8. This could be a reason for avoiding responsibility and disliking work in a matrix structured organization. Slovenian managers prefer predictability and stability. Unstable situations cause them stress. It is expected that superiors should provide answers to all questions, i.e. they prefer leaders who are the same time specialists. It is not desired from employees to break an organization's rules, even if this might be beneficial for an organization. Competition among employees also causes nervousness. Respondents were undecided whereas competition has positive or negative effects. Females and those with a lower level of education believe that it is rather negative.

A calculation of indexes separately for females and males illustrates that females are more risk averse than their male colleagues. Females appear to be "followers". They work hard, obey rules and instructions. They think of unpredictable situations as disturbing factors. Experimenting seems more suitable for males; usually they have more free time. Those with a lower level of education show greater uncertainty avoidance. They try to avoid unknown situations and vice versa. More educated respondents are more in favor of risk taking. They enjoy unpredictable situations and unknown environments.

Slovenian top managers explain a relatively high uncertainty avoidance with a need for security. Slovenian managers feel safest at home. Slovenians look for safety. This attitude starts with upbringing that aims towards obedience, restrictions, and failure avoidance.[19] Companies in Slovenia should work more on encouraging creativity, taking risks, and experimenting. They should avoid stimulating conservative behavior, average performance, and punishment. Every business is to some extent risky, since there is no development without risk. Top managers also suggest paying more attention to tolerance in families and in schools.

Tolerating opinions of others, doubts and diversity are also part of UAI values. A relatively high UAI index means that Slovenians are an intolerant, ethnocentric and xenophobic nation. They are not intolerant only to what is foreign, but also to what is Slovenian, but different. Intolerant people have difficulties living with others and seem to be introverted.

Uncertainty avoidance has its roots in specific history and in Catholic tradition. Trstenjak (1991) claims that Austria in times of the Habsburgs expected their citizens to be hardworking and disciplined workers. Slovenians always wanted to be good students as well as good teachers. A formula for a good student was to repeat teacher's lectures perfectly. "Different and creative thinking was never stimulated. It usually meant trouble to a teacher...discipline and the focus on a polite, obedient student and a teacher caused the so called vertical thinking of Slovenians, which was the opposite of lateral thinking that stimulates creativity" (Trstenjak, 1991). A Catholic church has had a strong influence on the upbringing focused on obedience and humility. The result of this inclination is uncertainty

---

[19] In schools the situation is similar. There is less room for doubts and relativity. Things need to be structured, goals must be clear, schedules must be written down. Pupils prefer questions where there is only one correct answer. They expect to be awarded for punctuality. It is recommended to agree with a teacher.

avoidance, decreasing the need for new experience, opposition to experimenting and oppressing wishes to be different. This is certainly not positive for a society that wishes to be innovative. Innovative people are not happy with rules. Changes are challenges. Innovative people are not so averse to changes, communication is less formal, they encourage creativity, a winning attitude and new ideas, and they are more tolerant of what is different.

The UAI dimension is not a universal value dimension, since it has no significant meaning among Asian values. Networks and personal relations, which are based on trust, are more important than laws and rules. Long-term orientation, which is so typical for Asian countries, causes a great deal of uncertainty. There is no room for absolute truth. The majority of Asian countries have lower UAI indexes.

e) Short-term/Long-term orientation. According to the LTO index (32.61), Slovenia is among relatively short-term oriented countries. Saving as a value is not expressed in Slovenia. Hard work does not necessarily mean a better life.[20] Free time is becoming an important factor. Striving for a better quality of life means living for today, satisfying plenty of various needs, both material and nonmaterial. The highest LTO index in Hofstede's research is 118 and the lowest one is 0.

Short-term/long-term orientation is the only dimension that originates in Asian and not in Western culture. Hofstede's research illustrates that Eastern Asian countries, especially China, Hong Kong, Taiwan, Japan and South Korea are mostly long-term oriented. The Netherlands is the most long-term oriented European country (Hofstede, 2001).

Slovenian women are more short-term oriented than men. It looks like they take care for a quality of life and do not pay much attention to what will happen in ten or more years. They satisfy the daily needs of their families, whereas men more often think of investments and objectives. The LTO indices show that respondents with a higher level of education are more short-term oriented. Those with a lower level of education who take care of themselves and their families cannot afford to live day by day. They are more long-term oriented. Since they are in a worse financial situation, they are inclined toward more systematic saving and have developed a positive attitude toward saving. Those with more money and better opportunities can more easily be short-term oriented. Money does not serve the same function to the rich and the poor.

Typical values of long-term oriented countries are: saving, self-discipline, a desire to learn. In Asia, free time is not a special value. Families carefully save money and think about the future. They behave pragmatically. People should adjust to circumstances. What is bad and what is good depends on a present situation. What is true and what is not true is less important than what works and how to achieve common goals. Family and business atmosphere are often linked together (Ralston et al., 1993). Intuition and common sense are as important as logic. (Hofstede, 2001).

Slovenian top managers believe that the existing short-term orientation is a result of a transitional nature of the Slovenian society. It is hard to be long-term oriented in such circumstances. Others think that there is no need for saving, as unemployment is not high and social security does not seem to be low either. The middle class is able to satisfy its relatively high material needs (house, car, vacation). Managers who are not owners have more short-

---

[20] Slovenians have a positive attitude toward work. At the beginning of the transition period, they considered saving as an important value. Moving away from a materialistic vision of the society, however, resulted in a loss of importance for saving (Poročilo o človekovem razvoju Slovenije 2000–2001 (Human Development Report, Slovenia 2000–2001)).

term goals than companies' owners. Short-term orientation is to some extent in accordance with uncertainty avoidance. Long-term goals bring along great uncertainty.

At the end we used cluster analysis (Ward Method) to classify countries by data for all five value dimensions into groups. Four groups of countries were formed (Picture 6.1.):

1. USA, Great Britain, Canada, Germany
2. the Netherlands, Sweden, Slovenia
3. Pakistan, the Philippines
4. Taiwan, South Korea, Brazil, Thailand, India, Hong Kong

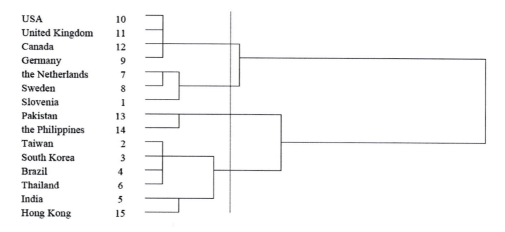

Source: Own work.

Picture 6.1. Classification of Countries According to Five Value Dimensions.

According to the above classification we can claim that Slovenian managers get along best with Dutch and Swedish managers and less so with managers from Asian and Latin American countries. Therefore, it is possible to conclude that Slovenians express a greater need for cross-cultural training when a difference between their own and a foreign culture is greater. Analysis of variance, which was used to test differences among groups, proves that group 2, which also includes Slovenia, differs from the group of Asian countries in all dimensions except in UAI (Jazbec, 2005).

CONCLUSION

Slovenians prefer equality in a society, they are individualists with feminine values, they want to avoid uncertainty and are not long-term oriented.

Slovenian companies have become fully aware of culture's influence on business when they started penetrating Asian markets. Top managers admit that they would be more efficient in doing business with these countries, if they better knew and understood their culture. Understanding a Chinese value system is relevant for Slovenian international companies. First impressions are instructive, and to some extent alarming. They warn that it is not enough to consider Confucius's values, as might be understood from the books about traditional Chinese philosophy. Slovenian companies will compete in developing the best pragmatic approaches to business operations.

Slovenian companies must act pragmatically, too. If cross-cultural communication with Asian managers is such an obstacle in doing business, it is essential to engage in an intensive research of markets that are culturally closer. Russia and Turkey, for example, are two big and, for most of Slovenian companies, still fairly unknown markets. Better knowledge of their culture and especially value dimensions would lead to a better understanding of managerial behavior. Nevertheless, being aware of culture's influence on business and understanding the necessity of cross-cultural training are crucial for recognizing, respecting and appropriately responding in a specific culture. People always do business.

REFERENCES

Adler, J. N. 1997. *"International Dimensions of Organizational Behavior."* Cincinnati: South-Western College Publishing.

Canary, J. D., Cody, J. M., and Manusov, L. V. 2003. "Four Important Cognitive Processes." In Galvin, M. K., and Cooper, J. P. (eds): *"Making Connections. Readings in Relational Communication."* Third Edition. Los Angeles: Roxbury Publishing Company: 35–42.

Cushner, K., and Brislin, W. R. 1996. "Cross-Cultural Interactions. A Practical Guide." Thousand Oaks: Sage Publications.

Deresky, H. 2002. *"International Management."* New Jersey: Pearson Education, Inc.

Fang, T. 2003. "A Critique of Hofstede's Fifth National Culture Dimension." *International Journal of Cross Cultural Management*, 3 (3): 347–368.

Glaser, R. 1984. "Education and Thinking: The Role of Knowledge." *American Psychologist*, 39: 93–104.

Goodall, K. 2002. "Managing to Learn: From Cross-Cultural Theory to Management Education Practice." In Warner, M., and Joynt, P. (eds): *"Managing Across Cultures: Issues and Perspectives."* London: Thomson Learning: 257–268.

Hall, T. E. 1959. *"The Silent Language."* New York: Doubleday.

Hofstede, G. 1997. *"Culture and Organization: The Software of the Mind."* New York: McGraw-Hill.

Hofstede, G. 2001. *"Culture's Consequences. Comparing Values, Behaviors, Institutions and Organizations Across Nations."* Second Edition. Thousand Oaks: Sage Publications.

Hofstede, G. 2002. "Images of Europe: Past, Present and Future." In Warner, M., and Joynt P. (eds): *"Managing Across Cultures: Issues and Perspectives."* Thomson Learning, London: 89–103.

Jandt, E. F. 2004. *"An Introduction of Cross-Cultural Communication."* Thousand Oaks: Sage Publications.

Javidan, M., and House, J. R. 2001. "Cultural Acumen for the Global Manager: Lessons from Project GLOBE." *Organisational Dynamics*, 29 (4): 289–305.

Jazbec, M. 2005. *"Medkulturno komuniciranje kot sestavni del poslovnega izobraževanja."* Magistrsko delo. Ljubljana: Fakulteta za družbene vede Univerze v Ljubljani.

Langguth, G. 2003. "Asian Values Revisited." *Asia Europe Journal*, February, 1 (1): 25–42.

Mead, R. 1990. "Cross-Cultural Management Communication." Chichester: John Wiley and Sons.

Musek, J. 1994. *"Psihološki portret Slovencev."* Ljubljana: Znanstveno in publicistično središče.

Poročilo o človekovem razvoju Slovenija 2000–2001. Hanžek, M., and Gregorčič, M. (eds). Ljubljana: Urad RS za makroekonomske analize in razvoj and UNP.

Ralston, A. D., Gustafson, J. D., Cheung, F., and Terpstra, H. R. 1993. "Differences in Managerial Values: A Study of U.S., Hong Kong and PRC Managers." [URL.: http://faculty-staff.ou.edu/R/David a.Ralston-1/uhp1993.html], 2005.

Samovar, A. L., and Porter, E. R. 1991. "Communication Between Cultures." Belmont: Wadsworth Publishing Company.

Schwartz, H. S. 1999. "A Theory of Cultural Values and Some Implications for Work." *Applied Psychology: An International Review*, 48 (1): 23–47.

Svetlik, I. 1998. "Oblikovanje dela in kakovost delovnega življenja." In Možina, S. (ed): *"Management kadrovskih virov."* Ljubljana: Fakulteta za družbene vede: 147–174.

Svetlik, I. 2000. "Work Values in the Course of Transition in Slovenia." In Adigun, I., and Svetlik, I. (eds): *"Managing Cultural Diversity – Implications for the EU Integration. Special Issue."* Ljubljana: Inštitut za družbene vede. Fakulteta za družbene vede: 9–17.

Terpstra, V. 1978. "The Cultural Environment of International Business." Cincinnati: South-Western Publishing Co.

Trstenjak, A. 1991. "Misli o slovenskem človeku." Ljubljana: Založništvo slovenske knjige.

Trompenaars, F., and Hampden-Turner, C. 2000. *"Riding the Waves of Culture."* London: Nicholas Brealey Publishing.

Tung, L. R. 1981. "Selection and Training of Personnel for Overseas Assignments." *Columbia Journal of World Business*, 16 (1): 68–78.

Ule, M. 2004a. "Nove vrednote za novo tisočletje: spremembe življenjskih in vrednostnih orientacij mladih v Sloveniji." In Mlinar, Z. (ed): "Demokratizacija, profesionalizacija in odpiranje v svet." *Teorija in praksa*, 41 (1/2): 352–360.

Ulijn J., Nagel A., and Liang, T. W. 2001. "The Impact of National, Corporate and Professional Cultures on Innovation: German and Dutch Firms Compared." *Journal of Enterprising Culture*, 1 (1): 21–52.

Yin, L. C. 2003. "Do Traditional Values Still Exist in Modern Chinese Societies?" *Asia Europe Journal*, February, 1 (1): 43–59.

Žižek, S. 1982. *"Zgodovina in nezavedno."* Ljubljana: Cankarjeva založba.

In: New Emerging Economies and Their Culture
Editors: J. Prašnikar, A. Cirman, pp. 85-99
ISBN: 978-1-60021-754-8
© 2007 Nova Science Publishers, Inc.

Chapter 7

COMPARISON OF CULTURAL PROFILES OF YOUNG MANAGERS FROM THE COUNTRIES OF SOUTH-EASTERN EUROPE AND RUSSIA

Janez Prašnikar, Marko Pahor and Hugo Zagoršek

INTRODUCTION

Mapping national cultures is a comprehensive, demanding and time consuming project. Until now only a few researchers have managed to collect comprehensive databases of comparable data for the majority of countries. On the basis of research conducted at the end of the 1970s, Hofstede (2001) researched four basic dimensions in approximately 60 countries worldwide. Ten years later, under the influence of Asian researchers, he added the fifth dimension. The research consortium GLOBE (House et al., 2004) has collected data on nine cultural dimensions for 62 countries. Trompenaars (1993; 2004) draws from a constantly growing database of more than 55,000 managers from over 50 countries.[21]

Eastern European countries are mainly not included in the above mentioned research. This particularly holds for countries on the territory of the former Yugoslavia, which represent a "blank spot" on the international map of national cultures. With the exception of Slovenia, internationally comparable data concerning the cultural profiles for these countries do not exist.

In this chapter we present the results of a comparative study of cultural profiles of young managers from certain countries on the territory of the former Yugoslavia (Slovenia, Croatia, Bosnia and Herzegovina, Serbia and Montenegro) and Russia. These are managers who have recently completed their education or are still included in post graduate studies of business sciences and therefore have little or even no work experience. Additionally, they come from transitional countries and perceive new social circumstances similarly, thus forming similar values, beliefs and points of view. On the other hand, they belong to different national cultures. Our research confirms the influence of both types of factors on the formation of

---

[21] More on various models of culture see Zagoršek and Štembergar (in this book).

managers' cultural profiles. Its significance is also in that it shows the usefulness of the methodology employed in such research.

In the next part we first present the results of the existing studies in selected countries. In the third part we present the methodology. We follow with the presentation of the results and the comparison of cultural profiles of different groups of managers. The concluding part contains the main observations.

BRIEF INTRODUCTION OF HOFSTEDE'S STUDY OF CULTURAL PROFILES IN STUDIED COUNTRIES

The cultures of the studied countries, all of which are Slavic, have a lot of commonalities as well as differences. However, being a large country and having played a substantial role in the history, Russian culture has excelled for centuries. On the other hand, cultures of the former Yugoslav countries have mainly been influenced by the Central European, Mediterranean, Eastern and Dinaric cultures (Goić, 2005). The Central European culture comes from the northwest, from the territory as well as the institutions of the former Austro-Hungarian monarchy. Eastern cultural influences were primarily brought by the Turks in times of their invasions from the southeast and have left an important impact in the invaded area. The Dinaric culture, present in the central hilly parts of the Western Balkans, could be described as autochthonous to this area. It had presumably existed long before the arrival of the Slavs. The dominant and distinctive culture in individual countries of the Western Balkans has certainly developed under the influence of a specific combination of all these influences. It may be broadly presumed that the intensity of individual influences was proportional to the distance from the transmitting source. According to this presumption the Central European and (to a lesser extent) the Mediterranean culture would have the greatest influence in Slovenia. In Croatia one can talk about a combination of the Central European, the Mediterranean and the Dinaric (especially in central parts) cultural components in different concentrations in individual parts of the country. In Bosnia and Herzegovina a combination of the Dinaric and the Eastern culture is present. The Dinaric culture is dominant in Montenegro, with some characteristics of the Eastern and (on the coast) the Mediterranean culture. In Serbia one can talk about a combination of the Dinaric and the Eastern culture, with specific (slightly less important) characteristics of the Central European culture (Goić, 2005).

Besides historical and geographical determinants, the contemporary culture in these countries has also been influenced by recent experiences and events. In the second half of the 20th century they were socialist countries. Four of these countries (on the territory of the former Yugoslavia) spent the majority of the previous century in the same country and therefore belonged to a uniform ideology. After the breakup of Yugoslavia at the end of the 20th century three of them were involved in a bloody ethnic conflict.

Little empirical data concerning the level of similarities or differences among cultures of the countries on the territory of the former Yugoslavia exist. Some stress that geographical and linguistic proximity and a shared history in the 20th century are reflected also in the cultural proximity of the nations in this area. Since people concentrate more on differences while taking similarities for granted, the former are often unjustly emphasized. Only by stepping out of a regional framework and observing ourselves in the world-wide context can we see how similar the cultures of these countries are compared to other European, American, Asian or African countries (Wachtel, 1998).

Others point out that the fact that we speak similar languages does not mean that we ascribe the same meaning to events around us. A nation's culture is rather stable. It is questionable to what extent the forced ideological homogenization during the time of Yugoslavia left its traces in the national cultures of individual nations. Significant disagreements at the breakup of Yugoslavia show that there might be more mutual differences than we imagine (Debeljak, 1986).

At the end of the 70s Hofstede (1980) included three of the then Yugoslav republics in his research: Slovenia, Croatia and Serbia (Table 7.1). Considering the intense social changes within the last 30 years the data are likely to be slightly out of date. They are also unreliable because of small samples, as in some republics fewer than 40 people answered the questions. The iteration of Hofstede's research, performed for Slovenia by Jazbec (in this book), shows that at least in Slovenia the current state on some dimensions differs from the one presented in Table 7.1[22]. However, the results of the original study show a high similarity in the way of thinking and beliefs of people of the then republics.

Substantial power distance or respect for hierarchy and authority is present in all three countries that arose from the former Yugoslavia. It is the highest in Serbia and slightly lower in Slovenia and Croatia. All three countries are quite collectivistic (putting community ahead of an individual). Croatia is the most individualistic although differences among countries on this dimension are almost negligible. Typically feminine values, such as good relationships, cooperation and general quality of life (in contrast with achievement, heroism, work and material success), prevail in all three countries. Slovenia stands out in the direction of femininity. In all three countries strong uncertainty avoidance is present – risk aversiveness and avoidance of unstructured, non-transparent and uncertain procedures and circumstances. In summary, the data from Hofstede's research confirm the thesis about substantial cultural proximity and similarity among the countries of the former Yugoslavia.

Table 7.1. Dimensions of National Culture According to Hofstede (2001) for Slovenia, Croatia and Serbia

	Power distance (PDI)	Individualism (IDV)	Masculinity/ Femininity (MAS)	Uncertainty avoidance (UAI)
Slovenia	71	27	19	88
Croatia	73	33	40	80
Serbia	86	25	43	92
Russia	90	50	40	90

Note: Numbers present an index of a country's ranking approximately on the scale between 1 and 100, where a higher number indicates a higher intensity of a specific dimension. Numbers for Russia are based on estimates (Hofstede, 1993).

---

[22] Results of the research performed on the sample of 563 Slovenian managers are: Slovenes are highly individualistic (IDV 107), inclined towards low power distance (IPD 28) and uncertainty avoidance (UAI 72), with prevailing feminine values (MAS 20) and relatively short-term oriented (LTO 33). For more on this see Jazbec in this book.

Russia is rather different. Power distance and the presence of individualism are high. The uncertainty avoidance is similar to the countries of the former Yugoslavia; however it differs from Slovenia in the degree of femininity – in Russia masculine values are more evident.

METHODOLOGY

Questionnaire. In our research we have used a questionnaire about national culture developed by Trompenaars (1993). The questionnaire includes various types of questions, such as short scenarios where an individual is forced to choose between two alternatives, questions where an individual among several statements chooses the most suitable one and classic Likert-type questions where an individual expresses his/her agreement or disagreement with a certain statement on a one-to-five scale. The questionnaire has been tested on numerous samples and has good psychometric characteristics (Trompenaars and Wooliams, 2004).

Trompenaars (1993) distinguishes seven basic dimensions of culture that represent key challenges of existence of a human as a social being. Dimensions of organizational culture are added to the dimensions of national culture. With their aid it is possible to form various types of current and ideal organizational culture. The four types of organizational culture are formed by combining two dimensions: 1) orientation towards a task or person and 2) hierarchy or egalitarianism (Trompenaars and Wooliams, 2004).[23]

Sample and course of research. The research of cultural dimensions was performed on ten groups of current and former postgraduate students of business sciences in seven countries. A total of 650 people participated in filling out questionnaires. Countries were not represented equally. Initially Turkey was also included in the research but was excluded due to insufficient number of participants (13).

The surveying took place in June and July of 2005. In each country young managers completed a questionnaire in their mother tongue but the method of acquiring the data differed among countries. In Slovenia the participants answered the questionnaire through a computer interface while in other countries they completed a paper version of the questionnaire (with identical questions) and the data was later transferred to a computer system.

Table 7.2. Basic Demographic Data of the Sample

	Slovenia	Croatia	B&H	Serbia	Montenegro	Russia
Age	35.5	31.9	33.7	28.6	29.5	31.9
Share of males	63%	38%	55%	45%	34%	49%
Years of education	17.4	16.2	16.2	16.6	16.7	16.2
Share of managers	71%	34%	61%	23%	46%	57%

Source: THT and own analysis.

---

[23] See Zagoršek and Štembergar (in this book) for a detailed description.

The choice of the sample is reflected in the demographic data – the participants in this comparison are relatively young, around 30 years old and well educated since they have on average completed more than 16 years of education, i.e. they have on average at least an undergraduate degree. The average education is highest in the Slovenian sample, which indicates the dominant share of active managers. The sample is well balanced in regards to gender. In Slovenia, and Bosnia and Herzegovina the share of men is slightly higher while in Croatia, Montenegro, and Serbia women prevail.

In researching cultural profiles of countries we use two types of data, both of which are based on the same questionnaire. When comparing only groups of young managers from the chosen countries we use raw data. By raw data we do not mean the answers to the questions but rather the dimensions derived directly from them. When groups of participants from the studied countries are placed in a broader group of countries, we use transformed data. In transforming raw data we have accounted for distributional characteristics of a certain dimension for all 55,000 managers from the Trompenaars database as well as demographic characteristics of an individual participant.

CULTURAL PROFILES OF YOUNG MANAGERS

Placement into a Broader Group of Countries

In this part we compare young managers in the studied countries with studies of managers' profiles around the world where Trompenaars' methodology has been used. The selected countries have been placed into a broader context of countries on the basis of the so called cultural profiles that are based on transformed cultural dimensions, which take into account the distributional characteristics of an individual dimension as well as the demographic specifics of an individual group – average age, gender structure and the like.

From the data in Table 7.3 below we can conclude:

1. Young managers included in the research are very similar among themselves on many dimensions. Index values range mainly between 50 and 60 and can therefore be placed somewhere in the middle compared to other countries.[24] Although they belong to a group of transitional countries, they differ from the already performed studies in those countries that used the same methodology by displaying higher adherence to the rules and procedures (universalism), higher care for the colleagues (lower individualism) and higher intertwinement of business and personal relationships (less relationship specific). Young managers give more importance to the internal locus of control and proactive behavior (mechanistic view of the environment). On the other hand, they differ from the old EU members (young managers: higher intertwinement of business and personal relationships and lower importance of achievements) as well as from Asian countries (young managers: higher universalism, lower intertwinement of business and personal relationships, lower importance of status and power). The results of a study of Russian young managers, who on the majority of dimensions agree with others, also lead to the conclusion that these groups of

---

[24]   Due to the use of transformed data we assume the mean of 50.

managers are similar. An individual's age and profession play an important role in determining a cultural profile, which is included also in the Trompenaars' research methodology.

Table 7.3. Comparison of Cultural Profiles – Transformed Data

		U (h) – P (l)	Ind (h) – C (l)	N (h) – A (l)	S (h) – D (l)	Ach (h) – Asc (l)	Int (h) – E (l)
Old EU members	Austria	67	45	58	49	56	55
	Greece	38	44	38	54	50	54
	Denmark	65	65	52	76	70	62
	Ireland	69	44	46	71	79	49
	Italy	70	46	45	73	62	57
	France	43	36	40	67	55	66
	Germany	62	53	59	67	61	49
	The Netherlands	56	63	46	84	61	48
	Spain	52	57	49	65	65	70
	Sweden	78	58	54	64	77	49
	Great Britain	66	60	62	68	75	56
New EU members	The Czech Republic	34	90	50	80	50	47
	Poland	43	83	55	72	47	49
	Hungary	62	74	29	63	44	37
	Australia	84	65	61	65	74	71
Other Western countries	Switzerland	82	61	54	70	62	46
	USA	76	67	68	90	78	76
Other countries of the Eastern block	Bulgaria	18	79	54	74	30	30
	Russia	18	84	57	57	37	31
	Israel	76	64	45	65	81	61
Middle East	Turkey	57	41	46	69	45	59
Far East	China	44	40	51	22	46	31
	India	33	17	57	26	42	42
	Japan	55	29	80	33	40	10
Young managers included in the research	Slovenia	52	57	59	51	55	56
	Croatia	53	59	59	50	52	50
	Bosnia and Herzegovina	50	60	61	51	47	51
	Serbia	48	54	65	51	47	54
	Montenegro	66	66	61	52	51	64
	Russia	38	59	65	60	53	46

Note: U – universalism, P – particularism, Ind – individualism, C – communitarianism, N – neutral, A – affective, S – specific, D – diffuse, Ach – achievement, Asc – ascription, Int – internal, E – external. The sign (h) means that this pole of the dimension is denoted by high values and the sign (l) means that this pole of the dimension is denoted by low values.

Source: THT Consulting, 2005 and own work.

2. Similarities in value dimensions of the Slovenian, Croatian and Bosnian young managers with certain dimensions of Austrian managers (exceptions being higher universalism and higher inclination towards communitarianism in the Austrian research) point to the similarities of national cultures. This is consistent with historical reasons, which was already pointed out by Hofstede's results. It is worth adding that the results of young Serbian managers do not vary much from the stated ones.

3. Although similar on many dimensions, the data on young Russian managers depart in particular on two dimensions, where they reach notably lower values: the bigger role of personal relationships over rules (particularism) and relationship with the external environment. The values on both dimensions are approaching values in the Trompenaars' Russian research and point out the significance of dimensions of national culture. Disregard for the rules and organic perception of the environment, on which an individual does not have much influence, are much more present in Russia than elsewhere.

4. The departures evident in the data from Montenegro are also interesting. Higher inclination towards respect for rules, higher emphasis on individualism than communitarianism and higher active involvement of an individual in the environment are slightly contrary to our understanding of Montenegrin culture.[25]

Differences among Selected Countries

In the previous part we saw that cultures of young managers in selected countries are relatively similar. Considering that this is a geographically limited area with a lot of common history, this is in a way understandable. However, certain differences among them exist. The similarities and differences of individual groups of young managers from different countries, are seen from Table 7.3. Here, in contrast with the previous part, we use raw untransformed data that are comparable among themselves but not directly with the data from other countries.

Universalism – particularism. Young managers from Montenegro stand out most in regards to respecting the standardized rules, with Slovenian and Croatian managers also scoring high on this dimension. On the other hand, young Russian managers stand out for their inclination towards particularism. With them the importance of individual circumstances and personal relationships is most evident.

Individualism – communitarianism. Young managers from Montenegro stand out on giving preference to individualism. Vukotić (2005) emphasizes that this is only partially true since they have a strong desire for individualism, but they have to behave in a traditional way despite their strong desire to dominate in a group. However, this level of individualism is not accompanied by the appropriate tendency to take risks. Closest to them are young managers from Russia. Others are quite similar among themselves and emphasize collectivistic values to a greater extent.

---

[25] As mentioned by Cerović and Aleksić (2005), the difference between the expected and the actual results could be a result of the sample of young managers in Montenegro who belong to a specific group that supports liberalism in this country.

Neutral – affective. Differences among groups on this dimension are relatively small. Only groups from Russia and Serbia stand out slightly. They are more neutral, as they try to exclude emotions from business relationships.

Specific – diffuse. Russian managers have the most specific culture among young managers. Croatian managers show the highest intertwinement of business and personal relationships (the difference is not statistically significant) while Slovenes are somewhere in the middle.

Achievement – ascription. Status is given the biggest weight by the young managers from the more eastern countries – those from Bosnia and Serbia. Young managers from Slovenia stand out for assigning bigger weight to achievements than status. Cerović and Aleksić (2005) interpret this as a consequence of people in Slovenia being evaluated mainly on the basis of what they have themselves achieved, while in Serbia they are evaluated according to their status and/or connections with certain social groups. This result is expected and in line with the findings from previous research. Another explanation for this could also be an undeveloped market and the industrial structure that still values inherited positions (Čičić, 2005).

Relationship towards the external environment. Managers from Montenegro are more mechanistic. They think they own their own destiny and can proactively affect the environment. According to Vukotić (2005) people in Montenegro have a feeling that they can change everything in a moment, although this is more a revolutionary zeal than the real state of affairs. Montenegrins are followed by the Slovenian and Serbian managers. Managers in Russia have the most organic culture, characterized by giving in to fate.

Further we describe a cultural dimension that we omitted in the previous part due to more difficult comparability. We also describe the current and ideal organizational culture as perceived by young managers from selected countries.

Relationship towards time. All young managers from the selected countries are more directed at the present and the future and consider past less important. Future is most emphasized in Montenegro. In their culture one does not live a present life now and for now but for the future and the future generations (descendents). Fruits of present labor and battles are meant for the future generations (Vukotić, 2005). Past is given most attention by young managers from Bosnia and Serbia. Young managers from Slovenia mainly perceive time synchronically. It is interesting that young Croatian managers stand out most on this dimension.

Young managers in the majority of the selected countries currently see the Family and the Eiffel Tower as the prevalent types of organizational culture. Those are hierarchical cultures, the former oriented towards employees and the latter towards task implementation. It is interesting that here young managers from Croatia and Serbia stand out, the Croats ascribing more significance to task implementation and the Serbs to family relationships. Young managers from Slovenia and Montenegro compare the current organizational culture more with the Guided Missile, characterized by orientation towards task implementation and the achievement of goals, which includes teamwork. However, they hardly notice any characteristics of the Incubator. In their judgment, formalization and hierarchy prevail over creativity and equality of mutual relationships.

In the opinion of young managers, the ideal types of organizational culture are mainly the Guided Missile and the Incubator, while the Family and the Eiffel Tower are much less desired. Their preference is therefore given to a more egalitarian organization compared to a hierarchical. Since the Guided Missile is in most cases ahead of the Incubator it seems that young managers want their work to be directed towards achievement of goals and tasks, which presents them a bigger challenge than developing conditions for creativity and their own development. Here the Slovenian managers, who see developing conditions for creativity as a contribution to ideal organizational culture, stand out.

Table 7.4. Cultural Profiles of Young Managers in the Studied Countries – Raw Data

	Slovenia (n = 153)	Croatia (n = 114)	B&H (n = 198)	Serbia (n = 31)	Montenegro (n = 67)	Russia (n = 74)
U (high) – P (low)	63.9 (20.1)	63.3 (22.6)	58.6 (22.7)	57.2 (25.0)	**76.9 (19.0)**	*45.6 (19.9)*
Ind (high) – C (low)	52.9 (23.2)	52.6 (19.2)	56.2 (21.6)	51.0 (19.9)	**66.6 (21.6)**	59.7 (20.3)
N (high) – A (low)	54.6 (18.0)	54.4 (17.0)	56.9 (15.5)	62.9 (17.2)	57.0 (14.8)	61.8 (15.7)
S (high) – D (low)	64.2 (23.1)	59.4 (23.6)	60.2 (27.2)	61.3 (25.7)	63.8 (23.1)	**69.6 (24.2)**
Ach (high) – Asc (low)	59.2 (13.3)	54.3 (14.6)	*48.1 (13.8)*	49.2 (15.8)	54.2 (13.9)	56.3 (15.2)
M (high) – O (low)	61.6 (21.4)	55.4 (20.7)	56.5 (20.3)	59.4 (24.8)	**72.1 (16.7)**	*49.9 (19.8)*
Relative meaning of past	*26.1 (6.6)*	26.4 (7.2)	28.2 (7.3)	28.4 (6.4)	27.1 (6.5)	28.1 (10.4)
Relative meaning of present	35.5 (6.2)	35.2 (7.5)	*32.9 (6.7)*	32.7 (5.1)	*32.1 (6.6)*	32.9 (7.3)
Relative meaning of future	38.4 (6.3)	38.3 (8.5)	38.9 (8.6)	39.0 (7.0)	40.8 (6.6)	39.0 (10.0)
Perception of time – Syn (high) – Seq (low)	64.5 (21.2)	*55.7 (24.9)*	59.3 (24.3)	60 (29.4)	57.0 (25.3)	**66.4 (22.7)**
GM – current	4.3 (2.7)	*3 (2.1)*	3.4 (2.4)	3 (2.4)	**4.4 (2.4)**	3.7 (1.9)
F – current	3.9 (2.1)	4.6 (1.9)	4.5 (2)	4.5 (2.1)	*3.3 (1.8)*	3.8 (1.9)
ET – current	4 (2.5)	**4.8 (2.5)**	4.1 (2.3)	4.4 (2.4)	4 (2.2)	4.2 (2.2)
Inc – current	1.7 (1.6)	*1.6 (1.3)*	1.9 (1.4)	2.1 (1.2)	2.3 (1.7)	2.3 (1.6)
GM – ideal	5.9 (2.3)	6.3 (1.9)	5.9 (1.9)	**6.9 (2)**	6.2 (1.7)	5.9 (1.9)
F – ideal	1.3 (1.1)	1.8 (1.2)	1.5 (1.3)	*1.1 (1.0)*	1.4 (1.0)	1.6 (1.2)
ET – ideal	*0.8 (1.2)*	1.2 (1.3)	1.6 (1.4)	1.2 (1.8)	1.2 (1.2)	1.9 (1.6)
Inc – ideal	6.0 (2.4)	*4.7 (1.9)*	5 (2)	4.7 (1.8)	5.2 (2.0)	*4.6 (1.9)*

Note: U – universalism, P – particularism, Ind – individualism, C – communitarianism, N – neutral, A – affective, S – specific, D – diffuse, Ach – achievement, Asc – ascription, M – mechanic, O – organic, Syn – synchronic, Seq – sequential; GM – Guided Missile, F – Family, ET – Eiffel Tower, Inc – Incubator.

Arithmetic means of raw data (standard deviations in parentheses). Bolded values are higher with statistical significance, italicized values are lower with statistical significance.

Source: THT and own analysis.

Differences among Young Managers and Managers from Three Companies in Slovenia

A group of young Slovenian managers in the study is comprised of three different populations. The first are the members of the Alumni Association of the International Full Time Graduate Program in Business Administration at the Faculty of Economics in Ljubljana

(70 replies out of approximately 300 members). The second group is represented by the participants of the Consortium MBA (KMBA) (40 replies out of 75 participants)[26] while the third group includes participants at last year's business conference in Portorož (43 replies out of 200 registered participants). The three populations differ among themselves in some characteristics. The first group primarily consists of young managers who are at the beginning of their careers, included in the second one are managers with a few years of experience who mainly hold positions in middle or higher management and are preparing to take over more responsible duties. In the third group top management is more represented than in the other two.[27] In the Table 7.5 we first present a comparison between the whole group of young managers (including all three mentioned groups) with the data on dimensions of organizational culture for the managers of the three companies that participated in our research and are covered later in this book (Droga, Helios and Trimo).

Table 7.5. Comparison between Managers from Companies and Young Managers

	Slovenia (n = 508)	Managers from companies (n = 355)	Young managers (n = 153)
Universalism (high) – Particularism (low)	65.6 (22)	66.4 (22.7)	*63.9 (20.1)*
Individualism (high) – Communitarianism (low)	53.7 (21.9)	54 (21.4)	*52.9 (23.2)*
Neutral (high) – Affective (low)	55.3 (15.9)	55.5 (14.9)	54.6 (18)
Specific (high) – Diffuse (low)	65.2 (23.2)	65.5 (23.2)	64.2 (23.1)
Achievement (high) – Ascription (low)	58 (14.1)	57.5 (14.5)	59.2 (13.3)
Mechanistic (high) – Organic (low)	57.5 (20.8)	*55.8 (20.4)*	61.6 (21.4)
Relative meaning of past	26.1 (6.8)	26.1 (6.9)	26.1 (6.6)
Relative meaning of present	36.3 (6.1)	36.6 (6)	*35.5 (6.2)*
Relative meaning of future	37.6 (6.8)	37.3 (7)	38.4 (6.3)
Perception of time – Synchronic (high) – Sequential (low)	67.1 (20.5)	67.8 (20.4)	*64.5 (21.2)*
Guided Missile – current	4.4 (2.4)	4.4 (2.2)	4.3 (2.7)
Family – current	3.7 (1.9)	3.7 (1.9)	3.9 (2.1)
Eiffel Tower – current	3.8 (2.1)	3.8 (2)	4 (2.5)
Incubator – current	2 (1.6)	2.1 (1.7)	*1.7 (1.6)*
Guided Missile – ideal	5.6 (2)	5.5 (1.9)	**5.9 (2.3)**
Family – ideal	1.6 (1.1)	1.7 (1.2)	*1.3 (1.1)*
Eiffel Tower – ideal	1 (1.3)	1.1 (1.3)	*0.8 (1.2)*
Incubator – ideal	5.7 (2.2)	5.6 (2.1)	6 (2.4)

Source: THT and own analysis.

Index values of individual dimensions that are lower with statistical significance are italicized and underlined. Statistically significant higher values for the group of young managers are bolded.

---

[26] Consortium MBA is a special form of MBA at the Faculty of Economics in Ljubljana, which consists of groups of managers from selected companies.

[27] 45% of the participants at the last year's conference identified themselves as top management (chairman of the board, members of the board). 75% of participants identified themselves as managers.

The groups are different with statistical significance on four out of six dimensions of organizational culture. Young managers are more inclined towards respecting the rules and put higher emphasis on collectivistic values.[28] They value achievement over status and think to a higher extent that they can actively influence events in the environment.

Young managers give more attention to the future than the present, which is understandable, considering the age difference between the two groups. Lack of work experience is probably also a reason that they perceive time more sequentially.

Young managers are more critical towards the current organizational culture than the group of managers from participating companies. The Family type of culture is according to them more present in the current organizational culture. They also estimate that there is a lack of atmosphere for the development of creativity, which is a characteristic of the Incubator. Although both groups put a strong emphasis on non-hierarchical organizational structure in the ideal scheme, the importance of the Guided Missile and the Incubator is higher with the young managers.

In Table 7.6 we compare groups of young managers among themselves. Members of the Alumni Association of the International Full Time Program in Business Administration are the most individualistic, separate their business and personal lives the most and believe most that the environment can be controlled and directed. Compared to others they perceive time more as a sequence of events and less as a harmony of past, present and future.

The group of KMBA students is interesting. They accept acting according to the rules more, are significantly more collectivistic and accept the intertwinement between business and other areas of life and work. They also go more with the flow than their colleagues (organic culture). They do not put much emphasis on the past but they perceive time more synchronically than other groups. According to them, the prevalent types in the current organizational culture are the hierarchical types of culture, in the mode of "respect your boss and the existing rules".

Participants at the business conference are more than others in favor of respecting the general rules and put less importance on personal relationships (universalism) but do not deviate on other dimensions of culture. They perceive time as a sequence of events more than others. Among all current types of organizational culture they perceive the Guided Missile the most, i.e. orientation towards the implementation of tasks and goals. The types of hierarchical organizational cultures are less important to them. That is why they favor culture that is oriented towards people and the development of their creativity, i.e. the Incubator.

Let us at the end point out the differences among the three companies (Droga Kolinska, Helios and Trimo). A detailed analysis of the organizational culture of individual companies will be presented in later contributions. We compare them taking in account the organizational units in Slovenia, only.

Our data reflects very well the issue of merging Droga and Kolinska into a new company, which was underway just in the period of our data collection. Managers who participated in the survey (their response rate was very low) have the lowest values on the neutral/affective dimension, which shows a high tolerance for expressing feelings in both companies. They are also in favor of less mixing of business and personal relationships. According to their opinion, the hierarchical types prevail in the current organizational culture, with the prevailing family component. Managers of Droga value the organizational culture that would

---

[28] As will be seen later, this is mainly due to the KMBA students.

be oriented towards equality and individuals, i.e. the Incubator, the highest among all companies.

Table 7.6. Comparison among Different Groups of Young Managers

	Young managers (n = 153)	MScBA Alumni (n = 70)	KMBA (n = 40)	Conference Participants (n = 43)
Universalism (high) – Particularism (low)	63.9 (20.1)	*60.5 (18.6)*	66.5 (19.6)	67 (22.5)
Individualism (high) – Communitarianism (low)	52.9 (23.2)	58.3 (23)	*46.5 (21.9)*	50.2 (23.2)
Neutral (high) – Affective (low)	54.6 (18)	53.6 (18.8)	55.4 (20.1)	55.6 (14.5)
Specific (high) – Diffuse (low)	64.2 (23.1)	**66.8 (25.1)**	*60.6 (21.8)*	63.4 (20.7)
Achievement (high) – Ascription (low)	59.2 (13.3)	58.5 (13.5)	60.6 (13.5)	59.2 (12.9)
Mechanistic (high) – Organic (low)	61.6 (21.4)	63.3 (21.2)	*59.5 (23.1)*	60.7 (20.4)
Relative meaning of past	26.1 (6.6)	26.7 (7.3)	*24.8 (6.2)*	26.5 (5.6)
Relative meaning of present	35.5 (6.2)	34.8 (6.9)	36.5 (5.1)	35.6 (6.1)
Relative meaning of future	38.4 (6.3)	38.5 (6.7)	38.7 (5.8)	37.9 (6.4)
Perception of time – Synchronic (high) – Sequential (low)	64.5 (21.2)	*62.6 (22.7)*	**69.6 (17.4)**	*62.8 (21.6)*
Guided Missile – current	4.3 (2.7)	4.2 (2.7)	3.6 (2.5)	**5.2 (2.8)**
Family – current	3.9 (2.1)	3.9 (2.2)	**4.5 (1.7)**	*3.3 (1.9)*
Eiffel Tower – current	4 (2.5)	4 (2.5)	**4.5 (2.1)**	*3.6 (2.6)*
Incubator – current	1.7 (1.6)	1.9 (1.7)	*1.5 (1)*	1.8 (1.8)
Guided Missile – ideal	5.9 (2.3)	6.1 (2.5)	6.2 (2)	*5.3 (2)*
Family – ideal	1.3 (1.1)	1.3 (1.1)	1.3 (1)	1.5 (1)
Eiffel Tower – ideal	0.8 (1.2)	0.8 (1.4)	0.7 (1.1)	0.8 (0.9)
Incubator – ideal	6 (2.4)	5.8 (2.5)	5.8 (2.4)	6.3 (2)

Source: THT and own analysis.

Color was recently acquired by Helios. A high degree of respect for rules is characteristic of both companies. A high level of impartiality in relationships is present in Helios. Managers give in to the environment less (the highest level of mechanistic culture) and in the current organizational culture see the highest value in the type of culture that builds on achieving goals and implementing tasks (the Guided Missile). Currently in Color a more formalistic and centralized type of culture (the Eiffel Tower) is present than elsewhere, for which one of the reasons might be the process of takeover by Helios.

Trimo differs from others on two cultural dimensions. The relationships in Trimo are the least partial and the least under the influence of emotions. On the other hand, business relationships intertwine with personal relationships. It is a company with the most democratic current organizational culture. There exists high orientation towards implementing tasks and achieving stated goals (the Guided Missile). The importance of orientation towards people and their creativity (the Incubator) is also the highest in Trimo among all companies. The opposite is true for both hierarchical organizational cultures, which are the least important in the current organizational culture. For Trimo the Incubator and the Guided Missile are the most desired types of organizational culture.

Table 7.7. Comparison among Managers from Different Companies

	Managers from companies (n = 355)	Kolinska (n = 6)	Droga (n = 33)	Color (n = 55)	Helios (n = 112)	Trimo (n = 149)
Universalism (high) – Particularism (low)	66.4 (22.7)	57.2 (35.2)	63.7 (19.8)	67.8 (23.3)	68.9 (21.6)	64.9 (23.4)
Individualism (high) – Communitarianism (low)	54 (21.4)	53.3 (16.3)	47.3 (17.2)	54.5 (19.4)	53.2 (21.9)	55.8 (22.6)
Neutral (high) – Affective (low)	55.5 (14.9)	45.8 (10.2)	47 (8.8)	51.7 (15)	**56.8 (14.7)**	**58.3 (15.2)**
Specific (high) – Diffuse (low)	65.5 (23.2)	**87.5 (13.7)**	71.2 (17.8)	68.6 (23.2)	64.7 (21.1)	62.8 (25.4)
Achievement (high) – Ascription (low)	57.5 (14.5)	57.3 (14.5)	53 (12)	58.4 (14.2)	59.8 (15.9)	56.5 (13.7)
Mechanistic (high) – Organic (low)	55.8 (20.4)	51.7 (14.7)	56.1 (16.2)	49.1 (22.7)	**59.3 (19.9)**	55.8 (20.4)
Relative meaning of past	26.1 (6.9)	29.6 (5.1)	28.4 (5.4)	26.7 (7.7)	26 (6)	25.3 (7.6)
Relative meaning of present	36.6 (6)	39.2 (6.9)	37.1 (6.2)	36.5 (6.8)	36.7 (5.3)	36.3 (6.2)
Relative meaning of future	37.3 (7)	31.2 (5.5)	34.5 (6.3)	36.8 (7.4)	37.3 (5.8)	38.4 (7.7)

	Managers from companies (n = 355)	Kolinska (n = 6)	Droga (n = 33)	Color (n = 55)	Helios (n = 112)	Trimo (n = 149)
Perception of time – Synchronic (high) – Sequential (low)	67.8 (20.4)	61.1 (19.2)	65.7 (18.2)	**71.1 (20.8)**	64.5 (21.3)	**69.9 (19.8)**
Guided Missile – current	4.4 (2.2)	2.7 (1.6)	2.9 (1.2)	3.4 (2.3)	**5 (2.1)**	**4.8 (2.1)**
Family – current	3.7 (1.9)	**5.3 (1.9)**	**5.3 (1.7)**	4.3 (1.7)	3.8 (1.9)	3 (1.6)
Eiffel Tower – current	3.8 (2)	4.5 (1.5)	4.9 (1.8)	**5.2 (2)**	3.4 (1.6)	3.2 (1.9)
Incubator – current	2.1 (1.7)	1.5 (0.5)	0.9 (0.6)	1.2 (1)	1.7 (1.3)	3 (1.8)
Guided Missile – ideal	5.5 (1.9)	5.7 (1)	5.5 (1.8)	5.9 (1.8)	5.8 (2.1)	5.2 (1.8)
Family – ideal	1.7 (1.2)	1.7 (0.8)	1.7 (0.9)	1.5 (1.2)	1.5 (1.1)	1.9 (1.2)
Eiffel Tower – ideal	1.1 (1.3)	1.5 (2.1)	0.6 (1.1)	0.9 (1.1)	1.3 (1.3)	1.2 (1.3)
Incubator – ideal	5.6 (2.1)	5.2 (1.6)	**6.2 (1.7)**	5.7 (1.9)	5.4 (2.3)	5.7 (2.1)

Source: THT and own analysis.

CONCLUSIONS

Groups of young managers who are still studying or have recently completed the study of business and organizational sciences have at least two common characteristics: they do not have significant work experience and have developed their cultural profile in similar circumstances, i.e. in the process of transition and business education. That is why the groups are relatively similar on cultural dimensions.

Through analysis we have also observed the cultural differences that stem from differences in national cultures. Young managers from Slovenia, Croatia, and Bosnia and Herzegovina, followed closely by young managers from Serbia, are on cultural dimensions very similar to Austrian managers. Differences can be observed on dimensions of universalism – particularism and individualism – communitarianism. Young managers are more particularistic and individualistic. On the other hand, young managers from Russia are on some dimensions approaching the profile of Russian managers, which was identified using the same methodology in other studies. Young managers from Russia are much more particularistic and less ready to intervene in social developments (they subjugate themselves more to the environment). Our research therefore shows that elements of national culture play an important role in defining young managers.

With the employed methodology we have identified differences and similarities in the culture of younger and older managers in Slovenia. There are slight differences between young managers and the managers from the three Slovenian companies, especially in the calmer judgments of the managers from these companies regarding certain questions about national and organizational culture. On the other hand, there are significant differences in judgments regarding individual dimensions of culture and types of organizational culture among the three studied groups of young managers. It seems that they are influenced by their position within a company. Young managers, members of the MScBA Alumni, are more particularistic and individualistic and emphasize the point of view that they can actively participate in changing the environment. Young managers, members of the KMBA, are more universalistic, put a larger emphasis on the organic view of the environment and on the hierarchy of the existing organizational structures. Because they mainly hold positions in middle and top management and have been employed for a longer period of time, their judgment is more influenced by practical experience. Participants at the Portorož business conference hold higher managerial positions compared to the other two groups. Their attention is focused towards higher universalism; among the current types of organizational culture they emphasize the inclusion of employees in the implementation of tasks and accomplishment of goals, while among the ideal cultural types they emphasize the creation of circumstances for creativity and innovativeness of individuals.

By using the Trompenaars' methodology we have in our research pointed out differences in organizational cultures of the three selected Slovenian companies: Droga Kolinska, Helios and Trimo. The first company is in the process of merging. The data display the post-merger uncertainties of the managers from both companies. The second company is due to the nature of its activity (follower in the area of R&D, orientation in market niches) very oriented towards the implementation of stated tasks and implementation of goals. The third company, which is based on project work for individual buyers, is more oriented towards the individual and creating circumstances for their creativity. Taken as a whole, the methodology has proven itself to be a useful tool in the study of cultural profiles of various groups of managers.

REFERENCES

Cerović, B., and Aleksić, A. 2005. "Komentar rezultatov za Srbijo." In Prašnikar, J. and Cirman, A. (eds): *"Globalno gospodarstvo in kulturna različnost."* Časnik Finance, Ljubljana: 135–140.

Debeljak, A. 1986. "Zastarelost jugoslovanstva." *Nova revija* 5 (52/53): 1389–1396.

Goić, S. 2005. "Komentar rezultatov za Hrvaško: pogled iz Splita." In Prašnikar, J. and Cirman, A. (eds): *"Globalno gospodarstvo in kulturna različnost."* Časnik Finance, Ljubljana: 147–151.

Hofstede, G. 1980. *"Culture's Consequences: International Differences in Work-Related Values."* Beverly Hills: Sage Publications.

House R. J. et al. 2004. *"Culture, Leadership, and Organizations: The GLOBE Study of 62 Societies."* Thousand Oaks: Sage Publications.

Jazbec, M. 2007. *"Slovenian National Culture And Cross-Cultural Training."* In this book.

Trompenaars, F., and Woolliams, P. 2004. *"Business Across Cultures."* Chichester: Capstone.

Trompenaars, F. 1993. *"Riding the Waves of Culture: Understanding Cultural Diversity in Business."* London: The Economist Books.

Vukotić, V. 2005. "Komentar rezultatov za Črno goro." In Prašnikar, J. and Cirman, A. (eds): *"Globalno gospodarstvo in kulturna različnost."* Časnik Finance, Ljubljana: 131–134.

Wachtel, A. B. 1998. *"Making a Nation, Breaking a Nation: Literature and Cultural Politics in Yugoslavia."* Stanford: Stanford University Press.

Zagoršek, H., and Štembergar, M. 2007. *"Culture and its Influence on Business Performance."* In this book.

In: New Emerging Economies and Their Culture
Editors: J. Prašnikar, A. Cirman, pp. 101-118

ISBN: 978-1-60021-754-8
© 2007 Nova Science Publishers, Inc.

Chapter 8

ORGANIZATIONAL CULTURE AND MANAGERIAL CONTROL AFTER AN INTERNATIONAL ACQUISITION

Adriana Rejc Buhovac and Sergeja Slapničar

INTRODUCTION

This study addresses the question of how a multinational corporation (MNC) integrates a newly acquired subsidiary into its network by combining a reconciliation of organizational cultures and the execution of managerial control. After an acquisition, synergies do not arise automatically. They are realized via consolidation of product groups within the corporation, costs cutting, down-sizing of excessive capacities, economies of scale, stronger market position or other strategies. Furthermore, MNC's headquarter decisions may restrict development of business functions, impose transfer prices, reallocate costs, restrict purchasing and selling, charge for know-how etc. to maximize corporate profit (Noerreklitt and Schoenfeld, 2000). Many of these strategies affect employee morale and motivation as they are related to reorganization of their work, performance measurement, tighter performance targets, and threat of dismissals. Moreover, information asymmetry and failure to include all relevant contingencies in the contracts leave space for opportunistic behavior despite rigorous formal control systems. While some of these features are typical of any complex business organization, the information asymmetry is much more problematic in an international context.

It has been increasingly realized that a common organizational culture can efficiently mitigate opportunistic behavior. Ouchi (1980) observed that organizational members must either trust each other or closely monitor each other. In fact, many corporate alliances result in a complete failure or poor realization of synergistic payoffs rather than achieving previously planned results, which is often due to a lack of congruence in organizational culture. In cross-border alliances the collusion of both organizational and national cultures occurs. Inherited systems of beliefs and values, management mentalities, and informal relationships may represent major impediments to the establishment of new organizational perspectives (Bartlett and Ghoshal, 1989).

The core problem is related to the design of an appropriate control system that considers differences in national cultures, but on the other hand brings about a new corporate culture. Control is a complex process in any diversified organization, more so when it comes to cross-frontier alliances in which efficiency in controlling subsidiaries is mitigated by geographical distance, cultural differences, and the institutional environment. It has been largely acknowledged that organizations in one national context exhibit similarities in their functioning (Bhimani, 1999) which arise from sharing common national values and beliefs. Consequently, most studies investigate the impact of the national culture on the design of control (see Harrison and McKinnon, 1999, for review). This approach clearly neglects the role of the organizational values. In other words, as formulated by Harrison and McKinnon (1999), should MNCs uncritically accept the national cultural dictates, or is it possible that through time and by applying socialization practices they can modify national cultural influences resulting in the creation of a cultural microclimate?

The present study aims to address the convergence of organizational cultures and the role of control mechanisms in this process. We analyze what mechanisms of formal control system parent companies put in place to direct the behavior and shape common organizational culture in the acquired companies. We argue that the choice of control mechanism to a large extent reflects the organizational culture of the parent company and indirectly also its national culture. The focus of the study lies on formal control systems, more specifically, on performance measurement and incentive systems.

We consider the European context, in which differences between national cultures may not be very contrasting but still discernible. We study the imposition of control from the perspective of a subsidiary. Our argument draws on data from three case studies: Lek, Slovenia, acquired in 2003 by Novartis – the Swiss pharmaceutical multinational corporation; Danfoss Trata, Slovenia, acquired in 1995 by Danfoss – the Danish corporation for heating, air conditioning and refrigerating systems; and Mora Moravia, the Czech Republic, acquired in 2005 by Gorenje – the Slovenian multinational corporation for household appliances.

LITERATURE REVIEW AND RESEARCH QUESTIONS

As this study is concerned with culture, we shall start with its definition. In general, culture is a system of knowledge, beliefs, implicit and explicit system of norms, and values. It is manifested in historically based preferences, behavioral patterns, practices, and their assigned meanings (Laurent, 1986; Henri, 2003). An all-inclusive definition of culture proposed by classical anthropologists (Radcliffe-Brown, 1952; Evans Pritchard, 1937, quoted in Dent, 1991) is that culture is a "total way of life" of a community. An organizational culture in particular is its own value set shared by members of an organization (or organizational sub-unit). These values are unobservable, but manifest themselves in the practices of that organization (Pratt and Beaulieu, 1992). The culture of the organization is typically created unconsciously, based on the values of founders of an organization, its top management, national cultural values and norms, industry, function of the unit (Chow et al., 2002) and the personal characteristics of employees, such as education, gender, age, and religion (Hofstede et al., 1990).

The concepts of control and organizational culture are strongly intertwined. Organizational culture often goes unnoticed until it comes under pressure for change. In an acquisition, such a pressure may be imposed on the subsidiary and its organizational culture is subjected to a purposeful harmonization with the organizational culture of the MNC. Change of the subsidiary's organizational culture may be accomplished through various control mechanisms, which help top managers delineate employees' behavior in the best interest of the corporation (Anthony, 1988; Chow, Shields and Wu, 1999). Authors typically distinguish between two types of control mechanisms (Leifer and Mills, 1996; Misztal, 1996; Simons, 1995; Martinez and Jarillo, 1989; Zucker, 1986; Bartlett and Ghoshal, 1989; Ouchi, 1979):

1. *Informal control* is related to mechanisms, such as selection, training, transfer, career path of managers, etc. (Martinez and Jarillo, 1989; Bartlett and Ghoshal, 1989), and communication of values and beliefs through the corporation's mission statements or other corporate documents (Simons, 1995). Informal control aims at creating a common system of values, which is by many organizational theorists viewed as the first best control mechanism (Zucker, 1986; Leifer and Mills, 1996; Misztal, 1996). All these activities are denoted as *socialization* or *acculturation*. Another type of informal control mechanisms involves direct actions and intervention of headquarter managers (Bartlett and Ghoshal, 1989). It is based on the *personal surveillance* of managers and labeled *behavior control* (Mintzberg, 1983; Ouchi, 1977).

2. *Formal control,* on the other hand, is a group of mechanisms that includes: (i) *departmentalization* or grouping of activities within organizational units, following the principle of labor division (Simon, 1976); (ii) *(de)centralization* of decision making through the hierarchy of formal authority, (iii) *formalization and standardization* expressed in written rules, policies, job descriptions, etc., (iv) *performance measurement* systems to monitor outcomes and correct deviations as well as to screen threats and opportunities from the external environment, and (v) *incentive systems* (reliance on fixed versus variable compensation, a basis for bonus determination and promotion). Due to their diversity, these mechanisms have received different names in the literature: Simons (1995) refers to them as boundary, diagnostic, and interactive systems, Child (1984) and Ferner (2000) label them bureaucratic control, Gupta and Govindarajan (1991) structural variables. Performance measurement and incentive systems are named *output control* (Ouchi, 1980).

Martinez and Jarillo (1989) notice that use of control mechanisms by MNCs has shifted from predominantly "hard" ones to an increased use of the "soft" ones – informal and subtler mechanisms. Soft mechanisms may not necessarily be "soft" in terms of permissiveness in contrast to the rigidity of formal mechanisms (see for example MacIntosh, Shearer and Riccaboni, 2005, for a description of General Electric's harsh socialization policy in subsidiaries). All in all, MNCs have acknowledged the vital importance of formal control systems' acceptability and the need to mitigate the probability of resistance to their implementation for maximum control efficiency (Ferner, 2000). Thus, deciding on control is not only merely choosing among different control mechanisms but also designing the way they are put in place.

Transforming an organizational culture is far from being an easy task. On one hand, many authors suggest that values arising from national culture are more persistent than values transmitted through organizational culture. As argued by Kilduff (1992), "the optimistic hope that MNCs can operate as melting pots within which cultural antagonisms disappear is controversial." Laurent (1986) for example reports that managers in MNCs, relative to managers in culturally homogenous organizations, appear to develop more extreme attitudes on scales measuring deep-seated cultural assumptions. He estimates that nationality is three times stronger in influencing the shaping of managerial assumptions than any other variable, such as age, education, function, position, or type of company. The national cultural background of managers appears to be quite insensitive to more transient organizational culture values. On the other hand, in trying to build a common organizational culture MNCs actually hope to supersede some of the not-fitting specificities of national cultures (Laurent, 1986).

Hofstede and his colleagues suggest that organizational culture reflects values and practices. They find that organizational values largely overlap with national values (Hofstede et al., 1990). Organizational practices, on the other hand, are also underpinned by values but they are much more diverse within one national context, which may be explained by other previously mentioned factors. It has been evidenced by Soeters and Schreuders (1988), Pratt et al. (1988), Hofstede et al. (1990), Chow et al. (2002) that only certain national values of a parent company are transmitted into the organizational culture of a subsidiary. As suggested by Pratt et al. (1988), the influence of national culture may depend on both, the character of the local company and the aggressive approach of the parent company. The aggressiveness of the parent company's organizational culture is certainly manifested in the form of control mechanisms. As suggested by Bhimani (2003), organizational culture characteristics become embedded into a design of management control. The inconclusive results challenge further investigation into the question of immense practical importance to MNCs.

Our research questions are summarized in Picture 8.1, which presents relationships among forces of convergence of organizational cultures. The hypothesized direction of impact is the following: the national culture of a company is to a large extent expected to underlie its organizational culture. The more similar the national cultures of the acquiring and acquired companies, the more similarities are to be expected in the organizational cultures arising from the same core values. In case of divergent organizational cultures of the two companies, the more divergent their organizational cultures, the higher are the costs of managerial control. As the headquarters establishes control mechanisms that start the process of submerging the organizational culture of a subsidiary into the one of the MNC, both formal and informal control mechanisms may be used. Formal control may include reorganization of processes, standardization and formalization of procedures and systems, in particular performance measurement and incentive systems. Informal control, on the other hand, may include training and other forms of motivating, putting "the right people in place", firing incompatible managers, and other approaches to influencing people's behavior and perceptions. The study focuses on three acquired companies that differ in the period in which they were merged into a multinational company: one company was acquired ten years ago, another one two years ago, and the third was acquired just recently.

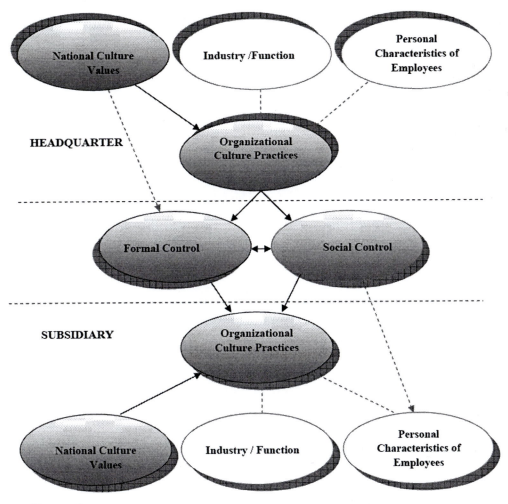

Source: Own work.

Picture 8.1. A Model of Relations in Integrating Organizational Culture of an International Subsidiary.

Taxonomy of National and Organizational Culture

Although there have been various attempts to define the taxonomy of a national culture, in particular its impact on business (e.g. Trompenaars, 1994; Trompenars and Woolliams, 2004), the majority of researchers have used Hofstede's methodology or his Values Survey Module (Hofstede, 1980a; 1980b; Hofstede and Bond, 1988): his Culture's Consequences has had an average of 94 citations per year in the last 18 years (Baskerville, 2003). For that reason we shall also rely on Hofstede's scores for national culture of countries of interest. Scores for Slovenia have recently been obtained by Jazbec (2005).

Based on an extensive survey of over 116,000 observations of employees of IBM subsidiaries from 64 countries, Hofstede (1980a) developed initially four and later a fifth dimension of national culture (Hofstede and Bond, 1988): (i) power distance, (ii) individualism vs. collectivism, (iii) masculinity vs. femininity, (iv) uncertainty avoidance and (v) long-term orientation.

Among several specifications of organizational culture dimensions (i.e. Trompenaars, 2003; Henri, 2004; Quinn, 1988; Quinn and Rohrbaugh, 1983) we again chose to make use of Hofstede's model of organizational practices (Hofstede et al., 1990). According to Hofstede, practices may be grouped along the following six dimensions: (i) process- vs. result- oriented culture indicates a concern for means as opposed to goals; (ii) employee- vs. job- oriented culture indicates a concern for people as opposed to concern for getting the job done; (iii) parochial vs. professional culture, whereby in a parochial culture employees derive their identity largely from the organization while in a professional culture they identify with their type of job; (iv) open vs. closed system is about the communication climate, whereby a closed system is seen as "closed and secretive" and an open system is "open to newcomers and outsiders" (Hofstede, 1998); (v) loose vs. tight control refers to the amount of strict unwritten codes and dignified behavior; and (vi) normative vs. pragmatic culture deals with the popular notion of customer orientation. Pragmatic organizations are market-driven, whereas normative organizations perceive their tasks as the implementation of inviolable rules (Hofstede. et. al., 1990).

Impact of National Culture on Organizational Culture

The literature suggests that certain national values are so strong they imbue the organizational culture and influence the development of certain practices, all other things equal. We research whether the dimensions of national and organizational culture are associated. Masculinity is more likely to be related to the development of job-oriented culture, in which pressure for getting the job done (Hofstede, 1998) is stronger than a concern for the overall welfare of employees. With respect to the parochial – professional dimension, it is evidenced by Chow et al. (2002) that in a highly individualistic culture employees are emotionally independent from the organization and have a calculative involvement with it, whereas in the collectivistic culture employees have emotional dependence and moral involvement with the organization. This suggests that individualism is likely to be linked to the development of professional culture. Power distance is related to attitudes about hierarchy (Pratt and Beaulieu, 1992). A low power distance culture prefers decentralization over centralization and flat organization over a very hierarchical one. The flatter the organizational structure, the more equal the employees and, hence, also more open to one another. The association of cultural openness with national affiliation has been supported empirically by Hofstede et al. (1990). Uncertainty avoidance is expected to play an important role in deciding whether an organization is pragmatic (defined as market-oriented) or normative. "Normative organizations perceive their task towards the outside world as the implementation of rules. Their major emphasis is on correctly following organizational procedures which are more important than results" (Hofstede, 1998). Uncertainty avoidance leads to formalization – many formal rules prevent quick reactions required by the market.

Dimensions of Performance Measurement and Incentive System

Literature defines the following five dimensions of performance measurement and incentive systems as central mechanisms of formal control: (i) selection of performance measures relates to the choice of performance indicators included in the performance measurement system; (ii) target setting refers to the targets set for selected performance measures. Here, employee participation in setting targets (generally and for their performance appraisals) and the use of external versus internal standards is considered; (iii) reliance on performance measures refers to flexible versus tight reliance on performance measures in evaluating performance and rewarding; (iv) group versus individual evaluations; and (v) performance contingent pay – in some organizations results are rewarded in the form of bonuses and long term incentives, whereas in others fixed compensations prevail while long-term results, commitment, and loyalty are rewarded only by promotion and fringe benefits.

Impact of Organizational Culture on Control Mechanisms

We investigate whether characteristics of organizational culture are transmitted to the subsidiary's organizational culture by the choice of the following control mechanisms:

Job vs. employee orientation might influence reliance on performance measurement and target setting. In an employee-oriented culture, reliance on performance measurement is expected to be flexible in terms of the use of performance evaluation and rewards for individuals. An individual is evaluated on the basis of an objective as well as subjective evaluation of the superior in the light of his past record and future prospects. In a job-oriented culture, reliance on short term results is supposed to be stronger and more consistent. With respect to target setting, Hofstede et al. (1990) found evidence that job- vs. employee-oriented cultures differ in whether targets are set internally or externally: they suggest that operating against external standards breeds a less benevolent culture than operating against internal standards (budget), the first being typical of a job-oriented culture and the second of an employee-oriented one.

Parochial culture is expected to embed group evaluations, as in such a culture exposure of an individual is less acceptable than it is in a professional culture. This is further related to remuneration practices: performance contingent pay is more effective if performance evaluations are individual, while in group evaluations, cause and effect relationships are less clear and less controllable from the point of view of the individual.

In a culture characterized by an open communication climate, it is expected that participation in a target setting and in the choice of performance measures for individual evaluation is higher than in a closed culture. A culture with a tight control is also supposed to rely more tightly on the formal performance measurement.

Finally, customer-oriented culture, pragmatism, is expected to be associated with the selection of financial and market performance measures as opposed to a normative culture which relies more on production measures. Although this association was predicted by Hofstede et al. (1990), they failed to find any supportive evidence which they ascribed to the large variation of organizational units under scrutiny. The choice of performance measurement seems to be more strongly correlated with the industry which might be an intervening variable between normative/pragmatic culture and the selection of performance measures.

METHODOLOGY

To inquire about the proposed relationships, we performed field research on three different post-takeover and national/organizational settings and studied the subsequent imposition of managerial control in the acquired companies. Our research methodology is supported by a survey and in-depth interviews.

In the survey, organizational culture was measured with a set of questions that were reconstructed organizational culture factors from Hofstede et al. (1990). We measured organizational culture in both the subsidiary and the parent company. In subsidiaries, respondents were key managers (usually second level managers and managers of business functions), while in parent companies, respondents were managers supervising the subsidiary (in each parent company only one or two managers). Dimensions of performance measurement and incentive systems in subsidiaries were measured with a set of statements such as "The performance of my organizational unit is measured predominantly with non-financial performance indicators (i.e. market share, customer satisfaction, quality measures) as opposed to financial indicators (profit, sales, profitability, cash flow etc.)." "My individual performance is measured comprehensively and on a long-term basis, predominantly with subjective evaluation by the superiors as opposed to objective indicators in short-term periods." Each statement addressed the practice before and after the acquisition. Respondents graded the statements on a scale from 1 to 5.

In each subsidiary, semi-structured interviews were then conducted to provide additional depth to the results and substantial context. In each of the three companies we interviewed the CEO and CFO. Semi-structured interviews provided in-depth knowledge of the company context, a better understanding of the managers' views of organizational culture, performance measurement and incentive systems and their use in the company, and an opportunity to get additional data. In interviews, we specifically covered broader mechanisms of control, such as reorganization, standardization of policies, socialization, etc.

DESCRIPTION OF COMPANIES

Novartis is a world leader in the research and development of products to protect and improve health and well-being. Novartis was created in 1996 from the merger of the Swiss companies, Ciby-Geigy and Sandoz. Its core business is pharmaceuticals, consumer health, generics, eye-care, and animal health. In 2004, the Group's businesses achieved sales of USD 28.2 billion and a net income of USD 5.8 billion. The Group invested approximately USD 4.3 billion in research and development. Headquartered in Basel, Switzerland, Novartis Group companies employ about 81,000 people and operate in over 140 countries worldwide. It is listed on the NYSE. Within the generics part of Novartis, Novartis Generics conducted a series of successful acquisitions in the past years, which resulted in a consolidation of the generics industry in Central and Eastern Europe. As a result, in 2003 Sandoz united all

Novartis generic companies under one single, global brand. Sandoz is thus a leading global supplier of high-quality generic pharmaceuticals, headquartered in Holzkirchen, Germany. In 2005, Sandoz acquired Hexal AG, Germany's leading generics company, and EON Labs, one of the fastest-growing generic pharmaceuticals companies in the US. Sandoz reported sales of USD 3.0 billion in 2004. By now, the combined company employs over 20,000 people in over 120 countries.

Lek, Slovenia, is one of the pillars of the leading generic pharmaceuticals company Sandoz. Lek operates as the global development center for Sandoz products and technologies, as a global manufacturing center for pharmaceutical active ingredients and medicals, as competence center for vertically-integrated products and for global development in biopharmaceuticals, and as the global supply center for Central, Eastern, and South-Eastern Europe. Funded in 1946 as Lek, the medical products factory, the company's fast growth was characterized by continuing investments, product portfolio expansions, an increase in the number of employees, and market growth. In 1991, Lek reorganized as a joint-stock company and a year later its shares were first quoted on the Ljubljana Stock Exchange. In 1995, Lek was the first Central European pharmaceuticals company to place a final product on the US market. In 2001, the company completed the acquisition of the Romanian pharmaceutical company Pharma Tech and became one of the leading manufacturers of antibiotics in the region. This was followed by the acquisition of Argon, Poland. The year 2002 was marked by the friendly takeover through which Lek became a member of Novartis Group. Today, Lek operates in more than 100 countries worldwide. In 2004, Lek achieved sales of USD 663 million (in 2002, USD 366 million), a net income of USD 112 million (in 2002, USD 42 million), and invested approximately USD 67 million in RandD (USD 42 million in 2002). There were more than 2,500 employees working in Lek by the end of 2004.

Danfoss is a leader within research and development, production, sales, and service of mechanical and electronic components for several industries. Owned by the Danish family Clausen (99.5%), it employs 17,500 employees. In some dependent companies, minority owners work as employees as well. The company was established in 1933 and is located in Nordborg, Denmark. Over 130 dependent companies operate in 56 countries worldwide. Danfoss's activities are divided into three main business areas: refrigeration and air conditioning, heating and water, and motion controls, each leading within its industry. In 2004, Danfoss Group achieved sales of USD 2.7 billion and a net income of USD 128 million. Danfoss owns three companies in Slovenia with a 100% ownership and another one with a 25% ownership. Altogether, it employs approximately 1,500 people in Slovenia and is placed among the ten largest exporters in Slovenia.

Danfoss Trata is a manufacturing subsidiary of Danfoss, located in Slovenia. The company develops and manufactures electromechanical products for district heating, heating, and air-conditioning control. Established in 1937, it reached a 90% market share in district heating and air-conditioning control in the former Yugoslavia in early 1990s. The collapse of Yugoslavia put the company in a serious financial crisis and managers considered a strategic alliance with Danfoss as the best solution. In 1995, Danfoss bought the majority share in Trata. The main purpose of this strategic acquisition was to establish a central center for development and manufacturing of electromechanical products for district heating, at that time dispersed over numerous Danfoss plants around Europe. Production from Denmark (in 1996), Sweden, and Germany (in 2004) was moved to a Slovenian manufacturing site. As a consequence, sales increased by 20% in 2004 and 30 employees were added to the payroll.

The centralization of business functions, warehousing and purchasing, in particular, is expected to further decrease the total manufacturing costs of electromechanical components for district heating. All in all, the successful acquisition resulted in a ten fold increase in sales and a net income of over USD 5 million.

Gorenje Group encompasses Gorenje Domestic Appliances – Gorenje d.d. – a joint stock company holding 47 integrated enterprises operating in 22 countries. The various Gorenje enterprises are organized into five divisions: household appliances, interior furnishing, heating and industrial equipment, services, and environmental protection and energy. Among these, the household appliances division, which includes the manufacture and sale of household appliances, represents 79% of total sales. In 2004, Gorenje Group achieved sales of USD 1.1 billion with an average 13% growth rate in the last five years. With 9,568 employees and a market value of USD 410 million, Gorenje Group is one of the biggest Slovenian companies. Despite increased competition in its main industry, Gorenje maintains its position among the eight largest domestic appliances manufacturers in Europe, and today, 86% of its production is exported. Its market share in South-Eastern Europe amounts to over 60% and its position is relatively secure in some Western European countries, such as in Denmark (12% market share).

In 2005, Gorenje acquired *Mora Moravia*, the Czech manufacturer of cookers, and further sustained its leading position in Central and Eastern Europe. Mora Moravia is located in Marianske Udoli, Moravia. Established in 1825, it became an important Czech producer of cookers with a significant market share in the Czech Republic, Slovakia, and some other countries of Eastern Europe. In 2004, the company's net sales amounted to USD 72 million with a net income of USD 518,000 while employing over 1,000 employees. Within the first year of acquisition, a 5% increase in sales and a significant increase in net income is expected.

FINDINGS

The first group of research questions deals with the relationships between different dimensions of national and organizational cultures. With respect to the notion that different characteristics of national cultures have an impact on differences in organizational cultures, Figure 8.1 compares the dimensions of national cultures of Switzerland, (Novartis), Denmark (Danfoss), the Czech Republic (Mora Moravia), and Slovenia (Lek, Danfoss Trata, and Gorenje). Results are taken from Hofstede's web site on countries' scores and Jazbec (2005) for Slovenia.

Figures 8.2 and 8.3, respectively, delineate characteristics of different dimensions of organizational cultures in studied companies as found in the survey. The extent of alignment of the patterns of organizational cultures shown with lines in Figures 8.2 and 8.3 reflects the actual state of harmonization of organizational cultures in respective companies. Figure 8.2 is specific in that it includes the organizational culture of Lek prior to the acquisition by Novartis. As can be seen in Figure 8.2, the organizational culture of Lek is shifting toward the pattern evidenced in Novartis. Figure 8.3 shows that after ten years, Danfoss and Danfoss Trata developed relatively parallel patterns of organizational culture, while in Gorenje and Mora Moravia (acquired in early 2005), organizational cultures are still further apart.

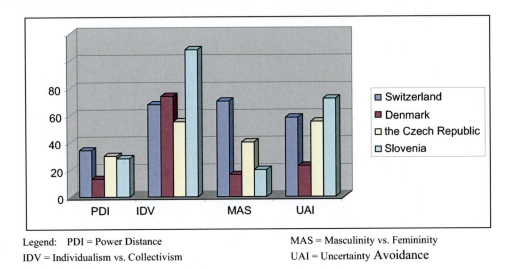

Legend: PDI = Power Distance   MAS = Masculinity vs. Femininity
           IDV = Individualism vs. Collectivism   UAI = Uncertainty Avoidance

Source: Own work.

Figure 8.1. Comparison of National Cultures of Switzerland, Denmark, the Czech Republic and
Slovenia.

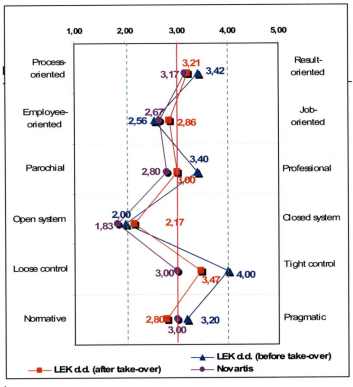

Source: Own work.

Figure 8.2. Organizational Cultures of Lek and Novartis.

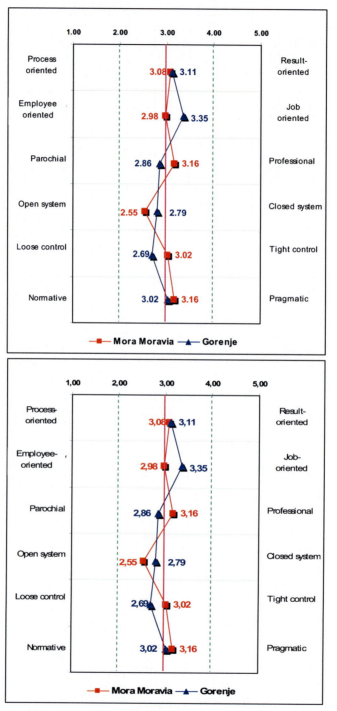

Source: Own work.

Figure 8.3. Organizational Cultures of Danfoss and Danfoss Trata, and Gorenje and Mora Moravia.

The influence of national culture on the characteristics of the organizational culture as well as the relationships between organizational culture and formal control propose:

(1) *National culture*, predominantly characterized by *masculinity,* is more likely to be related to the development of *job-oriented organizational culture*. In Novartis, where one would expect to confirm this hypothesis, empirical results do not provide sufficient evidence. In both the parent company as well as Lek, where there is a tendency toward femininity, organizational cultures are rather employee oriented. From this perspective, both organizational cultures are aligned, however, the Swiss national culture would imply the opposite. The second case confirms the hypothesis: the Danish national culture is dominated by femininity and the Danfoss organizational culture is strongly employee oriented. The same is true with Danfoss Trata.

In Gorenje, interestingly, the dominant feminine dimension of Slovenian national culture does not impact the employee- vs. job-oriented dimension of the organizational culture. Job orientation is evident. As of today, the company has not attempted to put in place any mechanisms to influence this dimension of organizational culture in Mora Moravia. As illustrated in Figure 8.3, Mora Moravia is characterized by an employee orientation which is in line with the dominance of femininity in the Czech national culture. *Employee orientation,* empirically evidenced as prevailing in the studied companies, is further hypothesized to be in relationship with *subjective and comprehensive evaluation of individuals and with the use of internal standards of performance* when targets are set. The cases of Mora Moravia and Danfoss Trata confirm this hypothesis. In Lek, employee orientation weakened after the acquisition but it still prevails over job orientation. Yet, the use of internal standards of performance and the subjective and comprehensive evaluation of individuals that one would expect to be present is rather poorly evidenced. A potential explanation of this phenomenon may relate to the fact that Novartis is listed on the NYSE and is thus subject to strict rules of financial reporting, external performance measures, and objectivity.

(2) *Individualism* is a specifically strong dimension of Slovenian national culture. It is suggested to be related to *professional* organizational culture. As can be seen in Figure 8.3, a professional organizational culture was dominant in Lek prior to acquisition. After joining the Novartis Group, characterized by parochial organizational culture, Lek's professionalism weakened and started to shift toward the parochial pattern of relationships typical of the parent company. In other studied countries, similarly, individualism prevails and is accompanied by rather professional organizational cultures in companies under study. This notion thus receives strong empirical confirmation. It is further suggested that professional organizational culture encourages individual evaluations and rewards and is also related to variable compensation. In Lek, the period after acquisition is marked by a relatively important rise in individual evaluations and rewards, which is contrary to the expected tendency of weakened professionalism. In line with this, variable compensation increased significantly as well. Before Danfoss Trata was acquired by Danfoss, performance measurement in the subsidiary was generally poorly developed and its importance increased immediately afterwards. The acquired company had to develop group (team) performance measures and performance measures at the company level, and has only recently developed criteria for performance appraisal of individuals, managers in particular. As a consequence, the extent of variable compensation is small but is increasing from year to year. All in all, the Danfoss Trata case does not provide proof for the proposed relationships. In Mora Moravia, a performance measurement system remains firmly set and the focus is on company performance measurement. Employee compensation is primarily fixed with subjective evaluations of individual performance. Gorenje, the parent company, is currently determined

to postpone the question of devising a joint compensation policy, which may be related to the current lack of individual evaluations and rewards at the second managerial level in their own organization.

(3) *Low power distance*, a characteristic of all four national cultures, is suggested to be related to *open systems*. All three cases confirm this notion. Danish national culture has the lowest power distance of all studied countries and Danfoss organizational culture is very open, too. It is further hypothesized that open systems are related to *participative target setting and choice of indicators*. Evidence from questionnaires from Lek and Danfoss Trata confirms this proposition. After acquisition, employees to a larger extent participate in target setting and in determining the right performance measures. Mora Moravia is an exception and may be explained by the initial requirements of the parent company, which strictly sets financial targets for the recently acquired subsidiary and whose organizational culture is characterized by a closed system.

(4) The relationships between *uncertainty avoidance* and the type of control – *loose/tight control* differ across the studied companies. Relatively small uncertainty avoidance is typical of Danish national culture but has not had much influence on the organizational culture in Danfoss, which is characterized by a tendency toward tight control. Further, Gorenje's organizational culture is marked by very loose control even though Slovenian national culture reflects high uncertainty avoidance. Clearly evident and theoretically sound, though, is the shift from rather tight control to predominantly loose control in Lek, the latter being characteristic of Novartis organizational culture. Tight control is further hypothesized to be related to tight reliance on performance measures when conducting performance appraisals and determining rewards for employees. This is particularly true for Lek and Danfoss Trata where the importance of tight reliance on performance indicators increased in the post-takeover period. In Mora Moravia, however, the incentive system is based on company performance measures which are beyond the influence of individuals.

(5) *Large uncertainty avoidance* is suggested to be in relationship with *normative* organizational culture. In Lek, a trend toward more normativism could be detected after joining Novartis Group, which represents a tendency to increased alignment of the two organizational cultures. In Danfoss Trata, quite the contrary, pragmatism prevails, which may well be related to insignificant normativism in Danfoss and is aligned with the typical Danish low uncertainty avoidance. From this perspective, Mora Moravia is similar to Danfoss Trata as it is characterized by a pragmatic organizational culture and is in harmony with the parent company's pragmatism. With the exception of Lek, normativism is far from being strongly present in the studied companies. In terms of the selection of performance measures, normativism is suggested to be related to increased emphasis on financial performance measures. All subsidiaries use balanced performance measurement systems – at the corporate level, financials are dominant but are supported by non-financial performance measurements of customer satisfaction, quality, productivity, and employee commitment. This relationship thus cannot be confirmed in our three cases.

Discussion and Conclusion

Each of the three studied takeovers has its unique characteristics and the diversity of these stories is most helpful in further contributing to the evolving theory of organizational culture convergence in an international takeover setting. In the case of Novartis, the parent company carefully planned the acquisition of Lek. Starting with due diligence (covering a thorough analysis of Lek products, technologies, research and development activities and competencies, distribution channels, and organizational culture traits), the parent-to-be-company swiftly recognized one of the finest qualities of Slovenian national culture, its adaptability. They counted on this specific characteristic in those rare dimensions of Lek organizational culture where it diverges from the pattern of the Novartis organizational culture. After two years of joining Sandoz, Lek organizational culture has changed evidently toward further alignment with the Novartis organizational culture, which explains the current relatively poor presence of formal managerial control. So far, the parent company has focused more on the geographical consolidation of the generic pharmaceuticals industry and has let acquired companies work on the necessary convergence of their organizational cultures by themselves. The consolidation, however, did include reorganization of key strategic processes. The first reorganization took place in the finance function where strict compliance with the SEC rules was put in place. A reorganization of purchasing followed with indirect purchasing being introduced. The new organizational structure of Sandoz further envisages direct reporting of specific business functions in subsidiaries to the global business functions at Sandoz level.

The story of Danfoss-Danfoss Trata is different in that it includes a ten-year post-takeover period. In line with expectations, the convergence of the two organizational cultures is almost exemplary. In spite of some national culture differences between the two countries, a relatively high alignment in all dimensions of organizational cultures is present. This may imply that a long enough period may help adapt and align otherwise divergent organizational cultures, also with formal control mechanisms, and thus weaken the influence of the national culture on organizational culture. Typical of the Danfoss Trata case is the shared common vision of top managers from early on – to concentrate manufacturing operations in Slovenia aiming to increase production at the local site and realize synergies in production costs and development at the group level. Shared values, frequent visits of Danfoss managers to the Slovenian subsidiary, and Danfoss network organization, in which Danfoss Trata plays a vital role, provide evidence that socialization and gradual reconciliation of organizational cultures has played an important role here. Among formal managerial control mechanisms, reorganization of activities and reallocation (transfer) of production facilities from other countries to Slovenia took place early on. Today, ten years after the takeover, the role of these mechanisms has faded away and is restricted to regular monthly financial reports. Most other areas of performance measurement and management control are localized.

Gorenje acquired Mora Moravia just recently. It approached to integration processes by appointing two Slovenian managers to top managerial position in Mora Moravia, by replacing some of the existing managers, by optimizing all business processes under strict surveillance of Gorenje managers, and by reorganizing purchasing and sales. These activities produced improved business results in the first year. Top management in Gorenje considers the implementation of joint politics in the area of performance measurement and incentive systems as subordinate to the above measures, as they believe personal control may quite sufficiently replace more formal mechanisms. Thus, the only formal control that took place in the first month after acquisition was executed through monthly accounting reports on budget realization.

A joint characteristic of the three acquired companies is that, after acquisition, they all improved their business results in terms of increased production, new markets, and sales growth. Different lengths of acquisitions and thereby different periods for parent companies to exercise managerial control and thus supplement softer organizational culture alignment processes, however, help form the following conclusions: personal surveillance, establishing sound foundations for trust, and early replacements of incompatible managers represent the mechanisms put in place first to help converge divergent organizational cultures. Among formal mechanisms, reorganization of critical activities and process optimization are vitally important to ensure the payoff on acquisition. Only after that an alignment of performance measurement systems and incentive systems takes place. As evidenced in our study, none of the parent companies attempted to change the existing performance measurement systems in the subsidiary extensively. They did and do require more frequent and complete reporting of financials, but let the locals determine most of other performance measures and targets.

REFERENCES

Anthony, R. N. 1988. *"The Management Control Function"*. Boston: Harvard Business School Press.

Bartlett C. A., and Ghoshal S. 1989. *"Managing Across Boarders. The Transnational Solution."* Boston, MA: Harvard Business School Press.

Baskerville, R. F. 2003. "Hofstede Never Studied Culture." *Accounting, Organizations and Society* 28: 1–14.

Bhimani, A. 1999. "Mapping Methodological Frontiers in Cross-National Management Control Research". *Accounting, Organizations and Society* 24: 413–440.

Bhimani, A. 2003. "A Study of the Emergence of Management Accounting System Ethos and Its Influence on Perceived System Success." *Accounting, Organizations and Society* 28(6): 523–638.

Child, J. 1984. "Organization. Second Edition." London: Harper and Row.

Chow, C. W., Harrison, G. L., McKinnon, J. L., and Wu, A. 2002. "The Organizational Culture of Public Accounting Firms. Evidence from Taiwanese Local and US Affiliated Firms." *Accounting, Organizations and Society* 27: 347–360.

Dent, F. J. 1991. "Accounting and Organizational Cultures: A Field Study of the Emergence of a New Organizational Reality." *Accounting, Organizations and Society* 16: 705–732.

Gupta, A. K., and Govindarajan, V. 1991b. "Knowledge Flow Patterns, Subsidiary Strategic Roles, and Strategic Control Within MNCs." *Academy of Management Proceedings:* 21–25.

Harrison, G. L. 1993. "Reliance on Accounting Performance Measures in Superior Evaluative Style – the Influence of National Culture and Personality." *Accounting, Organizations and Society* 18: 319–339.

Henri, J. F. 2004. "Organizational Culture and Performance Measurement Systems." *Accounting, Organizations and Society*, article in press, available online November 30, 2004.

Hofstede, G. 1980a. *"Culture's Consequences – International Differences in Work–Related Values."* London: Sage Publications.

Hofstede, G. 1980b. "Motivation, Leadership, and Organization: Do American Theories Apply Abroad?" *Organizational Dynamics* Summer: 42–63.

Hofstede, G. 1984. "The Cultural Relativity of the Quality of Life Concept." *Academy of Management Review* 9(3): 389–398.

Hofstede, G., and Bond, M. H. 1988. "The Confucius Connection: From Cultural Roots to Economic Growth." *Organizational Dynamics* 16: 5–21.

Hofstede, G., Neuijen, B., Ohayv, D. D., and Sanders, G. 1990. "Measuring Organizational Cultures: a Qualitative and Quantitative Study Across Twenty Cases." *Administrative Science Quarterly* 35: 286–316.

Hofstede, G. 1998. "Identifying Organizational Subcultures: An Empirical Approach." *Journal of Management Studies* 35: 1–12.

Jazbec, M. 2005. "Medkulturno komuniciranje kot sestavni del poslovnega izobraževanja." Magistrsko delo. Ljubljana: Fakulteta za družbene vede.

Kilduff, M. 1992. "Performance and Interaction Routines in Multinational Corporations." *Journal of International Business Studies* First Quarter: 133–145.

Leifer, R., and Mills, P. K. 1996. "An Information Processing Approach for Deciding Upon Control Strategies and Reducing Control Loss in Emerging Organizations." *Journal of Management* 22(1): 113–137.

Laurent, A. 1986. "The Cross-Cultural Puzzle of International Human Resource Management." *Human Resources Management* 25(1): 91–102.

MacIntosh, N. B., Shearer, T., and Riccaboni, A. 2005. "Transnational Corporations and Expert Management Control Systems: A Levinasian Philosophical Ethical Critique." Paper presented at European Accounting Association Annual Congress 2005, Gothenburg, Sweden, May 23–25, 2005.

MacLeod, W.B. 1995. "Incentives in Organizations: An Overview of Some of the Evidence and Theory". In H. Siebert (ed.): "Trends in Business Organisation: Do Participation and Cooperation Increase Competitiveness?" Chicago: Kiehl Institute World Press: 3–42.

Martinez J. I., and Jarillo J. C. 1989). "The Evolution of Research on Coordination Mechanisms in Multinational Corporations." *Journal of International Business Studies* Fall: 489–514.

Misztal B. A. 1996. "Trust in Modern Societies: The Search for the Bases of Social Order." Cambridge: Polity Press.

Noerreklit, H., and Schoenfeld, H. M. W. 2000. "Controlling Multinational Companies: An Attempt to Analyze Some Unresolved Issues." *The International Journal of Accounting,* 35(3): 415–430.

Ouchi, W. G. 1977. "The Relationship Between Organizational Structure and Organizational Control." *Administrative Science Quarterly* 22: 95–113.

Ouchi, W. G. 1979. "A Conceptual Framework for the Design of Organizational Control Mechanisms." *Management Science* 25(9): 833–848.

Ouchi, W. G. 1980. "Markets, Bureaucracies and Clans." *Administrative Science Quarterly* 25: 129–141.

Pratt, J., Mohrweis, L.C., and Beaulieu, P. 1988. "The Interaction Between National and Organizational Culture in Accounting Firms: An Extension." *Accounting, Organizations and Society* 18: 621–628.

Pratt, J., and Beaulieu, P. 1992. "Organizational Culture in Public Accounting: Size, Technology, Rank, and Functional Area." *Accounting, Organizations and Society* 17(7): 667–684.

Quinn, R.E., and Rohrbaugh, J. 1983. "A Spatial Model of Effectiveness Criteria: Towards a Competing Values Approach to Organizational Analysis." *Management Science* 29: 363–377.

Simon, H.A. 1976. "Administrative Behaviour." Third Edition. New York: The Free Press.

Simons, R. 1995. "Levers of Control. How Managers Use Innovative Control Systems to Drive Strategic Renewal." Boston: Harvard Business School.

Soeters, J., and Schreuder, H. 1988. "The Interaction Between National and Organizational Cultures in Accounting Firms." *Accounting, Organizations and Society* 13: 75–85.

Trompenaars, F. 1994. *"Riding the Waves of Culture."* New York: Irwin.

Trompenaars, F., and Woolliams, P. 2004. *"Business Across Cultures."* Chichester: Capstone Publishing Ltd.

Zucker, L.G 1986. "The Production of Trust: Institutional Sources of Economic Structure 1840-1920". In B. M. Staw and L. L. Cummings (eds.): *"Research In Organizational Behaviour."* Greenwich, CT: JAI Press: 8: 55–111.

PART III: TURKEY: TODAY'S CHALLENGE OR AN OPTION FOR THE FUTURE

In: New Emerging Economies and Their Culture
Editors: J. Prašnikar, A. Cirman, pp. 121-137
ISBN: 978-1-60021-754-8
© 2007 Nova Science Publishers, Inc.

Chapter 9

THE TURKISH ECONOMY: A RETROSPECTIVE ASSESSMENT AND RECENT DEVELOPMENTS

Bilin Neyapti

INTRODUCTION

This study provides a brief historical overview of the Turkish economy through episodes marked by major policy changes and reform attempts. The evolution of the Turkish economy is therefore told first by summarizing policies and their outcomes in the pre-1980 period; and then by giving a short account of the developments between 1980 and 2001, a period which itself may further be divided in two phases (1980–1989 and onwards), for a meaningful analysis. Finally, the developments after the 2001 financial crisis are evaluated.

Prior to the 1980s, the Turkish economy was a closed one. The import-substitution based industrialization strategy that the country adopted in the 1960s failed to bring about an economic upturn by the end of the 1970s. Coupled with this, the economic hardship the country experienced following the two oil crises in the 1970s led Turkey to go into a deep economic and political crisis. The 1980s, following an interruption to democratic life in 1980, portray a new phase: that of economic liberalization. Throughout the 1980s and 1990s, however, the liberalization of domestic and foreign transactions did not yield much higher growth performance than the preceding two decades: during the 1960s and the 1970s the average annual growth rate was 4.9% versus the 4.7% of the previous two decades. On the other hand, economic imbalances grew markedly over time; for example, budget deficits amounted to more than 10% of GDP in the beginning of 2002, as compared to 6% in the 1970s, and annual inflation rose on average to 64% during the 1980s and 1990s from 23% in the 1970s.

The accumulation of the various policy mistakes and economic mismanagement, reinforced by the effects of the Asian financial crisis in the late 1990s and severe effects of the 1999 earthquake, paved the way for a deep financial crisis in 2001. The crises rendered the launching of a wide-scale institutional reform efforts inevitable. The long term success of the new phase depends largely on the serious treatment of this reform impetus via building strong institutions of enforcement that would ensure continuity and credibility.

The structure of this chapter is as follows: the second section provides an overview of the status of the Turkish economy with respect to the world and other middle income countries, referring to the relative sizes and rankings of main economic and social indicators. The third, fourth and fifth section give overviews of the Turkish economy over three periods: pre-1980, 1980s and 1990s and after 2001. Finally, the sixth section evaluates Turkey's economic prospects.

THE CURRENT STATUS OF THE TURKISH ECONOMY IN THE WORLD

This section provides a comparative view of the Turkish economic and social indicators vis-à-vis the rest of the world, particularly with respect to the low and middle income (LMI) and middle income (MIC) groups of countries. The data is mainly from 2003, with the exception of certain data in the Appendix that were not available for 2003.[29]

As of 2003, Turkish per capita income (at purchasing power parity) stood at about 90th percentile of the world average, but was 68% and 21% higher than that of LMI and MIC countries, respectively. GDP growth in Turkey was about twice as much as the world average (2.55 times in per capita terms), although this performance was only slightly higher compared to the rest of MIC and LMI countries in 2003. Nevertheless, Turkey appears to lag behind both LMI and MIC countries with respect to savings and investment shares in GDP. The ratio of research expenditure to GDP in Turkey also lags behind both the world average and the average of LMI and MIC countries.

Turkey is more urbanized, but also has greater population growth and unemployment than the average of the rest of MIC countries and the world. The economic structure of Turkey still appears largely agricultural (three times higher than the world average and about the same as the LMI average) as the percentage of arable land in Turkey is at least three times higher than the average of both the world and LMI countries. Its employment share in the agricultural sector is lower than the MIC average, although the GDP share of value added in the same sector is greater. In the industrial sector the situation is reversed: the share of industrial value added is relatively low in Turkey while the share of industrial employment is greater than in MIC countries.

As for the comparison of social indicators, one can note that public education and health spending in Turkey are both slightly worse compared to the rest of MIC countries, and education spending is only slightly better compared to the world average and the average of LMI countries. Life expectancy and literacy rates are at a similar level compared to education spending. Atiyas and Emil (2005) note that income distribution in Turkey is generally worse than in other middle-income countries, though better than in Latin America.

The Turkish economy is slightly more open than the world economy on average (in terms of export and import to GDP ratios), but slightly less than the economies of the MIC countries. In the financial arena, domestic credit to GDP, private credit to total banking sector credit, and market capitalization of listed companies, which are all indicators of financial

---

[29]   The data mentioned in this section was obtained from the World Development Indicators of the World Bank, unless otherwise stated.

sector development, are much better in Turkey than in MIC or LMI countries. On the other hand, aid and foreign direct investment figures are relatively unfavorable for Turkey as compared to the world average and the average of LMI and MIC countries. Turkey's debt service to GDP ratio which exceeds the averages of both LMI and MIC countries is one apparent explanation. The ratio indicates a riskier business environment, which is also reflected in the index of legal rights of borrowers and lenders. On the other hand, procedures to enforce a contract, time needed to enforce a contract, to register property and to start a business are all much shorter in Turkey than in MIC countries, which presents a favorable ground for business.

In terms of overall aggregates, Turkey's GDP (at purchasing power parity) constituted only 0.9% of the world GDP, but it represented more than 2.1% of the total GDP of LMI countries and 2.6% of the total GDP of MIC countries in 2003. The Turkish population and labor force constitute about 1.1% of the world labor force, 1.3% of the labor force of LMI countries and more than 2% of the labor force of MIC countries. Its manufacturing value added totals 0.4% of the world value added, and 2% of value added produced by LMI countries. As for potential global influence, Turkish scientific and technical journal articles are about half of its population share in the world, and around three times as much as its population share in LMI and more than twice its population share in MIC.

Despite its average or below average performance with regards to many economic attributes, Turkey was the 17th largest economy in the world (in PPP terms) in 2003, which makes it an important economic power (Table A 9.2 in Appendix). It ranked 12th in the world in terms of the amount of arable land, 15th in terms of population size, and 7th in terms of agricultural value added. However, it was only 26th in terms of its industrial value added. Turkey ranked below 100th in terms of private capital inflows and aid per capita, but was as of 2003 the 2nd largest user of IMF funds and 8th in terms of long-term debt. In view of the indicators that may reflect the growth potential of countries, the following is observed: Turkey ranks 29th and 42nd with regards to gross fixed capital formation and net foreign direct investment inflows, respectively. It is 24th with respect to scientific and technical journal articles. To summarize, Turkey is a large developing country that does not yet perform at its full potential due to its prolonged structural constraints and accumulated economic problems.

FROM REPUBLIC (1923) TO THE 1980S: A BRIEF OVERVIEW

The Turkish economy was dominated by the agricultural sector.[30] The period until the 1950s is often referred to as an etatist period during which the import-substitution strategy dominated economic policy. During this period, the mining and agricultural sectors were largely subsidized while the private sector was less favored compared to the state sector. Targeting mainly the consumer and intermediate goods production, the textile sector was given the utmost emphasis.

The post Second World War years were characterized by the development of infrastructure to spur private sector growth. This policy increased domestic credit flows to the state economic enterprises, which then financed capital accumulation in the private sector through cheap state sector inputs. Partnerships between state enterprises and the private sector

---

[30]   45% of value added and about 80% of employment in the 1923–1932 period (Kepenek and Yenturk, 1994).

also meant the transfer of capital from the state towards the private sector. However, coupled with rapid population growth and urbanization, these policies failed to spur economic growth (per capita) and the 1950s ended with increased inflation and foreign debt.

The period between 1960 and 1980 was the period of planning that was agreed upon by the decision of (semi-civil, semi-military) bureaucracy to overcome the economic hardships and pursuant political repression. The planning emphasis was on industrialization through protectionism,[31] which was mainly directed towards the production of industrial and intermediate goods. Besides agriculture, transportation and construction works also appear to have been given emphasis in this period.

During this period, increased domestic credit expansion via central bank financing of state economic enterprises and the treasury was a notable factor in accumulated financial troubles. In addition, bank credits were not directed to productive sectors. Fiscal policies were ineffective in delivering equality, indirect rather than direct taxes were emphasized, and tax evasion became prevalent. The lack of discipline and prudence in both monetary and fiscal areas, the oil crises of 1974 and 1978, the following economic downturn in the neighboring countries and the Cyprus conflict all contributed to the chaotic economic and political circumstances in Turkey by the end of the 1970s. The foreign debt to GDP ratio rose from 13.6% in 1973 to 20% in 1979 and was accompanied by a decrease in the term structure and increase in interest rates.

THE 1980S AND THE 1990S

January 24, 1980 marks the beginning of a new period characterized by market- and outward-oriented economic reforms. The main pillar of this approach was price liberalization. An orthodox stabilization program reduced inflation that reached 110% in 1980 to around 30%.[32] Kepenek and Yenturk (1994) evaluate the results of the program by stating that while the problem of the black market could certainly have been prevented with market pricing, it also led to many monopolistic state economic enterprises (SEEs) to offer non-economic prices. Moreover, market prices that formed in non-monopolistic markets were still inefficient due to technological and distributional constraints. Without the necessary infrastructural adjustments that could improve the competitiveness of the domestic production sectors, price liberalization thus generated further economic problems.

Another manifestation of price liberalization was in the form of higher interest rates and the depreciation of the TL, both geared towards attracting foreign exchange. Figure 9.1 shows a trend of increasing inflation and interest rates and currency depreciation over time. The emergence and collapse of various brokers during the 1980s signaled the fragility that such deregulation could generate in the economy. The reforms also included additional non-market measures to encourage exports and legal measures to attract foreign capital. Indeed, among the main criticisms of this reform period was the lack of development considerations and sole reliance on the views of comparative advantage and laissez-faire, laissez passer.

---

[31]   Referred to as import substitutive industrialization.
[32]   All data is obtained from the Central Bank of the Republic of Turkey, unless otherwise indicated.

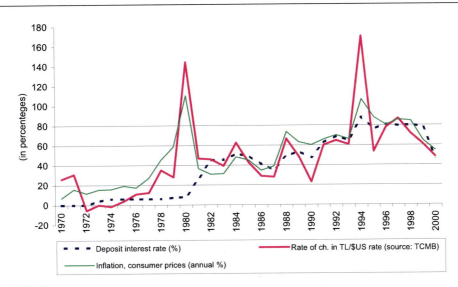

Source: TCMB.

Figure 9.1. Trends in Interest, Inflation and Devaluation Rate: 1970–2000.

As the second pillar that was consistent with the target of achieving a private-sector oriented economy, tight monetary and fiscal policies aimed at reducing the impact of SEEs in this period. In mid-1980s, open market operations provided a new financing channel for the government and eventually enabled the abandonment of the direct advances of the central bank, which was a step towards greater central bank independence. Liberalization of the foreign exchange regime was followed by capital account liberalization in 1989. Additional market institutions were introduced in the form of inter-bank money market in 1986 and Capital Market Board in 1987.

The 1980s certainly witnessed an increase in the trade (trade volume as percentage of GDP almost doubled in the 1980s as compared to the 1970s, see Figure 9.2), although this was accompanied by an average rate of currency depreciation of 55.3% and an average CPI inflation of 51.3% during the 1980s. Parallel to these trends, (deposit) interest rates also increased from 8% in 1980 to about 50% by 1990. While the public sector borrowing rate (PSBR) to GDP ratio was well contained in the first half of the 1980s, it reached the pre-program period levels by 1990 (8%). In the meantime, the share of investment spending in total government expenditure fell from 17.3% in the 1980s to 7.2% in the 1990s.

Boratav and Yeldan (2005) have investigate the causes of macroeconomic failures of the post-1980 period and attributed the lack of sustainability of the program's initial positive achievements also to the channeling of private investment to unproductive sectors such as construction. It is argued that the initial export boom was due to excess capacity inherited from the earlier decade and the failure to invest in technology-intensive areas led to unsustainable growth performance until the 2000s.

On the structural side the share of industrial value added rose from 20% of GDP in the 1970s to about 28% during the 1980s and 1990s, whereas the share of agriculture steadily fell from 34.3% in the 1970s to 16.5% in the 1990s; the share of services steadily grew to 55% during the 1990s from 45% in the 1970s. This structural transformation, however, also indicates the worsening domestic terms of trade for the agricultural sector as the labor force employed in agriculture remains relatively high (around 35% in 2004).

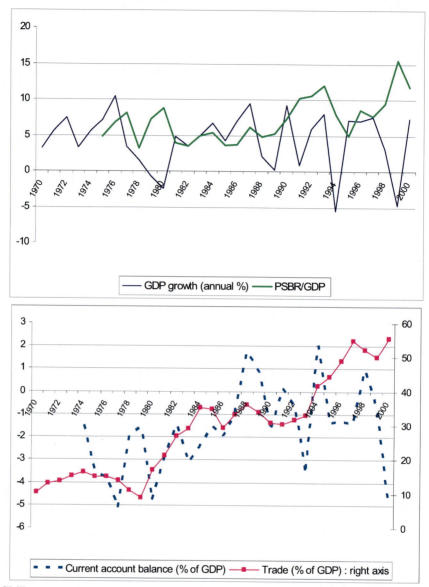

Source: TCMB.

Figure 9.2. Trade, Growth, Budget Deficits and Current Account Deficits: 1970–2000.

The period's benchmark is the 1994 exchange rate crisis that erupted due to the exit of hot money, initially attracted by high interest rates, as the government reduced the interest rate to reduce its debt burden. A very insightful and thorough survey of the Turkish economy in these two decades was provided by Ertugrul and Selcuk (2001). They attribute the boom-bust cycles in Turkey to the changes in and mismanagement of exchange rate policies that resulted in temporary overvaluations of the TL, leading to initial demand increases, followed by depreciation and reversal of fortune.

FROM THE MILLENNIUM ONWARDS

As public sector domestic borrowing increased over time, the Turkish banking sector became laden with debt instruments that paid increasingly higher interest.[33] Indeed, while the share of foreign currency in total deposits of private banks rose to 72% in 1999, increasingly speculative-oriented domestic investment activity rendered the financial system highly vulnerable to exchange rate risks.

The 1999 earthquake, following the East Asian and Russian financial crises, hit the economy hard, resulting in a 6% loss of GDP, coupled with PSBR to GDP ratio of 15.5% in 1999, up from 9.4% in the preceding year. The new economic reform program was launched in December 1999 with support from the IMF.[34] The program envisaged adopting an exchange-rate based stabilization program, stopping currency devaluation and the loss in the value of money via the management of net foreign assets. However, the program suffered greatly from a financial crisis in November 2000, when the inter-bank borrowing mechanism failed to support the overnight financing requirements of the short-term debt laden structure of the banking system. Finally, the program came to a severe stop in February 2001, which was politically triggered.[35] This led to the abandonment of the pegged exchange rate regime and resulted in a 96% (year-on-year) devaluation of the (average) value of the TL against the USD, or by 31% only in March of 2001 (Central Bank of Turkish Republic). The crises also led to a 9.5% fall in real GDP.

Following the crisis, the economic program needed to be revised, bearing in mind that economic recovery requires a radical and encompassing institutional reform. Needless to say, IMF reviews in the crises' aftermath stressed bank restructuring, fiscal and monetary transparency combined with a strengthened incomes policy. Indeed, various institutional reforms were launched even though the extent of their success varied over time. Below we briefly analyze some of the crucial institutional reforms of economic recovery, i.e. fiscal, monetary and financial reforms.

FISCAL OUTLOOK AND REFORMS

The average annual budget deficit in Turkey was 9.5% of GDP during the 1990s and averaged 10.7% between 2002 and 2003. While the deficit responded strongly to the booms and busts during the period, its increasing trend was certainly due to the accumulated imbalances in the form of high inflation, interest rates and debt. Indeed, the interest component of PSBR rose tremendously over the years, increasing to 29.3% in 1990s and to about 44% in the 2000–2003 period from 12.5% in the 1980s. Likewise, social security spending has been on an increase, doubling to about 8% of total government spending in the beginning of the 2000s compared to the 1980s. On the other hand, budget realizations have

---

[33] Interest payments on domestic debt increased from 2.1% of total government spending in 1980 to 14.3% in 1990 and to 40% in 2000 (State Planning Organization).

[34] Evrensel (2002) reports that Turkey was on a stand-by agreement (SB) with the IMF for 11 years between 1971, when it became a member of the IMF, and 1997. Adding 1999 means that Turkey spent 12 out of 29 years on an SB.

[35] The triggering effect is generally argued to be a press announcement by the prime minister stating that there is a deep political crisis, to which markets immediately react with soaring interest rates.

yielded primary surpluses during the 2000s, with a current policy target for primary surpluses of 6.5% of GDP.

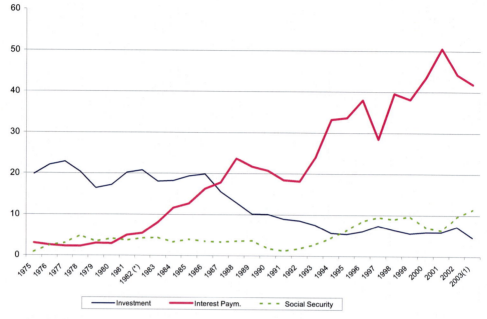

Source: TCMB.

Figure 9.3. Shares of Investment, Interest Payments and Social Security Spending in Total Spending of the Government.

To look further into the issue of accumulated imbalances, it helps to state that external debt to GDP on average totaled 37%, 43% and 66% for 1980s, 1990s and the 2002–2003 period, respectively. It is also worth noting that the share of short-term debt in total increased from 14.5% in the 1980s to 21.3% in the 1990s and fell to 14.2% during the 2002–2003 period. The medium and long-term component of external debt in GDP was 40% during the 1996–2000 period, it rose to 67% in 2001 and fell to 51% in 2003. Domestic debt stock reached 69% of GDP in 2001 and fell to 54% in 2003. The ratio of public debt stock to GDP also fell from 101% in 2002 to 75% in 2004 (TCMB Quarterly Report, 2004).

Recent data also indicate that the share of interest payments in total expenditure has decreased from 50.6% in 2001 to 41% in 2004, following the pattern of reduced inflation rates. Nevertheless, interest payments still constitute about 15% of GDP. Furthermore, the trend of government investment spending decreased in the post-1986 period and remained incredibly low in the 2000s: about 2% of GDP. Total investment fell from 24% of GDP during the 1990s to 14.7% during the 2000–2003 period.[36]

---

[36] Ismihan et al. (2003) argue that complementarity between public and private investment also suffered from macroeconomic instability.

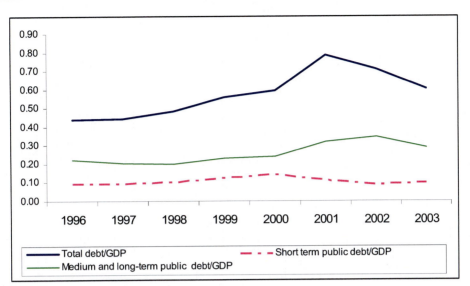

Source: TCMB.

Figure 9.4. Total Debt, Public Medium and Long Term and Public Short Term Components: 1996–2003.

Apart from increasing debt service, the increasing fiscal burden also originates from bad fiscal management in the sense of increasing reliance on indirect taxation,[37] the lack of accountability and transparency in budgetary operations and a large informal sector. In view of such problems that inhibit sustainable budgetary prospects, various reforms have been enacted since 2000[38]: in 2000, extra-budgetary funds were mostly eliminated[39] and government accounts were consolidated[40]; in 2002, the Public Procurement Law was adopted but half of its articles were later revoked in response to political pressures; in 2003, the Public Debt Management Law, the Public Financial Management and the Control Law were adopted to achieve transparency and better regulation; and in 2005, the Local Authorities Law was also adopted. Nevertheless, implementation issues still remain due to continued capacity constraints and accountability. In addition, although some consolidation with regards to social security has occurred, a comprehensive reform is still pending.

MONETARY OUTLOOK AND REFORMS

In the aftermath of the 2001 banking crisis, and after the realization that all possible price stabilization attempts had been tried and failed, the only credible way out appeared to be the adoption of an (implicit) inflation targeting mechanism that required the instrument independence of the central bank. The relatively transparent nature of this mechanism, which

---

[37] The share of indirect taxes in total government revenue reached about 50% in the 2000s as compared with less than 40% in the 1980s (State Planning Organization).

[38] See also Atiyas and Emil, 2005.

[39] The remaining ones are the Defense Industry Support Fund, the Privatization Fund and the Social Aid and Solidarity Incentive Fund.

[40] Currently the primary deficits are defined both with and without SEE's duty losses. The basic definition includes central government, local governments and social security institutions.

even though implicit, amounted to periodical public reports of the central bank on the progress, was an important feature of attaining the much needed credibility.

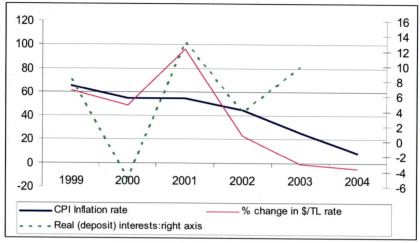

Source: TCMB.

Figure 9.5. Rates of Inflation (Annual Average) Exchange Rate Depreciation: 1999–2004.

The Central Bank of the Turkish Republic (CBRT) has gained independence in stages over the years since the end of 1980s: advances were already prohibited in 1997[41] and the CBRT law was revised to vest it with greater independence in 1999 and 2001. More importantly, however, the discipline in monetary policy making since 2001 started to indicate that CBRT has become an institution that is independent from political pressures in practice as well. This new era especially proved to be a testing ground for the central bank's independence due to the extent of economic hardships and the rising political pressures for loosening the monetary policy.

As a result of the monetary program's gained credibility, the CPI inflation (end of year) has been lower than the target rates since 2002: 30% versus 35% in 2002, 18.4% versus 20% in 2003 and 9.3% versus 12% in 2004. Figure 9.5 shows the stabilization of the value of currency and money, which records slight appreciation of the TL against the USD and the reduction of inflation rates to single digits since 2004. Appreciation of the TL, coupled with still high real interest rates, often causes concern about a widening current account balance and short term financing.

FINANCIAL SECTOR REFORMS

In 1999, a new banking law was enacted that involved much more comprehensive and/or strict provisions regarding capital requirements, management and lending practices, to name a few. In addition, the Bank Regulatory and Supervisory Agency (BRSA) was established in 1999 to harmonize the banking practice with the Basel standards.

---

[41]   See Berument and Neyapti, 1999.

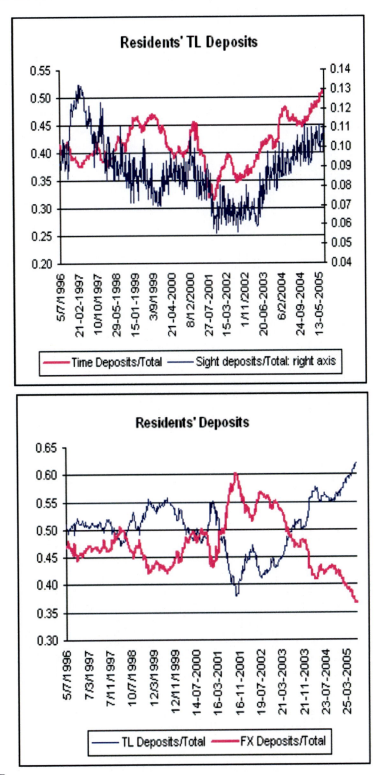

Source: TCMB

Figure 9.6. Residents Deposit Structure.

As a result of the BRSA's restructuring efforts banks were recapitalized and capital adequacy standards were generally met by 2005. What is more, the 100% deposit insurance that was put forward by the 1994 financial crisis has recently been relaxed. As a result of either liquidation (3), merger (14), or sale (5) of the problem banks, as of May 2005 there was only one bank remaining under the administration of the Deposit Insurance Fund, down from 23 banks that were listed initially.[42]

Between 2001 and 2003, which were the initial years of the recent reforms, a notable switch in the banking system deposits from domestic to foreign exchange (forex) by the residents occurred; forex deposits reached more than 60% of total deposits of residents in mid-2001. By mid-2005, this trend seems to have been completely reversed again, with the TL deposits totaling more than 60%. In the meantime, a sudden drop in time (TL) deposits of residents also recovered, reaching more than 50% of their total deposits by June 2005. The deposits, however, remains largely short term.

As for capital flows, there have been no notable FDI flows to Turkey till 2000: the FDI to GDP ratio was about half a percent for all years except for a few years of privatization of state-owned banks or monopolies that involved partnerships with foreign companies. Moreover, the per capita aid to GDP ratio has also been very low. Nevertheless, the medium- and long-term debt after 2001 started to increase as the share of short term debt in GDP fell. Total debt also fell after the initial crisis in 2001 was averted. Many researchers of the Turkish economy (e.g. Boratav and Yeldan, 2001; Ertugrul and Selcuk, 2001) have criticized the current policies for not averting the proneness of the entire system to crises, which are a consequence of high volume of short-term capital flows due to the persistence on high real interest rates. Nonetheless, in the 2000s, Turkey started to experience net FDI inflows precipitated by relative economic stability and the prospects of EU accession.

WHERE TO GO FROM HERE? A SWOT ANALYSIS

It appears appropriate to end this study with a SWOT analysis that provides a (rough) analysis of strengths, weaknesses, opportunities, and threats. This approach seems to be appropriate since Turkey does have both weaknesses and strengths. The latter can be utilized for a successful overturn of the Turkish economy in the next couple of decades, while recognition and elimination of the former is also greatly needed.

Turkey's strength lies mainly in its dynamic economy that recorded one of the highest growths among developing economies over the past decades. Turkey's serious educational reforms over the years and its young population certainly add to its strengths. The latest stabilization efforts, especially regarding inflation, have also been rather praiseworthy. In terms of location, Turkey benefits from major trade routes and from its proximity to the Eastern markets as well.

There are, however, various weaknesses persisting in the Turkish economy, as the above study reveals. Among them are the past record of lack of continuity due to high political turnover, the population's short memory and populist attributes of the bureaucratic and political structure, a large informal sector and still high real interest rates that prevent the financial sector from lending primarily to the production sectors. In addition, newly initiated

---

[42]   Source: www.tmsf.org.tr.

institutional reforms are prone to suffering from weak accountability and enforcement mechanisms.

Despite these weaknesses, several strong opportunities may be present in the path to success, such as the mutually reenforcing nature of the reform agenda and EU membership process (Turkey's young population, for example, appears to be a balancing feature for the social security problems in an aging EU). Further opportunities for trade diversification may emerge, especially as China and other countries in the Far East and South Asia, as well as former Russian economies continue to grow. A new phase of development planning that combines the identification of local potentials and initiatives with a central vision for long term growth is especially important in view of the effects of increasing global trade.

Furthermore, the realization of a more stable economy and thus improved business environment may increasingly attract foreign direct investment, part of which may originate from the stock of workers abroad. Moreover, the fact that the Turkish banking sector is currently rather small[43] indicates that there exists great room for its growth. While this may encourage foreign bank entry, the benefits of which are debatable, the prospects of a much greater volume of financial intermediation could also bring about growth. Such growth would certainly benefit from enabling the access of small and medium enterprises to financing and would eventually help to eliminate the informal sector. Healthy banking sector growth could materialize, however, only when it is accommodated by prudential regulation and supervision that Turkey has recently took steps towards.[44]

Among the external threats to Turkey's sustainable growth and development, one could count the possibility of a world depression signaled by low interest rates in the developed economies; increasing oil prices in the face of the still overwhelming oil-dependence and high oil taxes, and increasingly competitive world markets, not least of which is due to growing Chinese exports. As for the domestic threats, high current account deficits, political developments which have led to the elimination of a strong opposition to the incumbent, and the lack of a strong enforcement component in the current institutional reforms appear to make to the top of the list. Moreover, while the young population structure of Turkey can be an opportunity, it may also be a threat to development if the population growth continues to be high.

The overview in this study of the past decades' economic performance suggests that Turkey was held back from a sustainable growth path due to both policy mistakes, be it political short-sightedness or simply mismanagement, and structural and institutional constraints. Over time, all these led to the accumulation of imbalances and instability resulting in political and financial crises. Turkey is currently in a relatively optimistic phase of recovery that can set a perfect ground for the realization of longer term opportunities. This involves solidifying the institutional reforms that have been launched in the beginning of the 2000s so as to signal credible commitment to the goal of stabilization. Stabilization, however, needs to be accompanied by a new form of development planning that is geared to contribute to the business environment to stimulate both domestic and foreign investment.

---

[43]   As of 2003, domestic credit provided by the banking sector reached 53% of GDP as compared to the mere 20% at the beginning of the 1990s, while the world average stood at 162% and the middle and low income average was 79% in the same year.

[44]   As of May 2005, the share of foreign banks in the banking sector credits was about 11%, and 7% in total deposits (BRSA).

APPENDIX

Table A 9. 1. Turkey in Comparison with LMI and MIC

	Ratio to the World	Ratio to LMI	Ratio to MIC	
Main Economic Indicators:				
GDP growth (annual %)	2.05	1.11	1.18	
GDP per capita, PPP (constant 2000 international USD)	0.89	1.68	1.21	
GDP per capita growth (annual %)	2.55	1.08		
Gross fixed capital formation (% of GDP)	0.81	0.72	0.64	
Gross domestic savings (% of GDP)	0.95		0.72	(2002)
Government Policy:				
Health expenditure, public (% of GDP)	0.84	0.90	0.85	(2001)
Public spending on education, total (% of GDP)	1.09	1.10	0.96	
Economic Structure:				
Industry, value added (% of GDP)	0.92	0.76	0.61	
Manufacturing, value added (% of GDP)	0.85	0.77	0.59	
Agriculture, value added (% of GDP)	3.37	1.06	1.39	
Employment Structure:				
Labor force, female (% of total labor force)	0.95	0.96	0.92	(2000)
Employment in agriculture (% of total employment)			0.86	(2000)
Employment in industry (% of total employment)			1.26	(2000)
Unemployment, total (% of total labor force)	1.18		1.64	(2002)
Population Structure				
Urban population (% of total)	1.38	1.56	1.27	
Population growth (annual %)	1.32		1.74	
Population ages 65 and above (% of total)	0.83	1.03	0.85	
Population ages 0–14 (% of total)	0.98	0.92	1.08	
Size, in percentages:				
Population, total	1.13	1.33	2.37	
Labor force, total	1.10	1.30	2.18	
GDP, PPP (current international USD)	0.92	2.07	2.62	
Foreign direct investment, net inflows (BoP, current USD)	0.273	1.029	1.15	
Foreign direct investment, net (BoP, current USD)	3.92	1.75		
Long-term debt (DOD, current USD)		4.82		

	Ratio to the World	Ratio to LMI	Ratio to MIC	
External debt, total (DOD, current USD)		5.70	6.84	
Official development assistance and official aid (current USD)	0.214	0.218	0.627	(2002)
IBRD loans and IDA credits (PPG DOD, current USD)		2.38	43.70	
Workers' remittances, receipts (BoP, current USD)		7.29		
Financial Markets:				
Domestic credit to private sector (% of GDP)	0.12	0.28	0.25	
Domestic credit provided by banking sector (% of GDP)	0.33	0.68	0.63	
Stocks traded, total value (% of GDP)	0.50	1.71	1.92	
Market capitalization of listed companies (% of GDP)	0.32	0.65	0.64	
External:				
Trade (% of GDP)	1.26	1.02	0.94	
Imports of goods and services (% of GDP)	1.29	1.08	1.04	
Exports of goods and services (% of GDP)	1.22	0.96	0.85	(2000)
High-technology exports (current USD)	0.00	0.01		
Aid and FDI:				
Foreign direct inv., net inflows (% of gross capital formation)		0.26	0.26	
Foreign direct investment, net inflows (% of GDP)	0.42	0.29	0.27	
Aid per capita (current USD)	0.19	0.16	0.26	
Aid (% of imports of goods and services)	0.28	0.07	0.17	
Aid (% of GNI)	0.33	0.06	0.16	
Debt and Debt Service:				
External debt, total (DOD, current USD)		0.06	0.07	
IBRD loans and IDA credits (PPG DOD, current USD)		0.02	0.04	
Long-term debt (DOD, current USD)		0.05		
Short-term debt (% of total external debt)		1.00	0.91	
Total debt service (% of GNI)		1.86		
Public and publicly guaranteed debt service (% of GNI)		1.68	1.64	
Business Environment:				
Legal rights of borrowers and lenders index (0=less credit access to 10=more access)	0.20	0.22	0.22	
Time to enforce a contract (days)		0.87	0.82	(2004)

Table A 9.1. (Continued)

	Ratio to the World	Ratio to LMI	Ratio to MIC	
Procedures to enforce a contract		0.71	0.70	(2004)
Time to register property (days)		0.11	0.11	(2004)
Time to start a business (days)		0.18	0.18	(2004)
Social Indicators:				
Life expectancy at birth, total (years)	1.03	1.06	0.98	(2002)
Health expenditure, total (% of GDP)	0.65		1.09	
Health expenditure per capita (current USD)	0.33		1.58	
Health expenditure, private (% of GDP)	0.53		0.74	
Literacy rate, adult total (% of people ages 15 and above)	0.74		1.44	(2000)
Literacy rate, youth total (% of people ages 15–24)	1.10	1.11	0.99	(2000)
Potential Global Influence:				
Research and development expenditure (% of GDP)	0.29	0.89	0.97	(2000)
Scientific and technical journal articles	0.55	3.74	4.85	(2001)
International tourism, receipts (% of total exports)		1.03		
International tourism, receipts (current USD)		3.94		

Data from 2003, unless otherwise indicated.
Source: World Bank, World Development Indicators.

Table A 9.2. Turkey's Ranking in the World

	Rank in the world	Year
Size of the economy:		
GDP (constant 2000 USD)	21	2003
GDP, PPP (constant 2000 international USD)	17	2003
GNI, PPP (current international USD)	17	2003
GNI, Atlas method (current USD)	24	2003
in per capita terms:		
GDP per capita, PPP (constant 2000 international USD)	66	2003
GNI per capita, Atlas method (current USD)	64	2003
Land use, arable land (hectares)	12	2001
Labor force, total	16	2003
Population, total	15	2003
Land area (sq km)	36	
Economic Structure:		
Agriculture, value added (constant 2000 USD)	7	2002
Industry, value added (constant 2000 USD)	26	2002

	Rank in the world	Year
Capital flows:		
Gross private capital flows (% of GDP)	110	2002
Net capital account (BoP, current USD)	163	2002
Net financial flows, IDA (current USD)	133	2003
Net financial flows, IBRD (current USD)	127	2003
Use of IMF credit (DOD, current UD$)	2	2003
Long-term debt (DOD, current USD)	8	2003
IBRD loans and IDA credits (PPG DOD, current USD)	10	2003
Aid per capita (current USD)	146	2003
Growth potential:		
Scientific and technical journal articles	24	2001
Gross fixed capital formation (current USD)	29	2002
Foreign direct investment, net inflows (BoP, current USD)	42	2003
International migration stock, total	25	2000
Workers' remittances, receipts (BoP, current USD)	12	2002

Source: World Bank, World Development Indicators.

REFERENCES

Atiyas, I. and Emil, F. 2005. "Political Economy of Government Failures, Crises and Opportunities for Reform." Prepared for the Economic Research Forum and the Institut de la Méditerranée Project. Country Profile: Turkey. Ankara: August 13, 2005.

Berument, H. and Neyapti, B. 1999. "How Independent is TCMB?" *Isletme ve Finans*: 11–17.

Boratav, K. and Yeldan, E. 2001. "Turkey: 1980–2000: Financial Liberalization, Macroeconomic (In)Stability and Patterns of Distribution." Manuscript.

Central Bank of the Turkish Republic. [URL: http://www.tcmb.gov.tr].

Deposit Insurance Fund. [URL: http://www.tmsf.org.tr].

Ertugrul, A. and Selcuk, F. 2001. "A Brief Account of the Turkish Economy: 1980–2000." *Russian and East European Finance and Trade* 37 (6): 6–30.

Evrensel, A. 2002. "Effectiveness of IMF-Supported Stabilization Programs in Developing Countries." *Journal of International Money and Finance* 21: 565–587.

Kepenek, Y. and Yenturk, N. 1994. "Turkish Economy." Istanbul: Remzi Kitapevi.

Metin-Ozcan, K., Ismihan, M. and Tansel, A. 2005 "Macroeconomic Instability, Capital Accumulation and Growth: The Case of Turkey 1963–1999." Bilkent University: Department of Economics Discussion Paper: 02.

Pamukcu T. and Yeldan, E. 2005. "Country Profile: Turkey, Macroeconomic Policy and Recent Economic Performance." Manuscript.

In: New Emerging Economies and Their Culture
Editors: J. Prašnikar, A. Cirman, pp. 139-153

ISBN: 978-1-60021-754-8
© 2007 Nova Science Publishers, Inc.

Chapter 10

CONTEMPORARY TURKISH CONSUMPTIONSCAPE: POLARITY AND PLURALITY

Özlem Sandıkcı and Güliz Ger

INTRODUCTION

Marketing begins and ends with consumers. A company can survive only by correctly assessing and anticipating consumers' needs, and responding to them in an efficient and timely manner. Globalization, technological developments, the movement of people and products intensify competition and transform consumption practices in less affluent societies. Some believe that globalization leads to commercial, cultural, and technological standardization and as societies become richer their consumption practices resemble those of the Western world. Others argue that consumption cultures developed in the less affluent societies are neither unidirectional adoption of Western values nor a mere replica of Western consumption styles (Ger and Belk 1996; Miller 1995; Sandıkcı and Ger 2001).

In this paper we explore the contemporary Turkish consumptionscape and discuss how global and local economic, political, social, and cultural forces shape consumption patterns. As with many developing countries, Turkey suffers from an uneven distribution of income where a small percentage of the population enjoys very high levels of income. The significant gap between the haves and the have-nots becomes reflected in consumption behaviors. A small percentage of the population enjoys a lifestyle based on the global consumerist ideology, resides in million dollar residences, adorns themselves with designer clothing, dines at upscale Turkish and foreign cuisine restaurants, and travels abroad frequently. The majority of the population, however, struggles to maintain a decent living. In addition to the polarity observed between the consumption styles of different socioeconomic groups, the Turkish consumptionscape is characterized by a plurality of consumption practices that entail different interpretations of the modern and the traditional, the local and the global. Turkey is located between the West and the East not only in geographical terms but also in cultural and social terms. An inevitable effect of this is the emergence of hybrid forms of lifestyles and consumption dynamics that draw from multiple cultural resources.

This chapter first provides a brief economic and political background of Turkey and discusses major turning points in the history of the Republic. We then discuss the current consumption environment in relation to different socioeconomic groupings and outline variations in the income levels as well as consumption styles among different classes. Finally, drawing from data collected from different sources such as interviews, participant observations, archival data, and popular media, we discuss four different consumption practices – Islamist, spectacularist, nationalist, and historical – that have become increasingly visible. We suggest that contemporary Turkish consumptionscape is complex and multilayered where different adaptations of modern identity and modern consumption practices coexist.

BACKGROUND

The establishment of the Republic in 1923 marked a fundamental change in Turkish history. The social revolution undertaken by Mustafa Kemal Ataturk, the founder of the state, aimed at changing every aspect of the economy, culture, and society, and transforming a rural, traditional and religious empire to an industrial, modern and secular republic. In a short period of time everything from clothing style to the alphabet, from the civil code to the measurement units had changed. The new regime was paternalistic and authoritarian (Robins, 1996) and believed that only by adopting the principles of rationality, technology and science, Turkey could progress and become a prosperous, civilized and modern country. As Robins argues, for the Kemalist elite, "it seemed as if the principles of modernity could be accommodated only on the basis of a massive prohibition and interdiction of the historical and traditional culture" (1996). However, the ambitious social engineering program was far from being a smooth process. The country frequently experienced economic and political turmoil which led to the military coups of 1960, 1971 and 1980.

Until the 1980s, Turkey's economic development strategy was based on the import-substitution model. The semi-controlled mixed economy consisted of a domestically-oriented publicly and privately owned industrial sector and mostly privately owned small agricultural businesses. With many restrictions on foreign direct investment and high import tariffs, local companies were protected from global competition. During the early decades of the republic the model proved to be successful and managed to create an industrial base in consumption goods. However, by the end of the 1960s, it became clear that the economic boom experienced earlier was not sustainable and the import-substitution model was unsuccessful in developing industries that manufacture intermediate and capital goods (Tokatli and Boyaci, 1998).

Industrialization had been uneven across Turkey from the beginning, with businesses concentrating mostly in Istanbul and other big cities in the Western parts of the country. An inevitable effect of this was the influx of people from the rural Eastern parts to Istanbul and other developing cities with the hopes of finding employment and better living conditions. Those who migrated settled down on the peripheries of the cities, building shantytowns on the land belonging to the state or the municipalities. First seen during the early 1950s, shantytowns mushroomed in the coming decades as a result of increasing migration from Eastern Turkey (Keleş, 2002). The migrants did not only build illegal houses but also developed a culture of their own that combined rural traditions with the values of the city. Out of the shantytowns emerged *arabesk*, the culture of the migrant, that spoke of "a decaying city in which poverty stricken migrant workers are exploited and abused" (Stokes, 1992). As Robins observes "village people, religious people, Kurdish people have invaded the living space of the secular and westernized middle classes" (1996), bringing the geographically and socially peripheral Islamist revivalism and ethnic identification into the center, into the big cities.

Since the 1980s, Turkey's development strategy has changed drastically. Three years after the 1980 military coup elections were held and the military yielded power back to the parliament. The late Turgut Özal, whose Motherland Party gained a sweeping victory at the elections, became the prime minister. Özal was an avid believer in liberalization and globalization, and sought to develop the export potential of the country and open Turkey up to global competition (Öniş, 1991). The Özal era was characterized by a positive approach to foreign capital, expansion of the service and consumer goods industries, and restructuring of the financial and retailing sectors. During the 1981–1993 period, the economy experienced high rates of growth, averaging an annual rate of 5%. Despite the financial crises in 1994 and 2001, average income increased steadily over the years, and organized financial support in the form of credit cards, consumer credit, and installment options developed a solid consumption base among the relatively well off segments of the urban population.

In the 1990s, as a result of the liberalization policies, Turkish consumers found themselves bombarded with foreign brand name products that they had not heard of before or could only have purchased from the black market. Shopping malls, five-star hotels, office towers, gated communities, foreign cuisine, and fast food restaurants became the new landmarks of Istanbul and other big cities. With the privatization of television and radio broadcasting, several private television and radio channels emerged and dramatically transformed the nature and scope of advertising. However, the economic boom of the period was fueled by both legitimate and illegitimate means. Stories of people becoming excessively rich overnight occupied the public discourse. For the newly rich, conspicuous consumption and obsession with foreign brand names became the means of symbolic expression (Sandıkcı and Ger, 2002). However, while the recently prosperous upper-middle and upper classes enjoyed a global consumerist lifestyle, income distribution got worse over the years, especially in the two largest cities – Istanbul and Ankara – which comprise 28% of the population and 34% of total consumption expenditure (DIE 2004). The gap between the haves and the have-nots made its mark on the economic, social, and cultural environment, creating a consumptionscape which is characterized by both polarity and plurality.

SOCIAL CLASS, LIFESTYLE AND CONSUMPTION

In almost all societies power, authority, and prestige are unequally distributed, and access to resources such as education, housing, and consumer goods is largely determined by people's position in the social hierarchy. Social class consists of a complex set of variables including income, education, occupation, and family background, and describes the overall rank of people in a society. Social class, similar to other macro groupings such as ethnicity and religion, influences consumers' behaviors both directly and indirectly. On the one hand, it affects purchasing directly by determining how much money will be spent. On the other hand, it shapes one's identity, taste structure, and lifestyle, and indirectly affects how money will be spent. In this sense, "social class is as much a state of being as it is of having" (Solomon, Bamossy and Askegaard, 2002). The past decades have witnessed changes in the class structure and the relationship between class and consumption in many newly industrializing countries. As a result of the globalization of economies, development of consumer societies and relatively high levels of growth, upper income groups of the "new rich" have emerged (Arnould, Price and Zinkhan, 2004). On the other hand, due to ineffective allocation of wealth and corruption, the gap between the haves and the have-nots has also increased.

Similar to many less affluent countries, Turkey suffers from highly unequal income distribution. Despite minor improvements in recent years, income differences between social classes continue to be deep. According to the latest figures, while the richest 20% of households commands 48.3% of total disposable income, the poorest quintile's share remains at only 6% (DIE 2004). With a Gini coefficient of 42, Turkey ranks as the 40th worst income distribution economy among 113 countries (CIA World Factbook, 2005). As a result of the high urbanization rate, today 62% of the population lives in urban areas. The urban population possesses 71.5% of total disposable income and their spending constitutes 72.7% of total consumption expenditure (DIE 2004). On the other hand, 27% of the population lives below the poverty line.[45] This figure amounts to 35% in rural areas and to 22% in the cities. Around 15% of Turks experience relative poverty; i.e. they live below the society's average level of welfare (DIE 2004).[46]

According to the 2003 Household Budget Survey, on the average, housing and rent expenditure constitutes 28.3% of total consumption expenditure, followed by 27.5% spent on food and non-alcoholic beverages, 9.8% on transportation, 6.2% on clothing and footwear, and 5.7% on house furnishing and home care services (DIE 2004). Communication, restaurant and hotel services, and alcoholic beverages, cigarettes and tobacco product each constitute around 4%. Households allocate only around 2% of their total consumption expenditure to health, education, and entertainment and culture categories respectively (for the breakdown of consumption expenditure by income quintiles, see Table 10.1).

As the overall purchasing power is relatively low, per person consumption rates in many product categories are far below the European Union averages (Table 10.2). For instance, only 20% of households use toilet paper and 6% use paper towels (Capital, 2002). In addition to limited income, cultural factors play a role in low penetration rates. For example, in the dairy products category, although consumption rates are high, especially for milk and yogurt, the share of brand products remains very low. This, however, is expected to change in the long run with increasing education levels and women's employment rate. Nonetheless, with a population of 70 million and gradual improvements in disposable income, Turkey is a potentially lucrative market. The promising market attracts new global and local players; in many product categories, competition is tough with many suppliers (Table 10.3).

While average consumption rates across different product categories remain low, consumption styles and spending levels of different social classes vary significantly.

[45] Absolute poverty based on food and non-food expenditure.
[46] Relative poverty line was defined as 50% of the mean value of the consumption expenditure per equivalent individual (DIE 2004).

According to a 2002 survey conducted among the urban population, less than 600,000 people are categorized as belonging to the A socioeconomic group and they have an annual average disposable household income of USD 16,000 (Capital, 2003).

Table 10.1. Types of Consumer Products According to Income Quintiles, 2003 (Monthly Averages in %)

| | Income groups (%) | | | | |
| | Quintiles | | | | |
Types of consumer products	1	2	3	4	5
Foods and non-alcoholic beverages	13.1	16.9	19.5	22.2	28.2
Alcoholic beverages, tobacco products	11.3	15.3	18.8	23.5	31.0
Clothing and footwear	6.4	11.6	15.3	22.4	44.2
Accommodation expenses and rent	9.3	13.8	17.5	22.0	37.5
Furnishings, services for home	6.4	10.8	16.2	23.2	43.4
Health	9.1	12.4	17.3	17.8	43.5
Transport	3.8	7.3	11.0	19.6	58.2
Communications	6.2	11.0	15.4	23.0	44.5
Entertainment and culture	3.5	6.7	11.7	18.7	59.5
Education	1.2	4.5	8.3	16.9	69.1
Restaurants and hotels	6.2	9.9	15.5	23.0	45.5
Miscellaneous products and services	5.5	8.7	14.1	20.5	51.2

Source: Turkey's Statistical Yearbook, 2004.

Table 10.2. Consumption Levels According to Product Categories

Consumption level per capita		
Product categories	Turkey	Europe
Poultry (kg)	9.0	20.0
Meat (kg)	25.0	105.0
Pasta (kg)	4.5	6.4
Brand name yogurt (kg)	3.4	20.0
Ice cream (l)	1.0	8.0
Fruit juice (bottle)	13.0	114.0
Refreshing non-alcoholic beverages (bottle)	107.0	334.0
Beer (l)	1.0	114.0
Paper towels (kg)	0.1	3.3
Toilet paper (kg)	0.4	5.9
Mobile phones	33.0	70.0
Car	70.0	475.0
Products made of iron (kg)	191.0	308.3
Cement (kg)	370.0	600.0

Source: Adapted from Fırat, 2002.

Two and a half million people belong to the B socioeconomic group, with an average income of USD 12,000. Both C and D socioeconomic groups consist of approximately 15 million people and have annual average disposable household incomes of USD 6,000 and USD 3,600 respectively. Finally, there are around five million people who have an annual average disposable household income of USD 2,300 and are classified in the E socioeconomic group.

**Table 10. 3. Diversity According to Brand Name
and Models for Individual Product Categories**

Product categories	Number of brand names	Number of models
Cookies	95	1,650
Chocolate	41	446
Fruit juice	120	1,109
Cooking oil	148	1,021
Yogurt	121	881
Water	242	425
Refreshing non-alcoholic beverages	109	860
Beer	11	123
Processed meats	67	856
Pasta	60	328
Shampoo	112	1,363
Washing powder	65	724
Toilet paper	109	387
Sanitary pads	23	260
Deodorant	156	1,141
Car	56	4,200

Source: Adapted from Tekinay, 2002.

The upper socioeconomic class involves both old money holders and the newly rich, and their consumption patterns vary significantly. Among this group there are super rich industrialists and merchants, land and property owners, and CEOs of top 500 hundred companies, top level government bureaucrats, and media and sport stars. Most of these people are located in Istanbul, while others are in big cities like Ankara, Izmir, Bursa, Gaziantep and Adana. Those living in Istanbul live in million dollar villas or gated communities located along the shores of the Bosporus and in the newly developed suburbs. They socialize in elite restaurants and frequently travel and shop abroad. While those who possess greater cultural capital are more involved in high art and attend ballet and opera, those who are rich in economic capital but lack cultural capital are avid consumers of popular culture. All households in the A socioeconomic group own at least a car, and ownership rates of computers and mobile phones reach 87 and 81% respectively (Capital, 2003). This group also has the highest number of educated people in Turkey with 55% of the members holding university degrees.

The B socioeconomic group, or the upper-middle class, consists mainly of high level bureaucrats and managers, and medium-sized business owners. They possess most of the consumer durables but their car ownership rate is lower compared to the A status group.

Whereas the upper classes prefer to drive prestigious brands such as Mercedes Benz, BMW, Audi, and sport utility vehicles, the upper-middle classes typically own brands such as Opel, Volkswagen, and Peugeot (Capital, 2003). The middle class or the C socioeconomic group constitutes the majority of the non-shantytown urban population. Among the upper level Cs, the car ownership rate is around 50% whereas in the lower segment it falls to 25% (Capital, 2003). Computer ownership ranges between 18 to 24% and mobile phone ownership is between 30 to 45%.

The urban lower class, or the D socioeconomic group, is commonly located in the shantytowns or poor neighborhoods. Their income meets only the basic needs and the commonly possessed durables are a refrigerator and a television set. Around 20% of them, however, own mobile phones (Capital, 2003). Finally, the lowest social class, the E status group, consists of people living below the poverty line. They struggle to provide food for their families and almost all the family members, including children, work outside of home if they can find employment. However, the level of unemployment is the highest in this group.

Those with the highest income enjoy a lifestyle influenced by the global consumption ideology, exhibit high fashion consciousness and like to display their trendy and flamboyant consumption. The majority of population, however, struggles to maintain a decent living. Most of the urban and rural poor and the lower-middle classes consume to maintain a respectable lifestyle. "To live like a normal human being" is a commonly heard reason that motivates consumption. This is related to notions of deservingness and fairness – to have and use the things that other people have (Ger and Belk, 1999). For the poor, Coke, Fanta, and candy bars represent small luxuries purchased in an attempt to compensate for the lack of a "normal life" with abundant consumer goods and for the lack of meat at the dinner table, as well as to please the children who see desirable consumer objects on television and in the stores. The urban poor who cannot afford many things in the stores, or even in the supermarkets, engage in window shopping. This is usually done on weekends as a family outing and is their way of participating in the consumer society from which they are excluded. Especially after the 2001 economic crisis, many Turkish consumers have faced difficulties in providing the basic necessities and have become more price sensitive. During the economic crisis of 2001 some even took a large shopping cart, chose items with a lot of deliberation, filled their carts, only to leave the cart at a corner of the store after an hour or two of shopping, and left empty handed (Ger, 2003).

The situation was relatively better in 2005 and postponed demand in various product categories began to be transformed into purchasing behavior. However, the increasing unemployment rates and the amount of per capita unpaid credit card debt, which has now reached to USD 5,527, are worrying indicators (Milliyet, 2003). As Cizre-Sakallioglu and Yeldan (2000) note, "while most people, given the chance, would opt for Western standards of living, globalization has weakened the equitable delivery by the state of the requirements behind those standards."

Given the polarity in socioeconomic status, class differences and status- and respectability-seeking shape consumer behavior. Furthermore, polarity makes relative deprivation a significant aspect of the Turkish consumptionscape: relying on both temporal and current comparisons, the poorer consumers desire more goods than they can afford.

FACTORS THAT SHAPE CONSUMER BEHAVIOR AND "NORMAL" CONSUMPTION

As people in other marketizing societies, Turks have been learning to have consumer desires. The factors that fuel this process are numerous. One is the globalized consumer holidays such as Christmas, Mother's Day, Father's Day, and Valentine's Day. The second is the development of the market with prominent shopping malls, a great variety and proliferation of "new and improved" goods, hi-tech goods, and the increased advertising and merchandising. The third is the encounter with the Western styles of consumption on television, in the movies or in person: tourists, cosmopolitans, expatriates, Turkish migrants returning home for holidays. The fourth is the display by the *nouveau riches* and the conspicuousness of their flashy consumption styles in the media. The fifth involves the ideology and ideals such as the global ethos of consumerism, the notion of the "good life," and modernity and progress tied to consumption. These ideals are linked to the desire to move ahead, to be modernized, to leave the failed past behind, and to catch up with the Western world. Combined with an (over)confidence in the new/global/West versus a lack of confidence locally, these ideals and ideologies impel people towards an imagined "normal" modern consumption.

This last point implies that being or becoming a modern person/family is of utmost concern. A modern identity and a sense of joining the rest of the world (being like Westerners) are sought in the consumption of material things. Most people, especially the lower and middle classes, consume to communicate to themselves and to others their modern identity. To consume like Westerners or like other modern Turks and to be accepted by one's social circle are important motivations for consumption. While being modern is aspirational, it is also regarded as being "normal." Normal consumption is seen to entail using the standard mass produced goods of the world and buying for comfort, pleasure, fun, practicality, and convenience. Ideally, it is having products of good quality in abundance and to get the novel goods, the "new and improved" things that appear on the market, ceaselessly. Owning electronics, kitchen appliances, cell phones and detergents, eating McDonald's hamburgers and other fast food, drinking Coke and shopping in malls are regarded as constituting a normal modern life. Hi-tech goods and electronics are typically among the favorite objects. The yearning for a normal modern (which is at the same time respectable) life is so great that in poor villages where parents cannot afford to buy milk, they will buy candy bars for their children. Again, for the sake of modernity, people switched from producing and consuming olive oil, which had been used in the traditional Turkish cuisine for centuries, to Western sunflower oil in the 1970s. Only in late 1990s, after it became fashionable in the West, olive oil made a comeback, but now as healthy Mediterranean oil. Women who have grown up seeing their mothers make jam, tomato paste, and pickles, brew tea leaves, and make Turkish coffee now buy industrial and branded canned foods, jams, pickles, tomato pastes, ketchup, and teabags and instant coffee for the sake of modern convenience. Young girls, who like their international counterparts, are fond of chips and fast food develop cellulite problems before they reach their 20s and then frequent health clubs and resort to dieting to have a modern, slim shape. Such is the broad scene of modern consumption in Turkey.

The findings of a multi-site study on consumer desires support our argument that seeking a modern identity is a prevalent force in consumption in Turkey. Belk, Ger and Askegaard (2003) found that while Americans, Danes, and Turks all desire otherness, an altered state, an escape or a transformation to another time or a place, Turks also desire a total transformation, a permanent escape, and removal of constraints. Furthermore, while Americans and Danes desire to escape to nature, Turks wish to experience exciting night life in world cities and the "glittery life of Barbie."

The consumptionscape in Turkey is driven by these global and local market factors and ideals as well as by the identity-expressing strategies of various groups. In addition to the ideal of normal modernity, other cultural and political factors make for further plurality.

WAYS OF CONSUMING:
DIFFERENT CONSUMPTION PRACTICES

Since the mid-1990s, there has been an increasingly fragmented and vocal public sphere with different identity claims. The struggle to differentiate and legitimize identity of each of the different groups finds its symbolic expression in the domain of consumption. Next we discuss four consumption styles that to some extent cut across socioeconomic classes and are most visible and distinct from the conventional consumption manners of the middle and lower middle classes explained above.

Spectacularist Consumption

Some upscale urban consumers who have little cultural capital exhibit a highly fashion-conscious and display-oriented consumption. Immersed in popular culture, they are after trendy designer clothes, the latest models of cell phones and plasma televisions, and only the "in" restaurants, bars, and clubs. They frequent the increasingly prevalent beauty salons and fitness clubs to obtain trendy eyebrows, haircuts, manicures, make up, and slim bodies. Plastic surgery and liposuction produce fashionable lips, noses, faces, breasts, thighs, and hips. To outsiders, these young upscale urbanites all look alike, with their exact same eyebrows, make up, hair styles, nail colors, and clothes. "Fifteen-year-olds believe that they have to have that one brand of jeans in a particular bell bottom style; another bell bottom cut or brand simply does not work and becomes a source of shame" (Sandıkcı and Ger, 2002).

Termed "magazine" media, television shows, colorful weekly magazines and daily newspapers with large pictures exhibit the lifestyles of the celebrities such as singers, fashion models, VJs, DJs, soccer players, and television and movie stars. Many one to two hour "magazine" and "paparazzi" programs in which celebrities are interviewed on the streets, restaurants, bars, clubs, resorts, or luxury yachts occupy airwaves during prime time. In these programs, cameras zoom to the tattoos, bare bellies, low décolletage or exposed thighs and bottoms, the skimpy and fashionable clothes and accessories; and the outfits and the appearance of the celebrities are rated on a scale of ten. For example, the interviewer gives a rating of one to a fashion model that he encounters on a beach, calling her outfit hideous because her bikini is outdated. She angrily reacts to the commentator's decision: "But this bikini is Versace!"

While the rich and the famous engage in public display of their flamboyant consumption with pride, the mass media disseminate and spectacularize that type of life and consumption by making it visible in every home, poor or rich. The audiences consume the images of such consumption as they watch these programs with admiration, fascination, envy, but also criticism of the artificiality, meaninglessness, indecency, and wastefulness of it all. Such publicly displayed consumption parades as a spectacular model or antimodel, depending on the audience.

Nationalistic Consumption

A more modest and less advertised type of consumption pertains to objects that symbolize a nationalistic ethos. The most widespread version of nationalistic consumption, shared by the extreme and moderate nationalists and secularists pertains to objects, films, photos, and books about or associated with Atatürk (the founder of the republic), such as the popular Atatürk-embossed silver and gold brooches and lapel pins. Another form of nationalistic consumption, especially for those who cannot afford foreign goods, is the preference for domestic brands, justified with statements such as "*we* can produce electronics just as well as foreigners."

A more extreme form of nationalistic consumption, aligned politically with the Nationalistic Movement Party, involves baseball caps, t-shirts, flags, stickers, posters, calendars, pins, key chains, car decorations, bumper stickers, cell phone accessories, and other decorative items adorned with pictures and slogans associated with nationalism. One prominent symbol is the three crescents with the legendary wolf, which, according to the myth, saved the Central Asian Turkish tribes and led them to fertile lands. Youngsters sporting (American) baseball caps, t-shirts, and flags with the wolf and the crescent figures roam the streets during political events or when Turkish soccer teams win in international games. Books on Turkic Central Asian legends, CDs of nationalistic pop and rap music are among other items that appeal to consumers seeking national pride or who are politically nationalistic.

The most interesting version of nationalistic consumption is that of *Mehmetçik* objects, such as music CDs with songs about soldiers, greeting cards to be given to soldiers being drafted for compulsory military duty, and posters with pictures of an imagined *Mehmetçik*. All the soldiers in the army are called *Mehmetçik*, referring euphemistically to a soldier bravely and selflessly serving his country. There are television programs about the acts of bravery of various soldiers. Here it must be noted that opinion polls consistently indicate that the public has far more confidence in the military than in any other institution. In addition to the enormous confidence in the military, the importance of the image of *Mehmetçik* is probably also related to the prominent role of heroes who come along and save the people in many Turkic myths and legends. *Mehmetçik* has become a legendary hero among the folk in the rural areas (Mardin, 1993) and the objects symbolizing and glorifying *Mehmetçik* find eager consumers.

These forms of consumption express a longing for a sense of worth, for pride in national identity. Nationalism and nationalistic consumption emerge in response to a prevailing feeling of inferiority in relation to the hailed "West," a general devaluation of a past that failed to create a Westernized, modern country. Whether in the form of Atatürk pins, Mehmetçik posters and cards, or baseball caps with politically nationalistic symbols, such objects and experiences fashion novel local identities, drawing from secular republican, Anatolian, military, or ancient Central Asian symbols.

Islamist Consumption

While an almost mythical "Turkishness" is one source on which to build identity, Islam is another. Despite the secular legal system, Islam has played a prominent role in the political, sociocultural and economic domains since the 1980s. Liberalization and privatization of the economy during the 1980s changed not only the lifestyle of urban secularists but also created Islamic businesses and an Islamic bourgeoisie. This Islamic bourgeoisie is conservative in values but avant-garde in consumption practices. Accordingly, similar to secular media's dissemination of spectacularist consumption values, television and radio channels backed by Islamic capital play an important role in communicating religious lifestyles. A rich and prolific Islamic media ranging from Islamic pop music to romance novels, women's magazines, best sellers and movies, transmits popular Islamic culture.

Since the 1980s, a new style of "Islamist" consumption emerged in many domains such as decoration, leisure, and fashion. Families shop in malls as well as in department stores built inside mosques and in flourishing marketplaces set up on mosque grounds. Such marketplaces sell Korans, prayer beads and religious books as well as Islamic pop music tapes, CDs and romance novels, bright colored clocks with lights and a picture of Kaba in Mecca, landscape paintings or impressionistic reproductions framed with Koranic calligraphy, and many other items including stickers, posters, key chains, coloring books, calendars, greeting cards and decorative items decorated with Islamic symbols, pictures, or calligraphy. Several summer resorts, run by Islamic companies, cater to the religiously sensitive people with their separate swimming pools and beaches, separate entertainment and recreation activities for men and women.

The domain of fashion is the most visible indicator of Islamist consumption patterns (Sandıkcı and Ger, 2001). The rise of political Islam fostered a demand for religiously appropriate clothing items. The 1980s uniform large scarf with a loose fitting long overcoat transformed in the 1990s into heterogeneous dressing styles, signaling the rising fashion consciousness especially among the upper, upper-middle class, urban, well-educated, young religious women. Today, more casual, modern, distinctive, and youthful designs and fashionable colors are being sought. Pants and long jackets, skirts and shorter blazers, above-the-knee coats, or jeans and shirts, with smaller and more tightly tied scarves placed inside the shirt are commonly preferred. However, in public spaces one can easily come across covered women wearing tight long skirts with slits up to the thighs, very tight tops under transparent shirts or jackets, or sexy sparkly high-heeled sandals accompanied by fashionable handbags. Scarves by Hermes, Dior, Gucci, or prestigious Turkish brands such as Vakko or Aker are worn by the upper and less known brands by the middle and lower classes. Fashion shows and catalogues model religiously acceptable and modest yet tasteful, stylish and modern clothes. Depending on personal factors, such as age, work status, religious order and political alliances, some believe that loose fitting, long garments that do not reveal body contours are the proper style, others opt for pants and tighter and shorter jackets or shirts, which are deemed more suitable for the lifestyle of workingwomen.

The covering and dressing style operates not only as a signifier of whether one is religious but as an indicator of the sociocultural position of the wearer. The newly emerging urban, middle-class covered women do not simply differentiate themselves from the Westernized, secular Turkish women; they equally distance themselves from the traditional Islamic women who wear a headscarf out of a habit and from the "gaudy and pretentious" styles of the Islamist newly rich. Drawing both from Islam and local and global cultural resources, this elite crafts new consumption practices – modern, casual and trendy clothes, natural foods, traditional cuisine, Ottoman culture and artifacts, alternative vacation and traveling, books, intellectual debates, educational programs and documentaries on Islamic television channels – all in an attempt to differentiate itself from the secularist moderns and other groups of Islamists.

Historical Consumption

The last decade also witnessed a revival of interest in objects and customs constructed to represent "our own traditions" that belong to several collectively imagined pasts – Anatolian, Turkish, and Ottoman. One example is the phenomenally successful show titled "Sultans of the Dance" (the title is indeed in English) which is a Turkish version of the Irish River Dance and consists of stylized folk dances and music from various regions of Turkey with allusions to ancient Anatolian myths. Many proud spectators commented that "it is great to see that we can accomplish such a professional, world class show." Another example is a "return" to traditional wedding ceremonies, complete with a "henna night" party preceding the wedding night, in line with "our customs" (Üstuner, Ger and Holt, 2000). Since the late 1990s young people want full-fledged, large conventional wedding ceremonies, unlike the simpler, less ceremonial weddings preferred by the youth in the 1970s. These ceremonies, which are perceived to be "traditional," are in fact highly urbanized and Westernized and anything but "traditional" in a historic sense. Furthermore, new "traditional" restaurants are popping up in major cities, cookbooks of traditional cuisine are hitting the bookstores, and Turkish coffee, after its decline in the 1980s, when it yielded its traditional throne to first Nescafe and then cappuccino, espresso, and filter coffee is making a comeback. Along with the increasing popularity of Turkish coffee, the long gone hookah smoking in cafes is now a trendy pastime activity among young urban professionals.

In home and personal decoration, evil eye beads inserted in silver or porcelain decorative objects or stringed together with fashionable colorful beads have recently become prominent. Traditionally, evil eye beads were used in Turkey by pinning a small bead on clothing or hanging a larger one in the entrance hall of a home. Now, variously sized and shaped beads appear in necklaces, bracelets, vases, pots, plates, and even in heart-shaped Valentine's Day gifts. Although the pagan evil eye, like the henna night ritual, is not particularly Turkish, but rather has its origins in the Middle East, North Africa, and Asia, it is imagined to be so. Thus, figures, experiences, and objects construed to be traditional or historical are incorporated in consumption in new and recontextualized forms and ways.

A prominent form of historical consumption expresses itself in the nostalgic interest in the Ottoman culture, traditions, and lifestyle. Ottoman-inspired consumption clusters around leisure activities, cuisine, home decoration, art, and fashion. Several luxury hotels and resorts that opened up in the last decade make a direct reference to the Ottoman past. "For example, Çıragan Kempinski Hotel in Istanbul, which is located in the late Ottoman palace named Çıragan, offers five-star accommodation to its guests who are treated as Ottoman sultans. The guests can dine in one of the hotel's restaurants named "Tuğra" (imperial signature) that serves old Ottoman cuisine and then go its night club to enjoy a performance named "Sultan's Night" featuring classical Ottoman music and belly dancing. The hotel publishes a monthly newsletter titled "Ferman" (imperial edict) that includes stories about Ottoman palace weddings, Ottoman palaces, Turkish coffee, etc." (Sandıkcı and Ger, 2002). Similar developments are abundant in the culinary culture. Some restaurants offer traditional Ottoman meals to their patrons, with classical Ottoman music playing at the background.

Many are also interested in decorating their homes in line with Ottoman design principles and artifacts. Those who can afford them can acquire expensive Ottoman antiques. Objects ranging from paintings to miniatures, vases, various kitchen equipment and furniture are sold to an eager audience at periodic auctions and in antique stores. Alternatively, one can resort to upscale department stores or designers to help them furnish their homes with fabrics and furniture inspired by the textiles, velvets, caftans, robes, cushions, and sashes of the Sultans.

The cultural identity and the history of the Ottomans provide a new source to draw from in nostalgic consumption. Returning back to a past that is largely unknown in the contemporary republic and trying to rebuild it through a contemporary reading indicates the search for constructing an identity that is simultaneously traditional and modern.

Spectacularists, nationalists, Islamists, and historicists differentiate their identities from each other and from the mainstream middle classes by creating particular "modern" consumption styles. However, these different categories of consumption styles are not mutually exclusive: there are nationalist spectacularists, Islamic nationalists, and historical nationalists. On the one hand, while spectacularist consumption appears to have a modern/global style, it also has very local aspects. On the other hand, while the other three consumptionscapes appear to be "traditional," they also possess modern and global aspects. The emergence of the nationalistic, historical, and Islamic consumptionscapes is not simply a resistance, an assertion of local distinctiveness against the West/global, perhaps epitomized and exaggerated by the spectacularist consumption. That is because the nationalists, Islamists, and historicists do not abandon buying foreign goods, eating fast food, or engaging in otherwise Westernized or modern consumption and ways of life (Sandıkcı and Ger, 2001). Furthermore, this emergence is not a return to traditions either; the apparently "traditional" practices entail new and recreated forms. What we see are multiple new articulations of "modern" identities, class distinctions, and subcultures in Turkey.

CONCLUDING THOUGHTS AND IMPLICATIONS

Yearning for modernity and respectability, nostalgia, and a search for authenticity operate jointly in shaping consumer behavior in Turkey. The immense polarity in income levels and lifestyles, increased aspirations for a high level of consumption constructed and legitimized to be "normal" and modern across all social classes, and the profound relative deprivation experienced by the poor set the stage for the contemporary consumptionscape. This consumptionscape involves great plurality not only due to income and social class differences but also due to the diverse strategies of seeking and expressing modern, fashion-conscious spectacularist, nationalist, historic, and Islamist identities and ideals. In each case, the identity and the consumption that expresses it are simultaneously traditional and modern, as well as local and global. Modernity, fashion, nostalgia, traditional/historical/religious/national authenticity merge in hybrid forms of consumption such as Monet reproductions framed by Koranic verses, sexy sandals and headscarves, gameboys in remote rural homes, and Coke with traditional Turkish foods (e.g. "döner kebap"). Hybridization and recontextualization of various objects, forms, and uses culminate in multiple novel consumption styles.

REFERENCES

Arnould, E., Price, L., and Zinkhan, G. 2004. "*Consumers.*" New York: McGraw-Hill.

Belk, R., Ger, G. and Askegaard, S. 2003. "The Fire of Desire: A Multi-Sited Inquiry into Consumer Passion." *Journal of Consumer Research* 30: 326–351.

Büyük, S. S. 2003. "6 Grubun Yeni Kimliği." [The New Identity of 6 Groups] *Capital* 1: 70–73.

CIA. 2005. "The World Factbook."

Cizre-Sakallioglu, U., and Yeldan, E. 2000. "Politics, Society and Financial Liberalization: Turkey in the 1990s." *Development and Change* 31: 481–508.

Ger, G. 2003. "Delights and Discontents of Shopping." In Garrett, R., Root, D. and Tuer, D. (eds): "Public 27: Shop." Toronto, Public Access: 14–27.

Ger, G., and Belk, R. 1999. "Accounting for Materialism in Four Cultures." *Journal of Material Culture* 4 (2): 183–204.

Ger, G., and Belk, R. 1996. "I'd Like to Buy the World a Coke: Consumptionscapes in the Less Affluent World." *Journal of Consumer Policy* 19: 271–304.

Fırat, E. 2002. "Kişi Başına Hesabının Gücü." [The Power of Per Capita Calculation] *Capital* 8: 64–68.

Keleş, R. 2000. "Kentleşme Politikası." [Politics of Urbanization] Ankara: Imge.

Mardin, Ş. 1993. "Din ve İdeoloji." [Religion and Ideology] Sixth edition. Istanbul: İletişim.

Miller, D. 1995. "Consumption as Vanguard of History." In Miller, D. (ed): "Acknowledging Consumption." London: Routledge: 1–57.

Milliyet. 2003. "Kredi Kartı Alacaklarının Yüzde 7si Batık." [7% of Credit Card Debt is Defaulted]. August 5, 2003.

Önis, Z. 1991. "Political Economy of Turkey in the 1980s: Anatomy of Unorthodox Liberalism." In Heper, M. (ed): "Strong State and Economic Interest Groups: The Post-1980 Turkish Experience." Berlin: de Gruyter: 27–39.

Robins, K. 1996. "Interrupting Identities: Turkey/Europe." In Hall, S. and du Gay, P. (eds): "Questions of Cultural Identity." London: Sage: 61–86.

Sandikci, O., and Ger, G. 2005. "Aesthetics, Ethics and Politics of the Turkish Headscarf." In Kuechler, S. and Miller, D. (eds): "Clothing As Material Culture." London: Berg: 61–82.

Sandikci, O., and Ger, G. 2002. "In-Between Modernities and Postmodernities: Investigating Turkish Consumptionscape." *Advances in Consumer Research* 29: 465–470.

Sandikci, O., and Ger, G. 2001. "Fundamental Fashions: The Cultural Politics of the Turban and the Levi's." *Advances in Consumer Research* 28: 146–150.

Solomon, M., Bamossy, G., and Askegaard, S. 2002. "Consumer Behavior: A European Perspective." Essex, UK: Pearson Education Limited.

Stokes, M. 1992. "The Arabesk Debate: Music and Musicians in Modern Turkey." Oxford: The Clarendon Press.

Tekinay, A. 2002. "Demokrasi Sendromu." [The Syndrome of Democracy] *Capital* 8: 5660.

Tokatli, N., and Boyaci, Y. 1998. "The Changing Retail Industry and Retail Landscapes." *Cities* 15 (5): 345–359.

State Institute of Statistics. 2004. "Turkey's Statistical Yearbook." Republic of Turkey: Prime Ministry.

Üstüner, T., Ger, G., and Holt, D. 2000. "Consuming Ritual: Reframing the Turkish Henna-Night Ceremony." *Advances in Consumer Research* 27: 209–214.

In: New Emerging Economies and Their Culture
Editors: J. Prašnikar, A. Cirman, pp. 155-176

ISBN: 978-1-60021-754-8
© 2007 Nova Science Publishers, Inc.

Chapter 11

STRATEGIC AND CULTURAL FIT ASSESSMENT IN A DIVERSIFIED COMPANY: DROGA KOLINSKA CASE– POSSIBLE ENTRY INTO TURKISH MARKET

Ljubica Knežević Cvelbar and Monika Lisjak

INTRODUCTION

The two biggest Slovenian food processing companies, Droga and Kolinska, merged in May 2005 with the aim of improving competitiveness in international markets by exploiting synergy effects resulting from joined purchasing, logistics, and marketing functions. The merged company, Droga Kolinska, employs 1,640 employees and is a regional player in the food and beverage industry since most of its operations are focused in South-Eastern Europe. The vision of the newly created company is to become one of the leading food producers in South-Eastern Europe (qualitative interviews, 2005). The company intends to pursue a strategy of product and market diversification through organic growth and acquisitions of local food companies. In fact, Droga Kolinska is building a production plant for Argeta pâté in Bosnia and Herzegovina, which can be a starting point for entering the Turkish and Middle Eastern markets. Furthermore, the company acquired Grand and Soko Stark in Serbia and Montenegro, a strategic move that improved its position in the existing South-Eastern European markets.

Strategic fit assessment consists of the evaluation of resource complementarities and it is crucial in decisions regarding mergers and acquisitions (M&A), particularly among firms operating in the same or related industries (Pennings and Lee, 1996). Besanko et al. (2004) point out that through strategic fit, a merged firm's resources exceeds the sum of its organizational processes. In other words, activities or processes of different firms complement each other so that the combined effect is greater than the sum of its parts. Thompson and Strickland (1999) propose to measure strategic fit by performing a portfolio analysis. The GE matrix offers a framework for evaluating each strategic business unit's (SBU) competitive strength and long-term industry attractiveness. In this way, a firm can identify SBUs that have a great investment potential and match up well with the corporate portfolio. However, the GE matrix does not evaluate synergies between SBUs. Thus, it is necessary to upgrade the analysis in order to determine the strategic fit among business units along the value chain and define the potential synergies.

Cultural fit evaluates culture compatibility, complementarity, and harmony among merging organizations. It does not imply cultural identity but rather a set of common, similar, and completely different cultural elements that are needed to empower merged culture (Ulijn et al., 2003). Pennings and Lee (1996) advanced the hypothesis that firms operating within the same industry with similar size, history, and strategic orientation (so called structural determinants) should experience higher cultural compatibility, thus improving chances for a merger success. Despite these general guidelines, each case should be analyzed separately.

This chapter addresses the issue of strategic and cultural fit in merging organizations from an academic and managerial perspective. Its objective is therefore twofold. The first objective is to present an operational framework for assessing strategic and cultural fit in M&A deals, while the second objective is to assess the fit in the case of Droga Kolinska. This assessment will in turn provide the basis for developing the company's future strategy.

The chapter is divided into three main sections. A description of methodology used is provided in the first section. Analysis of strategic and cultural fit on the case of Droga Kolinska is presented in the second section. Managerial recommendations are given in the last part of the article. A possible entry of Droga Kolinska on the Turkish market is evaluated in the Appendix.

METHODOLOGY

Strategic fit was assessed according to a two step analysis. In the first step we used a business portfolio framework to examine and compare the different SBUs that make up Droga Kolinska, and to evaluate their current effectiveness and vulnerabilities. A nine-cell matrix, which was developed by McKinsey and Co. for General Electric Company, was utilized to identify high and low potential business units. SBUs were first rated according to their business strength and industry attractiveness (Thompson and Strickland, 1998; Zagoršek and Štembergar, 2006), and then plotted on the resulting GE grid. Graphically, SBUs were depicted by bubbles, the size indicating the share of revenues produced by an individual SBU within the portfolio, and the center of the scale representing the average of all scores from the SBUs (Thompson and Strickland, 1998).

The research encompassed an evaluation of market attractiveness within six industries (nonalcoholic carbonated beverages, mineral water, baby food, condiments and spices, tea and coffee, cereals, rice, canned food). Each industry was ranked according to thirteen relevant factors[47] on a ten point scale. Relevant factors were later weighted according to two criterias: their importance for achieving Droga Kolinska's strategic objective, and their fit with the company's needs and capabilities. The assessment is based on the industry's

---

[47] The relevant factors for evaluating industry attractiveness are: projected growth; market size; intensity of competition; threat of potential entry; competition from substitutes; power of suppliers; power of customers B2C; power of customers B2B; emerging industry opportunities; resource requirements; social, political, regulatory and environmental factors; industry profitability; and the degree of uncertainty and business risk.

secondary data. The sum of the weighted ratings for all the factors provides a quantitative measure of the industry's long-term attractiveness.

The competitive strength evaluation of Droga Kolinska's SBUs is based on ten factors.[48] A ten point scale was adopted. Factors and weights were partly defined from the qualitative interviews with five Droga Kolinska managers and expanded using secondary data. Business units' strength in Eastern and Western markets was analyzed separately due to a difference in industry life cycles and market infrastructure.[49] When estimating the competitive advantage of business units in Eastern Europe, only those markets in which Droga Kolinska is already present (markets of the former Yugoslavia, Russia, Slovenia) were taken into account. However, a different approach was adopted for Western markets. Since the company has limited presence in Western Europe, potential markets were also considered.

As portfolio analysis does not consider interactions between SBUs, value chain analysis was performed in the second phase of strategic fit assessment. Synergy analysis for each SBU was carried out according to the adapted Porter value chain model (Porter, 1998 in Thomson and Strickland, 1998).

The cultural fit in Droga Kolinska was assessed according to a two-step analysis as well. In the first step, a structural determinants analysis was performed based on secondary data obtained from the companies' annual reports, their web sites, and newspaper articles. Determinants under investigation were the size of the companies, their markets, history, vision, mission, and values.

In the second step the dimensions of organizational culture were analyzed based on the quantitative research conducted among 1,000 production and administrative employees of Droga Kolinska between July 15 and June 6, 2005. The response rate was 29% and the sample included 290 employees. What is unique about our analysis is that it focuses on analyzing organizational culture fit between two merging organizations. In fact, the survey was performed at the very beginning of the merger. Only production and administrative workers were targeted, due to the fact that the management structure was changing during the merger process and the rest of management was under pressure or unwilling to participate in the research. The questionnaire was divided in two parts. In the first part we assessed the company's culture according to the cultural dimensions proposed by Hofstede and Verbeke's (a description of the six cultural dimensions is presented in Table 11.1). In the second part we measured some demographic and psychographic characteristics of respondents.

The analysis was further broadened with five semi-structured in-depth interviews with middle management representatives in order to gain an in-depth perspective of cultural similarities and differences between the organizational cultures of merged companies.

---

[48] The relevant factors for evaluating competitive strength are: relative market share; profitability relative to competitors; competitive advantage – ability to match or beat rivals on key products attributes; ability to compete on cost; how well resources are matched to the industry key success factors; brand name reputation/image; power of suppliers; power of customers B2C; power of customers B2B; and management know-how.

[49] Euromonitor classification was used when defining markets as Eastern and Western Europe.

Table 11.1. Hofstede and Verbeke's Cultural Dimensions

Cultural dimension:	The concept of dimension:
Process vs. result orientation	It reflects the degree to which organization encourages and expects that employees will be oriented toward the achievement of results in contrast to tight task and process performance.
Employee vs. job orientation	It reflects the way the organization supports the employees in terms of education, attention to personal events in contrast to task performance.
Open vs. closed	It reflects the way the employees and management deal with criticism when they make mistakes and how they publicly cope with it.
Loose vs. tight control	It reflects the way management actually controls the members of the organization, dealing with their daily work regulations such as arriving on time or taking breaks and dealing with expenses.
Social responsibility vs. self interest	Socially responsible organizations act in order to bear in mind the interests of all stakeholders involved and ethics, honesty and responsibility to all interest groups are core values in business process in contrast to more profit orientation.
Market vs. internal orientation	It shows how organization as a whole interacts with customers and competition.

Source: Verbeke, 2000.

In every research and analysis there are also some limitations and disadvantages that have to be taken into consideration. First, the strategic fit analysis that builds on the GE portfolio matrix has important limitations. In fact, the evaluations of industry attractiveness and business strength ratings and weights depend on the quality of information and personal managerial judgment. Second, the cultural fit analysis is based on a sample frame that includes only production and administrative employees. This limitation was alleviated by conducting in-depth interviews with middle management. Finally, the analysis is based on the assumption of probability sampling, although a convenience sample was used for the analysis (all employees that were present at work on the day the survey took place and were willing to participate in the survey).

DROGA KOLINSKA STRATEGIC FIT

Portfolio Analysis – The GE Matrix for Eastern European Markets

According to the portfolio analysis (Picture 11.1), the most promising industries for Droga Kolinska in the long-term in Eastern Europe are mineral waters, canned meat, and baby food. The brands with highest competitive strengths and business position in the former Yugoslav (including Slovenian) and Russian markets are Grand, Barcaffe, Donat Mg, Argeta, and Cockta. When considering both industry attractiveness and strength of individual businesses, it is apparent that Donat Mg (mineral water), Argeta (pâté), Grand, and Barcaffe (coffee) have top investment priority in these markets. The recommendation for those brands is to grow and build selectively.

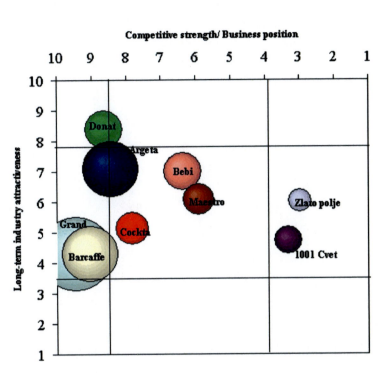

Source: Own analysis.

Picture 11.1. The GE Industry Attractiveness – Competitive Strength Matrix for Eastern Europe.

Based on the GE Matrix for *Eastern Europe* (Picture 11.1), the strategic implications for Droga Kolinska brands are the following:

DONAT Mg: Donat Mg operates in a highly attractive industry fueled by emerging trends toward healthy lifestyles and healthier beverages. Its competitive strengths and business position are also high due to its uniqueness and a high market share in Slovenia and Croatia (Kolinska Annual Report, 2004). In 2004, it produced revenues in the amount of USD 15.7 million, which represents 7.8% of total revenues from all nine Droga Kolinska brand categories (Kolinska Annual Report, 2004). The proposed strategy for Donat Mg is to heavily invest in growth, especially in foreign markets. Although Eastern European markets represent a potential for Donat Mg, its entrance in Western European markets is a priority. Huge investments in advertising and promotion due to the special use of Donat Mg are needed.

ARGETA: Argeta is a brand of pâté that enjoys high competitive strengths in Eastern Europe as it is a market leader in Slovenia (20% market share), Kosovo (75% market share), Macedonia (38% market share), and Bosnia and Herzegovina (20% market share), while it is a niche player in Croatia (9%), Serbia and Montenegro (no data available), and Austria (13%

market share) (internal company data, 2004). Argeta's revenues in 2004 were USD 34.8 million, accounting for 17.4% of total revenues from all nine Droga Kolinska brands (Droga Annual Report, 2004). The pâté industry in Eastern Europe is also promising due to the adoption of western consumer lifestyles that drive the demand for prepared food. Argeta is therefore a star in the Droga Kolinska portfolio. The proposed strategy for Argeta in Eastern Europe is to invest heavily in the most attractive foreign markets and secure its position in the existing markets. Due to expansion of production capacities in Bosnia and Herzegovina, also Turkey has become a potential market for Argeta internationalization.

BARCAFFE: Strong competition from local as well as multinational companies makes the coffee industry in the Eastern markets less attractive (local companies account for 40% and multinational companies for 60% of market share). Barcaffe is the most known coffee brand in Slovenia but the brand recognition in other markets is minimal. Its revenues in 2004 were USD 37.8 million, which represents 17.7% of total revenues within the analyzed Droga Kolinska portfolio (Droga Annual Report, 2004). According to the position in the GE matrix, the recommended strategy is to build selectively. However, consumer preferences for coffee are very local and influenced by tradition, thus the Barcaffe strategy should be less focused on geographical expansion and more on protecting its strong position in the domestic market.

GRAND: This brand operates in the coffee industry. Thus the industry attractiveness situation of Barcaffe and Grand is the same. However, the two brands differ on the business strength dimension. In fact, Grand has a higer business strength due to its strong position in the former Yugoslav markets. Grand is the only regional brand that has achieved brand recognition at a multinational level. Grand's revenues in 2004 were USD 60 million, which accounts for 30% of total revenues from all nine Droga Kolinska brands (Grand Prom Annual Report, 2004). According to the GE matrix, the recommended strategy for Grand is similar to Barcaffe's: securing a position in the markets where it enjoys a leading position (Serbia and Montenegro, Bosnia and Herzegovina, Macedonia).

COCKTA: Cockta is in an industry of average attractiveness, which is growing slowly. Emerging regions, such as Eastern Europe, have for the most part seen strong growth of consumption of carbonated beverages over the past five years, whereas the less mature countries, such as Romania and Ukraine, have held sway. Volume growth of total carbonated beverages (on-trade plus off-trade) in Eastern Europe was 18% for the 1998–2003 period (Milenkovic, 2004). Cockta has a reasonably good business strength since it is made of natural ingredients, is free of any orthophosphoric acid and caffeine and therefore differs from its main rivals (Coca-Cola, Pepsi etc.). The business strength of Cockta is also expected to improve due to Cockta's great potential in the former Yugoslav markets, where awareness, recognition, and preference for Cockta is high. Cockta's revenues in 2004 were USD 11.9 million, which is 6% of Droga Kolinska's examined portfolio (Kolinska Annual Report, 2004). Protecting the existing businesses and investing in attractive segments (children and teenagers) appear to be logical strategic directions according to the GE matrix. This could be achieved by adopting an integrated marketing communication approach and by increasing the intensity of the distribution.

BEBI: Bebi operates in an attractive industry in Eastern Europe, mainly due to high opportunities in the Russian market. Bebi has an average business strength in current markets and the brand is not well known in the area of the former Yugoslavia. But on the other hand, Bebi has established a solid position in Russia with a 30% market share (Kolinska Annual Report, 2004). Bebi's revenues in 2004 were USD 15.7 million, which represents 7.8% of the analyzed portfolio revenues (Kolinska Annual Report, 2004). The recommended strategy is to concentrate investments in high profit, low risk segments, and defend the position in the current markets. Therefore, it is reasonable to position Bebi as a premium product in the Russian market.

MAESTRO: Industry attractiveness of condiments and spices is with an 8% growth rate above average in Eastern Europe (Mudgil, 2005; Euromonitor August 2000; July 2001). Concerning business strength, Maestro is in a similar position as Bebi due to its significant market share in the Slovenian and former Yugoslav markets. Maestro's revenues in 2004 were USD 11.3 million, which represents 5.7% of total revenues from all nine Droga Kolinska brand categories (Droga Annual Report, 2004). According to the GE matrix, the recommended strategy is to protect its position on current markets, especially among the premium product line.

1001 CVET: The brand operates in the tea industry that is mature and stagnating (0.2% growth rate in 2003); it is expected to grow by 2.7% by 2008 (Euromonitor, 2004). In addition, sales profitability is deteriorating due to price wars (Coffee Executive Brief, 2005). However, the situation in Eastern Europe is different as markets are developing due to increasing purchasing power and emerging business opportunities. Besides low industry attractiveness, 1001 Cvet has a low level of business strength as it does not substantially differ from the competition. Its revenues in 2004 were USD 9.3 million, which amounts to 4.6% of revenues of the Droga Kolinska investigated portfolio (Droga Annual Report, 2004). According to the GE matrix, the recommended strategy is selective expansion, meaning that management should only pursue expansion opportunities that carry minimal risk. In case there are no such opportunities, management should aim at minimizing investment and rationalizing operations.

ZLATO POLJE: Zlato polje as a healthy food product is positioned in an attractive industry, but the competitive strengths and business position are weak because of strong local and multinational competition. This is reflected in revenues generated by Zlato polje, which were the lowest among all nine Droga Kolinska brands, accounting for USD 5.9 million in 2004 and representing 3% of all revenues (Droga Annual Report, 2004). According to the GE matrix, Zlato Polje should pursue expansion opportunities that carry minimal risk as well as increase its brand image among consumers.

Portfolio Analysis – The GE Matrix For Western European Markets

According to the GE matrix, the most promising industries in the long-term for Western Europe are mineral waters; healthy food products; canned meat; spices, sauces and semi-prepared food. Analyses show that Donat Mg, Argeta, Zlato polje, and Maestro have top investment priority in Western markets. These brands have potential as niche market players that serve smaller segments of sophisticated consumers.

Based on the GE Matrix for *Western Europe* (Picture 11.2.), the strategy implications for each Droga Kolinska brand categories are the following:

DONAT Mg: Donat Mg operates in a highly attractive industry in Western Europe due to the increasing health awareness among consumers. It has a strong business position compared to other Droga Kolinska brands in Western Europe and high competitive strengths because of its uniqueness and therapeutic effects (no direct competitors). The brand should invest heavily

162   Ljubica Knežević Cvelbar and Monika Lisjak

in most attractive segments and markets (Italy, Austria, and Germany). However, high investments in advertising and promotion are required in order to effectively communicate its benefits. The potential threats are strict restrictions regarding packaging, advertising, and promoting of mineral waters.

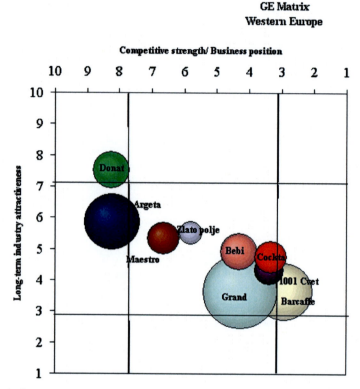

Source: Own analysis.

Picture 11.2. The GE Industry Attractiveness – Competitive Strength Matrix for Western Europe.

ARGETA: Argeta's industry is less attractive in Western than in Eastern Europe due to health trends, which lean towards less meat consumption and are enhanced by BSE and bird flu scares. However, Argeta is very successful in Austria with a 13.4% market share, which might indicate the brand has great potential also in other markets, such as Germany, Switzerland, and Sweden. Thus, Argeta should protect its position on existing Western markets and invest in the most attractive segments. At the same time, entrance on the new markets is recommended.

ZLATO POLJE: Zlato polje as a health food brand is more attractive in Western than in Eastern Europe. Although Zlato polje has not been launched in Western markets yet, it is reasonable to reposition the brand in the health food segment and to make good use of healthy lifestyle trends by pursuing strategies of brand expansion. However, management will need to adopt more offensive marketing approaches in order to counter competition.

MAESTRO: The condiments and spices industry has a similar position regarding long-term attractiveness as in Eastern Europe, but Maestro has a higher competitive strength compared to other Droga Kolinska brands in Western Europe. The reason is that Maestro will expand to include semi-prepared foods, whose distinctive advantage will be its original Mediterranean flavors. The most reasonable strategy is to protect existing markets and to build up ability to counter competition in the Western European markets.

BEBI: The baby food industry is in a mature stage in Western markets, whereas it is expanding in Eastern markets. The industry position in Western markets is worsening due to decreasing birth rates, and its long-term industry attractiveness in Western European markets is lower compared to Eastern Europe. Besides, corporate and brand awareness are significantly lower in Western European markets. The proposed strategy is to expand selectively and to pursue opportunities (in Switzerland, Greece, Turkey, Belgium, the Netherlands, UK, Ireland, Finland) with minimal risk; if there are no such opportunities, it is recommended to minimize investment and rationalize operations.

1001 CVET, BARCAFFE and GRAND: Attractiveness of the tea and coffee industry in Western Europe is similar to that in Eastern Europe. Although the Western European market is the largest market for hot drinks, it is mature and growth is very weak. There has been a slight increase in demand for green and herbal teas due to health trends. However, brand strength in Western markets is lower compared to Eastern markets. Furthermore, 1001 Cvet, Barcaffe, and Grand business units have neither the resources to build a strong brand nor the chance to compete on cost with strong multinationals.

COCKTA: The nonalcoholic carbonated beverages industry is less attractive in Western Europe than in Eastern Europe, as the market has remained static over the last five years (Milenkovic, 2004). Although Cockta is already available in some Austrian retail chains, like Merkur and Billa, it remains a local product. Thus, Cockta should protect the existing markets in Eastern Europe and pursue opportunities to expand with minimal risk also in Western European markets.

Portfolio analysis suggests that Bebi, Cockta, 1001 Cvet, Grand, and Barcaffe business units are even less promising in the Western markets than in the Eastern ones. The reason is that the intensity of competition makes it too costly for Droga Kolinska to compete profitably and those markets are nearing the mature stage of the market life cycle, therefore growth is less likely to be the best direction. The "stars" in the Western and the Eastern markets are Donat Mg and Argeta, which have high investment priority according to their competitive advantage and present trends in the industry.

Value Chain Analysis

The next phase in evaluating the strategic fit is value chain analysis. Synergy analysis for each SBU has been performed according to the adapted Porter value chain model (Porter, 1998 in Thomson and Strickland, 1998), presented in Picture 11.3. The analysis is based on primary (in-depth qualitative interviews with Droga Kolinska representatives) and secondary sources. Value adding activities – supply and logistics, technology (processes), production, marketing and sales, distribution, and human resources – are analyzed for each business unit separately. Columns show individual activities along the value chain, whereas rows represent separate business units. Similar patterns denote synergies among analyzed business units (see key), while different colors are used in order to define synergies between specific business units.[50]

	Suppliers Logistics	Technology (Process)	Production	Marketing Sales	Distribution	Human Resources
Cockta	→			→	→	→
Donat	→			→	→	→
Grand	→	→	→	→	→	→
Barcaffe	→	→	→	→		→
1001 Cvet	→	→			→	→
Bebi					→	
Zlato polje	→	→	→	→	→	→
Argeta					→	
Maestro	→	→	→	→	→	→

Opportunities to combine purchasing activities and gain leverage with suppliers (supply chain management)

Opportunities to share technology, transfer technical skills, and combine R&D

Opportunities to combine/share sales and marketing activities, leverage the use of a common brand name and after-sale activities

Opportunities to utilize common distribution channels and transport

Opportunities to combine human resources

Opportunities to combine production capacities

Source: Own analysis.

Picture 11.3. Analysis of Business Units' Synergies Along the Value Chain.

Synergy analysis along the value chain among the nine Droga Kolinska brands under investigation can be summarized as follows:

---

[50] Red defines synergies between Cockta and Donat Mg within the supply and logistics function; blue defines synergies between Grand, Barcaffe and 1001 Cvet within the supply and logistics, etc.

- Supply and logistics: Cockta and Donat Mg can reach synergies by developing common procurement (especially for packaging and labeling material); Grand, Barcaffe, and 1001 Cvet can experience potential synergies with logistics and procurement of basic raw materials, mainly with discounts on large quantities. Similar synergies can be expected between Zlato polje and Maestro.
- Technological processes: synergies are possible between Barcaffe, Grand, and 1001 Cvet; and between Zlato polje and Maestro.
- Production: the same machines can be used for producing Barcaffe and Grand, as well as for Maestro and Zlato polje.
- Marketing and sales: synergies can be reached between Donat Mg and Cockta, Barcaffe and Grand (and 1001 Cvet in the HoReCa sector[51]), and between Zlato polje and Maestro (particularly when approaching smaller retail shops with a narrower assortment).
- Distribution: synergies are possible between all business units (transport, warehousing, etc.)
- Human resources (know-how): possibilities for synergies exist between Cockta and Donat Mg; between Grand, Barcaffe, and 1001 Cvet; and between Zlato polje and Maestro.

Based on the research results, there are limited possibilities for synergies that can be reached between SBUs in Droga Kolinska. Most of the identified synergies were present in both companies before the merger (in Droga between Zlato polje and Maestro and between Barcaffe and 1001 Cvet, or in Kolinska between Donat Mg and Cockta), with the exception of Barcaffe and Grand.

Post merger synergies between Droga Kolinska's SBUs could be reached due to shared services regarding general administration (centralization of human resource management, accounting and finance; optimization of capacities; automation of transactions, IT) and procurement (a better negotiation position with regard to existing suppliers due to increased volume and market position; chance to enter into new supply arrangements; supply chain management; enterprise resource planning; improved materials management) and are the result of process rationalization. More sustained synergies can be achieved due to common marketing and shared market channels (cost savings regarding advertising; marketing knowledge exchange; cross-selling activities; implementation of multi-channels strategies; rationalization of brand portfolio).

ANALYSIS OF ORGANIZATIONAL CULTURES IN DROGA AND KOLINSKA

The analysis of organizational cultures in Droga and Kolinska was conducted by using two approaches: the structural determinants analysis, and the cultural dimensions analysis.

---

[51] Hotels and restaurants sector.

Analysis of Structural Determinants

First, cultural fit was assessed according to structural determinants analysis. Determinants under investigation were the size of the companies, their markets, history, vision, mission, and values.

Size. In order to determine and compare the companies' size, several accounting, financial, and market indicators were chosen. From the table below it can be seen that the companies are similar according to assets size, capital, revenues, and the number of employees. Although most financial indicators of Droga and Kolinska are similar, companies have substantially different NOPAT.[52] There is also a noticeable difference when comparing ROA and ROE. Kolinska has higher ROA and ROE ratios than Droga in both years. As far as markets are concerned, Droga is more oriented towards the South-Eastern European markets, while Kolinska follows a more diversified internationalization strategy.

Table 11.2. Comparison by Size

	Droga 2003	Droga 2004	Droga avg. growth since 2001	Kolinska 2003	Kolinska 2004	Kolinska avg. growth since 2001
Assets	117,943*	109,701*	-1.14%	105,264*	127,984*	4.81%
Avg. no. of empl.	631	594.29	-2.89%	588	545	-3.73%
Capital	83,755*	83,651*	0.83%	84,916*	87,636*	2.53%
Current ratio	2.08	2.63	16.79%	2.05	1.83	29.06%
Debt to assets	28.85	23.4	-8.15%	19.31	31.48	6.05%
NOPAT	4,539*	2,813*	15.91%	6,015*	4,792*	0.46%
ROA	3.81	2.47	19.22%	5.88	4.11	-7.92%
ROE	5.5	3.36	14.62%	7.25	5.55	-2.68%
Total revenues	92,166*	98,091*	0.82%	92,254*	94,243*	0.1%

* - in 000 USD

Source: http://www.fipoplus.com.

Table 11.3. Comparison by Markets

	Droga	Kolinska
Market sales in 2004:	- Slovenia 51% - South-Eastern Europe 41% - EU (mainly Sweden and Austria) 7.4 % - Russian Federation, the Near East and Other foreign markets 0.6 %	- Slovenia 65 % - Countries of the former Yugoslavia 21.2 % - Western Europe 2.5 % - Eastern Europe 9.2 % - USA 1.4 % - Other 0.3 %

Source: Annual Reports, 2004.

Industry. Droga and Kolinska both operate in the food processing industry. However, their product assortments differ substantially in terms of breadth and depth. Kolinska's product assortment consists of a wider variety of product groups, while Droga's product

---

[52]   Kolinska in 2003 had 32.5% and in 2004 70.3 % higher NOPAT than Droga.

portfolio is more comprehensive and concentrated compared to Kolinska's. Droga in fact builds its marketing strategy on strong brands (Barcaffe, 1001 Cvet, Argeta, Zlato polje, Maestro, Argo and Droga). Each product category is composed of several products that differ in taste and is offered in different packing options (Droga and Kolinska web sites).

History. Kolinska has a longer history than Droga, since production under the Kolinska name commenced in 1904. On the other hand, Droga's production heritage goes back to the late 13th century, but the firm was not established until 1964. Both companies experienced several M&As. The first time Droga and Kolinska entered international markets was in 1991 and 2002, respectively (Droga and Kolinska web sites).

Vision. The two companies have very similar visions. However, they pursue different strategic goals. In fact, Droga's goal is to become the leading provider of food and hot beverages (coffee and tea) in the region and the largest European producer of chicken pâté in 2004. Also, Droga is hoping to penetrate the markets of the Near and Far East with this brand. Kolinska, on the other hand, wants to become one of the leading producers, retailers, and suppliers of food and non-alcoholic beverages in Slovenia and in some other foreign markets, such as the Balkan region and Russia. Besides, Kolinska is mainly interested in increasing the company's market value, thus guaranteeing its owners an appropriate return on equity and enabling its employees to enjoy social security, professional, and personal development (Droga and Kolinska Annual Reports and web sites).

Mission. Both companies have similar missions. They both stress the importance of supplying high-quality, tasty, and safe food. Both missions also emphasize the companies' commitment to satisfying customers' needs. In addition to Droga, Kolinska in its mission statement stresses the importance of satisfying its employees and shareholders (Droga and Kolinska Annual Reports).

Values. The principal value of both organizational cultures is to supply high-quality food and beverages to their customers. In addition, Droga amplifies business success, employees' training, and company care for the natural and social environment. Similarly, Kolinska presents itself as a socially responsible company. In fact, Kolinska engages in different activities to guarantee the safety and health of its employees, who are one of the company's most important sources of competitive advantage, aid the local community (e.g., through donations and sponsorships of cultural and sport events etc.), and cooperate with external institutions, such as faculties and research institutes. (Droga and Kolinska Annual Reports).

To sum up, it can be said that a comparison of analysis of structural determinants has revealed that Droga and Kolinska are similar. They both operate in the food processing industry, are comparable in size and have similar missions and corporate values. Minor differences are revealed in regards to history and vision. Also, organizational culture is not systematically developed in either company.

Analysis of Cultural Dimensions

In the second step cultural fit was assessed by analaysing how the two companies score on Hofstede and Verbeke's cultural dimensions. The analysis begins with a description of the organizational cultures of Droga and Kolinska according to the proposed methodology. Then, the two cultures are compared. Finally, an assessment of the companies' subcultures follows.

Organizational Culture in Kolinska

According to methodology developed by Hofstede and Verbeke, Kolinska employees are more result- and less process-oriented, meaning that the accomplishment of results is highly encouraged by the organization, which implies that employees are able to overcome personal interests and work together in order to achieve stated goals. Achieving results and assuming responsibility is therefore among the most important values. The importance of accomplishing goals is also reflected in the fact that managers in Kolinska are more job- than employee-oriented. Although managers do not pay a lot of attention to employees' personal problems and rarely understand them individually, the organizational culture in Kolinska is more loose than tight. This means that the level of control the management has over employees regarding daily regulations, such as arrival time at work and performance of routine operations, is limited. Similar types of regulations and restrictions are therefore unnecessary, since employees are more result-oriented and ready to take over responsibilities to accomplish stated goals. Although Kolinska follows the profit motive, it acts as a socially responsible company and encourages its employees to consider the interests of all social groups involved in the company business (Figure 11.1).

Organizational Culture in Droga

Droga employees were equally process- and result-oriented. Similarly, Droga employees perceived the organization to be equally oriented towards their personal development and task accomplishment. Droga's organizational culture is, like Kolinska's, more loose than tight. On the other side, managers in Droga are less prone to publicly deal with their mistakes and to accept employees' comments. Employees less often solve interpersonal problems with their colleagues, which demonstrates the closeness of Droga's culture. However, employees believe the company is socially responsible, since it cares for employees, customers, and community's interests (Figure 11.1).

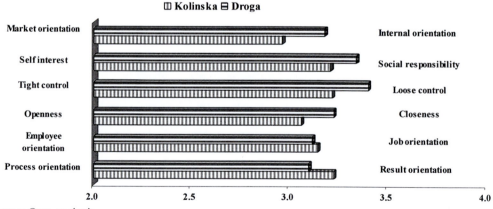

Source: Own analysis.

Figure 11.1. Comparison of Organizational Cultures in Droga and Kolinska.

Differences between Organizational Cultures in Droga and Kolinska

As it is evident from the description above, Droga and Kolinska share similar cultures, although some differences emerged. According to Hofstede and Verbeke's methodology, the investigated cultures differ in the dimension of market orientation. Kolinska is more market oriented, meaning that the company as a whole interacts more with customers and competitors compared to Droga, which is more internally oriented. Consequently Droga gives higher importance to internal affairs — planning and organizing processes, managing employees, dealing with personal and cross-departmental conflicts — than to events in the business environment. In fact, Droga recently introduced an integrated management system (which is a tool that enables the management to achieve set goals), composed of a human resource system, information protection, and a constant improvement system based on useful suggestions. In addition, Droga also has fewer product groups than Kolinska and its selling activities, which lean on the main product groups (coffee and meat sales represented 60% of revenues in 2004; Droga Annual Report, 2004), are more concentrated in the markets of the former Yugoslavia. On the other hand, Kolinska has a more diversified market and product portfolio. For example, the Unilever program represents 25% of revenues, water 17%, baby food 17%, and the nonalcoholic program 13% (Kolinska Annual Report, 2004).

Analysis of Subcultures (Production vs. Administration)

The analysis of subcultures identified major differences in cultural dimensions between the production and administrative employees. Administrative employees in both companies are more inclined towards organizational goals compared to production employees. This is to some extent logical due to the fact that the production employees are expected to work according to instructions, while the administrative employees are expected to be more result-oriented and should assume responsibility for their work. It follows that the administrative employees in both companies are prepared to take over other people's tasks in order to achieve common goals. They are also used to looser controls compared to the production employees, meaning that management does not prescribe and sanction everyday behavior. Consequently, the administrative employees have more maneuver space in regards to their work compared to the production employees. Being up-to-date with information about the market is therefore more common for them as they also know more about customers and competitors. On the other hand, the production employees in both companies are more concerned with following established routines. They especially focus on internal processes and less on market dynamics and are exposed to a higher level of management control (Figure 11.2).

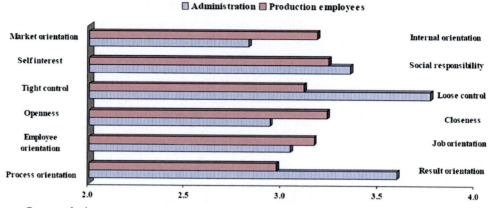

Source: Own analysis.

Figure 11.2. Comparison of Organizational Professional Subcultures in Droga and Kolinska.

The analysis also showed that differences exist between production employees and administration in the two companies. Production employees in Droga are less open compared to production employees in Kolinska. This reflects in a lower level of communication between hierarchical levels, meaning that Droga's management is less inclined towards open criticism compared to Kolinska's management. Droga production employees are more internally-oriented compared to Kolinska employees. This means that they are more focused on the internal processes than on market events. However, employees in Droga appear to be more socially responsible than in Kolinska. This is also supported by the secondary data (Droga and Kolinska annual reports and websites). Accordingly, Droga wants to increase the welfare of all interest groups involved, while Kolinska is more focused on the shareholders' value maximization. This is also evident from Kolinska's vision statement, which emphasizes the interests of shareholders over those of stakeholders (Droga and Kolinska Annual Reports, 2004).

CONCLUSIONS AND RECOMMENDATIONS

This paper presents an evaluation of strategic and cultural fit in the case of Droga Kolinska. The performed analysis can easily be adapted to other merging organizations, therefore providing an operational framework for assessing the fit between merging partners. Importance is given to both strategic and cultural aspects of the mergers and the main outcomes are future strategic guidelines for newly merged company.

Research results showed that there is an organizational fit between Droga and Kolinska's organizational cultures. This is mainly due to the fact that both organizations are part of the same national culture, are similar in size, operate in the food processing industry, have similar mission statements and corporate values, all of which reduces the likelihood of a cultural misfit. Nonetheless, some differences were revealed regarding history and vision statement. The analysis of organizational culture, based on Hofstede and Verbeke's cultural dimensions, showed that organizational cultures significantly differ in only one out of six cultural dimensions, i.e. the market orientation dimension. Namely, employees in Kolinska are more market-oriented and more focused on the market dynamics than are employees in Droga, who are more internally oriented. Larger differences, and consequently cultural incompatibility, were recognized at the professional subculture level, particularly among production and administrative employees, which is the case in most of the companies.

The performed analysis shows that cultural fit between the two organizations exists and that cultural clashes are not expected. This is good news for company management given the fact that the organization will need to undertake structural changes in order to improve its product portfolio and exploit the synergies between strategic business units.

Strategic fit analysis in Droga Kolinska shows that its product portfolio is unbalanced and highly dependent on the coffee market. Coffee sales account for almost half of the revenues from all nine Droga Kolinska brands. At the moment, this can be seen as a benefit, due to high industry profit margins. However, Barcaffe and Grand are successful regional brands that essentially fulfill local consumers' preferences. The brands' internationalization on new markets is highly improbable. Long-term coffee dependence may therefore expose Droga Kolinska to significant business risk.

The most promising brands are Argeta and Donat Mg, the former due to its popularity and high recognition among consumers and the latter due to its uniqueness and therapeutic effects. Both brands account for about a quarter of the revenues from all nine Droga Kolinska brands. Their competitive advantage is built on a strong market position in the domestic and in selected former Yugoslav markets. Both also have potential for success in new markets. Therefore internationalization of Argeta and Donat Mg is highly recommended. Research results show that Donat Mg has great potential to penetrate the Western European markets, where the product could be targeted to a niche segment of health conscious consumers, while Argeta has potential to succeed in the Turkish market, which could be well served by the production plant that is going to be located in Bosnia and Herzegovina (in Appendix).

APPENDIX
ENTRANCE INTO TURKISH MARKET

Motivations for Market Entry

Portfolio analysis has defined Argeta as one of the most promising brands of Droga Kolinska, with high possibilities to assert its position also in international markets. The brand has already exhausted the possibilities of the current markets, which is why expansion to new markets would be the next logical step.

Argeta pâté is a success in the markets of the former Yugoslavia and has become a strong brand in Bosnia and Herzegovina, Kosovo, and Macedonia. The conditions for doing business successfully in the challenging Muslim markets were assured by obtaining the Halal certificate, which guarantees that the product does not contain pork and that the complete process of meat preparation is in accordance with the requirements of Islam. After success in the former Yugoslav markets, the company started to consider the entry to other Muslim markets, including Turkey.

Argeta pâté differs a lot from all products available on the Turkish market and as such represents in the eyes of consumers an innovation in the food product market. The fact that Argeta is unlike any other product in the Turkish market can be an advantage as well as a disadvantage. On one hand the brand uniqueness represents an advantage because the product does not have any direct competitors. On the other hand, however, Argeta is a completely new product, still unknown to the customers and as such not a part of the Turkish diet.

Droga Kolinska also has an unknown corporate and product brand in the Turkish market, which can be an obstacle for success. Sandikci and Ger (2006) claim that brand is a highly important element within the purchasing decision of the Turkish consumer. Besides brand name, the authors state that price is another highly important purchasing decision factor, due to the unevenly divided income and relatively low purchasing power of the Turkish population. This can represent another disadvantage for market entry. Due to high tariffs for meat products (122.8%), the estimated price for 100 grams of Argeta pâté in retail stores is €0.7574. This price is significantly higher than the prices of Argeta's indirect competitors. However, it is also important to know that Turkish consumers associate the price of a product with its quality (Karakitapoglu, 2002) and high price for certain consumers means higher quality.The pros and cons for choosing Turkey as a potential market are summarized in Table A 11.1.

Market Entry Strategy

Droga Kolinska could enter the Turkish market by using several different market entry modes (e.g., export, direct investment etc.). The exporting entry mode carries low business risk, reduces entry costs, and allows the company to gradually understand and adapt to the market. At the same time, exporting is the fastest foreign market entry mode that exploits already existing production capacities. The disadvantages of the exporting mode are limited access to local information, and the fact that consumers perceive the brand as foreign. The highest obstacle for exporting Argeta is certainly a high customs level, which is 122.8%. Exporting Argeta to Turkey from Bosnia and Herzegovina is also an option, since Droga Kolinska is building a new production plant there. The production of pâté in Bosnia and Herzegovina can bring the Turkish market nearer, since these two countries have signed a bilateral free trade agreement. There is no customs duty for exporting meat and meat products from Bosnia and Herzegovina to Turkey if the meat itself originates from Bosnia and Herzegovina or Turkey. The production plant in Bosnia and Herzegovina also brings other advantages, such as investment incentives and lower taxes, which will allow Droga Kolinska to lower its price and thus be more competitive on the Turkish market. A good and long cooperation between Bosnia and Herzegovina and Turkey, as well as the familiarity with the Turkish business environment on the part of Bosnian managers are also very important. Droga Kolinska could export to Turkey with the help of an agent, which is a common decision among medium-size food companies (like Droga Kolinska) that do not have globally established brands. Choosing the right agent and maintaining a good relationship is the key to success.

Opportunities	Threats
• High market potential – approximately 71 million inhabitants, high fertility rates, high population concentration in large cities, young population • Globalization results in adoption of the western life style, thus global wants and needs • Only 15% of the population lives according to the rules of Islam • Spreads are widely consumed and deep-rooted in the Turkish eating habits • Turkey is striving to become an EU member (liberalization of the trade policy) • Slovenian membership in the EU (can increase its brand power due to the fact that the product is produced in the EU)	• Rigid legislation concerning food production (long and difficult export procedure) • Unstable economic environment and high business risk • Increasing future domestic and foreign competition • Distribution channels include many partners in the value chain, which leads to extracting industry profits by the intermediates • Piracy (local producers can start producing pâté) • Choice of the "right" partner (agent) • Knowledge about the Turkish market and customer behavior is limited
Advantages	Disadvantages
• A meat (poultry) product (Turks eat a lot of meat and meat products) • The product does not contain pork and has Halal and TSE certificates • Primary (focus group) results showed that Turkish consumers recognize the product as practical and nutritious and that it does not need additional adaptations • The product is suitable for all age groups • Argeta does not have a direct competitor in the Turkish market • The product is a "success" on the Muslim markets of the former Yugoslavia • Building a production plant in BiH (traditionally good relations between BiH and Turkey)	• First mover disadvantage (population not familiar with the product) • Unknown corporate and product brand (Turks prefer to buy products with recognized brands) • High tariffs for export from Slovenia (122%) • The price of Argeta is significantly higher than the price of indirect competitors • Turks are loyal to domestic products and producers • Droga Kolinska is entering the market with only one product (hard to find an agent) • Lack of established distribution channels • High bargaining power of distributors and retailers

Table A 11.1. SWOT Analysis

Another option for Droga Kolinska is to enter the Turkish market by using an intermediary entry mode (e.g., licenses, strategic partnerships, etc.). In this case the risk and necessary investments grow significantly, however, the company avoids customs limitations, it acquires access to local resources and market, and is able to build Argeta's recognition as being a domestic product. This particular option would deserve greater attention in case Turkish consumers were more willing to buy a domestic than a foreign brand.

The last option for Droga Kolinska is to invest in Turkey, i.e. through building new local production capacities. In the current phase this possibility might prove to be very risky and would demand excessive financial support. However, this approach can be used if Turkish consumers accepted the product and the market showed high development potential.

Considering all stated options, Droga Kolinska evaluated that entering Turkey by exporting from its subsidiary in Bosnia and Herzegovina would be the most sensible option.

Target Markets and Consumer Behavior Patterns

The potential target markets for Droga Kolinska can be divided into end consumer markets (B2C) and other business entity markets (B2B). Potential target segments on B2B markets include restaurants, hotels, schools and other educational institutions, importers and/or agents, wholesalers, retailers. Due to the fact that the most favorable entry mode is export, and that export in Turkey will go through an agent, those segments will not be further analyzed. Potential end consumers target markets include spectacularist consumers, ethno consumers, tourists, and meze consumers. The characteristics of those segments are analyzed and presented below.

Among four major consumption styles[53], the most promising target segment for Droga Kolinska is the "spectacularist consumption". The segment involves upscale urban consumers. When buying food products, they trust well established brand names, which guarantee quality. They find both the product brand and the retailer very important. The research shows that consumers buying well established brands or shopping in huge shopping centers pay less attention to other factors that otherwise influence shopping decisions in the case of food products. (Sandıkcı and Ger, 2006)

A niche target segment for Argeta pâté is the so-called "ethno consumer"[54], who comes from the former Yugoslavia and now lives in Istanbul. Their nutrition is similar to the nutrition of consumers in the markets of the former Yugoslavia; they know pâté as a product and have a tendency to follow western lifestyle. The danger in targeting the ethno market is the unwanted positioning of Argeta pâté by the other segments, associating it with ethno markets.

Since millions of tourists go to Turkey every year[55], tourists represent another niche target market. Argeta could be offered for breakfast and/or as an appetizer in two or three star hotels in tourist destinations like Antalya or Izmir. The focus would be on European tourists, who know the product and the way it is used.

Consumers whose diet includes "meze" are also interesting for Droga Kolinska. A traditional Turkish dinner starts off with appetizers or "meze"[56] plates, consisting of small quantities of different dishes accompanied by wine or rakia (a type of brandy). Despite the fact that "meze" dishes are appetizers, they are frequently ordered on their own and can substitute for the whole lunch or dinner. "Meze" as such is a widely used form of nutrition throughout Turkey and also represents a way of socializing within a family or/and among friends at home or in restaurants.

Students would also be a potential target segment in the phase of expanding Argeta's market share, i.e. when consumers are already informed about pâté. They have lunch during or after school/lectures in canteens at school/university or close by. Especially younger students bring light meals or lunch boxes from home. Argeta can be used as a spread in

---

[53] Four major consumption styles in Turkey include spectacularist consumption, nationalistic consumption, faithful consumption, historical consumption (Sandıkcı and Ger, 2005).

[54] In Istanbul there are more than half a million people from the former Yugoslavia and their descendants: Turkish Macedonians, Bosnians, Albanians from Kosovo, Muslims from Sandzak (Milevoj, September, 2003).

[55] In 2004 for example 17 million foreign tourists visited Turkey, out of which 12 million stayed at hotels. On average a foreign tourist spends 4.3 nights, average spending per person is 784$ out of which 25% is spent on food and drink (Turkey Retail Food Sector Report 2001, 2001).

[56] "Meze" consists of cold or hot dishes: various salads, cheeses, boiled vegetables, fried eggplants, cucumber with yoghurt dressing, rice, shells, spiced beef, lamb, seasoned liver.

sandwiches; however, it has to be mentioned that Turkish consumers mainly eat warm meals, such as kebabs, for lunch or light meals, which is why cold sandwiches are not widely consumed. For that reason offering Argeta as an appetizer or "meze" in canteens and self-serving restaurants would be a much better opportunity.

Within the presented potential market segments, the "spectacularist" and "meze" consumers are found to be the most attractive. For Argeta to be successful on the Turkish market, huge investments and serious marketing efforts will be necessary, because the primary demand has not been created yet and consumer behavior patterns have not been changed. Obstacles that might arise in the process of entering Turkey will originate from the fact that Argeta is a completely new product without an established place in Turkish nutrition habits.

REFERENCES

Annual Report Droga. 2004. [URL: http://www.droga.si/default.asp?id=362]

Annual Report Grand Prom. 2004. [URL: http://www.grandkafa.com]

Annual Report Kolinska. 2004. [URL: http://www.kolinska.si/financne_informacije-letno_porocilo.php]

Besanko, D., et al. 2004. "*Economics of Strategy.*" Third Edition. Hoboken: John Wiley and Sons, Inc.

Bowditch, L. J., and Buono, F. A. 1989. "*The Human Side of MandA. Managing Collisions Between Employees, Cultures and Organizations.*" San Francisco: Jossey-Bass Publications.

Capon, C. 2000. "*Understanding Organizational Context.*" London: Pearson Education Limited.

Carleton, J. R., and Lineberry, C. S. 2004. "*Achieving Post-Merger Success.*" San Francisco: Pfeiffer.

Cartwright, S., and Cooper, C. L. 1993. "The Role of Culture Compatibility in Successful Organizational Marriage." *Academy of Management Executives* 7 (2).

Euromonitor. 2000. "Canned Food." *Market Research Europe.* October 2000.

Euromonitor. 2001. "Packaged Food in Eastern Europe." *Market Research Europe.* July 2001.

Euromonitor. 2002. "Eastern European Hot Drinks." *Market Research Europe.* January 2002.

Fipoplus.2004. [URL: http://www.fipoplus.com]

Habeck, M. M., Kroeger, F., and Traem, M. R. 2000. "*Čas združitev. Sedem strategij za uspešno integracijo po združitvi podjetij.*" Ljubljana: DZS.

Home page. 2005. [URL: http://www.droga.si] [URL: http://www.kolinska.si]

Horwitz, F. M., et al. 2002. "Due Diligence Neglected: Managing Human Resources and Organizational Culture in Mergers and Acquisitions." *Emerald Research Register.*

House, R. J., et al. 2004. "*Culture, Leadership and Organizations: The GLOBE Study of 62 Societies.*" Thousand Oaks: Sage Publications, Inc.

Internal company data. 2004. Droga. Internal material with market shares.

Milenkovic, Z. 2004. "Carbonates: The Battle for Share in Emerging Markets – March 2, 2004." [URL: http://www.euromonitor.com/article.asp?id=2758]

Mudgil, V. 2005. "Condiment Category Grows, But Not All Segments Gain." *Retail World; Rozelle* 58 (1): 23.

Pennings, J. M., and Lee, K. (1996). "Mergers and Acquisitions – Organizational Fit and Outcomes. [URL:http://www- management.wharton.upenn.edu/pennings/research documents/smjlee11.doc]

Rejc Buhovac, A., and Slapničar, S. 2007. *"Organizational Culture and Managerial Control after an International Acquisition."* In this volume.

Thompson, A. A., and Strickland, A. J. 1998. *"Strategic Management: Concepts and Cases."* Tenth Edition. Boston: Irwin/McGraw-Hill.

Trompenaars, F., and Woolliams, P. 2004. *"Business Across Cultures."* Sussex: Capstone Publishing Ltd.

Ulijn, J., Duijsters Schaetzlein, R., and Remer, S. 2003. *"Culture and Its Perception in Strategic Alliances, Does It Affect the Performance? An Exploratory Study into Dutch German Ventures."* Eindhoven: Technische Universiteit Eindhoven.

Verbeke, W. 2000. "A Revision of Hofstede et al.'s (1990) Organizational Practices Scale." *Journal of Organizational Behavior* 21 (5).

Weber, R. A., and Camerer, C. F. 2003. "Cultural Conflict and Merger Failure: An Experimental Approach." *Management Science* 49 (4).

Zagoršek, H., and Štembergar, M. 2007. *"Culture and Its Influence on Business Performance."* In this volume.

PART IV: SOUTH – EASTERN EUROPE: ECONOMIC TRENDS AND EU INTEGRATION PROSPECTS

In: New Emerging Economies and Their Culture   ISBN: 978-1-60021-754-8

Editors: J. Prašnikar, A. Cirman, pp. 179-193   © 2007 Nova Science Publishers, Inc.

Chapter 12

SOUTH-EASTERN EUROPE: ECONOMIC TRENDS AND THE EU INTEGRATION PROSPECTS

Mojmir Mrak

INTRODUCTION

A decade and a half has now passed since the transition from a planned to market economy started in Central and Eastern Europe (CEE). In this period, countries of the region have had to overcome the legacy of an inefficient planned economy and adopt market principles. The challenges have been enormous, especially in South-Eastern Europe (SEE).[57] Bosnia and Herzegovina, Croatia, Macedonia, and Serbia and Montenegro have had to deal with internal conflicts, and all of the countries – including Albania, Bulgaria, and Romania – have faced, to varying degrees, political uncertainty, a rather low level of development and an infrastructure weakened by years of neglect.

The transition process has been unique in each country of the SEE region, and the countries have made a very different progress in this process. Bulgaria and Romania, for example, are at the door step of their accession to the EU in 2007. Croatia opened its membership negotiations in the second half of 2005, while Macedonia received an EU candidate country status at the end of that year. The other SEE countries are well behind the two groups of front runners with respect to both, the achieved level of transition and institutionalization of their relationship with the EU.

This contribution has a two-fold objective. The *first one* is to give a regional overview of recent economic trends in the countries of the CEE. The *second objective* of the paper is to provide an assessment of EU integration prospects for the region as a whole and for their individual countries.

---

[57] For the purpose of this paper, South-Eastern Europe covers Albania, Bosnia and Herzegovina, Bulgaria, Croatia, Macedonia, Romania, and Serbia and Montenegro. The paper reflects the situation as of March 2006.

Recent Economic Trends in South-Eastern Europe Output Growth

SEE's transition from planned economies to market structures has been occurring alongside an ambitious effort to restore peace and social stability in the region. The 1990s were characterized by dramatic collapses of output in SEE. By 2001, the region had reached only 74% of its pre-transition (1989) level of economic activity. In comparison, the five most developed CEE economies (the Czech Republic, Hungary, Poland, the Slovak Republic, and Slovenia) had increased their combined output to 115% of 1989 levels (World Bank, 2004).

SEE has now recovered from the recession of the 1990s. The region as a whole grew at an average annual rate of between 4 and 5% between 2001 and 2004. Table 12.1 shows that with exception of Macedonia whose economic activity remained at a practically unchanged level in 2000 and 2004 (mainly as a result of the internal conflicts in 2001), all other countries of the region increased their output by around one fifth.

This relatively high growth continued in spite of the continuous decline of external assistance to the Western Balkan countries and continued challenges stemming from a fairly weak global economic environment. An even quicker and more robust rebound of economic growth has been impeded by the slow pace of the economic restructuring caused at least partly by the absence of effective market-based institutions to protect property rights, fair competition, and financial discipline. Low levels of domestic and foreign investment have hindered economic development in SEE as well.

Not all sectors of the SEE economies were equally hit by their transformation from centrally-planned to market-based systems. Trade liberalization, the new power of consumer preferences, the cut-back of defense spending in some countries, and the conflicts in the Western Balkans are only some of the reasons explaining why industrial production suffered even more than the GDP growth during the 1990s. This process of deindustrialization has been slowed down in the recent years and in some countries of the region, like Bulgaria, even reversed.

Table 12.1. GDP of the SEE Countries, 2001–2006
(Net Change in % Against the Preceding Year)

Country	2001	2002	2003	2004p	2005f	2006f	Index 2004/1990	Index 2004/2000
Albania	7.6	4.7	6.0	6.0	6.5	6.5	144	127
B&H	4.5	5.5	3.5	6.0	5.0	5.0	…	121
Bulgaria	4.1	4.9	4.3	5.6	5.0	5.0	98	120
Croatia	4.4	5.2	4.3	3.7	3.5	3.5	102	119
Macedonia	-4.5	0.9	3.4	2.0	4.0	4.0	93	102
Romania	5.7	5.0	4.9	7.8	5.0	5.5	106	126
SandMN	5.3	3.8	2.0	7.0	5.0	5.0	58	119

p – preliminary, f – forecast
Source: WIIW database.

As shown in Table 12.1, rather strong economic growth of the SEE countries at an annual level of around 5% is expected to continue also in 2006. Assuming the continuation of market oriented reforms, the Western Balkan economies have the potential to grow at an even faster pace over the medium to long term. This would allow the countries of the region to reduce the large unemployment and increase the still low living standard of the population.

In spite of relatively high economic growth in the region as a whole over the recent years, SEE countries continue to be rather poorly developed not only vis-à-vis the Western European countries but also vis-à-vis the CEE. In 2004, per capita GDP in PPP terms in the region ranged from below USD 6,000 in the cases of Albania, Bosnia and Herzegovina, Macedonia and Serbia and Montenegro to close to USD 10,000 in the case of Croatia. The corresponding figures for Slovenia and Greece were around USD 20,000 in that year and USD 25,100 for the EU as a whole (Investment Guide for Southeast Europe, 2004).

Employment

Transition from centrally-planned to market economies has been associated with major changes in the level of employment throughout the SEE region. Similarly to other transitional countries open unemployment was almost non-existent in the region prior 1989. The situation reversed dramatically then after, when following the output collapse in the beginning of 1990s, registered unemployment grew sharply throughout the region. Revival of the output growth in recent years has so far not lead to a significant revival of registered employment. As a consequence, unemployment remains uncomfortably high at the levels between 8% in Romania and over 30% in Bosnia and Herzegovina and Macedonia (Table 12.2).

The persistently high and stagnating level of unemployment can at least partially be explained by the continuing process of labor shedding and is in contrast with initial expectations that economic growth revival and growth of the private sector will be able to absorb a significant proportion of the labor force previously employed by the state sector. When unemployment figures are discussed they should be put in the context of the large informal sector throughout the Western Balkan region. The only exception in this respect is Croatia. According to various estimates, a shadow economy represented around one third of the output in many countries of the region around the year 2000 (Gligorov, 2004).

Table 12.2. Rate of Unemployment in the SEE Countries, 2003–2006
(in % of Labor Force)

Country	2003	2004	2005f	2006f
Albania	15.0	14.4	14.0	13.5
B&H	42.0	42.0	42.0	42.0
Bulgaria	13.7	12.0	11.0	10.0
Croatia	14.3	13.8	13.5	13.0
Macedonia	36.7	37.0	35.0	35.0
Romania	7.0	7.5	8.0	8.0
SandMN	15.2	15.0	15.0	15.0

f – forecast.

Source: WIIW database.

Inflation

The process of disinflation in the SEE region made significant progress over the recent years. This is mainly due to the stabilization macroeconomic policies carried out under significant influence and sometimes even pressures from multilateral financial institutions, mainly the IMF and the World Bank. In 2004, five countries of the region had one-digit inflation rate while in Romania and Serbia and Montenegro the rate was at the level between 10 and 12%. There is little doubt that achieved disinflation (it has in several countries converged to the level required by the Maastricht criteria) has been one of the most remarkable macroeconomic achievements of the SEE countries in the recent years. As shown in Table 12.3, the disinflation trend is expected to continue also in 2005 and 2006.

Table 12.3. Inflation Rate in the SEE Countries, 2001–2006
(Net Change in % Against the Preceding Year; Measured as Consumer Price Inflation)

Country	2001	2002	2003	2004p	2005f	2006f
Albania	3.1	5.2	2.3	2.9	4.0	3.0
B&H	3.1	0.4	0.6	0.2	0.5	0.5
Bulgaria	7.4	5.8	2.3	6.2	4.0	4.0
Croatia	4.9	1.7	1.8	2.1	2.0	2.0
Macedonia	5.2	1.4	2.4	0.9	2.0	2.0
Romania	34.5	22.5	15.3	11.9	9.0	7.0
SandMN	88.9	16.5	9.4	10.8	10.0	10.0

p – preliminary, f – forecast
Source: WIIW database.

Public Finances

Consolidation of public finances is another component of the macroeconomic stabilization strategy carried out rather successfully by the SEE countries in recent years. The strategy usually designed and implemented in close cooperation with the IMF typically consists of a policy mix that combines a fixed exchange rate regime with restrictive monetary policy and tight fiscal policy.

In spite of the generally positive trend of public finances, fiscal consolidation of the SEE countries advances at a very uneven pace. As shown in Table 12.4, a quite impressive and maybe even dramatic adjustment took place in Macedonia where the general government deficit was reduced from 6.3% of GDP in the conflict year of 2001 to only 1.3% in 2004. Similarly good results were achieved also by Bosnia and Herzegovina. There the share of public expenditure in GDP was reduced by 10 percentage points between 2000 and 2003 (from 57% of GDP to 47% of GDP) (Transition Report, 2004). As a result, the government budget was almost balanced in 2003 and 2004. In Albania and Serbia and Montenegro the pace of fiscal adjustment is less pronounced. Strong fiscal pressures continue also in some other countries, especially in Croatia where the general government deficit, though halved in the 1999–2004 period, was still above 4% of GDP in the last year of that period.

Table 12.4. Public Sector Balance in SEE Countries, 2000–2004
(as % of GDP)

Country	2000	2001	2002	2003e	2004p
Albania	-9.2	-8.2	-6.7	-4.5	-6.5
B&H	-3.1	-2.5	-2.4	-0.2	-0.9
Bulgaria	-1.0	-0.9	-0.6	-0.4	-0.4
Croatia	-6.5	-6.7	-5.0	-6.3	-4.5
Macedonia	1.8	-7.2	-5.6	-1.6	-1.5
Romania	-4.0	-3.5	-2.6	-2.4	-1.6
SandMN	-0.9	-1.3	-4.5	-4.2	-3.4

Source: Transition Report 2004, 2004.

External Imbalances – Trade, Current Account, External Debt

Trade balance. The SEE region as whole runs a large and persistent trade deficit. In the Western Balkan countries the trade deficit was equivalent to more than 25% of their GDP in 2003 and 2004. In Bulgaria and Romania, the deficit was a bit lower but still high by international standards. It was around 13% of GDP in the case of Bulgaria and around 8% in the case of Romania.

There are several reasons for these large trade imbalances of the countries in the region. First of all, SEE countries are characterized by a relatively low level of foreign trade, expressed as a percentage of their GDP, in particular given the modest size of their domestic economies. Large trade deficits also reflect the need to satisfy growing imports for domestic consumption and investment, a common feature of most transition economies. There are several other more region-specific reasons explaining large trade deficits of the Western Balkan countries, including civil wars and trade sanctions, and the fact that some of these countries have still not succeeded in recovering from the virtual breakdown of the former SFRY's market. Furthermore, the Western Balkans had difficulties in fully taking advantage of the asymmetric trade measures granted by the EU, due chiefly to the lack of productive capacity, but also due to an insufficient ability to comply with EU quality standards.

Current account. Unilateral transfers from official and private sources together with positive balances of services contributed to limiting current account deficits of the SEE countries to a single digit figure for the countries of the region with the exception of Bosnia and Herzegovina and Serbia (Table 12.5). According to the conventional theory on stages of development, a modest current account deficit is acceptable and even desirable for countries at relatively low levels of development as is the case of all CEE countries. The problem, however, is how to define what is a sustainable current account deficit and when this deficit becomes unsustainable, i.e., when a country loses its ability to regularly service its external debt obligations.

What can be said for the SEE countries is that the existing current account position of these countries is highly vulnerable and is not sustainable over a longer period of time. There are two sets of arguments supporting this conclusion. The first one relates to the unsustainability of several current account revenue sources. Though still very important, the volume of official grants to the region has been continuously declining. In 2003, for example, they were equivalent to between 2.2 and 2.4% of GDP in the cases of Albania, Macedonia, and Serbia and Montenegro (European Commission, 2004). On the other hand, unilateral transfers from private sources continue to play a very important role for all the Western Balkan countries with the exception of Croatia. These transfers are mainly composed of workers' remittances, even though they may partly hide unrecorded transactions. As far as balances of services are concerned, they are positive throughout the region. Their size is, however, not really significant. The only exception is Croatia where tourism revenues play an extremely important role in financing the large trade deficit of the country.

Table 12.5. Current Account Deficit in the SEE Countries, 2003–2006 (% of GDP)

Country	2003	2004	2005f	2006f
Albania	-6.7	-4.3	-6.0	-5.0
B&H	-30.2	-27.7	-24.3	-21.7
Bulgaria	-8.6	-7.2	-6.1	-5.6
Croatia	-7.3	-6.1	-5.6	-5.3
Macedonia	-3.3	-7.1	-6.7	-6.5
Romania	-6.1	-7.7	-7.7	-7.4
Serbia	-10.2	-13.5	-15.0	-14.4
Montenegro	-7.3	-5.7	-5.0	-5.0

f – forecast

Source: WIIW database.

Table 12.6. FDI Inflow in the SEE Countries, 2001–2004
(in EUR Per Capita, in % of GDP)

Country	2001		2002		2003		2004	
	EUR pc.	% of GDP	EUR pc.	% of GDP	EUR pc.	% of GDP	EUR pc.	% of GDP
Albania	67	4.9	46	3.0	57	2.9	107	4.2
B&H	31	2.4	69	4.7	99	5.4	130	6.0
Bulgaria	103	6.0	115	5.8	268	10.6	334	10.8
Croatia	352	7.9	253	4.9	460	7.1	242	3.1
Macedonia	217	12.8	39	2.1	47	2.0	75	2.8
Romania	52	2.9	52	2.5	102	3.9	233	6.9
Serbia	21	1.6	63	3.3	181	7.1	128	4.3
Montenegro	16	0.9	137	6.9	72	2.9	99	3.4

Source: WIIW database.

Long-term sustainability of current account deficits in CEE countries is questionable also from their capital accounts point of view as a relatively small proportion of the region's current account deficits is currently financed with non-debt creating FDI (Table 12.6). The Table clearly shows that countries that are more advanced in their transition and EU accession processes have also been the main destination of FDI inflows. A significant proportion of FDI inflows has been a result of privatizations. FDIs associated with privatization may in the next few years still represent an important source of the funds required to finance their growing balance of payments deficits. In the medium term, however, it is realistic to expect that countries in the region will have to rely on debt financing to a much greater extent than now. This means that the possibility of new debt servicing problems should not be excluded, at least in some Western Balkan countries, especially in those ones that will not be able to establish themselves as more important destination for FDIs in the form of "greenfield investments".

External debt. The level of external debt in the region expressed as a percentage of GDP was estimated at around 65% in 2000. Since then, it came down to around 46% by the end of 2004, mainly as a result of the decline of the external debt in Serbia and Montenegro following the conclusion of rescheduling agreements with foreign creditors. As a result of these agreements the external debt of the country was more than halved, from 132% of GDP in 2000 to 55% of GDP in 2004. This is still higher than in any other country of the region with exception of Croatia where the external debt is equivalent to around 80% of its GDP (Vuković, 2005). This figure should, however, be judged in the context of significantly higher debt servicing capacity of Croatia in comparison to other Western Balkan countries.

Conclusion on external imbalances. The key to the longer term sustainability of the external position for countries in the region is the strongly export-oriented economic development of their economies. Only through intensive structural reforms will SEE countries be able to substantially increase both economic growth and exports and thus reduce the level of their balance of payments deficits to a long-term sustainable level. Otherwise, these countries will be unable to break the vicious circle of low economic growth, restricted imports and balance of payments problems.

Structural Reforms

If the major objective of the macroeconomic policies is to create a stable environment, then the major objective of the structural reforms is to actually accomplish the transition and make a transition economy a viable and competitive long-term actor on the international market. Macroeconomic reforms alone, although necessary, do not lead automatically to supply responses needed for a comprehensive transformation to a market economy. These reforms do not deal systematically with structural weaknesses in a country's economy, with the lack of entrepreneurial cadres as well as managerial and supervisory personnel, and also with the inadequacies in technological, financial accounting and marketing areas.

Structural reforms in transition economies reforms could be classified into three large areas. The first one involves reforms where the task of the state is *to withdraw from all economic responsibilities.* These reforms include liberalization of prices, of trade and of the market for foreign exchange and have typically been done very fast and in the early period of the transition process. The second area of reforms involves reforms that require *redistribution of assets,* such as small- and large-scale privatization. The third area of reforms are those ones that involve building and/or rebuilding of institutions, i.e., enterprise restructuring, banking sector reform, introduction of competition policy and the establishment of securities markets and non-bank financial institutions. The last two groups of structural reforms are due to their complexity and controversies typically extended over a much longer period of time.

During recent years, the CEE countries have taken further steps in the process of structural reforms in all three areas. Good progress has been achieved in some segments of the reforms that involve liberalization, especially in the trade liberalization area. In the context of the Stability Pact for South East Europe (SEE), a Memorandum of Understanding on Trade Liberalization and Facilitation was signed in June 2001 by all the seven countries of the region. In spite of an improved infrastructure for intra-regional trade, its volume remains rather limited, with only a few countries importing from their SEE neighbors more than a quarter of total imports. For all the SEE countries the EU continues to be the main trading partner. The main reason for poor intra-regional trade among the SEE countries is strong concentration of their export base on products with similar specialization patterns (mostly in labor-intensive and basic products) which limits the intra-regional trading opportunities.

Another area where transition has been practically completed is the area of the privatization of SMEs. In contrast, the so called large-scale privatization, i.e., privatization of former state-owned enterprises, has proved to be more complicated than originally thought and as a consequence, the advances here have been, in general, much slower and also less uniform across the countries of the region. The slower pace of large-scale privatization has been typically caused by one or a combination of the following reasons: major restructuring needs, restitution problems, the lack of clarity on existing liabilities and ownership rights, debt resolution negotiations, social considerations, the lack of administrative capacity and the lack of interest from foreign investors. While some countries, like Albania and Macedonia, have made significant progress in the process of large enterprise privatization, the situation of loss-making public enterprises with all the negative consequences on the budget and jobs remains particularly difficult in Bosnia and Herzegovina as well as in Serbia and Montenegro.

One of the major challenges for the region as a whole is how to strengthen economic growth and reduce unemployment. In order to achieve these two objectives, considerable progress will still be needed to establish an attractive framework conducive to investment driven by private sector development. A weak investment climate undermines the prospects for economic growth and poverty reduction and jeopardizes the stability of the region. But to create a climate that will attract investors, the countries must establish robust and enduring basic market institutions. There are several areas where the scope for improving the climate conducive to domestic and foreign investors is still large. One of them is the absence of market-based institutions to protect property rights, fair competition, and fiscal discipline. The establishment of a transparent legal system and its enforcement through an effective judiciary remain the key conditions for the promotion of a business friendly environment. The reform of the cadastre and the clear definition of ownership rights over land remain bottleneck issues in most countries of the region which prevent or delay important investments and should be considered as a key priority. The reform of public administration and the management of public finances is another area that poses important challenges to the countries of the region over the medium term.

EU INTEGRATION STATUS OF THE SEE REGION AND ITS PROSPECTS

Status of the SEE Countries' Relations with the EU[58]

More than two years after the EU, at the June 2003 Thessaloniki European Council, reconfirmed its commitment to the states of the Western Balkans that they share "a common European destination," countries of the SEE have reached very different positions along their road to the EU. Bulgaria and Romania are clear front runners. The two countries (they are *de-facto* an integral part of the big bang Eastern enlargement) completed their EU accession negotiations in 2004 and are expected to become members as of January 2007. If the two countries are compared among themselves, Bulgaria is being considered as better prepared for the membership than Romania.

The relations of Western Balkan countries with the EU are progressing within the framework of the so-called Stabilization and Association Process opened to five countries of the region: Albania, Bosnia and Herzegovina, Croatia, Macedonia, and Serbia and Montenegro. This Process is a strategy explicitly linked to the prospect of the EU accession for the countries of the region and is adjusted to the level of development of each of the countries concerned, allowing them to move at their own pace. In return, countries of the region are expected to demonstrate a sufficient level of economic and political commitment to stabilization and development of the region. The Copenhagen criteria for accession remain entirely valid as well.

Croatia signed the Stabilization and Association Agreement (SAA) agreement in October 2001. Today, the country has a status of an EU candidate country, and started accession negotiations in the second half of 2005 after getting a clearance about its full cooperation with the Hague Tribunal. The country has established its structures that are needed for effective negotiations with the EU. Under a very optimistic scenario, Croatia may be able to conclude its EU accession negotiations in three years, which would open the way for full membership either in 2010 or 2011.

Macedonia is another Western Balkan country that signed SAA in 2001, and this happened even a few months earlier than in the case of Croatia. Unfortunately, internal political problems, especially the 2001 unrests, have slowed down the country's EU accession dynamics. After receiving a positive avis of the European Commission, the country was granted a status of an EU candidate country at the December 2005 European Council. It is not realistic to expect that accession negotiations with Macedonia will start before the parliamentary elections scheduled for the fall of 2006.

The remaining three Western Balkan states are a long way behind not only Croatia but also Macedonia. All three are still without the signed SAA agreement. Albania began negotiations for an SAA in early 2003, but with no tangible results as the country has shown inadequate progress toward reforms in some crucial areas, including the fight against organized crime and corruption. The remaining two countries, Bosnia and Herzegovina and Serbia and Montenegro, started their SAA negotiations only in the late 2005. This means that under a very optimistic scenario they would be able to conclude the SAA negotiations

---

[58] The text discusses only those direct forms of contractual cooperation between the EU and the SEE countries. It therefore does not address cooperation of the region with various EU-sponsored institutions, like the Stability Pact, the European Investment Bank, and also the European Bank for Reconstruction and Development.

sometime in 2006 or 2007. Consequently, full membership for these countries can not be realistically expected well before the end of the next decade.

In order to strengthen the EU accession process in the Western Balkan countries, the June 2003 Thessaloniki Council endorsed the conclusion to introduce "European Partnerships," inspired by the Accession Partnerships for candidate countries. These partnerships have identified priorities for action supporting efforts of the countries in the region to move closer to the EU. At the same time, these partnerships should provide guidance for financial assistance provided by the EU and its member states financial assistance to the region and should reflect the particular stage of development of each of the countries.

The EC assistance provided under CARDS accompanies the Stabilization and Association process notably through institution building and gradual alignment with the acquis. The main objective of the CARDS program is to support the Stabilization and Association process in the Western Balkans. In more operational terms, the CARDS program has the following four objectives: (i) reconstruction, democratic stabilization, reconciliation and return of refugees, (ii) institutional and legislative development, including harmonization with EU norms and approaches, to underpin democracy and rule of law, human rights, civil society, the media, and the operation of a free market economy, (iii) sustainable economic and social development, including structural reforms, and (iv) promotion of closer relations and regional cooperation among countries and between them, the EU and the (then candidate) CEE countries.

The CARDS program works on two levels – regional and country – and for realization of its objectives, strategic priorities and actual programs are being established at both levels. Yet, CARDS strategic priorities vary according to individual countries. The strategic priorities and programs are stipulated in Country Strategic Papers (CSP) prepared on a six-year basis. The total volume of funds available under CARDS for the 2000–2006 period is close to EUR 5 billion. Table 12.7 provides information about the country-by-country allocation of the CARDS assistance in the 2002–2004 period.

Table 12.7. Indicative EU Assistance to the Western Balkans, 2002–2004 (in EUR Million)

Country	2002	2003	2004	Total
Albania	44.9	46.5	52.5	143.9
B&H	71.9	63.0	58.0	192.9
Croatia	59.0	62.0	68.0	189.0
SandMN	195.0	255.0	210.0	660.0
Kosovo	154.9	50.0	40.0	244.9
Macedonia	41.5	43.5	43.5	128.5
Regional projects	45.0	35.0	0.0	80.0
Total	612.2	555.0	472.0	1,639.2

Figures for 2002–2004 include allocations from the Integrated Border Management regional envelope, but exclude any allocations for budgetary support.
Source: www.seerecon.org/gen/eu-see.htm (as indicated in the CARDS Strategy papers 2002).

Prospects of the EU Integration for the SEE Countries and Expected Patterns of the EU Accession Negotiations

The membership of Bulgaria and Romania in the EU can be considered a closed case and it is not important whether it will actually happen in 2007 or a year later. As far as further SEE enlargement is concerned the situation is much less clear. True, the EU has made a political commitment to bring all the SEE countries into the EU membership, but this commitment has been given without a defined timetable. As already mentioned, for the Western Balkan countries, the SAA provides an institutional framework which gives all of the countries of the region the prospect of eventual accession. This could, however, happen within a couple of years, as will probably be the case with Croatia, or within a decade or more which will probably be the case with the rest of the Western Balkans. Is should be clearly understood that the exact timing of accession does not depend only on the preparations of would-be members. It also depends greatly on how the EU itself develops after its 2004 Eastern enlargement, after the EU constitution refusals at referendums in France and the Netherlands, and once the accession negotiations start with Turkey and Croatia.

It is realistic to expect that EU accession negotiations with Croatia, to be hopefully joined in the not too distant future also by Macedonia, will in many respects differ from the EU negotiations that were completed in 2002. Some of the differences that can be envisaged are the following. *First,* this will not be a convoy type of negotiations as was the case with the big bang Eastern enlargement. This means that "individual treatment" of each of the candidate countries will not be only a proclaimed principle in negotiations but a principle that will actually be implemented in practice. It is reasonable to expect that the speed of the negotiations will to a much larger extent depend on individual merits of each candidate country. *Second,* it is a fact that enlargement that will include the Western Balkan countries will be lower on the political priority list of the most EU member states than was the case with the last enlargement. There is no doubt that "enlargement fatigue" is pretty strong in several old member states and that it will have a negative influence on the dynamics of the enlargement process in the years to come. *Third,* in contrast to the last EU enlargement when the enthusiasm of the old member states was based on both political and economic interests, in the case of the Western Balkan countries the predominant pro-enlargement argument is stability. In some EU member states, the membership offered to these countries is considered as a kind of an insurance policy for stability and peace in the region, and consequently in Europe as whole. *Fourth,* based on experiences from the previous accession cycle, it is realistic to expect that implementation of the commitments made by candidate countries will be much more in the center of the negotiation process than before. *Fifth,* the very fact that a candidate country has to negotiate with 25 or 27 member states is by itself an additional complication in comparison to the negotiation process with the 15 members. It should not be forgotten that negotiations with candidate countries very often involve intense negotiations among the EU member states.

EU Financial Assistance to the Western Balkan Countries in the Next Medium-Term Period

Similarly as in the case of the CEE countries, the accession process of the Western Balkan countries will also be supported by the financial assistance provided by the EU. As the accession process for countries of this region will be extended well into the next decade it makes sense to take a closer look at the volume of financial resources earmarked for the candidate countries in the next medium-term financial perspective of the EU covering the period between 2007 and 2013.

According to the proposal of the European Commission, financial resources to prospective members will be governed through the so called Instrument for Pre-Accession Assistance (IPA) establishing a unified instrument for pre-accession assistance. As such, it will replace not only the Phare Regulation, but also the SAPARD, ISPA, Phare CBC and Co-ordination Regulations as well as the Turkey and CARDS Regulations.

According to the draft IPA regulation, beneficiary countries will be divided into two categories, depending on their status as either candidate countries or potential candidate countries. *Potential candidate countries* are listed in Annex I of the regulation, and at this moment include Albania, Bosnia and Herzegovina, Macedonia and Serbia and Montenegro. *Candidate countries* are listed in Annex II, and at this moment include Croatia, Macedonia and Turkey. A country can move from Annex I to Annex II only after the decision of the Council giving it candidate country status.

The IPA sets five components: (i) *Transition Assistance and Institution Building* to help countries meet the accession criteria and improve their administrative and judicial capacity, (ii) *Regional and Cross-Border Cooperation*, (iii) *Regional Development* to help prepare for Structural Funds ERDF programs and Cohesion Funds, (iv) *Human Resources Development* to help prepare for Structural Funds ESF programs, and (v) *Rural Development* to help prepare for Agriculture and Rural Development.

There will be a clear differentiation within the IPA between assistance provided to potential candidate countries listed in Annex I of the regulation, and to candidate countries listed in Annex II of the regulation. For potential candidate countries, the assistance will consist of institution building, in particular to strengthen the Copenhagen political criteria, enhance administrative and judicial capacity and selectively promote some alignment with the *acquis* in areas of mutual advantage. This will be complemented by regional and cross-border cooperation, investment to promote economic and social development and other transition measures to foster stabilization and reconciliation throughout the Western Balkans. The potential candidate countries will, therefore, benefit from the following two components: (i) Transition and Institution Building Component, and (ii) Regional and Cross-Border Cooperation. They will, therefore, receive a level of funding less than that proposed for candidate countries. For the candidate countries, however, the full pre-accession package will apply. The institution building effort will, therefore, focus on full rather than selective alignment with the *acquis,* and these countries will also benefit from the other three components of the Instrument designed to help prepare candidate countries for EU Funds after accession.

The total volume of financial resources under the proposed by the Commission was at the total level of around EUR 14 billion for the 2007–2013. The draft IPA regulation sets out the total envelope of funds available for assistance to both candidate and potential candidate countries, but not the allocation for each country. However, it does state the principles for allocation of funds to candidate countries, i.e., to Turkey, Croatia and, in a not too distant future, Macedonia. The draft regulation states that the future candidate countries should be broadly treated the same way as the past candidate countries. Taking into account the size and absorption capacity of Turkey, a somewhat different principle is applied for this country. Calculated on these principles, Table 12.8 provides a rough estimated allocation of IPA funds among the three candidate countries.

Table 12.8. Estimated Allocation of Assistance Under the IPA for "Candidate Countries", 2007–2013 (in EUR Million)

	2007	2008	2009	2010	2011	2012	2013	Total
TOTAL	1,426	1,631	1,734	1,977	2,294	2,441	2,564	14,067
- Croatia*	120	120	120	120	120	120	120	840
- Macedonia	54	54	54	54	54	54	54	378
- Turkey	1,000	1,150	1,300	1,450	1,600	1,750	1,900	10,150
- "Potential candidates"	252	307	260	353	520	517	490	2,699

* If Croatia becomes an EU member during this period, it will no longer be supported under this budget line, and its projected funding will be available to other pre-accession states.
Source: Breaking Out of the Balkan Ghetto: Why IPA Should Be Changed, 2005.

In contrast to candidate countries of Croatia and Macedonia that would according to these estimates have an average annual aid intensity of EUR 27 per capita over the 2007–2013 period, the comparable aid intensity of the remaining three Western Balkan countries – with a formal status of "potential candidates" – would be significantly lower (Table 12.9).

This budget allocation provides a very clear EU assumption concerning the progress of "potential candidates" through the accession process. The assumption suggests that candidate status for this group of countries is not expected before 2010 making the membership realistic well beyond the end of the next financial perspective.

Table 12.9. Estimated Allocation of EU Assistance under the IPA to "Potential Candidates", 2007–2013 (in EUR million)

	Population	2007	2008	2009	2010	2011	2012	2013	Total
Serbia	8.0	113	138	117	159	234	233	220	1,214
Kosovo	1.8	25	31	26	35	52	52	49	270
Montenegro	0.6	10	12	10	14	21	21	20	108
Albania	3.2	45	55	47	63	94	93	88	485
B&H	4.1	59	71	60	82	119	118	113	622
Total	17.8	252	307	260	353	520	517	490	2,699
Per capita		14	17	14	19	29	29	27	

Source: Breaking Out of the Balkan Ghetto: Why IPA Should Be Changed, 2005.

International Commission on the Balkans and its Recommendations

The "conventional" scenario of the EU accession process for the Western Balkan countries outlined in the previous subchapters has been challenged earlier by the International Commission on the Balkans composed of 18 distinguished individuals both from the region and from outside the region.

In its report which came out in 2005, the Commission stated that the Stabilization and Association Process strategy adopted five years ago which put high expectations on regional cooperation has simply failed. The Commission's conclusion was that "the Balkans needs a new strategy if it is to translate Brussels' stated political aim to integrate the region into reality. Despite the commitment made at Thessaloniki, the dream of European integration has not yet proved powerful enough as a force for transforming the societies of the Balkans, especially if we agree that the basic indicator of success is the progress of each country on the road to the EU" (The Balkans in Europe's Future, 2005). The Commission argued that the region is facing a kind of a status quo situation caused by the expectation gap (people do not trust their leaders being in position or in opposition), the development gap (instead of catching up with the rest of the continent, the Balkan countries will fall further behind), and the integration trap (the dysfunctional states and protectorates that characterize the region actively hinder the inclusion of the Balkans into the European mainstream). The Commission further stated that "despite the scale of the assistance effort in the Balkans, the international community has failed to offer a convincing political perspective to the societies in the region. The future of Kosovo is undecided, the future of Macedonia is uncertain, and the future of Serbia is unclear. We run the real risk of an explosion of Kosovo, an implosion of Serbia and new fractures in the foundations of Bosnia and Macedonia" (The Balkans in Europe's Future, 2005).

Based on the assessment that all Western Balkan states with the exception of Croatia are characterized as weak states, the Commission recommends that the new EU accession strategy for the countries of the region should be "a mixture of classical state-building policies with those aimed at transforming nation states into member states. What we face in the Balkans is a need for a "member-state building" strategy. The Stabilization and Association Process is simply not strong enough as a framework for building member states". In more specific terms, the Commission recommends the following: "In autumn 2006 the EU should sponsor a Summit that aims to present all Balkan countries with their accession road maps. The Summit should review the achievements of individual states in satisfying the Copenhagen criteria and, on the basis of this, the EU will decide whether to start direct negotiations on membership or to sign a pre-accession Europe Agreement on member-state building with those countries that do not yet qualify for accession talks. Second, in the view of the Commission it is realistic for these countries to start accession negotiations around 2009/2010, in the belief that the Europe Agreements will contribute to meeting the Copenhagen criteria. The objective of accession could be set towards 2014/2015" (The Balkans in Europe's Future, 2005).

REFERENCES

2004. *"Investment Guide for Southeast Europe."*

EBRD. 2004. *"Transition Report 2004."* London.

European Commission. 2004. *"The Western Balkan in Transition."* Brussels: DG ECFIN.

European Stability Initiative. 2005. *"Breaking Out of the Balkan Ghetto: Why IPA Should Be Changed?"*

Gligorov, V. 2004. *"Southeast Europe: Development and EU Integration Processes."* Presentation. Ljubljana.

The International Commission on the Balkans. 2005. *"The Balkans in Europe's Future."*

The World Bank. 2004. *"Building Institutions in South Eastern Europe."* Washington, D.C.

Vuković, N. 2005. *"Vprašanje vzdržnosti plačilnobilančnih primanjkljajev v državah Zahodnega Balkana."* (mimeo).

In: New Emerging Economies and Their Culture
Editors: J. Prašnikar, A. Cirman, pp. 195-207

ISBN: 978-1-60021-754-8
© 2007 Nova Science Publishers, Inc.

Chapter 13

TRANSITION IN SERBIA AND MONTENEGRO: FROM RECURRENT CRISES TOWARDS EU INTEGRATION

Milica Uvalić

INTRODUCTION: THE SLOW PACE OF TRANSITION IN SERBIA AND MONTENEGRO

The transition to a market economy and multiparty democracy has been more complex in Serbia and Montenegro (the Former Republic of Yugoslavia until February 4, 2003)[59] than in many other countries of the former socialist world. Since 1991, a number of essentially politically determined processes have had very negative economic implications for the country – including the 1991 break-up of SFR Yugoslavia, four military conflicts in which Serbia/FR Yugoslavia has been directly or indirectly involved,[60] nationalistic policies which gave priority to political over economic objectives, policies of ethnic cleansing leading to massive migrations of the population, severe international political and economic sanctions against FR Yugoslavia throughout most of the 1990s, culminating in eleven weeks of NATO bombardments in 1999. These political events have had destabilizing effects for the whole SEE region, but the implications for the Yugoslav economy have been particularly profound and long lasting. FR Yugoslavia has also experienced substantial delays in political reforms, postponing democratization and the establishment of a functional state, as well as in more radical economic and institutional reforms, both of which have had direct implications for its slow process of integration with the European Union (EU).

---

[59] The Federal Republic of Yugoslavia, consisting of Serbia and Montenegro, was constituted in April 1992. On March 14, 2002, the representatives of three governments – the federal government of FR Yugoslavia, of Serbia, and of Montenegro – signed the Agreement on Principles of Relations of Serbia and Montenegro. A new Constitutional Charter started being prepared, which after having been finalized and adopted in February 2003, led to the change in the country's name into "Serbia and Montenegro". After the referendum in Montenegro in May 2007, Serbia and Montenegro became two independent states in June 2007.

[60] In chronological order: Slovenia (1991), Croatia (1991–1992), Bosnia and Herzegovina (1992–1995), and Kosovo/FR Yugoslavia (1999).

FR Yugoslavia has thus remained, throughout the 1990s, a country of major political and economic instability, characterized by recurrent economic crises, reform backsliding, reversals in macroeconomic stabilization, inward-oriented economic strategies, and international isolation. Today, the country faces a number of specific economic problems and internal constraints on growth and development. Still, the overall prospects have significantly improved after 2000, due to both internal political developments – the fall of the Milosevic regime in Serbia in October 2000 – and to the fundamental change in international strategies towards South-Eastern Europe (SEE). After the 1999 Kosovo conflict, the EU launched its Stabilization and Association Process (SAP) for the five countries in the so called "Western Balkans" (or the SEE-5: Albania, Bosnia and Herzegovina, Croatia, FYR Macedonia and Serbia and Montenegro), which offered these countries generous trade concessions, contractual relations through the signing of Stabilization and Association Agreements (SAA), a new major program of financial assistance (CARDS, envisaging some EUR 5 billion of aid over the 2000–2006 period), political dialogue, and even prospects of EU membership.

This contribution looks at the largest (in terms of population and territory) of these "Western Balkan" countries, Serbia and Montenegro. Although it is a country that is presently in various respects lagging behind most other SEE countries, both the present EU candidates (Bulgaria, Croatia, Romania, FYR Macedonia, Turkey) and the non-candidates (Albania, Bosnia and Herzegovina,), it has achieved a lot of progress over the last five years and thus also hopes to soon be in line for EU membership.

In what follows, we will consider some of the main economic features of Serbia and Montenegro today and the likely prospects for the future. Although according to UN Security Council Resolution 1244, Kosovo is still officially part of Serbia and Montenegro, it is explicitly excluded from the analysis, since after 1999 it has been under the special mandate of the UN Mission in Kosovo (UNMIK).[61] In addition, a part of the analysis will refer primarily to the recent developments in Serbia, as the prevalent part of the economy (contributing over 95% of GDP), although the statistical data reported in the paper refers to the whole country. We will consider, in a comparative perspective, Serbia and Montenegro's recent macroeconomic performance (section 2), progress with transition-related institutional reforms (section 3), and its current position with respect to the EU (section 4). Some concluding remarks, also regarding future prospects, are given at the end (section 5).

MACROECONOMIC PERFORMANCE

Following the break-up of SFR Yugoslavia, FR Yugoslavia experienced extreme macroeconomic instability, hyperinflation and the rapid worsening of most macroeconomic indicators,[62] which prevailed throughout the 1990s. The economic turnaround came only after the October 2000 political changes in Serbia, when more radical economic reforms started

---

[61] All statistical data on Serbia and Montenegro in the post-1999 period do not include Kosovo (unless otherwise indicated).
[62] In 1993, FR Yugoslavia had an average inflation rate of 116.5 trillion, or one of the highest hyperinflations ever recorded in history (see EBRD, 2004; for more on economic policies in FR Yugoslavia in the 1990s, see Uvalic, 2001).

being implemented. The new course of transition has given impressive results in some areas, though more limited achievements or even lack of more substantial change in others.[63]

One of the most immediate tasks of the 2001 Serbian/Yugoslav government was *price liberalization,* which enabled the elimination of major price distortions caused by the frequent recurrence of the pre-2001 government to price freezes. These measures initially led to a very high average *inflation* rate, of over 90% in 2001 (Table 13.1). Notable progress was achieved in disinflation over the next few years, as average inflation was reduced to 21% in 2002, further to 11.5% in 2003, and to a one-digit figure in 2004, together with a relatively small depreciation of the nominal exchange rate (therefore real appreciation), introduction of internal convertibility of the national currency (the dinar), and a substantial increase in foreign exchange reserves (in 2005 over USD 3 billion).[64] Despite clear signs of improvement, average inflation again jumped to 15% in 2005, mainly due to higher oil and electricity prices, and wages increasing more than productivity, though a further decline to around 11% was expected in 2006. Therefore, Serbia and Montenegro has reached a certain degree of macroeconomic stability, but it remains among the few countries in the SEE region (together with Romania) to still have a relatively high inflation rate.

The achievements have been less impressive regarding *fiscal accounts.* Over the last few years Serbia and Montenegro's public deficit has not been particularly high, even before grants (-3.1% of GDP in 2004; see Table 13.1), generally lower than in some other SEE countries, including Albania and Croatia. However, the structure and level of public expenditure has not changed substantially.

Table 13.1. Serbia and Montenegro – Main Macroeconomic Indicators, 1998–2006

	1998	1999	2000	2001	2002	2003	2004	2005	2006
Inflation rate (annual average,%)	30.0	41.1	70.0	92.5	21.5	11.6	9.8	15.5	11.4
General gov't balance (before grants,% of GDP)	-5.4	Na	-0.9	-1.4	-4.5	-4.2	-3.1	N/A	N/A
General gov't balance (after grants,% of GDP)	N/A	N/A	-0.2	-0.7	-3.4	-4.0	-2.7	N/A	N/A
Real GDP growth rate (%)	6.7	-18.0	5.0	5.5	4.0	3.0	8.0	4.0	5.0

Source: Commission of the EU (2004b); except for the 2004–2006 inflation and real GDP growth rates: Economist Intelligence Unit (2005), June and September.

Although radical fiscal reforms have been in course since 2001 (a major simplification of the tax system, the passage to gross wages for social contribution purposes, the recent introduction of the value-added tax), general government expenditure remains one of the highest in the SEE region, in 2003 amounting to 47% of GDP (similar to that in Bosnia and

---

[63] Since Montenegro started many economic reforms independently of reforms and economic policies in Serbia, part of this section refers primarily to macroeconomic policies in Serbia.

[64] The analysis of exchange rate policies refers only to Serbia, since Montenegro has established its own central bank and introduced the DM (and later the Euro) as legal tender in 1998, which has been used ever since. The dinar depreciated nominally against the Euro by only 5% during 2001–2002, by 11% in 2003 and by 8% in the first eight months of 2004. In real terms, the exchange rate therefore appreciated by some 50% during 2001–2002, remained appreciated by 2% in 2003, and depreciated by 3.4% in the first eight months of 2004 (Commission of the European Communities, 2004b). On exchange rate policies in the Western Balkan countries in recent years, see Daviddi and Uvalic (2004).

Herzegovina, but lower than in Croatia; see EBRD, 2004). Government revenues have been unstable under the impact of ongoing fiscal reforms, while the government's tax collection capacity has not improved much until 2003–2004, when a number of measures were introduced to decrease the informal economy and regulate all payments (e.g. introduction of fines for non-issuing of receipts). The problems on the fiscal side could, however, prove to be a serious impediment for preserving macroeconomic stability, if certain structural reforms are not seriously addressed soon (e.g. pension reform).

Growth performance has been rather satisfactory since 2000, as real GDP registered relatively high growth rates of 4 to 5%. A major slowdown was recorded in 2003, when real GDP grew by only 3%, while industrial production registered a 3% decline. In 2004, real GDP growth rate was exceptionally high (8%) and was expected to be relatively high also during 2005–2006, at the level of 4–5% (Table 13.1). Despite strong economic recovery during the last five years, these high growth rates have been largely insufficient to compensate for the earlier very substantial fall in output.[65] Although during the 1990s most other SEE countries also experienced reversals in the trend of economic recovery, so that by 2003 none of the countries, except Albania, had reached its 1989 GDP level (Table 13.2), Serbia and Montenegro is by far in the worst situation: by 2003 it had reached 52% and by 2004 56% of its 1989 real GDP (Table 13.3).

Serbia and Montenegro thus remains one of the poorest countries in the SEE region also in terms of other indicators (Table 13.3). In 2004, it had a GDP per capita at market exchange rates of USD 2,820 (marginally higher than that of Albania or FYR Macedonia); or according to estimates of the Economist Intelligence Unit, of around USD 5,800 at Purchasing Power Parity (PPP), therefore only ahead of Albania.

Table 13.2. Growth in Real GDP in SEE Countries, 1989-2004 (in %)

	1989	1990	1991	1992	1993	1994	1995	1996	1997	1998	1999	2000	2001	2002	2003 Est.	2004 Proj.	GDP 2003 (1989 = 100)
Albania	9.8	-10.0	-28.0	-7.2	9.6	8.3	13.3	9.1	-7.0	12.7	8.9	7.7	6.8	4.7	6.0	6.2	129
BH	n.a.	-23.2	-12.1	-80.0	-10.0	0.0	20.8	86.0	37.0	15.6	9.6	5.5	4.4	5.5	3.5	4.0	57
Bulgaria	0.5	-9.1	-11.7	-7.3	-1.5	1.8	2.9	-9.4	-5.6	4.0	2.3	5.4	4.0	4.8	4.3	5.5	84
Croatia	-1.6	-7.1	-21.1	-11.7	-8.0	5.9	6.8	6.0	6.5	2.5	-0.9	2.9	4.4	5.2	4.3	3.7	91
Macedonia	0.9	-9.9	-7.0	-8.0	-9.1	-1.8	-1.2	1.2	1.4	3.4	4.3	4.5	-4.5	0.9	3.1	2.5	78
Romania	-5.8	-5.6	-12.9	-8.8	1.5	3.9	7.1	4.0	-6.1	-4.8	-1.2	1.8	5.3	4.9	4.9	5.8	92
S & M	1.3	-7.9	-11.6	-27.9	-30.8	2.5	6.1	7.8	10.1	1.9	-18.0	5.0	5.5	4.0	3.0	8.0	52
Avr 27 trns C	0.3	-3.3	-7.9	-9.2	-4.9	-5.5	-0.1	0.2	2.5	-1.0	3.4	6.0	4.3	4.0	5.6	6.1	85

Source: EBRD (2002) and EBRD (2004).

---

[65] It ought to be recalled that GDP in FR Yugoslavia in only three years (1991–93) fell by over 70%, while in 1999 (after the NATO bombardments) it fell by another 18%.

Table 13.3. Level of Development of SEE Countries

	Population 2004 (mln)	GDP per capita in USD at market exch. Rates 2003	GDP per capita in USD at market exch. rates 2004	GDP per capita in USD at PPP 2003	GDP per capita in USD at PPP 2004	Real GDP 2004 (index, 1989 = 100)	GDP per capita in EUR at current prices and exch. rates 2003
Alb	3.2	1,959	2,560	4,560	5,121	131.6	1,685
B&H	4.2	1,660	1,960	6,160	7,029	70.9	1,897
Bulg	7.7	2,550	3,130	7,570	8,261	92.0	2,257
Croat	4.4	6,300	7,760	10,620	11,390	94.7	5,745
Mac	2.0	2,300	2,590	6,920	7,147	83.5	2,121
Rom	22.4	2,550	3,150	6,990	7,800	100.6	2,317
S&M	10.5	2,390	2,820	5,110	5,772	55.7	2,232

Source: Economist Intelligence Unit (2004 and 2005). Last column: Commission of the European Communities (2004b).

According to the EU Commission data, Serbia and Montenegro in 2003 had a GDP per capita (at current prices and exchange rates) of EUR 2,232, which is slightly higher than Albania, Bosnia and Herzegovina, or FYR Macedonia, and close to that of Bulgaria. Considering that GDP per capita at PPP in the EU in 2004 was around USD 25,000, Serbia and Montenegro was in 2003 still at about 23% of the EU average.

The social costs of the transition have been particularly high in Serbia and Montenegro. From 2001 onwards, despite measures to create new jobs for laid off workers, the registered unemployment rate was extremely high and continued to increase: from 27% in 2000, to 28% in 2001 and to 32% in 2004. Similar problems are present in most other SEE countries; particularly in Bosnia and Herzegovina and FYR Macedonia, where the registered unemployment rates are even higher (Uvalic, 2003; 2004). These very high figures, however, clearly overestimate the effective number of unemployed workers, as they do not take into account that a relatively large portion of activities in Serbia and Montenegro still takes place in the unofficial (informal) economy. According to most estimates of the size of the informal economy in transition economies, it is generally larger in the SEE than in the CEE countries, though smaller than in many CIS countries. In Serbia and Montenegro, unemployment in any case remains a key economic and social problem. With the further implementation of enterprise restructuring and privatization, additional measures will clearly be necessary to stop or reverse such negative trends.

Serbia and Montenegro's *external sector* is characterized by even more fundamental problems, linked to the structural weaknesses of the economy. Foreign trade has been highly unbalanced in recent years, the value of imports being two to three times the value of exports. The trade deficit reached historical records in recent years, increasing from 20% of GDP in 2000 to 25% of GDP in 2004. The limited restructuring and modernization of key industries, fairly low FDI until a few years ago, low domestic investment, and real appreciation of the dinar (until recently) are among the main reasons for the sluggish export performance. Serbia and Montenegro's current account deficit is also among the highest in the SEE region, primarily due to very poor export performance: whereas in 2000 it was still only 4% of its GDP (after grants), it continued to grow ever since to more than 11% of GDP in 2004 (it is higher only in Bosnia and Herzegovina, amounting to 15% of its GDP). Since 2001, Serbia and Montenegro has relied heavily on large inflows of foreign aid to cover the current account deficit, but in view of the substantial reduction of foreign donations expected in the forthcoming years, it is questionable whether the situation is sustainable (although the forecasts for export market growth are rather optimistic, see below). Serbia and Montenegro's external debt remains very high (in 2004 around EUR 10 billion). There has been a very remarkable improvement over the last four years, as external debt declined from over 100% to 55% of the country's GDP by 2004, due to the favorable write-off of a large part of the debt owed to the Paris and London Club of creditors and Russia,[66] which also permitted a substantial fall in the debt/export ratio (Table 13.4). Nevertheless, Serbia and Montenegro remains the most indebted country in the SEE region.

Table 13.4. Serbia and Montenegro – External Sector Indicators, 1998–2004

	1998	1999	2000	2001	2002	2003	2004
Trade balance (% of GDP)	-13.1	-15.9	-20.8	-24.5	-24.9	-24.3	-24.8
Current account (before grants,% GDP)	-4.8	-7.5	-7.1	-9.7	-12.8	-12.6	-13.0
Current account (after grants,% GDP)	-4.8	-7.5	-3.9	-4.6	-8.8	-10.2	-11.6
External debt (% GDP)	76	103	132	103	73	69	55
External debt (billion EUR)	9.0	10.6	12.2	13.5	11.3	11.9	10.5
Debt–export ratio (%)	267	500	448	436	365	360	280
FDI (million EUR)	101	105	27	184	597	1,235	620

Source: Commission of the EU (2004b).

Table 13.5. Export Market Growth in SEE

	2003	2004	2005	2006
Albania	2.8	4.8	1.4	2.9
Bosnia and Herzegovina	6.5	7.3	5.4	6.1
Bulgaria	7.9	7.0	5.4	5.8
Croatia	6.0	9.3	5.5	6.9
Macedonia	5.0	7.5	4.1	4.7
Romania	5.6	7.8	3.8	4.6
Serbia and Montenegro	5.2	7.5	5.0	5.9
SEE total	5.6	7.3	4.4	5.3
5 CEE total	4.8	7.5	4.1	5.0
3 Baltic states total	5.5	9.1	6.3	7.1

Source: Economist Intelligence Unit (September 2005).

Forecasts of the Economist Intelligence Unit on export market growth for the next few years, based on import demand in 20 leading partner countries, are rather optimistic, as they place Serbia and Montenegro favorably in comparison with other SEE countries. Although the country's export market growth was somewhat lower in 2003 than the SEE average,

---

[66] In 2004, a total of around USD 2.5 billion of foreign debt was written off as a result of deals with the London Club, the Paris Club and Russia.

during 2004–2006 it is expected to be above not only the SEE average, but also of the average export market growth of the five CEE incoming EU member states (Table 13.5).

Foreign direct investment (FDI) has been steadily increasing since 2001 and was particularly high in 2003, when Serbia and Montenegro attracted an impressive amount of over EUR 1.2 billion in FDI. However, the largest part of FDI in recent years has been secured through a few successful privatization deals. Moreover, until the political changes in late 2000, Serbia and Montenegro had attracted an extremely limited amount of FDI (Table 13.6): if we consider the cumulative net inflow of FDI into Serbia and Montenegro during the 1989–2003 period, it amounted to USD 3.1 billion, or only around 10% of the total in all seven SEE countries. In per capita terms, the figures are even less impressive: the cumulative net inflows of FDI to Serbia and Montenegro, during 1989–2003 were only USD 374 per capita (Bosnia and Herzegovina is the only SEE country that attracted less FDI in per capita terms). However, as a proportion of GDP, in 2003 Serbia and Montenegro was one of the two major recipients of FDI among the SEE countries (together with Bulgaria), both having attracted FDI corresponding to 7% of their GDP.

PROGRESS WITH INSTITUTIONAL REFORMS

Since late 2000 Serbia and Montenegro has also undertaken radical economic and institutional reforms. In Serbia, in particular, many reforms have been moving forward at accelerated speed over the last four years. In some areas progress has been impressive, whereas in others the achievements have been much less evident. In 2001, the EBRD evaluated Serbia and Montenegro as "the fastest reformer" among all 27 transition economies. There are many important measures which have been undertaken by the Yugoslav/Serbian government in 2001–2003.

Table 13.6. Net Inflows of Foreign Direct Investment in SEE, 1989–2004 (in USD Million)

Country	Cumul. net FDI inflows 1989-96	FDI net inflows (annual)								Cumulative FDI inflows 1989-20031989-2003		FDI inflows (% BDP)	
		1997	1998	1999	2000	2001	2002	2003	2004	Mln USD	p.c. USD	2002	2003
Albania	295	42	45	51	143	204	135	178	377	1.114	352	3,0	3,0
B&H	/	0	67	177	150	130	230	320	420	1.073	282	4,0	5,0
Bulgaria	450	507	537	789	1.003	641	876	1.398	2.000	6.235	795	5,6	7,0
Croatia	564	347	835	1.420	1.085	1.407	591	1.700	1.100	8.204	1.857	2,6	6,0
Macedonia	38	18	118	32	176	439	77	94	150	1.002	501	2,0	2,0
Romania	1.434	1.267	2.079	1.025	1.051	1.154	1.080	1.528	2.100	10.536	486	2,0	3,0
S&M	0	740	113	112	25	165	562	1.395	600	3.112	374	4,0	7,0
Ttl. FDI in:													
SEE-5	897	1.147	1.178	1.792	1.579	2.345	1.595	3.687	2.647	16.867	/	/	/
SEE-7	2.781	2.921	3.794	3.606	3.633	4.140	3.551	6.613	6.747	31.276	664	3,3	4,7
FDI in 27 trns. C.	42.002	19.926	24.329	26.591	25.604	26.578	30.345	19.004	30.094	220.626	928	5,0	4,3
SEE-5 share (%)	2,1	5,8	4,8	6,7	6,2	8,8	5,3	19,4	8,8	7,6	/	/	/
SEE-7 share(%)	6,6	14,7	15,6	13,6	14,2	15,6	11,7	34,8	22,4	14,2	/	/	/

Sources: Calculated from data of the EBRD (2004), EBRD (2003), and earlier data of the EBRD.

Privatization was initiated according to a new law adopted in 2001, based on cash-based sales to strategic investors at tenders and auctions, which fundamentally changed the privatization strategy away from the insiders' model applied in the 1990s towards commercial sales; during the first two years of its application, some 1,200 firms were privatized (out of 3,000 planned for privatization). *Foreign trade liberalization* has occured through the elimination of quotas and other quantitative restrictions and substantial lowering of the average tariff rate (to around 9%) and accompanied by other positive developments, including the signing of free trade agreements with all other SEE countries.[67] The country was also able to benefit from EU trade concessions extended to Serbia and Montenegro in late 2000, which enable duty-free access to EU markets for most goods, and obtained observer status in the WTO with the intention of soon becoming a member. Legislation on *foreign direct investment* (FDI) has been improved, giving foreign partners national treatment, removing various restrictions that previously existed regarding foreign activities in certain sectors, and simplifying registration by reducing burdensome bureaucratic procedures. Reforms of *labor legislation* have also been implemented, with the 2001 adoption of a new Labor Act which has enforced flexibility in labor relations and clarified the responsibilities of the employers and the employees. *Banking reforms* have also started: a number of loss-making banks were closed at an early stage, including four of the largest banks, representing 55% of total assets of the banking sector, and permitting the entry of foreign banks (Société Générale, Raiffeisen Bank, HVB Bank, National Bank of Greece, etc.).

Although there was a certain slowdown in the pace of economic reforms in 2003,[68] further progress in many areas was achieved in 2004–2005 with the adoption of numerous new laws. In the 2004 Doing Business Survey of the World Bank, Serbia and Montenegro ranked as the top reformer of the year: it led in making the kinds of reforms that can spur growth at the company level, having been evaluated favorably in eight of the ten areas studied, including the capital requirement for starting a company (which was recently cut from EUR 5,000 to EUR 500), the time required to start a new business (reduced from 51 days to 15), labor legislation (recent changes make it easier to hire temporary workers), the time to resolve commercial disputes (it has been substantially reduced, due to a new code of civil procedure), and further fiscal reforms (payroll and sales tax were replaced by value-added tax). These measures have indeed led to a substantial increase in new registered companies as their number in 2004 jumped by 42%.

If we consider some recent indicators on progress in transition of the European Bank for Reconstruction and Development (EBRD) in mid-2004, we see that Serbia and Montenegro has made progress in many areas in recent years. Indeed, there are no large differences between results achieved in comparison with some other SEE countries regarding certain economic reforms which were generally easier to implement, such as price liberalization, reforms of the trade and foreign exchange systems, or small-scale privatization (Table 13.7).

---

[67] FR Yugoslavia has signed a free trade agreement with all the other SEE countries, as envisaged by the Stability Pact's June 2001 Memorandum of Understanding on Trade Liberalization and Facilitation.

[68] The main reasons for the slowing down of economic reforms in 2003 are primarily political. After the 2003 presidential elections, it took several months of negotiations to form a minority government by the coalition of the DSS, the G17 Plus and the SPO-NS Renewal Movement. The tragic assassination of Prime Minister Djindjic in March 2003, the split in the DOS, the delays in adopting a new Constitutional Charter, linked to the continuing difficult relationship between Serbia and Montenegro, the unsatisfactory situation in Kosovo even five years after the conflict, are among the most important elements of recent political instability.

Table 13.7. Progress in Transition in SEE, Mid-2004

Country	Enterprises					Markets and trade			Financial institutions			Infrastructure
	Private sector share of GDP (in%) mid-2004	Large-scale privatization	Small-scale privatization	Governance and enterprise restructuring		Price liberalization	Trade and foreign exchange system	Competition policy	Banking reform and interest rate liberalization	Securities markets and non-bank financial institutions		Infrastructure reforms
Albania	75	2+	4	2		4+	4+	2	3-	2-		2
B&H	50	2+	3	2		4	4-	1	3-	2-		2+
Bulgaria	75	4	4-	3-		4+	4+	2+	4-	2+		3
Croatia	60	3+	4+	3		4	4+	2+	4	3-		3
Macedonia	65	3+	4	2+		4	4+	2	3-	2		2
Romania	70	4-	4-	2		4+	4+	2+	3	2		3+
S&M	50	2+	3+	2		4	3+	1	2+	2		2

Source: EBRD, 2004.

Serbia and Montenegro has also achieved fairly good results in these areas, considering that it started implementing more radical economic reforms only in 2001. There are, however, other reforms where progress has been much slower. The most critical areas include enterprise governance and restructuring, banking reforms, the development of securities markets and non-bank institutions, and competition policies, although far-reaching reforms in these areas have been substantially delayed in most other SEE (and CEE) countries as well.

Table 13.8. Characteristics of the Banking Sector in SEE in 2003

	Number of banks	Total banking sector assets % of GDP	State ownership % of ttl capital	Foreign owner-ship % of ttl capital	Concen-tration: 3 largest banks Assets in% of total	Loan-to-deposit ratio %	Net interest spread %
Albania	16	50.2	4.4	95.6	68.5	81.9	5.9
B & H	37	58	10.0	70	-	79.8	6.8
Maced.	22	41.2	13.0	48	66	87	8.0
S & M	57	43.7	36.9	26.8	33	74	12.7
Serbia	47	46	37.5	26.3	30	71.4	13.2
Montenegro	10	32.3	25.0	36.2	59	95.6	8.9
Kosovo	7	44.1	0	61.0	70	45.3	12
SEE-4	140	46.9	22.7	48.8	46.3	76.2	10.1
SEE-3	106	-	24.2	-	58.8	94	2.8
CEE-8	217	-	-	-	-	111	2.6

Source: Commission of the European Communities (2004a).

Regarding corporate governance and restructuring, although the private sector share in GDP by now exceeds 50%, privatization has left many problems unresolved and poor corporate governance remains characteristic. Enterprise restructuring has been delayed, as many loss-making companies not yet privatized have been waiting for the new bankruptcy law, whose adoption has been postponed several times, while FDI has gone into a few of the best companies. Moreover, large-scale privatization has been delayed, and some of the largest and strategically most important companies, which were nationalized in the early 1990s, are only now scheduled for privatization (e.g. the oil company NIS).Another critical area is the financial sector. Despite radical banking reforms, the indicators presented in Table 13.8 show that privatization of the banking sector in both Serbia and Montenegro has been lagging with respect to other SEE countries: state ownership in 2003 still represented a relatively high percentage of total banking capital (37% in Serbia and 25% in Montenegro), while foreign ownership was the lowest (26% in Serbia and 36% in Montenegro). Other indicators for the SEE countries also show that the net interest spread has remained the highest in Serbia (in 2003 still over 13%), higher by some 3% than the average in the four Western Balkan countries, and by 10% higher than the average in Bulgaria, Croatia and Romania.

TOWARDS GREATER INTEGRATION OF SERBIA AND MONTENEGRO WITH THE EU

After a decade-long isolation of Serbia and Montenegro from the outside world, non-membership in the United Nations and other international organizations, and disruption in its relations with the EU, the situation started improving after the radical change in the political regime in Serbia in October 2001. Integration of Serbian-Montenegrin and EU markets through a general expansion of trade has been in course since early 2001. EU trade concessions introduced for the Western Balkan countries were extended to FR Yugoslavia in November 2000, allowing duty-free access to EU markets for most products, which has very favorably affected trade patters over the next few years. Since 2001 Serbia and Montenegro has been registering impressive growth rates of its exports to the EU, although the volume still remains relatively low. Today the EU is its main trading partner on both the export and import side. In the meantime, Serbia and Montenegro has also been one of the major beneficiaries of the EU CARDS program of financial assistance for the western Balkans. Over the 2001–2004 period, it has received over EUR 3.5 billion of financial assistance.

Serbia and Montenegro has also greatly delayed establishing contractual relations with the EU. Since its inclusion into the SAP in early 2001, the process which should have prepared the ground for starting negotiations on the SAA has been extremely slow. Serbia and Montenegro has had a series of joint meetings with the EU: starting in June 2001, five Consultative Task Force meetings and another seven Enhanced Permanent Dialogue meetings, at which a lot of technical work was done. Nevertheless, at the beginning of 2005, Serbia and Montenegro was the SEE country that had advanced least in the SAP. The main stumbling block, apart from the sensitive political issues,[69] pertained until recently to the very complex relations between Serbia and Montenegro.[70] Initially, the EU Commission insisted

---

[69] The critical political issues included the still unresolved constitutional issues (relationship between Serbia and Montenegro, the future of Kosovo, and collaboration with the Hague Tribunal.

[70] The two republics have taken somewhat different transition paths ever since FR Yugoslavia was created in April 1992. Only some areas of economic activity were under the authority of the federation, while a number of specific economic reforms have been carried forward by Serbia and Montenegro separately. In addition, after 1998 Montenegro has tried, for political reasons, to distance itself from Serbia by establishing independence in various areas, including monetary, fiscal, and foreign trade policy. As mentioned previously,

on full harmonization of a number of economic laws which are very different in the two republics, including the foreign trade law,[71] and measures which would ensure the functioning of a common market in the country as a whole. The process was stalled by the inability to reach a mutually acceptable solution, leading to a significant postponement of a positive Feasibility Report which would have enabled negotiations on the SAA to start. Although an Action Plan on harmonization and the internal market was prepared and most tariffs were actually harmonized, what remained critical was the harmonization of tariffs for some 56 agricultural products on which no agreement was reached. The Action Plan was a failure, as the two republics clearly have very different economic systems and different economic interests.

Important new developments occurred from October 2004 onwards. The EU finally decided not to insist on the harmonization of economic legislation, but adopted the "twin track" approach. The twin track approach essentially meant that the EU would deal separately with the two republics on policies which Serbia and Montenegro conduct separately, notably trade, economic and sectoral policies, while continuing to work with the country as a whole where it is the State Union that is the competent authority, for example, on international political obligations and human rights. The Feasibility Report was re-launched and approved by the Council of Ministers on April 25, 2005. A further step forward was taken on October 3, 2005, when the Council approved the beginning of negotiations with Serbia and Montenegro on the SAA. However, in May 2006 the negotiations on a SAA were suspended, due to Serbia's insufficient collaboration with the Hague Tribunal (essentially the non-delivery of general Mladic). After Montenegro and Serbia became two independent states in June 2006, the EU concluded a SAA with Montenegro (early 2007), but not yet with Serbia, due to the very same reasons which led to the suspension of negotiations in May 2006.

Nevertheless, today EU membership is a top political priority for both Serbia and Montenegro. On October 13, 2004, the National Parliament of the Republic of Serbia adopted a *Resolution on Association with the European Union,* confirming that an accelerated entry of the Republic of Serbia into the EU as a full member and the joining of the Partnership for Peace is a strategic and national objective to which the National Parliament of the Republic of Serbia will in the future give full and continuous support. Other documents have been prepared and adopted in the meantime, including the Action Plan and the Strategy on EU integration, in line with the main objectives of the European Partnership.

CONCLUDING REMARKS

Until only a few years ago, Serbia and Montenegro was a country characterized by high political and economic instability, lagging behind many other transition countries in implementing fundamental economic and political reforms. Due to the political changes in Serbia in October 2000, the country has undertaken bold economic and political reforms in practically all areas and today is not very different from several other countries in the SEE

Montenegro uses the Euro (and no longer the dinar), has its own fiscal and other laws, and a foreign trade system which is somewhat more liberal than the one in Serbia (lower average tariffs, although it has retained quantitative restrictions). Some reforms were implemented earlier in Montenegro than in Serbia, although in general their respective economic systems are not very dissimilar.

[71]   At that time, the average tariff in Montenegro was as low as 3%, whereas in Serbia it was 9%.

region. Serbia is a relatively small economy that could benefit enormously from closer economic links and cooperation with other European countries. This trend is well on its way and is likely to continue further in the near future. Today, the EU is already Serbia's main trading partner (both in terms of exports and imports) and there is no doubt there will be increasing trading opportunities in the future.

FDI has been on an upward trend, and despite the slowdown registered in 2004, could indeed be expected to increase further, especially considering the positive changes adopted in 2004 which have substantially improved the business environment. There are some possible comparative advantages and potential opportunities which could render Serbia attractive today for foreign partners.

Location: The geographical and geo-strategic position places Serbia in the very center of the Balkan region. In terms of territory and population, it is the largest country among the SEE-5 and the second largest among the SEE-7 (after Romania). These features could make it a preferred location for foreign investors.

Fast growing economy: Although still below 60% of its GDP attained in 1989, the potential for growth in Serbia is high. Most estimates of international organizations predict that it will be one of the fastest growing economies in the SEE region in the years to come. In case of joint projects with foreign partners, this growth potential could be exploited by foreign investors.

Qualified and relatively cheap labor force: Serbia has a well educated and qualified labor force in many sectors, and labor costs are still relatively low with respect to some other transition economies in the SEE region.

SEE regional market: Serbia is today a country that has opened to the rest of the world and has introduced important measures of trade liberalization with other countries in the SEE region and much wider. The bilateral free trade agreements signed with the other SEE countries, which cover around 90% of these countries' trade, have practically created a large regional market with over 55 million consumers. This is another opportunity that could be attractive for foreign partners. The free trade agreement Serbia concluded with Russia is another potential advantage, which could also be beneficial for foreign companies investing in Serbia.

Despite these opportunities, Serbia and Montenegro today still faces a number of complex problems – economic, social, legal, and not least, political. The primary responsibility clearly lies with Serbia to carry forward all the economic reforms that so far have been implemented only half-way, but also all the legal and institutional reforms which have been realized only partially and without which the economic reforms in course cannot be fully effective (including e.g. legal reforms of the judiciary to ensure the rule of law, or more substantial reforms of the public administration). However, regarding the critical political issues, a part of the responsibility also lies with the wider international community, considering that these problems have become increasingly internationalized. Unless the EU puts major efforts to help resolve the remaining very complex political issues, which presently clearly cannot be handled by the country itself – the final status of Kosovo and therefore also of Serbia – the unsettled question of state borders will continue to be an element of instability.

The challenges in front of Serbia are numerous and the tasks manifold. Still, the overall prospects for its future are today much brighter than they were only five years ago. With further implementation of the transition to a market economy and democratization, regional integration and measures facilitating its access to EU markets, international assistance from the EU and other international donors, announced prospects of future EU membership and possibly increasing inflows of FDI, the overall conditions for achieving more permanent stabilization and sustainable growth are likely to substantially improve. This should in turn facilitate the future integration of Serbia into a wider Europe, despite all uncertainties regarding future EU integration processes. What is probably most important, is that these processes are now irreversible, since eventual political changes in Serbia may influence the speed of transition, but not its generally positive course.

REFERENCES

Commission of the European Communities. 2002. "European Economy. The Western Balkans in Transition." Brussels: *Occasional Papers*: 2.

Commission of the European Communities. 2004a. "European Economy. The Western Balkans in Transition." Brussels: *Occasional Papers*: 5.

Commission of the European Communities. 2004b. "European Economy. The Western Balkans in Transition." *Enlargement Papers*: 23.

Daianu, D., and Thanos, V. (eds). 2001. "Balkan Reconstruction." London: Frank Cass.

Daviddi, R., and Uvalic, M. 2004. "Currencies in the Western Balkans on their way towards EMU." in Torres, F., Verdun, A., Zilioli, C., and Zimmermann, H. (eds). 2004. *"Governing EMU: Economic, Political, Legal and Historical Perspectives."* Florence: European University Institute. Proceedings of the 1st Alumni Conference. October 3 and 4, 2003: 291–310.

Economist Intelligence Unit. 2005. *"Economies in Transition – Eastern Europe and the Former Soviet Union – Regional Overview."* London. Various issues (last issue: September 2005).

European Bank for Reconstruction and Development. *"Transition Report."* London. Various issues.

United Nations Economic Commission for Europe – UNECE. "Economic Survey of Europe." Geneva. Various issues.

Uvalic, M. 2001. "FR Yugoslavia." *Journal of Southeast Europe and Black Sea Studies* 1 (1). Frank Cass. Also in Daianu and Veremis (eds). 2001.

Uvalic, M. 2003. "Economic Transition in Southeast Europe." S*outheast European and Black Sea Studies* 3 (1): 63–80.

Uvalic, M. 2004. "The Impact of the 2004 European Union Enlargement on South-Eastern Europe." Ost-West Gegeninformationen (in German). Also in Italian (L'impatto dell'allargamento dell'Unione Europea nel 2004 per l'Europa sud-orientale). In Tramontana, A. (ed). 2004. L'Unione Europea. Università degli Studi di Perugia: Facoltà di Scienze Politiche. In Serbian (*Medjunarodna politika*), 54 (1110): 24–30. April–June 2003.

In: New Emerging Economies and Their Culture
Editors: J. Prašnikar, A. Cirman, pp. 209-228

ISBN: 978-1-60021-754-8
© 2007 Nova Science Publishers, Inc.

Chapter 14

HELIOS GROUP'S INVESTMENT IN SERBIA: IS THERE A STRATEGIC AND CULTURAL FIT?

Nada Zupan and Robert Kaše

INTRODUCTION

Company growth through mergers and acquisitions has become a frequently used strategy over the last few decades (Huang and Kleiner, 2004). The same trend can also be found in Slovenia, where companies have often chosen the former Yugoslav republics for their venue for internationalization through foreign direct investment (Damijan and Polanec, 2005). The period of the 80s and 90s in the world's paint industry can also be labeled as a period of consolidation. However, this does not hold for the Slovenian paint industry where these processes have only been present in the last few years. Helios started its growth strategy of takeovers after 2001 and among the companies that were taken over are Zvezda from Serbia and Montenegro and Color from Slovenia. The acquisition of Zvezda Helios is also in the center of attention of this case study analyzing the strategic and cultural fit of his acquisition.

Both of these fits are very important because company acquisitions are complex procedures that involve a high degree of uncertainty and often result in failures. According to the existing studies, approximately three quarters of acquisitions do not achieve the expected results (Huang and Kleiner, 2004). Very early the studies have cited as one of the most frequent reasons for failure an insufficient level of corporate cultural fit between companies (Buono and Bowditch, 1989) as well as an insufficient understanding of the importance of works and procedures which harmonize corporate culture. With insufficient cultural fit the relationships between employees and the way work is performed can show anomalies which can result in productivity decrease and incapability of organizational strategies execution on the tactical level.

The aims of this chapter are to analyze the strategic and cultural fit in the case of Helios Group's (hereafter the Group) investment in Serbia. The most important questions we will try to answer are: 1) is the acquisition of Zvezda Helios an effective undertaking from the business perspective view of the Group, 2) what are the differences in organizational culture and how do they affect the process of integration between Zvezda Helios and Helios Group, 3) how does the existing organizational culture in chosen Helios Group companies (mother company Helios, Zvezda Helios and Color) fit business strategy, 4) what changes are needed to improve the strategy of organizational culture fit in the future.

As a method we used an in-depth case study, with a combination of qualitative and quantitative methods. The data for the strategic fit analyses were gathered through company reports and by structured interviews in the period between April and September 2005 at Helios headquarters. During this time eight interviews took place. Executive managers of strategic business units (SBU), the total quality management (TQM) manager, the human resources (HR) manager, the executive finance manager and the executive director of Zvezda Helios were interviewed. The data were analyzed with standardized tools for analyzing a company's strategy and strategic fit in a group of companies. For the organizational culture analysis we used the survey and focus group methodology. The questionnaire used was developed by Trompenaars Hampden-Turner (hereafter THT questionnaire) and was used to depict existing and desired organizational culture as well as dimensions of personal culture and because of the already existing data bases it also allowed for cross-national comparison.[72] The focus groups provided us with the data for qualitative analysis. The surveys were conducted in June 2005 among managers and employees with higher levels of education in three companies: Helios, Zvezda Helios and Color. In total, 243 questionnaires were used for the analysis. Two focus groups were conducted in September 2005 after the initial results of the questionnaires were gathered.

The structure of the chapter flows from introducing the Group through some basic data to analyzing the strategic fit of the Zvezda Helios acquisition as well as cultural fit, where the third company, Color, is included. We proceed with analyzing the fit between the corporate business strategy and the existing as well as desired organizational culture as expressed by employees through questionnaires and focus groups. Finally, we propose the ideal organizational culture according to business strategy and identify needed changes and actions which would help the Group achieve long-term fit between its strategy and culture.

THE GROUP'S PROFILE

The Group is the largest producer of paints and coatings[73] in South-Eastern and Central Europe. According to the most reputable American branch magazine, Coatings World (2005), it is ranked 42nd among the world's largest paints and coatings producers. Recently, the business group has expanded towards Eastern and South-Eastern Europe. Besides the headquarters in Slovenia, the Group presently consists of fourteen companies in Slovenia, Croatia, Serbia and Montenegro, the Czech Republic, Poland and Russia. Among them are companies which Helios acquired between 2001 and 2004: Chromos (2001, Croatia), Zvezda Helios (2003, Serbia and Montenegro) and Color (2004, Slovenia). These companies have increased the manufacturing capacities of the Group in the domestic market as well as abroad.

---

[72] For more on this methodology, see in Zagoršek and Štembergar, 2007, chapter in this book.
[73] The Group manufactures wide palette of products in the following manufacturing programs: synthetic resins, decorative paints and coatings, car finishing and refinishing coatings, metal coatings (corrosion-resistant coatings), wood coatings, powder coatings and materials for horizontal road signalization.

In 2004 there were 1,748 employees employed in the Group, of which 478 were employed outside Slovenia. They created USD 208.8 million of turnover and achieved net income of USD 17.49 million. The total market capitalization of the company was approximately USD 263 million at the end of 2004, while the Group's stock was among the most frequently traded and the fastest growing in the Ljubljana Stock Exchange's free market (Helios Annual Report 2004).

The Group creates more than half of its turnover in Eastern and South-Eastern Europe (Figure 14.1). These markets are still developing and consequently incur higher business risk. The Group is willing to accept these risks since: 1) it has developed strong market knowledge through traditional presence on these markets, 2) higher risk is also compensated for with high growth opportunities,[74] and 3) especially in the markets of the former Yugoslavia the competition is less fierce.

The Group competes in a mature and highly competitive industry where low production and ecological costs play a crucial role. It encounters two types of competitors: 1) large global players that have already entered into Eastern and South-Eastern European markets, and 2) small local producers. Compared to the global players, Helios's main competitive advantage lies in strong market knowledge and higher flexibility, whereas lower potential to benefit from economies of scale and scope is a relative disadvantage. The situation is reversed when the Group is compared to local producers. In this case, Helios is able to compete on economies of scale and scope but is relatively less flexible. Therefore, Helios has a unique competitive position. It is very similar to large global players (i.e., Akzo Nobel, PPG, BASF) in terms of its portfolio and organizational structure, but smaller in size.

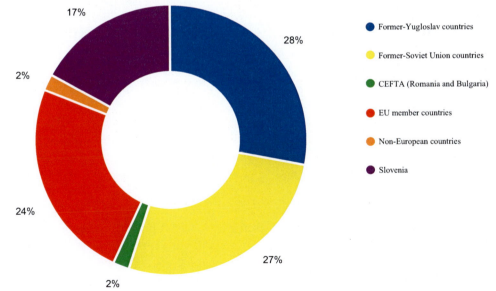

Source: Helios Group Annual Report for 2004.

Figure 14.1. Breakdown of the Helios Group's Turnover in Key Markets.

---

[74] Jotischky (2004) argues that the average consumption of paints and coatings in these regions is approximately 5 kg per capita, while in Western Europe and in the US it is above 20 kg, which indicates a large potential in these developing markets.

STRATEGIC FIT

The main strategic objective of the Group for the next five years is to become one of the ten leading manufacturers of paints and coatings in Europe. The corporate strategy that they pursue to achieve this goal can be characterized as *related diversification* (Johnson, 2004). Diversification is a strategy that takes the Group into both new markets and products, while the adjective related implies that diversification is pursued within the core capabilities of the Group. The specific features of Helios's strategy are:

- geographical and product diversification
- control of costs by economies of scale and scope
- long-term customer relationships
- imitation rather than innovation
- fast growth and creation of synergies through acquisitions

Similar to many large global paints and coatings producers the Group has become widely diversified in both product and geographical dimensions. From the perspective of product (program) diversification, the Group is horizontally and vertically integrated. The horizontal dimension of integration relates to the current and planned product portfolio in which many complementary products for painting and coating of various surface types are present. The vertical dimension of integration, on the other hand, relates to the backward and forward integration within the Group. Namely, the production of paints and coatings in Helios is backward integrated into synthetic resins production. Also, the company is forward integrated into the distribution network. Extensive diversification and backward integration in the value chain are the main factors that help the Group achieve economies of scale and scope, and in turn a better competitive position in their strategic markets.

Another feature of the corporate strategy is geographical diversification. Recently, Helios started to pursue a global strategy (Bartlett et al., 2003). In this case, the Group has been penetrating new (regionally) scattered markets by offering relatively standardized products and thus exploiting economies of scale and scope. At the same time value-adding activities have been concentrated in a very limited set of locations, mainly at the corporate center in Slovenia. The Group has started to follow this strategy after acquiring several production facilities in Slovenia, Croatia, and Serbia and Montenegro and is only in the beginning phase of product-line specialization.

Further, the Group emphasizes long-term relationships with customers and focuses on its capability to quickly apply existing technological knowledge in practice rather than search for breakthrough innovation. Long term relationships in both business-to-business (i.e. traditional business ties and networks) and business-to-consumer (i.e. well known, established brand names) markets have been crucial for the Group's current favorable position in the South-Eastern and Eastern Europe. The notion of the Group's expanding markets also implies that they cannot pursue radical innovations. Combining rapid international growth with radical innovation would excessively strain the Groups' resources and jeopardize their effectiveness. In addition, basic research in this industry incurs large fixed costs that due to their size only leading global players can afford.

The primary method for the Group's strategic development is growth through acquisitions,[75] which are focused on defending and consolidating positions in the domestic market and on developing or strengthening them in the new ones. Acquisitions in the new markets enable Helios to get hold of existing production facilities, established local brands, and local intellectual capital relatively quickly (compared with greenfield investment). Being aware of the implications of such a strategy Helios is faced with a problem of a diminishing potential targets, particularly in Central Europe (former CEFTA countries), where global players have been very active in the past. Helios therefore sees potential for acquisition activity mainly in Slovakia, Romania, and several former Soviet Union countries, especially in Russia and Ukraine.

While the company strives for achieving synergies and portfolio fit within the Group, there is also a specific rationale behind every single acquisition made. In the following subsections we discuss these dimensions of strategic fit and their implications in the case of the Group's recent acquisition in Serbia.

The Rationale for the Investment in Serbia

The Group entered the Serbian market following typical internationalization steps. It first exported paints and coatings to the Serbian market using local distribution systems, then it developed its own distribution system located near Belgrade and recently acquired a local company Zvezda (with operations in the paints and coatings industry) in Gornji Milanovac. The reason for the acquisition was further development of the Serbian market and enhancement of growth opportunities in South-Eastern European markets, while the background triggering mechanism was the Slovenian full membership in the European Union.

As a consequence of Slovenia becoming a full member of the European Union, tariffs for trading with countries of the former Yugoslavia and the former Soviet Union have increased. By owning production facilities in Serbia and Montenegro Helios has, besides advantages for doing business in the local market, become eligible to utilize trade agreements between Serbia and Montenegro and other countries in strategic markets that are far more favorable.

Further, implementation of stricter EU ecological legislation is going to prevent Helios from producing most of the solvent-based products in Slovenia. By 2007, only the production and sale of ecologically friendly, water-based paints and coatings will be allowed in the EU area. Therefore, Helios has been adjusting production lines in Slovenia and already has used water as the base in the major part of its product portfolio. However, strong demand for solvent-based paints and coatings still exists in South-Eastern and Eastern Europe. Looser ecological legislation in Serbia and Montenegro enables the Group to continue producing these products and thus service their strategic markets properly. At the same time, these discrepancies between the EU area and South-Eastern and Eastern European markets put pressure on Helios because it has to manage a wide product portfolio, which is very costly.

Finally, the acquisition of Zvezda has provided the Group with growth opportunities in the Balkans. Now that Helios's position in the former Yugoslav markets has been

---

[75] Helios also pursues market development and gathers additional knowledge through joint ventures. It cooperates in successful joint venture with a global company PPG in the auto finishing coatings program in the Russian market. Furthermore, it is considering forming new strategic alliances with its partners to penetrate the Asian markets.

strengthened, the Group can exercise their option and penetrate markets of other South-Eastern European countries (i.e. FYR Macedonia, Bulgaria, Romania, Albania). The acquired company Zvezda Helios and the distribution center near Belgrade provide the Group with production, logistic, research, training and customer support capabilities which can be seen as a springboard to new markets in this geographical area.

Portfolio Fit between the Parent Company and Zvezda Helios

A very important aspect of strategic fit is also product portfolio fit within the Group. We examine the introduction of Zvezda's product portfolio into the parent company's portfolio and discuss potential (mis)fits between them before product line specialization took place (Picture 14.1).

Clearly, by acquiring Zvezda the Group gained a production line for powder coatings[76] and production facilities for paints for plastics (masterbach). In addition, the Group's synthetic resins production facilities have been promised additional synergies through providing inputs for Zvezda Helios's paints and coatings at a lower cost.[77] Thus, a relatively strong fit is evident in these segments of the portfolio.

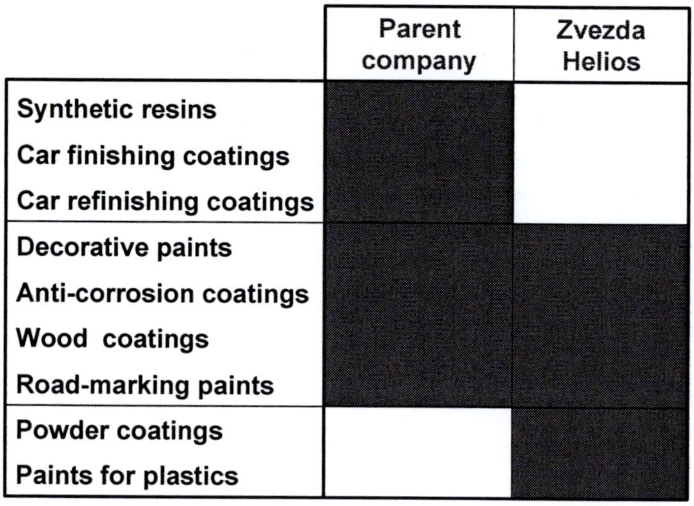

	Parent company	Zvezda Helios
Synthetic resins	■	
Car finishing coatings	■	
Car refinishing coatings	■	
Decorative paints	■	■
Anti-corrosion coatings	■	■
Wood coatings	■	■
Road-marking paints	■	■
Powder coatings		■
Paints for plastics		■

Source: Own work.

Picture 14.1. Portfolio before Specialization of Product Lines.

Alternatively, the first impression comparison of the middle section of both portfolios, as depicted in Picture 14.1, suggests a very limited fit and replication of production facilities. In road-marking paintings, for example, production specialization is not even expected, since this segment is highly price sensitive and transportation costs are an important factor when

---

[76]   A more recent acquisition of Color (Slovenia) provided the Group with a better production line for powder coatings. Although complementary, the powder coatings technology differs from the one based on synthetic resins as inputs and does not contribute to the economies of scale and scope related to the production of synthetic resins by the Group.

competing for government tenders. Currently, due to less efficient production in Zvezda Helios, applying to tenders in Serbia and Montenegro is coordinated by the corporate center to avoid double-bidding by the parent company and Zvezda Helios. In the future, the corporate center should transfer the know-how and provide inputs for competitive local production of road-marking paintings. Similarly, decorative paints, anticorrosion and wood coatings are also produced in the parent company as well as in Zvezda Helios. Yet the production line specialization potential is much greater in these segments and has to a certain extent already been performed.[78] Acknowledging that every segment in the portfolio has a water- and solvent-based dimension, the apparently weak portfolio fit becomes much stronger. When the production of solvent-based paints and coatings is moved to Zvezda Helios, the portfolio elements of the parent company and Zvezda Helios become almost completely complementary.

To sum up, the current portfolio fit between Zvezda Helios and the parent company is weak, but the potential to strengthen it through product-line specialization (i.e., moving production of solvent-based products to Zvezda Helios) is substantial.

Appropriateness of Zvezda Acquisition with Regard to Strategic Fit

In order to evaluate the appropriateness of the Zvezda acquisition, we considered both positive (synergies) and negative effects of the acquisition. In the case of Zvezda, synergies can be classified with regard to the timeframe and viability of their realization.

Several acquisition synergies, such as the effects of centralized purchasing and common distribution channels, economies due to common vertical value-chain activities (e.g. synthetic resins production) and advantages of transferring market-related knowledge and information, were enacted instantly after the acquisition. Then there are also potential synergies, such as common value-chain activities (e.g. shared research and development), transfer of know-how and the effects of product-line specialization which require more time and are contingent on consolidation and post-acquisition integration activities. While some of these have to a certain extent already been realized, the majority of their potential still awaits realization.

At the same time the Group is facing some negative aspects of the acquisition. The most obvious negative effect is overdiversification. The richness in product portfolio has reached the level where some streamlining would be beneficial. At the moment, the Group is still replicating production of some segments of the portfolio (based on the same solvent) on both locations, which is not cost-efficient. Likewise, an extensive number of the Group's products present in the former Yugoslav markets and multiple distribution channels that to a certain extent compete among each other call for a more streamlined approach. Further, production facilities in Zvezda Helios are technologically inferior to the facilities of the parent company and will require investments. This implies that the efficiency of Zvezda Helios is lower, causing the (temporary) need to replicate the lines in the parent company. As with the potential synergies, a significant part of these negative effects would disappear with product-line specialization.

---

[77] Car finishing and refinishing coatings are not produced in Zvezda Helios, thus within the Group portfolio they are complementary to Zvezda Helios's products.

[78] Some of the products in these segments are present in the same markets. The Group tries to address this issue by positioning products differently with various marketing and servicing activities.

We can argue that the Group's investment in Serbia and Montenegro contributes to achieving its strategic objectives. The acquisition strategy focusing on core business companies is appropriate. The main advantage of this strategy is faster market development, which is necessary in the paints and coatings industry in this region. Practically all global competitors have started or already have penetrated these markets and only by creating first-mover advantages can Helios achieve its ambitious strategic objectives. The second advantage of the acquisition strategy is gaining access to the local intellectual capital, which is very limited in these poorly developed markets. Creating intellectual capital from scratch requires a substantial amount of time that the Group, with respect to market circumstances, does not have.

However, first-mover advantages, quickly realizable synergistic effects and access to local intellectual capital can only contribute to the Group's temporary competitive advantage in their strategic markets. To realize all potential synergies created by the acquisition and to achieve sustainable competitive advantage the Group will have to make further actions in post-acquisition integration and consolidation. The effectiveness and efficiency of these activities will show how much added value the Group has created by acquiring the company. It is especially important that the Group continues with the production-line specialization and that it creates a unique Group corporate culture that will support it. The latter depends on the cultural fit between the parent and acquired company, which we discuss in more detail in the next section.

CULTURAL FIT AMONG HELIOS, COLOR AND ZVEZDA HELIOS

Research and practice of acquisitions in the past few decades show that cultural fit is an important element of achieving the synergies and expected results through acquisitions, even more so in international acquisitions. Appelbaum et al. (2000), for example, claim that confrontation with a new culture and a possible mismatch of organizational cultures of involved companies are possible reasons for the failure of an acquisition. However, like many other companies engaging in mergers and acquisitions, Helios did not explicitly take into consideration the question of organizational culture. The reason for this might be knowing the market and culture of the former Yugoslav republics and therefore no cultural shocks were anticipated when entering these markets. Since the number of companies within the Group is increasing, the importance of organizational as well as cultural fit is increasing. That is why Helios has decided to take part in the project of research of organizational culture in its three companies: the parent company Helios, which is the acquiring company, Zvezda (acquired in 2003) and Color (acquired in 2004).

The first important overall observation is that the Group has not yet systematically dealt with the issue of organizational culture. The company has never formally defined company values, which is why they are not included as guidelines on the strategic documents and internal publications. However, the focus group participants were somewhat cohesive in describing the basic values of the Group. The ones that were mentioned most often were self-initiative, flexibility, readiness to take risk, efficiency, quality and team work. In addition, knowledge and its effective usage in practice have been mentioned as another important feature of Helios's overall values. Other explicit values are good working habits, positive personal characteristics, employee productivity and identification with the company. The last value is particularly obvious in Helios where employees have developed higher levels of identification with the company compared to Color and Zvezda Helios. At the same time the conversation within the focus group showed that some desired values are relatively underrepresented. Employees are insufficiently aware of what to expect from the future when competition will be more severe. In some environments, especially in Color, there is a lack of self-initiative. As a participant in a focus group explained, employees in Color are "… not aggressive enough, especially in the field of marketing." Moreover, other participant said that employees in Color are not prepared enough to seek better results. The same goes for flexibility which is in Helios expressed as a value to accomplish a task, no matter what the circumstances. Most often the employees in Helios do this by accommodating work time and working behavior. However, according to opinions of the participants of the first focus group, employees in Color are less flexible and are not prepared to work more than what is just enough.

It is evident that activities of disseminating the desired organizational culture to all of the employees are somewhat unclear. The Group did not give any major formal attention to the organizational culture of the acquired companies and to the issue of compatibilities of various organizational cultures. The emerging question is: what is an organizational strength within the Group? Our analysis suggests that there is a rather strong organizational culture in Helios, which is expected, considering that this is the mother company and, according to the focus group participants, where the company's values are the clearest. In Color and Zvezda Helios there is a higher degree of agreement among employees about what is desired organizational culture in the near future compared to the current one. We can conclude that present organizational culture in these two companies cannot be labeled as "very strong".

To better understand the findings of the comparative analysis based on THT questionnaires, we prepared a graphical presentation where the position of every figure in the graph shows the presence of each cultural profile or the importance of its dimensions. The more a certain figure is distant from the origin, the more important this cultural type is. As it can be seen from Picture 14.2, the Family type of organizational culture is most strongly present in all three companies. This type of organizational culture is oriented towards people, but is on the other hand very hierarchical - power in the company is more or less concentrated in one center where all important decisions are made. The second most strongly manifested type is the Guided Missile, which is characterized by orientation towards tasks and goals, successful problem solving and decentralized operations. However, here we can observe significant differences. This type is significantly less important in Color as it is in the other two companies. In Color it has a lower value than the second most important profile, i.e. the Eiffel Tower, which is also task-oriented but is very hierarchical, which is an indicator of authoritative leadership in the company and desire for order and accuracy. The last type, the Incubator, which is characterized by orientation towards people and equality of workers and promotes team work, constant learning and the flexibility of employees, is less expressed in all three companies. It is significantly less expressed in Color than in Zvezda Helios. These findings were confirmed by the members of the focus group. All of them recognized Color as the most hierarchical company, where formalism is most explicit.

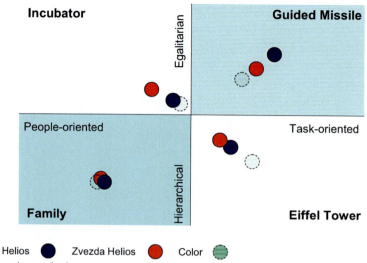

Source: Questionnaire analysis.

Picture 14.2. Current Organizational Culture Profiles in the Group.

The comparison of organizational culture profiles of Helios and Zvezda Helios revealed that they are similar. This similarity can be explained by similar positions on the market - in the recent history both companies were successful on their own market. It is also a consequence of the cultural transfer that followed the merger. The fact is that a very important member of Zvezda Helios's management team is a member of the parent company. Color has had a different fortune in the last few years. It has been faced with poor business results, frequent changes of owners and top management and uncertainty about the company's future. This type of a situation, where employees have difficulties identifying themselves with the company and are not prepared to accept new tasks, calls for a more autocratic leadership style.

The dimensions of personal culture of employees are also important for understanding the organizational culture. They are shown in Table 14.1. In general, we can see that in all three companies there is a relatively high level of adherence to the standardized rules (universalism). Individualism is also relatively highly expressed, whereas levels of intertwinement of business and personal relationships and acceptability of expressing emotions are low, which means that business and personal relationships are largely separated (specific culture) and emotions in business are kept under control (neutral culture).

The only significant difference between companies concerns status and power. In Helios and Color the power of employees is based on competency and achievement, while in Zvezda Helios a formal position and status related to that position are still prevalent. Although time is structured sequentially in all three companies, meaning that employees perceive time as a sequence of events and employees are mainly oriented towards future and present, we can also observe that in Zvezda Helios the past is more emphasized than in the other two companies. This is easier to understand if we know that Zvezda was very successful in the past and employees like to remember those times.

We may conclude that overall there are no differences between Helios and Color in the personal dimensions of the culture but Zvezda Helios differs from them on two dimensions, which surely reflects differences in national culture. The analysis shows that power in the

Serbian culture is significantly more based on status and not so much on the achievements compared to the Slovenian national culture. Orientation towards past is also more emphasized in the Serbian culture.

Table 14.1. Profiles and Dimensions of Personal Culture According to the THT Questionnaire for Helios, Color and Zvezda Helios

Dimensions	Helios	Color	Zvezda Helios
Universalism vs. Particularism	58/42	59/41	57/43
Individualism vs. Communitarianism	60/40	58/42	58/42
Neutral vs. Emotional	61/39	58/42	60/40
Specific vs. Diffuse	52/48	54/46	54/46
Achievement vs. Ascription	55/45	54/46	44/56
Time orientation - past	26	26	29
Time orientation - present	37	37	36
Time orientation - future	37	37	35
Attitude to external environment	48/52	53/47	51/49

Source: Questionnaire analysis.

Values and Organizational Culture Fitting the Group's Strategy

For each of the dimensions of corporate strategy that were explained before, we have tried to define ideal values that would represent the foundation of the ideal organizational culture types. The core of the Group's business strategy is the achievement of geographical and program diversification, therefore the most appropriate values would be knowledge, flexibility and mobility. They would facilitate fast reaction in the constantly changing business environment and according to market needs, cooperation and teamwork, exchange of experience and transfer of knowledge among employees in the companies in the Group. Furthermore, this would reduce the time interval between innovation and imitation and would neutralize risk exposure related to the implementation of new products and penetration into new markets. Sustainable synergies and cost cutting values such as efficiency, goal achievement and orientation towards future are important for achieving fast growth. These values would facilitate self-initiative, speed and quality in the process of task accomplishment, search for constant improvement, development and progress of all employees and the company's operations. Finally, to support the strategy of establishing long-term, continuing customer relationship, the value orientation towards customer should be emphasized. The empowerment of employees would be necessary for its establishment, because this will give them more responsibilities in activities relating to customers. The description of a typical employee in a company with all the above mentioned values would be: "The right person at the right place at the right time", which was already described as an ideal state by a member from the first focus group.

Based on these proposed values we can suggest the most appropriate organizational culture types according to Trompenaars Hampden-Turner typology. Although they propose the before mentioned four types of organizational culture (the Guided Missile, the Incubator, the Family and the Eiffel Tower), in practice all four types are interrelated but one of them usually dominates (Trompenaars and Woolliams, 2004). In this context also the ideal organizational culture of the Group might not be a single cultural profile but should be a combination of at least two cultural profiles with different intensities. The Guided Missile type, emphasizing task orientation and equality, should be the dominating cultural profile, while the combination with the Incubator would add the people orientation dimension. With these two cultural profiles all the ideal values such as knowledge, flexibility, mobility, efficiency, orientation towards future and orientation towards customer would be represented. A significant problem of establishing these values can be related to a high presence and influence of the hierarchy dimension represented by the other two cultural profiles.

FIT BETWEEN CORPORATE STRATEGY AND ORGANIZATIONAL CULTURE

Many researchers that study organizational culture (for example Schein, 1992; Cameron and Quinn, 1999) suggest that the true power of organizational culture in enhancing company performance is found when the fit between business strategy and organizational culture is achieved. Following this rationale, we first tried to define the ideal organizational culture reflecting the Group's corporate strategy and then analyzed how the current organizational culture matches the ideal types and also if the desired changes of organizational culture depicted from the THT questionnaire analysis are in line with the ideal types of organizational culture.

Strategy and Current Organizational Culture Fit within the Group

Current organizational culture in the Group consists of all four types of organizational culture (Picture 14.3). The most distinctive current organizational cultural types are the Family and the Guided Missile, whereas the Eiffel Tower and the Incubator are not emphasized. The existence of all cultural types makes sense but the problem is their unsuitable intensities that reduce the fit between the business strategy and organizational culture of the company. What is even more important is that the existence of hierarchy present in the Family and Eiffel Tower types reduces the fit between strategy and the current organizational culture. Moreover, the Family type of organizational culture can also deter the business strategy of the Group to become a global player. Namely, with tight interaction of employees around the centralized power the two-way flow of information between subordinates, superiors and each business unit weakens. This could consequently deter the realization of ideas and the self initiative of employees could fade away.

The second most distinctive existing cultural type, the Guided Missile, contributes to the Group's business strategy because task orientation supports achieving good business results through growth, synergies and cost reduction. This part of the business strategy is also supported by management by objectives and the company's vision. The Guided Missile is just the opposite of the Family, affecting the hierarchy-egalitarianism dimension. We can conclude that equality in the Group is present but is not at the level necessary for effective and successful implementation of the business strategy.

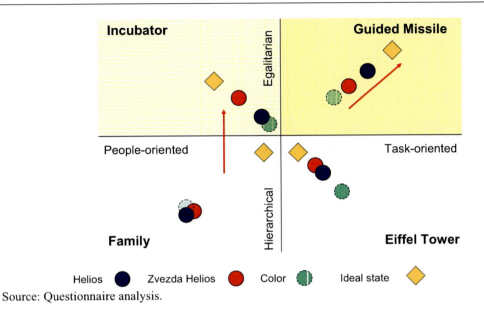

Source: Questionnaire analysis.

Picture 14.3. Comparison of Current and Ideal Types of Organizational Culture.

In order to improve the fit with business strategy we would thus need the intensification of the cultural type Guided Missile and the transformation of the Family type into Incubator.

Strategy and Desired Organizational Culture Fit within the Group

If we now focus our attention on examining the fit between the ideal and desired organizational culture, we find out that the most distinctive desired organizational culture types in all companies inside the Group are the Guided Missile and the Incubator, whereas the Family and the Eiffel Tower do not stand out as desired types (Picture 14.4). The existence of both most desired cultural types is otherwise in line with the business strategy, but not at the level of intensity that the results show. The intensity of the Incubator is too strong, since one of its characteristics, i.e. no need for a leader, in no way fits the strategy of expanding to the foreign markets and achieving growth and synergies through acquisitions, where leadership is very important and leaders have to be involved in all activities. Another Incubator characteristic that does not fit with the strategy of the Group is emphasizing an organization whose only purpose is to serve the needs of its members. However, the Group is an organization which values customers and long-term and continuous relationships. Therefore, it would be necessary to achieve a fit with the business strategy to correctly balance both cultural profiles, which would mean stipulating greater importance to the Guided Missile than the Incubator.

Based on our analysis we can say that the gap between the ideal and the current organizational culture is larger than between the ideal and the desired organizational culture. The gap between the ideal and the current organizational culture is the largest in Color, whereas the gap in Helios and Zvezda Helios is smaller and of approximately equal size in both companies. The gap between the ideal and the desired organizational culture is the smallest in Zvezda Helios, where the mentioned cultural profiles practically fit, whereas the gap in Helios and Color is a bit larger and approximately equally sized in both companies. However, the biggest problem is the unsuitable intensity of desired cultural types – the Incubator is overemphasized while the Guided Missile is underemphasized.

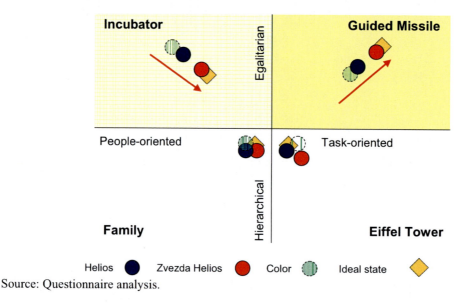

Source: Questionnaire analysis.

Picture 14.4. Comparison of Desired and Ideal Types of Organizational Culture.

From this we can conclude that certain changes would be necessary in all three companies but especially in Color, where the gap between the current and the ideal organizational culture is the largest. The need for change is also confirmed by the employees' way of thinking, because their expressed attitudes in the THT Questionnaires have shown significant differences between the current organizational culture and the desired one. What is positive for the Group is that employees actually think in the right direction concerning changes of the organizational culture but the intensity of desired cultural profiles does not exactly match the ideal cultural profile.

ACTIONS FOR ACHIEVING LONG-TERM STRATEGIC AND CULTURAL FIT IN THE GROUP

Our analysis of strategic and organizational culture fit based on the case of Helios's acquisition of Helios Zvezda (and with regard to organizational culture also the case of the acquisition of Color) suggests that the Group should undertake some actions in order to materialize potential synergies and goals by adding value to group performance. The main propositions can be summarized in six actions (Picture 14.5). We are fully aware that the process of post-acquisition integration is a very difficult one and thus we suggest that all actions should be assessed in terms of their importance and difficulty of execution.

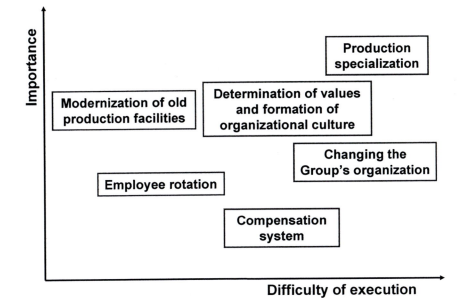

Source: Own work.

Picture 14.5. Proposed Actions for Achieving Long-Term Strategic and Cultural Fit in the Group.

Based on this rationale we propose that the Group first concentrates on the efforts to modernize old production facilities (especially at the Zvezda Helios location) in order to increase levels of productivity as well as the quality of products. Through implementing new technologies it would also be possible to gradually change organizational culture (Johnson et al., 2004). New ways of dealing with technologies can cause new perceptions, values and basic norms to form. In the second focus group it was stressed that in the Group so far there has been no major transfer of technologies or technical standards. Every company in the Group has its own standards and introducing common standards is not needed, according to the statements of the focus group participants. According to one participant of the focus group, the transfer of technology only happens when it is decided at the Group level that "some products will either partly or completely be produced in Color or in any other company." For the Group this is a technology or a technical standards project for a specific product and not a project of transferring technical standards for the purpose of unifying production processes. We think that transfer of organizational culture can be dealt also through a transfer of technology and technical standards. We believe that it would be wise to reconsider a possibility of unifying the production processes in the Group in the long run.

Another group of activities which is not so difficult to implement pertains to employee rotation or, even broader, to staffing changes in general. Bringing in new employees presents one of the most influential ways of introducing new points of view, convictions and ways of behaving in an organization. This is especially true when they are introduced through management. On the other side, the departure of individuals who do not agree with new ways and means of working also leads to the key elements of influencing organizational changes (Mesner Andolšek, 1995). In the second focus group it was explicitly said that organizational culture was transferred from the mother company to other companies through executive managers in an informal manner. Afterwards other employees took their part in transferring organizational culture, especially employees who had more contact with the acquired companies. These employees were technology experts, industrial plant managers and other employees constantly in contact with production. We believe that as an important action the policy of employee rotation within the Group's companies for a certain time would not only increase the transfer of organizational culture but would also increase familiarity among employees of the companies. By doing this the intellectual capital of the Group would also be increased. In the long run, making the desired modifications to the organizational culture would be possible only by clearly defining the values of the Group and transmitting them into the working habits of the employees. In this way we would increase the strength of the organizational culture and bring it closer to the ideal organizational culture that supports the strategy of the whole Group. The determination of basic values should be an essential task of management, who would then be responsible for spreading these values to all employees (Shearer et al., 2001). Management should be an example of how to spread the basic values and should assure that these values actually come true by means that are thoroughly explained later. In this way a common organizational culture would gradually form and would at the same time be in line with the business strategy as well as be adequately strong in order to successfully achieve business goals.

In the second focus group it was expressed that so far there has been no major systematic change to organizational culture. According to a participant of a focus group "...all procedures and formal transmission of organizational culture would be a total loss of time." Because of an obvious misfit between the existing organizational culture and the company's strategy and for the sake of superseding the informal transmission of organizational culture, we believe that the Group should seek direct and formal transmission of organizational culture as well (this should be the first step).

Although compensation systems are a rather sensitive issue in transitional economies and many companies are reluctant to implement substantial changes, they enable an effective translation of business strategies, goals and values of the company into employee behavior if suitable measure and forms of rewarding are included in the system (Zupan, 2001). Management can thus use a reward system as a tool for letting employees know what behavior is important from the business strategy's perspective. It also shows what values and beliefs are upheld in the organization. As such, the compensation system can also be a tool to unify organizational culture in the whole Group. According to the statements of participants in the second focus group, Helios intends to introduce a reward system that will emphasize rewards for acquiring desired goals. A similar system has so far been introduced in Zvezda Helios. The system would be modified before being accepted by all companies. The biggest modification would be rewarding according to the achievement of long-term goals.

Changing the group organization can also be an effective device for transmission of organizational culture (Cameron et al., 1999). Reorganization of human resource management function in the way which would establish only one central Human Resource Department responsible for strategically managing people in the whole Group could be justified through achieving synergies and sharing of best practices within the group. An extreme version of reorganization of the human resource function and also other activities with the intention of effectively transferring organizational culture would be a restructuring of the Group in a one single entity corporation. From the point of view of introducing a unified organizational culture this would be a plausible solution. However, from the business point of view, such a solution would certainly be difficult to accomplish (long and expensive legal procedures, managers dealing with a merger and not with the core business of the company). Moreover, restructuring is more or less a one way ticket because it would be impossible to return to the previous state if circumstances required that. However, at least partial restructuring could be an important and powerful instrument of transmitting organizational culture to the acquired companies.

The final set of activities pertains to the purely business issue of managing the Group's product portfolio. Current acquisitions have brought some less then optimal solutions for the whole group and some problems with a too diverse portfolio are emerging. In the future one of the most important but also most difficult actions would be product specialization in a way that a company within the Group with the best capabilities would be the producer of a certain line of products so that both synergies and optimal use of resources would be attained.

Of course, no matter which actions will be undertaken in the Group, special attention needs to be given to direct interaction with employees in terms of communication, training and participation, because the success of all changes depends on the willingness of people to implement them (Shraeder and Self, 2003) Communication among employees should increase the support for proposed changes and the flow of information and control over it should improve. Group problem solving is one of the best means for forming common convictions and points of views. According to the statements of the second focus group, the Group is already executing the transfer of organizational culture via organized meetings where formal discussions end up with various informal activities (sports and the like). Some organizational units, such as sales, have introduced several meetings on a yearly basis which deal with specific issues. Conferences for production programs are organized as well. It would be wise to further develop group cooperation for employees to feel more connected, which would consequently lead to a better flow of information and to a reduced power of hierarchy. Also, formal ways of communication should be devised and constantly evaluated for their effectiveness. When introducing any kind of organizational change it is very important that employees are constantly trained and thus capable to deal with new situations. This is especially true for members of management teams, who usually have to act as change agents. However, for changes to be effective, the appropriate amount of training should be extended to all employees at all levels.

CONCLUSION

We may conclude that overall the investment of Helios in Serbia has so far yielded positive results and has more or less materialized the possible synergies. The Group has strengthened its position in the Serbian market and also created a good base for further expansion in the region. However, as we have mentioned, for long term effectiveness some actions would be necessary in order to eliminate possible inefficiencies (old production lines and too much diversification in the product portfolio). Also, our analysis has shown that for the long term success some changes in organizational culture would be needed as well. Organizational culture is an important factor that influences the success of an acquisition and should therefore be treated adequately – appropriate analysis of existing organizational culture is thus needed as well as the implementation of activities to achieve fit between corporate strategy and organizational culture. After performing the analysis we claim that values supporting the strategy of the Group are as follows: knowledge, flexibility, mobility, effectiveness, achieving goals, future and customer orientation. These values are the most present in the following dimensions of organizational culture: employees' orientation toward achieving goals, equality among employees and orientation toward people. In this context, the Guided Missile type and, to some extent, the Incubator type of organizational culture would be most aligned with the Group's strategy. Present organizational culture in the Group with the Family as the most emphasized type therefore does not fit its business strategy. Desired organizational culture, as expressed by employees in THT questionnaires, in which elements of the Incubator should be prevalent, is closer to the ideal organizational culture. This shows their progress towards future-oriented thinking as well as possible major dissatisfaction with the Family type of organizational culture, which is opposite to the Incubator. On the other hand, the heavily stressed Incubator even exceeds the demands of current business strategy and would only make sense if the Group included in their own strategy a switch from imitator to innovator. Employees' wishes could give a signal to reconsider a partial change of business strategy in the Group. In general, it is wise to change organizational culture towards the alignment with the chosen business strategy while on the other hand it is necessary to develop a new business strategy, which considers present and desired organizational culture (Trompenaars and Woolliams, 2004).

We believe that because of some identified differences between the present, the desired and the ideal organizational culture in the Group, some changes should be introduced. Bringing these changes to life will presumably be more difficult and will take more time at points where the present organizational culture is stronger, easier and less time consuming at points where it is weaker. We can assume that bringing changes in organizational culture to life in the Helios mother company, where the organizational culture is powerful, will be more difficult and more time consuming compared to Color where the organizational culture is weaker. Nevertheless, the complexity of solutions in Color is also the largest because most changes are needed in that company. It would be wise in any case to formally define the elements of organizational culture that would support the business strategy of the Group. The role of management here is crucial because the management is responsible for implementing the defined organizational culture.

The case of the Helios Group and the so far accomplished acquisitions of companies show that in Slovenian companies as well as elsewhere the field of organizational culture receives too little attention. Here are the hidden reserves that could contribute toward faster implementation of business strategy. From this case we can conclude that powerful organizational culture can be developed despite the fact that no systematic approach toward this issue exists in the company. The question arises whether in this case organizational culture develops in the direction that is best for the successful performance of the company's business strategy and its long lasting effectiveness. Although it would be almost certainly impossible to find a company with no gap between the present, desired and ideal organizational culture, we can nevertheless assume that with systematic introduction of changes this gap could be reduced. For this to happen we first need an analytical foundation with which we can investigate the organizational culture in the mother company and in the acquired companies and learn about their characteristics and gaps between the various states that suggest the needed changes. It may be interesting to stress the fact that in the case of the Helios Group, it was shown that gaps in organizational cultures are even bigger between the two companies in Slovenia compared to Zvezda Helios in Serbia and Montenegro. Although the impact of organizational culture on the success of acquisition is believed to be greater in international undertakings due to differences in national cultures, we can learn from this very case that organizational culture can be an obstacle also in acquisitions in the domestic environment and should for this reason not be neglected.

REFERENCES

Appelbaum, H. S., Gandell, J., Yortis, H., Proper, S., and Jobin, F. 2000. "Anatomy of Merger: Behavior of Organizational Factors and Processes throughout the Pre-During-Post-Stages (Part 1)." *Management Decision* 38 (9): 649−661.

Bartlett, C. A., Ghoshal, S., and Birkinshaw, J. 2003. "Transnational Management." New York: McGraw Hill.

Buono, A. F., and Bowditch, J. L. 1989. *"The Human Side of Mergers and Acquisitions: Managing Collisions Between People, Cultures, and Organizations."* San Francisco: Jossey-Bass.

Cameron, K.S., and Quinn, R. E. 1999. *"Diagnosing and Changing Organizational Culture, Based on the Competing Values Framework."* California: Addison−Wesley Publishing.

Data on European paints and coatings industry, 2005. [URL: http://coatingsworld.com]

Data on paints and coatings industry, 2005. [URL: http://paintandcoatings.com]

Harrel, G. D., and Kiefer, R. D. 1993. "Multinational Market Portfolio in Global Strategy Development." *International Marketing Review* 10 (1): 60−72.

Helios Accounting Reports. 2004. [URL: http://seonet.ljse.si/menu/default.asp]

Helios Group Annual Report 2004.

Helios. 2004. Publication for the 80th Anniversary.

Huang, C.T.W., and Kleiner, B.H. 2004. "New Developments Concerning Managing Mergers and Acquisitions." *Management Research News,*27/4−5: 54−62.

Johnson, G., Scholes, K., and Whittington, R. 2004. *"Exploring Corporate Strategy."* Edinburgh: Prentice Hall.

Jotischky, H. 2004. "Paint Retailing in Central and Eastern Europe: Perspectives for the Future." *Coatingsworld*, October 2001: 66−75.

Mesner Andolšek, D. 1995. *"Organizacijska kultura."* Ljubljana: Gospodarski vestnik.

Damijan, J. P. and Polanec, S. 2005. "Export vs. FDI Behavior of Slovenian Firms: Does FDI Substitute for Trade Flows?" In J. Prašnikar (ed.): *"Medium-Sized Firms and Economic Growth."* New York: Nova Science Publishers.

Schein, H. E. 1992. "Organizational Culture and Leadership." San Francisco: Jossey-Bass Publishers.

Schraeder, M., and Self, D.R. 2003. "Enhancing the Success of Mergers and Acquisitions: An Organizational Culture Perspective." *Management Decision,* 41/5: 511−522.

Shearer, C.S., Hames, D.S., and Runge, J.B. 2001: "How CEOs Influence Organizational Culture Following Acquisitions." *Leadership and Organizational Development Journal,*22/3: 105−111.

Thompson, A. A., and Strickland, A. J. 1998. *"Strategic Management: Concepts and Cases."* Tenth Edition. Boston: Irwin/McGraw-Hill.

Trompenaars F., and Woolliams, P. 2004. *"Business Across Cultures."* Oxford: Capstone Publishing Ltd.

Zagoršek, H., and Štembergar, M. 2007.: *"Culture and its Influence on Business Performance."* In this book.

Zupan N. 2001: *"Nagradite uspešne."* Ljubljana: Gospodarski vestnik.

PART V: RUSSIA: REBIRTH OF A GIANT

In: New Emerging Economies and Their Culture
Editors: J. Prašnikar, A. Cirman, pp. 231-239

ISBN: 978-1-60021-754-8

Chapter 15

RUSSIA'S FUTURE

Sergei Guriev

INTRODUCTION

In recent years Russia has demonstrated outstanding economic performance. Russia's GDP per capita has been growing at about 7% a year. In dollar terms, Russian GDP tripled since 1998. In terms of purchasing power parity, Russian GDP has reached USD 10,000 per capita.

This growth has benefited all parts of the economy and the society. Poverty and unemployment decreased by one third. Wages doubled in real terms and quadrupled in dollar terms. Mobile phone penetration went up from less than 1% in 1998 to almost 40% (and reached 100% in the city of Moscow). Internet use is up from 2% to 15%. Real estate prices doubled. Retail lending is taking off: the stock of loans to households has been doubling every year since 2000, and is expected to reach 6% of GDP in 2006. Car ownership went up by more than 10% as did the quality of the car fleet. While cheap and outdated domestic cars still dominate in Russia, the growth rate of imported cars and foreign cars assembled in Russia is astounding. For the first time in Russian history, the total value of foreign cars sold exceeded that of the domestic cars.

Russia has become a net creditor to the world with its foreign exchange reserves exceeding the sovereign debt. In 2005 alone, the Russian government paid USD 15 billion sovereign debt ahead of schedule and has still amassed almost USD 30 billion in the stabilization fund; the fund has been growing at USD 3 billion per month. Russia's foreign debt is now below 20% GDP (compared to 50% GDP in 1998). All the three major rating agencies have awarded Russian debt investment grade.

What explains this growth? Can it be sustained? What are the short-term, mid-term and long-term perspectives of the Russian economy? In order to answer these questions I first analyze the success of the first term of Putin's presidency, provide a snapshot of the present state of Russia's economy and political economy, and lay out a framework for understanding Russia's future.

RUSSIA'S PERFORMANCE IN 1999-2004

Since 1998, the Russian economy has been growing like never before. The GDP annual growth rate averaged 7% per year; coincidentally this is the rate equivalent to doubling the GDP in ten years, the task set up by Putin for his government in 2002. As discussed above, the growth benefited the rich, the poor, and the emerging middle class alike.

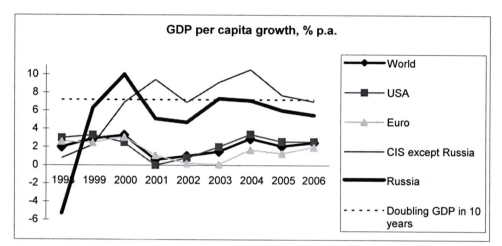

Source: IMF, World Economic Outlook, April 2005.

Figure 15.1. Growth of GDP Per Capita in Selected Countries.

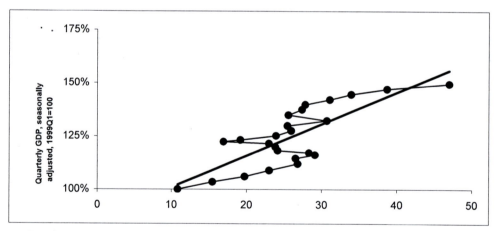

Source: Russian official statistics, US Department of Energy, 2005.

Figure 15.2. Quarterly GDP (bold line) and Oil Prices (thin line) in 1999–2004.

While there is not yet enough data for a quantitative decomposition of the growth performance into specific factors, there seems to be a consensus on the most important explanations. First, the initial conditions in 1999 were quite positive. These included unused capacity and cheap skilled labor. Second, Russia has benefited from a spectacular growth in world oil prices. Prices for natural gas and metals have also been very strong, providing

Russia with extremely fortunate terms of trade as these commodities account for the majority of Russian exports.

High resource prices contributed to growth in several ways. Huge inflow of export revenues helped stabilized government finances, strengthened the ruble, and triggered investment in the private sector. Prior to 1999, Russian firms were struggling for cash; given the underdeveloped financial system, they could not even finance their working capital. The export revenues were directed into other sectors either through the supply chain or through mergers and acquisitions and subsequent capital investment. Finally, high personal incomes earned by the rich and by the middle class working for commodities exporters created a demand for services which in turn reinforced growth in the non-tradable sector.

Third, Putin's government maintained a very sound macroeconomic policy. The government ran a substantial fiscal surplus five years in a row and used oil revenues to pay off foreign debt, much of that ahead of schedule. On top of that, the government saved USD 30 billion in the so called stabilization fund – to protect the fiscal balance from lower oil prices in the future. The Central Bank built up substantial foreign exchange reserves that are now fifth largest in the world. All of those kept real interest rates and real exchange rate of the ruble low. While the ruble has appreciated substantially since 1999, the appreciation would be much larger in the absence of Putin's macroeconomic policy and would result in a Dutch disease.

Fourth, following the turbulent 1990s, the government managed to restore political stability which further reassured foreign and domestic investors. Capital flight finally came to a halt. Overall, the stock market index increased sevenfold in dollar terms and foreign direct investment increased from negligible levels to 1.5% of GDP.

Putin has also undertaken a number of important reforms. While the impressive Gref Reform Program adopted in 2000 has not materialized in full, a few crucial elements were implemented. These included deregulation of small business, tax reform, and a Land Code that assured private property for land.

The policies have resulted in substantial adjustments at the microeconomic level. Small business has felt an easing of the burden. The regular survey of a representative survey of 2000 small businesses in 20 Russian regions conducted by the Center for Economic and Financial Research (CEFIR, www.cefir.org) has shown a substantial improvement in the regulatory environment for small businesses, even though the improvement was not as impressive as hoped by the reformers. In the regions where this improvement was especially large, small business growth was significantly higher. The regular survey of a representative sample of 1,000 medium and large industrial enterprises conducted by IET (Institute for the Economy in Transition, www.iet.ru) and CEFIR has shown that these firms have substantially improved their corporate governance and their investment has gone up.

RUSSIA IN 2005

The situation changed dramatically in 2004 following Putin's crackdown on big business (the Yukos case) and on opposition parties, free press, and civil society. The present economic trends are unfortunately somewhat different from the rosy picture above. The economy is already slowing down (even though oil prices continue to remain high), capital flight is accelerating, and all major reforms are delayed. Even the political stability is no more as the administration is facing the challenge of transferring power in the 2008 presidential elections. These developments are explained by the political economy of Putin's rule.

Box 1

Oligarchs

Russia's largest industrial tycoons or so called "oligarchs" built their conglomerates mostly in the 1990s and in the aftermath of the 1998 crisis. The World Bank's Country Economic Memorandum for Russia (2004) estimates that 22 of largest industrial groups control about 40% of Russian industry, more than all other private owners combined. After establishing full control over their assets (often through dilution and expropriation of other owners) the oligarchs started to restructure and invest in their firms. The microeconomic data show no evidence of oligarchs stripping the assets of their companies. On the contrary, there is preliminary evidence that oligarchs' companies outperformed other private- and state-owned companies in Russia in 2003 while still lagging behind the performance of foreign-owned firms. Sectors dominated by oligarchs include oil, metals, ore, pulp and paper – the very industries that were the engine of Russia's recent growth. While they possess substantial market shares in many industries, there is little reason for worries in terms of monopoly power as most of those industries are subject to global competition. What is more important is the so called "political antitrust" – a policy to prevent oligarchs from influencing policymaking.

Given underdeveloped democratic and judiciary institutions, lack of civil society, and widespread corruption, it is very hard to achieve. While Putin's government managed to purge oligarchs from federal politics, there is no chance to eliminate the institutional economies of scale: in Russian economics and politics, size still matters.

Putin's policy towards the oligarchs has been related to the popular attitude to their property rights. About 75% of Russian voters believe that oligarchs (and especially those who participated in the notorious loans-for-shares auctions of in the mid-1990s) have appropriated their assets in an illegitimate way. Hence, the president can always appeal to the median voter by repossessing the assets. This was demonstrated in the Yukos case and remains a clear and present threat to other oligarchs.

Source: Country Economic Memorandum for Russia, World Bank (2004); Guriev and Rachinsky: "The Role of Oligarchs in Russian Capitalism." Journal of Economic Perspectives, 2005.

The New Political Economy

During his first presidency, Vladimir Putin pursued consolidation of political power. Essentially, he struck a number of deals with some interest groups and crushed others. First, he offered oligarchs property rights protection in exchange for their retreat from politics. This deal was supported by the median voter's negative attitude to the oligarchs which could be used as a threat; the Yukos affair proved that this was a credible threat. Second, he offered pro-reform liberals a carte blanche for reforms in exchange for consolidation of political power in the hands of the President. Third, he effectively offered the population to reap the benefits of economic growth in exchange for political consolidation. By the end of his first term he had fully achieved his goal. The most important interest groups – oligarchs and regional governors – have lost any impact on federal politics.

Yet, it was not clear what the President was going to do with all this power. Apparently, Putin's government was to rebuild Russia as a great global player which indeed required catching up with the OECD countries in 10 to 20 years. While this was never officially acknowledged, the President seemed to follow the Chinese model of authoritarian modernization. On September 13, 2004, Putin announced a political reform that recentralized power in the hands of the federal center[79] and of the ruling party.

It turned out that the Chinese approach may not be as successful in Russia:[80] in the absence of checks and balances, opposition, independent press, and civil society, Putin's bureaucracy cannot function effectively. Since 2004 there have been a number of serious flaws in all areas: internal and external politics, security and reform.

- The government is losing the war on corruption. According to two surveys of 2,000 and 3,000 respondents conducted in 2001 and 2005, respectively, by the independent think tank INDEM (www.indem.ru), corruption has increased dramatically. While the number and frequency of bribes remained the same, the average bribe from businesspeople increased tenfold in dollar terms. It is even more important to compare the data from the BEEPS survey conducted by the World Bank in 2005 to be released in the Fall of 2005 to the BEEPS 1999 and 2002 results.

- The expropriation of Yukos has undermined the independence of the judiciary, protection of property rights and investment climate in Russia. Moreover, the climax of the case – the Yugansk auction – was carried out in a very shady way similar to the infamous loans-for-share of the 1990s. This may have long-lasting implications for protection of property rights in years to come.

- The attempt to intervene in elections in Ukraine failed despite massive resources spent to support the pro-Russia candidate. The attempt per se was undertaken by the Russian government as it was misinformed on the true preferences of Ukrainian voters.

- The attempt to reform the social benefits system failed as the reform was badly designed and executed. This resulted in mass street protests. Mindful of a Ukrainian-type revolution, the government backtracked from any additional reforms. Indeed, given the lack of checks and balances, independent press and civil society, the bureaucratic machine can neither design nor implement reforms in a way that would not antagonize large parts of the electorate. It is therefore unlikely to expect any large-scale structural reforms until 2008.

---

[79] This reform included replacement of electing regional governors with appointing them by the president, which is equivalent to making Russia a unitary rather than a federal state.

[80] One important difference between China and Russia is the stage of development: the authoritarian modernization works in moving from a rural to an industrial economy, while Russia needs to restructure an already-industrialized economy and move into a post-industrial stage. Another explanation of the difference is the ideology-driven political party in power in China and the success of economic decentralization coupled with political centralization (what Bardhan and Mookherjee call "Blanchard-Shleifer-Sonin model" in their survey of decentralization; see Bardhan, P. and D. Mookherje "Decentralization, Corruption and Government Accountability: An Overview," in S. Rose-Ackerman (ed.) *International Handbook of the Economics of Corruption,* Edward Elgar Co, 2006).

Challenges

Besides corruption which seems to be on the rise, the most important challenges Russia is facing are related to its human capital. The education system is deteriorating. According to multiple studies and international comparisons, while numbers of students are going up, the quality of education and research is decreasing. Healthcare is in an even worse shape. The Russian population is both aging and shrinking; this process is expected to continue for decades. Since the beginning of the economic transition, Russia has experienced a serious mortality crisis caused mostly by increased alcohol consumption and psychological stress (Brainerd and Cutler's paper in the Journal of Economic Perspectives, 2005). As the most dramatic increase in mortality occurred among the working age males, this has created long-term implications for the size and age structure of the population. Aging and depopulation in the Russian Federation are more serious than in most European countries. According to the World Population Data Sheet, the rate of natural increase in Russia is the world's second lowest (-0.6% after -0.8% in Ukraine). In addition, WPDS projects a population change in Russia between 2004 and 2050 at -17% (declining from 144 to 119 million), which is only slightly higher than -19% in Eastern Europe, but lower than in Russia's neighbors, Northern Europe (8%), Western Asia (60%), South Central Asia (89%). The United Nations provides an even lower estimate for population in Russia by 2050 (112 million).

While the population in Russia has been gradually falling since 1992, the decline in the working age population will be especially severe after 2007, especially in the central regions, as a long-term consequence of the birth rate behavior in the 1980s. In order to fully compensate for this drop, there should be an annual inflow of about 1 million working-age migrants, which is three times as much as the average net inflow between the 1989 and 2002 censuses. According to a demographic forecast for 2050 the share of population in the working age group (between 16 and 55 for females and 60 for males) will be close to 50%, which is considerably lower than 61% according to the 2002 Census.

The only solution to the aging population problem is an enhanced internal and external migration. Internal labor mobility is still low. Some regions lack labor and have zero unemployment rates. In others, unemployment is in double digits and rising. If the natural unemployment rate is assumed to be between 5 and 5.5%, Russia has an excess pool of 2 to 2.5 million people who could be reallocated from regions with high unemployment to those with low unemployment. However, it is unlikely to see growth in internal migration until there are developed financial and housing markets, as well as a sensible spatial development policy. These will very likely take many years to materialize.

The situation with external immigration is very different. The bureaucracy is corrupt and cannot effectively regulate migration; hence a large pool of undocumented labor migrants has emerged, estimated between four and five million people, mostly from the former Soviet Union countries. It is very likely that this pool will grow further in the coming years and Russia will have to undertake an immigration amnesty.

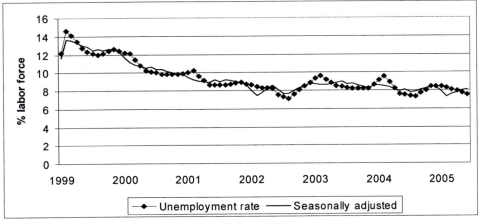

Source: Russian official statistics, author's calculations, 2005.

Figure 15.3. Unemployment in 1999–2004.

There seems to be no progress in reforming either education or health. One of the lessons from the reform of social benefits is that a corrupt and inefficient bureaucracy cannot implement any complex reforms without antagonizing voters, which the government cannot afford prior to the elections in 2008.

RUSSIA'S FUTURE(S)

The Nearest Future

In the coming two to three years, Russia's economic performance will depend on two major factors: world oil prices and the effectiveness of government bureaucracy. If the latter does not fall apart completely, the oil prices will drive economic growth in Russia. It is unlikely that oil prices will decrease to USD 25 per barrel; and if they stay above USD 30, Russia will maintain a positive fiscal balance and the Russian economy will continue to grow. The exact forecast is rather meaningless – the growth depends on the oil prices which are highly volatile. Each USD 10 per barrel change in world oil prices has a direct effect of 3% on GDP; there is also an indirect effect through the channels described above. If the oil prices remain as high as they are, Russian growth will probably stay at 5–6% per year. Russia will probably join the WTO in 2006.

The 2008 Challenge

Putin's administration is facing a very serious challenge in 2008. The Russian Constitution is quite clear on the two terms limit which requires Putin to step down in 2008. However, the ruling elite needs a loyal successor to protect the assets accumulated in the recent years. However, if the successor is weak, he/she may not be able to win an honest election and will therefore lack legitimacy, which will undermine his/her ability to protect the elite's property rights. If the successor is strong and sufficiently charismatic, he/she may initiate investigations of the present elite (even though not of Putin himself). This is fully plausible: in Russia, the president has almost no constraints on his power between elections. Also, if the next president is strong and enjoys majority support from voters, he/she will have no problem crushing vested interest – just as Putin himself demonstrated in the cases of Gusinsky, Berezovsky, and Khodorkovsky. It is possible that in this case Putin will probably be protected by his respect for the previous leader, Yeltsin, and by lawfully stepping down after two terms.

The Ukrainian and Georgian revolutions add an important dimension to this challenge: if votes are miscounted or if the spirit of the Constitution is violated, it is not unlikely to see street protests.

The government has considered a possibility of a legal solution that would allow Putin to stay in power without violating the letter of the Constitution. However, there are two problems. First, Putin would immediately lose the respect of his G8 colleagues. Second, street protests will become even more likely as the third-term president will be even less legitimate than a successor elected in a fraudulent election.

Therefore, there are very serious risks of political upheavals in Russia in 2007 and 2008. The most optimistic scenario is to find a strong successor who would then press for reforms both in the economy and in politics; hence one can hope for competitive elections in 2012.

One should however emphasize that no political upheaval can threaten foreign investment. Whatever government is in charge in Russia, it will have very little interest in isolating Russia from the West; the economic interdependencies have become too important.

The Long-Term Perspectives

The long-term outlook for the Russian economy is much less certain. On one hand, provided the comprehensive reforms are implemented, there is no reason to believe that Russia cannot grow at the rate of 6–8% per year. Indeed, the accumulated inefficiencies are so large that the TFP growth of 3% (demonstrated by the East Asian economies) seems to be well within reach. The remaining part of growth will come through investment in physical capital (the convergence effect). These rates would imply reaching 50% USD GDP per capita in 2025. Russia would probably be able to join OECD before 2015.

However, the success of the reforms is a big "if". First, in order to continue reforms, the Russian government must reform itself. Designing and implementing the reform of government bureaucracy is hard in all societies, and is even more difficult in Russia, given a very limited experience with democracy and civil society. The second crucial challenge is the education reform. Although Russia has inherited an impressive stock of human capital from the Soviet Union, it is deteriorating at an increasing rate. Without building a modern education system, Russia will soon (before 2010) lose its main comparative advantage (human capital) and will therefore become just another middle-income developing country. As such, Russia will not catch up with the OECD countries in any foreseeable future.

APPENDIX

Table A 15.1. Country Statistics and Main Indicators

Product categories	1999	2003
Population		
Population (millions)	46.3	143.4
Population growth (annual%)	-0.4	-0.4
Life expectancy (years)	66.0	65.7
Fertility rate (number of births per woman)	1.2	1.3
Infant mortality rate (per 1,000 live births)		16.0
Mortality rate under 5 years of age (per 1,000 children)		21.0
Births attended by skilled health staff (% of total births)	99.1	
Immunization, measles (% of children aged <12 months)	97.0	96.0
Prevalence of HIV (% of population aged 15–49 years)		1.1
Literacy rate, adult male (% of total males aged 15 years and above)	99.7	
Literacy rate, adult female (% of total females, aged 15 years and above)	99.4	
Primary completion rate (% of total population)		93.0
Economy		
GNI, Atlas method (current USD in billions)	258.1	374.8
GNI per capita, Atlas method (current USD)	1,760	2,610
GDP (current USD in billions)	195.9	432.9
GDP growth (annual %)	6.4	7.3
GDP deflator (yearly growth in %)	72.4	14.4
Agriculture, value added (% of GDP)	7.3	5.2
Industry, value added (% of GDP)	37.2	34.2
Services, value added (% of GDP)	55.5	60.7
Exports (% of GDP)	43.2	31.7
Imports (% of GDP)	26.2	20.8
Gross capital formation (% of GDP)	14.8	20.3
Revenue, excluding grants (% of GDP)		27.4
Cash surplus/deficit (% of GDP)		2.2
Trading and financial sector		
Trade in goods (% of GDP)	58.8	48.2
Trade in goods (% of goods GDP)	116.1	103.6
High-technology exports (% of manufactured exports)	14.9	18.9
FDI, net inflows (current USD in billions)	3.3	8.0
Present value of debt (current USD in billions)		184.2
Total debt service (% of exports of goods and services)	13.7	11.8
Short-term debt, outstanding (current USD in billions)	15.7	30.8
Aid per capita (current US$)	13.3	8.7

Source: World Development Indicators 2005.

In: New Emerging Economies and Their Culture
Editors: J. Prašnikar, A. Cirman, pp. 241-250

ISBN: 978-1-60021-754-8
© 2007 Nova Science Publishers, Inc.

Chapter 16

CROSS-CULTURAL ASPECTS OF DOING BUSINESS IN RUSSIA

Stanislav Pirogov and Svetlana Tvorogova

INTRODUCTION

Development of the global market has resulted in extensive contacts between nations. An ever increasing number of national companies operate on an international level and through work millions of people meet members of different cultures. Cultural differences among business partners impact the establishment of a business relationship and its development, negotiations, resolution of disagreements, motivation and decision making.

As business operations become increasingly global, the success largely depends on the ability of representatives of different cultures to cooperate. Cultural differences have sometimes subtle yet powerful impacts on understanding the behavior of others as well as decision making by contributing to the formation of preferences and expectations. Culture defines the set of values, on the basis of which people decide what is attractive and what is not and what is right and what is wrong. The main features of national culture and values that stem from the past tend to be rather stable and survive for centuries. Russia is an example of a country where recent social and political changes have caused greater cultural dynamics.

Studying the Russian culture of today is quite a challenge because the turbulent period of economic transition is causing numerous changes in national and consequently organizational culture as there is a close relationship between the two types of culture. It is very difficult, if not at all impossible, for companies to develop an organizational culture that differs substantially from the prevalent culture of the country companies operate in. Awareness of specifics of national culture offers a valuable opportunity for businesspeople to understand people's mindsets and the way business is done and capitalize on that knowledge.

The knowledge of cultural differences and one's own culture has a positive effect on reducing frustrations connected with complicated cross-cultural situations in the business environment since it allows the participants to be aware of hidden prejudices and stereotypes that could interfere with business communication. It helps establish good business relationships that are based on trust and mutual understanding. This allows the business partners to avoid false expectations and choose suitable business strategies.

RUSSIAN CULTURE IN THE PERIOD OF TRANSITION

The last 20 years in Russia have been marked by dramatic changes that were started by Mikhail Gorbachev's perestroika (rebuilding) in 1986 when he announced a move from a centrally planned to a market economy. At the time the government did not have a clear economic doctrine and the means to implement the transition. The process therefore lead to a destruction of internal economic structure and a decline of industries, health and education systems, which used to be on a high level during the times of the Soviet Union.

Gorbachev's program of economic, political and social restructuring directly triggered the collapse of the totalitarian state that functioned for more than 70 years. Year 1992 was the start of the period of inflation, which by the end of 1997 increased by 10,000%, changing not only the economy but also the lives of millions of people. The government granted freedom of religion, assembly, speech, the right to strike and the right to democratic elections with multiple candidates. Communist values, reinforced by the governing party for more than 70 years, were proclaimed to be of no importance and condemned. For years the situation was extremely unpredictable and almost completely unregulated.

This period distinctly marked the new generation of Russians. Those who were ten years old at the beginning of perestroika in 1986 are now in the economically most active age. Their upbringing was not influenced by the ideological pressure of the totalitarian regime but by unstable social and economic environment in the time when officially accepted social values were deeply revised.

The new type of Russian businesspeople operating in the present has not been fully studied yet but is quite different from the type of businesspeople who started their careers in the early 1990s and were brought up and educated under the communist regime, planned economy and within numerous restrictions. The process of political and economic transformation took place parallel to the changes in the value system, behavior patterns and business ethics.

Along with other countries Russia feels the effects of globalization, the effect of which dramatically increased in 1993 with the arrival of the internet. By the end of 2004 there were 147 internet users per 1,000 people, ranking Russia 44th among 59 countries (IMD World Competitiveness Yearbook, 2005). The number of internet users is increasing rapidly, but most of the users are in Moscow, St. Petersburg and other big cities. Despite rapid development the means of communication are not at the level that would completely satisfy the needs of the economy.

Internet access and other mass media have enabled the flow of information about politics, economy and culture from the part of the world that used to be on the other side of the Iron Curtain. Unlimited flow of information has introduced people to new, mainly Western, values.

One of the most striking examples of dramatic changes in Russian culture during the period of transition can be observed in the attitude toward religion. The number of believers has experienced an extraordinary increase, while their numbers are decreasing in the West

European countries. During the last years of the communist rule there were 10–15% of believers in cities and 20–25% in rural areas. Research at the beginning of 1990s stated the percentage of believers between 40–45%, while at the end of 1990s the number was already between 40–60% (Lopatkin, 2000). In the 2002 national census, 85% of adults claimed to be believers. Only 15% claimed to be atheists, while 62% were Orthodox and 6% Muslim. Other religions comprised 7%, each individual one representing less than 1%, and 14% of adults claimed to be believers but did not belong to any religion (Egorazyan, 2005).

The general data correspond to the value study that was conducted among the 1st year students at the University of Humanities in Moscow. The question "Do you believe in God?" received 62.5% of positive and 18.4% of negative answers, while 19.1% of participants could not make up their mind (Namlimanskaya, 2005). The percentage of believers seems to be quite high if we take into account that studies conducted in Moscow usually produce results that highly reflect the orientation of the West.

The fact that the percentage of believers in Russia has increased so much in a relatively short time period can be a consequence of the removal of the ideological pressure and the authorities' religious discrimination. To understand this phenomenon one has to consider the attitude of the communist regime towards religion. When assuming power the communists fought religion with exceptional violence. According to them, religion represented one of the main obstacles in establishing unlimited influence and power over people. Discrimination of the believers and the families of priests meant that members of religions did not have access to higher education and could not hold influential positions. "Scientific atheism" was a compulsory subject in undergraduate programs and was supposed to train the "ideology personnel", i.e. teachers, managers, journalists and others who were in any way related to the media, culture, education, management or politics. In this way the communists annihilated the traditional spiritual values and replaced them with the communist ideology.

The government policy changed at the end of 1980s when Gorbachev announced the freedom of religion. As soon as the pressure was removed people started to turn to traditional spiritual values. In the survey conducted in 2005 by the Russian Center for Public Opinion Studies only 1% of the participants expressed that it was difficult for them to exercise the freedom of conscience (VTSIOM, 2005).

VALUE SYSTEM AS THE BASIS OF CULTURAL DIFFERENCES

The core of culture is comprised of values that determine its main features. This area was carefully studied by Geert Hofstede (1980) who defined values as "a higher tendency to prefer certain states of affairs and things to others". An individual obtains the main values at a very early age and is usually not aware of them. Values are reflected through individuals' acts. Our own values seem to us the most rational and natural. One of the most difficult aspects of cross-cultural communication and doing business is the acceptance of different values.

Observations about the main trends in changes of work-related values in Russian national culture enable the understanding of today's Russian business culture. In this contribution we present analyses that were performed in line with Geert Hofstede's (1980; 2001) theory of dimensions of cultural differences: uncertainty avoidance, power distance, individualism/collectivism and masculinity/femininity.

In 1980 Hofstede published data for 50 countries and compared their culture on the basis of various indicators and cultural dimensions and identified differences in cultural values. Dimension scores for individual countries give us an idea to what extent these characteristics are present in a country's culture. In 1980 Russia was not included in the research since, during the Cold War, Western researchers were not allowed to conduct any social studies in the communist countries of the Eastern block.

Political changes have enabled such research and the newest data on national culture were included in the 2001 edition of the Hofstede's book. Scores were traditionally obtained on the basis of surveys and observations. Russian data sources included unpublished studies by Bollinger (1988) and Bradley (1998) as well as observations and descriptive data.

In 1995 and 1996 Naumov (1996) conducted a survey in accordance with Hofstede's theory. Most of the respondents in his study were not directly connected with the business world; they were students, teachers and scientists. Although the results might not provide the best insight into the business culture, they can give us some idea about the mentality of this level of society. Another research based on the same questionnaire and analytical method used by Naumov was conducted by Strukova and Pushnykh in 2003.

One of the reasons for such research were further changes in the social, economic and business life that took place over eight years after Naumov's analysis. The survey included the city of Tomsk and the surrounding region. All 370 respondents were employed by small and medium size business. The data therefore represent the regional and occupational specifics and the mindsets of entrepreneurs and businesspeople of the time. Table 16.1 also presents the research results obtained by Latova (2003), who in accordance with Hofstede's methodology surveyed students of humanities in Moscow.

The power *distance dimension* refers to the extent to which the less influential members of institutions and organizations within the country expect and accept that the power is distributed unequally (Hofstede, 1994) Institutions are the basic elements of society, like family, school and community; organizations are places where people work.

Table 16.1. Studies of Dimensions of Cultural Differences According to Hofstede

	Low vs. High Power Distance	Individualism vs.Collectivism	Masculinity vs. Femininity	High vs. Low Uncertainty Avoidance
Hofstede (2001)	93	39	36	95
Naumov (1996)	40	41	55	68
Latova (2003)	40	67	60	54
Strukova and Pushnykh (2004)	35	39	47	40

Hofstede's score on this dimension for Russia is very high (93). Russia has many qualities that are characteristic of high power distance countries. In the area of business organizations cultures with high power distance centralize power in the hands of few individuals. Subordinates prefer to receive orders than to make decisions and take responsibilities for their decisions. Superiors are expected to be autocratic and are entitled to certain privileges. Relationships between superiors and their subordinates are often emotional. There is a wide gap between salaries in individual companies. So far the middle class has not developed in Russia, another characteristic of large power distance cultures.

Another characteristic of high power distance countries is a one-party political system, as it existed in the Soviet Union. Almost a century ago the communists gained power by using violence. The present soft shift to democracy cannot be compared to that one in terms of violence.

In countries with high power distance the subordinates consider the ideal boss to be a benevolent autocrat or a "good father". After some experiences with "bad fathers" the employees may from the ideological point of view completely reject the superiors' authority while in practice they are willing to adjust (Hofstede, 1991). This statement can to a great extent be applied to society in the Soviet Union. In spite of carefully planned and conducted propaganda and state attempts to cultivate great respect and emotional attitude toward the communist leaders, the population rejected their authority. The reason was mainly the gap between the ideological propaganda and practice. People complied with the leaders but did, due to lack of respect for the communist authority, remain emotionally independent, even when they had to take part in demonstrations and carry huge portraits of leaders given to them by their company. Such demonstrations were organized mainly for the Russian people to witness the affinity of the population and not so much for the outside world to see. Foreigners might have been deceived by this, but the natives were not, so the communists' efforts were wasted in this respect. The lack of government's authority made it possible for democrats to take over the power during the first serious attempt.

The differences observed between Hofstede's (2001) power distance score of 93 and the scores obtained by Russian researchers – Naumov (1996) 40, Latova (2003) 40 and Strukova and Pushnykh (2004) 39 – might reflect the change in people's attitude to the studied dimension. Society in a more democratic Russia is less tolerant of inequality. This trend may not yet be noticed by an outside observer but it indicates the lowering of power distance.

Individualism vs. Collectivism: individualism refers to the degree to which the society reinforces individual and collective achievements and interpersonal relationships. It pertains to societies in which the ties between individuals are loose: everyone is expected to look after themselves and their immediate family. Collectivism is present in societies in which people are integrated into strong, cohesive in-groups from birth onwards (Hofstede, 1994).

Hofstede's score of 39 for Russia means that collectivism is present and is also reflected in the business culture. The group interests play an important role in hiring – relatives of the already employed have preference over others – which reduces risk but can lead to nepotism. People in collectivistic countries are more likely to consider themselves as members of a group and not merely individuals. That is why management in such societies is the management of groups, where incentives, praise and criticism are addressed to the group and not individuals.

The norm of an individualistic society that everybody should be treated the same (universalism) is not usually followed in a collectivistic culture, such as the Russian. The differentiation between "our group" and "other groups" is rather strong. The preferential treatment of friends (particularism) is often a part of business practice. That is why it is so important that personal relationships and trust are established before any business cooperation starts. Achievement-orientation, which is typical of businesspeople from individualistic cultures, can present an obstacle since personal relationships have preference in collectivistic societies.

Hofstede's (2001) score of 39 for individualism in Russia almost completely coincides with Naumov's (1996) 41 and is identical to Strukova and Pushnykh's (2004) score. Latova's (2003) high score of 67 suggests that the group of students of humanities from Moscow is much more individualistic. The reason might be that because of the subject of their study the students are better acquainted with the Western culture and its individualistic values. Higher average knowledge of foreign languages enables them to use foreign information sources directly. A possible explanation for a high score on individualism might also be a more individualistic orientation of the individuals who decide to study humanities. Since there is a relationship between the wealth of the country and the level of individualism, there is a possibility that together with the development of economy also the Russian society is becoming more individualistic.

Masculinity vs. Femininity: Masculinity is characteristic of societies where gender roles are clearly defined. Men have the leading role in the society and in the country. It is important to win and business takes precedence over relationships. People live to work.

Low masculinity score indicates that the differentiation and discrimination between genders are low. Both genders are treated equally in business and social life. Conflicts are more likely to be solved by compromise and relationships are more important than business.

With Hofstede's masculinity score of 36, Russia is a feminine country. Women's contribution to the social and business life of Russia is large and this is not only because they are more numerous. According to the 2002 census there are 67.7 million men and 77.6 million women in Russia. Women outnumber men in the generation older than 32 years. One of the main reasons is that life expectancy for men in Russia is 59 years while for women it is 72.5 years. Women want education more than ever before. For the first time in history the ratio of women with higher education has surpassed that of men (Table 16.2).

There are several reasons for the increase in the share of college level educated inhabitants in the transition period. Due to the economic recession a lot of people lost their jobs and women were the first and most affected by this. Therefore more and more women chose to acquire college level education. The fact caused the increased desire among females to receive higher professional education.

Unprecedented rates of inflation made it impossible for people to rely on their savings. Security could only be provided by information and knowledge that could be applied in the new social and business environment. Hundreds of private institutions of higher education appeared all over Russia.

Table 16.2. Number of People with College Level Education per 1.000 Inhabitants According to Gender

	1989	2002
Males	117	156
Females	110	163

Source: Federal State Statistics Service, 2005.

According to the data from the IMD World Competitiveness Yearbook (2005), women comprise 48.6% of the total labor force. This places Russia in the second place after Estonia and ahead of Finland, Sweden and Scotland. In 2002 women comprised 37% of total judges, workers holding senior positions and managers, ranking Russia 7th in the world. The comparison between women's and men's income ranks Russia 10th in the world. With decreasing birthrates more women are both available and needed in the workforce. As their number increases their values also become more visible.

Modesty is an important characteristic of feminine culture. Representatives of these cultures tend to take a passive role and do not try to sell themselves, as people from masculine cultures tend to do. This can be seen in the writing of CVs since in the feminine culture it is expected that the interviewer will discover the candidate's qualities. As feminine culture is in general more characterized by solidarity and mutual care, management control should be group based. Competitiveness within the group is not encouraged.

Hofstede's masculinity score for Russia is 39 (Table 16.1) and is lower than the score obtained by Russian researchers. The score for Naumov's sample of students and professors is 55, while the score for Strukova and Pushnykh's sample of businesspeople and entrepreneurs is 47. Latova arrived to the score of 60.

The number of women occupying leading positions in management increased from 12,000 in 1999 to 26,000 in 2000, while the number of men in such positions remained unchanged at 47,000.

Strukova and Pushnykh's score of 47 is higher than general Hofstede's score, which can be explained by the fact that business women experience tougher competition and are therefore more assertive and result-oriented. They strive for achievement and look for recognition, which is a masculine characteristic.

The masculinity score for students of humanities in Moscow is the highest (60). This is again due to the exposure to the American values and through individualism also masculinity. Compared to Russian managers and businesspeople the students and university professors from Naumov's sample (score 55) are also more characterized by masculinity.

Uncertainty avoidance can be defined as the extent to which the members of a certain culture feel threatened by uncertain or unknown situations (Hofstede, 1996). The level of tolerance for uncertainty and ambiguity within the society is different. Laws and rules are used in the society to prevent unstructured situations. A society with low tolerance prefers laws, rules and regulations that reduce the degree of uncertainty. In cultures with strong uncertainty avoidance the need for rules is emotionally conditioned. People feel more comfortable when situations are standardized, regulated by rules and thus more predictable. To avoid uncertainty people prefer similar leadership. In countries with low uncertainty avoidance rules are established when needed. People are more comfortable accepting the unknown and are more tolerant of deviations from norms. In the business context low uncertainty avoidance represents lower anxiety at the workplace. High uncertainty avoidance coincides with people's preparedness to work hard. Time and punctuality are very important. In countries with low uncertainty avoidance time does not play such a key role and people do not have the urge to be constantly active. Punctuality does not come naturally to the representatives of these cultures, although it can be achieved if needed. Innovations are encouraged since the fear of new ideas is smaller. Low uncertainty avoidance cultures are innovative but innovations are easier implemented in cultures with high uncertainty avoidance, since that demands persistence and punctuality.

The value of this index based on Hofstede's data is very high (95). Scores obtained by Naumov (68) and Latova (54) are lower. The value of the index of uncertainty avoidance is the lowest (40) in the most recent study conducted by Strukova and Pushnykh that included businesspeople and entrepreneurs. This means that the respondents are more independent and the uncertainty is higher. Besides, during the last 15 years the Russian business environment has changed so often and in such unpredictable ways that uncertain situations have become a norm for young Russian businesspeople and managers (Naumova and Pushnykh, 2004).

RUSSIAN BUSINESS ETIQUETTE

Business practices in Russia are also changing dramatically. Businesspeople have more opportunities to travel abroad, observe foreign customs and gain cross-cultural experience. In Russian companies the number of western-educated businesspeople is increasing. Those who get business education in Russia study Western business courses and are familiar with the Western norms. Business customs in Russia are generally similar to those in the West; however, some differences exist.

As already mentioned, third party in the role of an intermediary will be very helpful in establishing business contact in Russia because it will speed up the building of trust and good business relationships. It is important to gain access to people at the highest possible levels, as subordinates are reluctant to take risks and responsibility and prefer to follow directions. Bureaucracy is considered a big obstacle but can occasionally be circumvented. It is by no means worth using illegal approaches and putting business in danger. Establishing close personal relationships with business partners is of key importance since a subjective opinion strongly influences the decision making. It is typical of Russians that in the relationships they take into account the individual's status. Negotiations require a lot of patience since many times the "final" offers can be improved. The custom of drinking alcoholic drinks when socializing is well reflected in the Russian saying that what is on the sober man's mind is on the drunken man's tip of the tongue. A dinner with plenty of alcohol can be considered as a quick way to reveal the true nature of the business partner. Toasts and drinking at the same time with your host are typical. Drinking a full glass is not obligatory. People are not offended if you explain that you cannot drink because of your beliefs or health. Relaxed attitude and friendliness are the most important. It is advisable to arrange business meetings in advance and it is necessary to call the day before to confirm. Although Russians are considered to be rather flexible in terms of time, foreigners are generally expected to arrive on time. Russian businesspeople claim that it is absolutely inappropriate to be more than 15 minutes late, yet such occurrences are not so rare. Showing impatience if your business partner is late is considered impolite. Meetings usually take longer than expected and time after the meeting is a good opportunity for informal communication. Deadlines are not always very strictly observed so it makes sense to set early deadlines. Unsigned documents have less credibility and are usually a reason for slower decision making. Many Russian businesspeople and employees speak English. Russians differ from other nations that put large emphasis on relationships in that they are very direct when expressing their opinions.

RUSSIA AT THE CROSSROADS

In the period of transition and numerous economic, social and political difficulties many changes took place in the Russian culture. Communist values have been rejected by vast majority. After the removal of the atheistic pressure from the state, people have returned to traditional religious values and in the 2002 census 85% of the population classified themselves as believers.

Uncertainty and instability of the changing economical environment have caused a boom in higher education and motivated people to get prepared for the unpredictable changes in the business environment. The share of women with college level education is for the first time in history higher than the share of men. The role of women in Russian business and social environment continues to gain in its importance.

At the beginning of the 21st century, during the first years of president Putin's leadership, the governing elite and western oriented democrats seemed to have successfully introduced the western culture to the Russian society. Economic development was not possible without investments, managerial experience and technology from the West. Partnerships with Europe and the USA expanded rapidly and the influence of the western culture increased. The high standard of living and western values have started to attract people.

But the trend in the last years has been the opposite. Close integration has brought the acceptance of western values and transformation of the society, but the development did not continue in this direction despite economic cooperation. The idea of the peculiar Russian way of social development has become more popular among people. Surveys show (VTSIOM, 2004) that Russian citizens do not wish to integrate with the European culture. 48% of respondents identified themselves as citizens of Russia, 2% considered themselves European and 3% considered themselves to be citizens of the world. The majority of the latter are extremely successful and affluent individuals from Moscow and St. Petersburg that very likely do business at the international level.

Still one cannot say that the ones who do not wish to follow western values are in the majority, since the opposite trend is also very widespread. Final choice has not been made yet. The public opinion poll (VTSIOM, 2004) has shown that 46% of the participants wish to maintain their national identity while 40% of the participants support the political forces that are in favor of convergence with the Western civilization.

REFERENCES

Egorazian, V. 2005. "Prezident Roccii Musliman?" (The president of Russia - a Muslim?) *Ekspert.*

Egorov, B. K. 2002. "O kulturno-istoričeskih obrazah Rocii i sovremenih problemah teorii i praktiki kulturi." (On cultural and historical characteristics of Russia and modern cultural problems in theory and practice.) *Almanah Vipusk.*

Hofstede, G. 1980. "Culture's Consequences: International Differences in Work-Related Values." Beverly Hills: Sage Publications.

Hofstede, G. 1994. "Cultures and Organizations: Software of the Mind." New York: Harper Collins Publishers.

Hofstede, G. 2001. "Culture's Consequences: Comparing Behaviors, Institutions, and Organizations Across Nations." Second edition. London: Sage Publications.

IMD World Competitiveness Yearbook. 2005. Switzerland, IMD International: World Competitiveness Center. [URL: http://www.imd.ch/wcc].

Latova, N. V. 2003. "Rossiyskaya ekonomicheskaya mentalnost: kakoy ona stala v 1990-e gody I kakoy tip rabotnika sformirovalsya v resultate." [Russian economic mentality: what it became in 1990 and what type of workers was formed as the result.] Moscow: Russian Academy of Science.

Lopatkin, P. A. 2000. "Sovremenaja religiozna situacija v Rosiji: (Modern religious situation in Russia.) Sociologičeski analiz. (Sociological analysis.) Ot politiki gosudarstvenovo ateizma – k svobode covesti (From the politics of economic atheism to the freedom of consciousness.). Moscow.

Mjasojedov, C. P. 2003. "Osnovi kroskulturnovo menedžmenta kak vesti biznes s predstaviteljami drugih stran." (Basics of cross-cultural management: how to do business with foreigners.) Moscow: Delo.

Namlimanskaya, O. O. 2005. "Cenostie orientacii pervokursnikov Moskovskovo gumanitarnovo univesriteta. Znanije. Ponimanij. Umenie." (Values of orientation of 1st year students of the University of Humanities in Moscow. Science, understanding, knowledge.) Moscow: University of Humanities.

Naumov, A. N. 1996. "Hofstedovo izmerenie Rosii." (Hofstede's measurements of Russia.) *Management*, 3:70-103.

Russian Federal State Statistics Service. 2005. [URL: http://www.gks.ru].

Strukova, O. C., and Pushnykh, B. A. 2004. "Delovaja kultura po Hofstedu: Izmerenije po Hofstedu." (Working culture of Russia: measurements according to Hofstede.) *Menedžment Rosii za rubežom*: 2.

Trompenaars, F., and Woolliams, P. 2004. *"Business Across Cultures."* Chichester: Capstone Publishing Ltd.

VTSIOM. 2005. VTSIOM Predstavlyaet. *"Kak mi dumali v 2004 godu: Roccija na perepute."* (How we thought in 2004: Russia at the crossroads.) Moscow: Algoritm.

In: New Emerging Economies and Their Culture
Editors: J. Prašnikar, A. Cirman, pp. 251-267

ISBN: 978-1-60021-754-8
© 2007 Nova Science Publishers, Inc.

Chapter 17

CULTURAL FIT AS A MEANS OF STRATEGY IMPLEMENTATION: THE CASE OF TRIMO TREBNJE, D.D. AND TRIMO VSK

Metka Tekavčič, Vlado Dimovski,
Darja Peljhan and Miha Škerlavaj

INTRODUCTION

In this chapter we present the case of Trimo Trebnje d.d. (hereafter Trimo), which in 2001 together with a Russian partner established a joint venture in Kovrov (approximately 250 km from Moscow), the manufacturing company, Trimo VSK. Trimo has a 51% stake in the joint venture. Trimo has built its strategy on internationalization (Dimovski et al., 2005a). For internationalization to be successful it is important that the company knows the culture of the foreign (in our case Russian) market it is entering. The national culture of whichever country a company does business in has an effect on that company's organizational culture (Bartlett et al., 2004). It is the culture that is often blamed for marketing blunders, merger failures and unsuccessful transfers of best practices (Johansson, 2004). In Russia, Trimo would like to develop an organizational culture that will be based on the same values, standards and beliefs as the culture in Trimo Trebnje and thus create a uniform organizational culture. Trimo is, however, aware that organizational cultures in both companies will not be identical due to differences in national cultures.

The purpose of our research has been to comprehensively study the organizational culture in the case of Trimo d.d. (Trebnje, Slovenia) and Trimo VSK (Kovrov, Russia). We have been primarily interested in what the prevalent profile of the organizational culture in the company is, how strong the company's culture is, what the level of homogeneity of the culture in the company is and what the cultural fit within individual departments in the companies and within the analyzed companies is. Our goal has been to find out how much organizational cultures in Trimo Trebnje and Trimo VSK differ between each other and what the desired organizational cultures of both companies are. We have further looked into what could hinder the transfer of Trimo values and practices to Trimo VSK, which practices and values should be transferred at all for the culture to support the strategy as much as possible and which tools should be used to make the transfer of Trimo's culture to Trimo VSK smooth and fast.

TRIMO: A PROFILE OF THE COMPANY

Trimo is a joint-stock company with USD 115.8 million total revenue in 2004 and USD 40,800 value added per employee. It is internationally-oriented, exporting 70% of its products, mainly in Europe and it operates in approximately forty countries. Their main products include pre-fabricated steel buildings, steel structures, façades, roofs, containers, and sound-isolating systems. Trimo's pre-fabricated steel buildings represent endless possibilities of use since they are suitable for office buildings, commercial buildings, sports facilities, warehouse facilities, industrial and other facilities (URL: http://www.trimo.si). Trimo's main product is called "complete solutions" and includes a mix of all the products and services Trimo offers (especially steel constructions, roofs and façades). Trimo provides complete solutions in the area of steel pre-fabricated buildings: from idea and draft to the finished building. Such a system offers a wide range of buildings: industrial, commercial, shopping, business, sports, cultural, as well as buildings of prestigious importance. Trimo has for many years been the leading Slovenian company for the production and assembly of pre-fabricated steel constructions and one of the most important European manufacturers of pre-fabricated buildings and living units.

According to Slovenian legislation, Trimo is a large Slovenian company with almost 500 employees. In the 2005 "Finance Top 101 Slovenian companies" (Finance, 2005) it ranked 28th among Slovenian companies in terms of performance measures and size. On the same list, it ranked 32nd in terms of sales revenues, 19th in terms of operating profit growth, 9th in terms of value added per employee, 30th in terms of return on assets (ROA), 30th in terms of return on equity (ROE), 35th in terms of EBITDA[81] to revenues share and 70th in terms of size. On the "Slovenian Biggest Exporters" list Trimo moved from the 74th place in 1996 to the 37th place in 2001 (URL: http://www.gvin.com/Lestvice). Trimo is the market leader in the area of roofs and façades from mineral wool panels in Western and Central Europe and in the area of steel constructions in Slovenia (Kranjec, 2003).

Trimo's management firmly believes that this vision can be achieved only through the involvement of all employees. The statement known as "Trimo Way" is based on clear values and teamwork with regard to customer focus and total quality management. Through extensive training and communication, Trimo has been developing and continuously improving its products and services. Strong leadership and an action-oriented management style have facilitated the whole process of change management.

The main strategic guideline has been the long-term growth of the company. The basic elements of Trimo's core business strategy are presented in Table 17.1.

With the intention to expand business, Trimo has developed a network of six representative offices, nine companies and seven agencies (URL: http://www.trimo.si). Trimo opened its first manufacturing facility abroad in Russia, Trimo VSK (Kovrov), with approximately 150 employees, and a representative office, Trimo Rus, which deals with sales

---

[81]   i.e. Earnings before Interest, Taxes, Depreciation and Amortization.

operations. Trimo Rus offers mostly products made in Slovenia and a small portion of products from Kovrov, while Trimo VSK sells only products produced in Russia. Production in Trimo VSK is currently limited to facades and roofs because these are products with the highest potential for growth and sales revenues on the Russian market.

Table 17.1. Elements of Trimo's Core Business Strategy

- Expanding business in foreign markets combined with a constant development of new products that would ensure long-term profits, backed up by brand-name building and patent protection.
- Using the principles of TQM to achieve company mission and goals.
- Developing human capital (i.e. employees) into a sustainable competitive advantage.
- Ensuring that all employees are aware of the company's mission, goals and organizational culture in order to participate actively in their implementation.
- Constant improving of all elements that result in customer satisfaction.

Source: Trimo, 2004b; 2005.

Trimo has developed a set of critical success factors. The most important factor deals with employees, whose knowledge, skills, creativity, and innovativeness assure a sustainable competitive advantage for Trimo. All company activities are directed towards employee satisfaction and hence continuous improvements. Trimo devotes special attention to cooperation with strategic customers and suppliers with whom they form long-term partnerships. Together with suppliers they constantly develop new materials and implement improvements.

Trimo is a pioneer on the Russian market with the competition trying to copy its innovations. Trimo's way of work demands a highly qualified workforce, and recruiting, which was not a problem in Kovrov due to the right timing of entering the region. Trimo was able to hire quality technical personnel, who remained unemployed after the closure of military programs operating in the region. Russian employees adapt fast and the quality of their technical educational system is on a high level. More attention needs to be directed towards their independence.

Trimoterm panels have a competitive advantage in terms of quality and flexibility. At the moment their main disadvantage is the lack of variety and thickness, which is necessary in certain parts of Russia in order to protect against cold weather. With a new production line, which will be established in 2006, they plan to eliminate this setback. Due to the fact that Trimo has some difficulties with the quality of materials from local Russian suppliers, it would be reasonable to consider integrating this part of the value chain or at least consider strong cooperation with local suppliers in implementing quality standards in their operations. Trimo products are internationally well known and recognized by their quality. The brand name contributes to the implementation of the niche strategy in Russia. However, in the long-term the sustainability of such an approach is questionable, due to local companies trying to follow and copy Trimo. Intellectual property rights in Russia are not protected enough, a fact that poses a great threat to Trimo.

TRIMO AND ITS ORGANIZATIONAL CULTURE

Trimo strives to be a learning organization and implements several of the elements of the FUTURE-O® learning organization model (Dimovski et al., 2005). In particular, they emphasize the value of an educated workforce and constant innovation and improvements. As a result, various projects and programs are currently in place supporting such innovation and learning-oriented culture and consequently the company strategy. The most important approaches and tools applied in Trimo are (1) Continuous Improvement Process (CIP); (2) Total Quality Management (TQM) and Cost-Value-Driver-Analysis (CVDA); (3) Total Property Care (TPC); and (4) competencies maps.

The Continuous Improvement Process (CIP) fosters creativity among employees. Employees make proposals and submit initiatives for improvements in their environment and are actively involved in the introduction of initiatives through teamwork. The main characteristics of the CIP projects are higher economic efficiency, decrease in costs and increase in quality of products as demanded by customers, greater turnover and profit, improvement of quality and safety at work, reduction of factors that may impact the environment. The implementation of CIP projects results in greater employee satisfaction and a higher level of loyalty through the empowerment and involvement of all employees.

One of Trimo's strategic goals is process improvement which is accomplished by CIP and TQM. The main difference between CIP and TQM is that CIP concentrates on improvements within departments while TQM links different departments. TQM goals are the following: stable growth, value added growth, satisfied customers, competitive and satisfied employees, development of teamwork and project work, and process improvements with the inclusion of all employees. In order to achieve these goals, Trimo has updated the current TQM with CVDA. Under CVDA value drivers and cost drivers are analyzed and classified into three groups. These groups are set according to the contribution to added value. In group A there are drivers with the highest and in group C those with the lowest added value. These groups represent a starting point for process improvements. It is important that these drivers are determined by employees and not by managers. Later on, the process improvement is facilitated through the "promoter approach". A "promoter" is a leader and a representative of a department for process improvement and an employee motivator. Their main job is formal leadership of employees towards process improvements. TQM promoters have the liaison role of facilitating vertical and horizontal communication among employees (Peljhan, 2005). The selection of promoters is based on selection rules such as: a promoter is not the leader of a department, but is a true "Trimo Employee" (Picture 18.2) and acts as a Trimo leader. The leader of all promoters is the TQM coordinator, who plans and controls the implementation of process improvements and communicates with the managing director. Implementation of each process improvement is recorded in a "key file", where the goals of process improvement, estimated savings and activities that lead to improvements are introduced. "Key files" serve as a control for process improvements realization. In order to motivate employees to cooperate in process improvements, initiators of improvements, project leaders and other project members are offered additional rewards.

The Total Property Care (TPC) program was introduced in 1996. It facilitates the involvement of all employees in implementing changes, improving efficiency, reducing bottlenecks and costs, and improving quality, safety and the company's image. TPC has been an important part of Trimo's quality strategy ever since. This is a concept based on the involvement of all employees in the process of building organizational excellence through the development of cultural and technological relations, improvement of care for equipment and its maintenance, cost reduction, improvement of quality, working conditions, safety, and company reputation (Tekavčič and Peljhan, 2004). Each of Trimo's tangible assets, be it an office, equipment or inventory, is assigned to an employee whose responsibility is that it is kept in best possible condition. These employees carry out regular inspections of their assigned property and are required to write regular reports. Their work is inspected on a monthly basis and reported to top management. The delegation of responsibility for company property is a form of employee empowerment and aims at achieving higher quality of the working process and final products, and at enhancing employee loyalty (Trimo, 2004a).

Trimo has recently focused intensively on systems for knowledge management according to learning organization philosophy. Knowledge management is primarily seen as a way of taking advantage of the scale and scope of the accumulated experience generated within the company. Another key aspect is to diminish the importance of the individual and of personal experience. The idea is that ideas and experiences that developed in one project can be recycled and reused with minimal adaptation in other projects. The premise is that experience can be codified and rationalized in a way that suits database storage and retrieval. Here, the most important approach is building "competencies maps". We would like to emphasize that Trimo is also innovative in this respect as many companies build knowledge maps, whereas Trimo focuses on all competencies, taking into account that knowledge is only one part of competence. Knowledge is necessary, but not sufficient, especially when working in Trimo's organizational culture of innovative and task-oriented approach to performance management (Peljhan, 2005).

A clear company mission and business strategy along with extensive R&D efforts have become a basis for Trimo's success. Trimo's management believes that in order to achieve this, the company's mission and business strategies have to be communicated to every employee in advance to set an appropriate basis for understanding why the changes are important. In Trimo, top management uses special questionnaires to check the understanding of the mission, vision, values and the whole organizational culture among employees. The results for 2002 show that 98% of employees know the essential company values (Trimo, 2005a).

In order for a new business philosophy and related practices to be embedded into the decisions and actions of every employee, the philosophy of Trimo's management was written down in "Trimo Standards", comprising the basic principles all employees are expected to follow. Trimo Standards[82] are as follows (Trimo, 2002a):

- Our customers are the focus of our attention.
- We deliver total quality.
- Our resources management is efficient and effective.
- We continually improve working processes.
- We take care of our personal development and education.
- We take responsibility.

---

[82] Here we present the company-wide standards. Nevertheless, we have to emphasize that these standards are further elaborated for each sector in the company.

- We communicate with dignity.
- We are highly motivated.
- We keep company secrets.
- We measure the results of our work.

These standards are communicated continually to all employees in annual workshops and are also an important part of the training programs for newly hired employees. Standards are underpinned by four sets of core Trimo values (Picture 17.1).

PEOPLE: Employees are the key strength of Trimo . Company's power depends on the management and all employees. Values are teamwork , goal orientation , creativeness, innovativeness and individual talents .

CUSTOMERS: Enthusiastic and satisfied customer is measure of our success . We develop and improve original and complete product and service solutions for our customers .

VALUE ADDED: Profit and value added growth and cash flow available enable quicker company development .

ENVIRONMENT: We take care of well-organized factory and are friendly to our environment . All employees ' health is the value accomplished by the healthy way of living .

Source: Trimo, 2002.

Picture 17. 1. Trimo's Core Values.

In Trimo, core values are outlined for the company as a whole as well as for the individual employee in the form of a description of a "Trimo Employee" as a value-driven code of business conduct (Picture 17.2). In Trimo, every employee is expected to know the mission, vision, basic goals and organizational culture of the company and has to help implement them. According to Trimo Standards, only the people that are responsible, loyal to the company, display self-initiative and creativity, will be able to carry out the business strategy. The latter is also the framework that determines the "Trimo Employee". It is not necessary for employees to know the elements of a "Trimo Employee" by heart, but they have to work and live in accordance with them.

Organizational culture in Trimo (Picture 17.3) presents a very interesting mix of task-oriented performance driven culture and an innovative culture. This is a real demonstration of tension between control and flexibility in corporate values. There is a very strong focus in Trimo on outputs and on delivering assignments on time. This focus on the task is typically viewed as a strength since it contributes to make Trimo recognizable as a reliable and trustworthy business partner that delivers what it promised. The company is well known for its capacity to deliver on time. This is an outcome of the amount of resources in the company making it possible to put in extra people if needed, but what is perhaps even more important is a broadly shared mentality around the significance of delivery on time. The company has a strong "delivery culture". At the same time, much appreciated values are creativeness, innovativeness, and capabilities development. Trimo facilitates these values by programs like CIP and key files. This mix of task-/performance-oriented innovation culture works because of Trimo managers' leadership style facilitates employees' belief in Trimo's values.

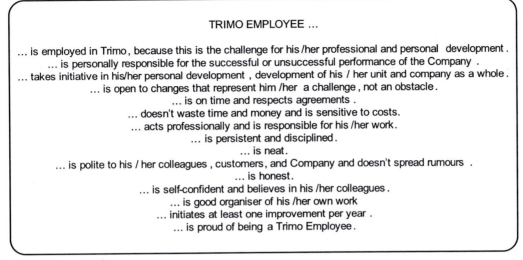

TRIMO EMPLOYEE ...

... is employed in Trimo, because this is the challenge for his /her professional and personal development.
... is personally responsible for the successful or unsuccessful performance of the Company .
... takes initiative in his/her personal development , development of his / her unit and company as a whole.
... is open to changes that represent him /her a challenge , not an obstacle.
... is on time and respects agreements .
... doesn't waste time and money and is sensitive to costs.
... acts professionally and is responsible for his /her work.
... is persistent and disciplined.
... is neat.
... is polite to his / her colleagues , customers, and Company and doesn't spread rumours .
... is honest.
... is self-confident and believes in his /her colleagues .
... is good organiser of his /her own work
... initiates at least one improvement per year .
... is proud of being a Trimo Employee.

Source: Trimo, 2002.

Picture 17 2. Trimo Employee.

Managers and other employees in Trimo strive to establish the culture of cooperation to balance the interests of all stakeholders : customers, employees , shareholders , and environment .

Every employee takes care of excellent performance as we want to be known after our quality and professionalism in all areas of our business .

We want to be the first choice of our customers . We do business according to high ethical standards . We keep our promises .

We all take part in continuous improvement process (CPI) to enable the long -term growth of the company .

We foster changes in all aspects of our business .

We foster and support talents who are capable of innovations .

Source: Trimo, 2002.

Picture 17. 3. Trimo's Core Values.

Trimo's organizational culture was developed to support the company's strategy on the long term growth of the company because it encourages creativity, which is necessary for the company's growth. It is based on a set of values and standards (Pictures 17.1, 17.2 and 17.3) and centered around employees, who are expected to contribute to the implementation of the company's strategy and consequently its success. For its success Trimo needs an educated, active, innovative and stimulated workforce. Trimo sees itself as a learning organization and is constantly working at improving the education and skill levels of its employees. In 2004 it provided each employee with fifty hours of training on average. They also have several procedures in place (e.g. TQM, CIP, Trimo dialogues, competencies maps), which are used to encourage employees to actively participate in the process of continuous improvements. Both a compensation and a promotion system that actively support continuous learning and employees' active involvement have been developed. Trimo has also developed a 360-degree evaluation for its management, called Trimo Leader, with which they measure and improve the quality of management. The evaluation consists of self-evaluation and evaluation provided by the supervisors and the subordinates. It is intended to evaluate managers according to their goal-orientation, strategic acting, motivation, communication and organization (Briški, 2005).

METHODOLOGY

The purpose of our research has been to comprehensively study the organizational culture in the case of Trimo d.d. (Trebnje, Slovenia) and Trimo VSK (Kovrov, Russia). Employees from both companies were included in the research (254 from Slovenia and 117 from Russia). They completed either the electronic or the paper version of the questionnaire, developed by Trompenaars Hampden-Turner[83] (available at www.7e-culture.nl after providing a password). Our goal has been to find out how much organizational cultures in Trimo Trebnje and Trimo VSK differ between each other and what the desired organizational cultures of both companies are. Further, we have looked into what can hinder the transfer of Trimo values and practices to Trimo VSK, which practices and values should be transferred at all for the culture to support the strategy as much as possible and which tools have to be used to make the transfer of Trimo culture to Trimo VSK smooth and fast.

The first part of the questionnaire refers to the dimensions of national culture (Trompenaars, 1993; Zagoršek and Štembergar, in this book), while the second part contains questions regarding types of organizational culture (Trompenaars, 1993; Zagoršek and Štembergar, in this book). The questionnaire covers both the current and the ideal type of organizational culture. For purposes of this research the employees in the Slovenian company were divided into 11 groups (Top Management, Middle Management, Low Management, Manufacturing, Development and Design, Procurement and Sales, Project Management, Quality Assurance, Accounting and Finance, Human Resource Management and General Affairs, Organizational Development and IT). The Russian company Trimo VSK is a manufacturing company and was for the purposes of this research divided into three groups: Management, Manufacturing, Others. In the empirical research we used quantitative (e.g. descriptives and tests of differences between groups, i.e. t-tests, ANOVA, LSD) and qualitative methods. We have also conducted in-depth interviews with Trimo's managing director, Trimo's human resources director and Trimo's total quality management coordinator. We would like to point out that in some departments the sample sizes are small. The analysis has been performed on the basis of the data received from THT. The comparison between the THT and our results is limited because the data used in our research have not been normalized while THT performs their analyses on normalized data.

---

[83] Hereafter THT.

ANALYSIS OF CULTURE AT THE COMPANY LEVEL

At the company level we researched and compared the dimensions of national and organizational culture in Trimo Trebnje and Trimo VSK. In Figures 17.1 and 17.2 the dimensions of national and organizational culture[84] for Trimo Trebnje and Trimo VSK are presented (Tekavčič et al., 2005).

In Trimo Trebnje a lot of emphasis is placed on planning and punctuality (i.e. sequential culture), and adherence to standardized rules and procedures (universalism) is supported. Results of our research have shown that employees of Trimo Trebnje are achievement-oriented and lean towards internal control, which means that they do not go with the flow but instead try to act proactively in the environment. They emphasize future and present more than past. In Trimo VSK they emphasize more the significance of the status and power based on one's position in the hierarchy than status and power based on competences and achieved results. In the Russian company they differentiate more strictly between business and personal relationships among people (higher specificity), emphasize strict adherence to plans even more and ascribe higher importance to the past than in the Slovenian company.

In Trimo the Guided Missile is the prevailing organizational culture, which can be seen in the following characteristics (Trompenaars and Wooliams, 2003; 2004): task and project orientation, low level of centralization, orientation towards the achievement of goals, orientation towards successful problem solving, great importance of vision and mission of the company, great importance of achieving results and success, great importance of the knowledge and professionalism of the employees, teamwork.

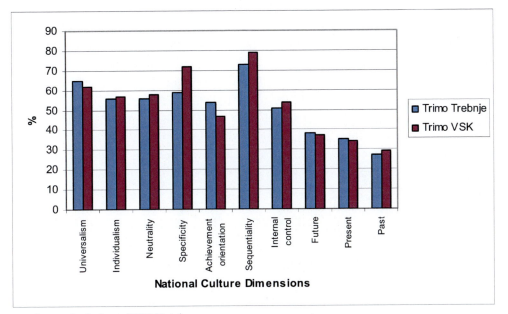

Source: Own calculations, THT Database.

Figure 17.1. Comparison of Dimensions of National Culture between Trimo Trebnje and Trimo VSK.

---

[84]   For description of dimensions, see Zagoršek and Štembergar, 2007.

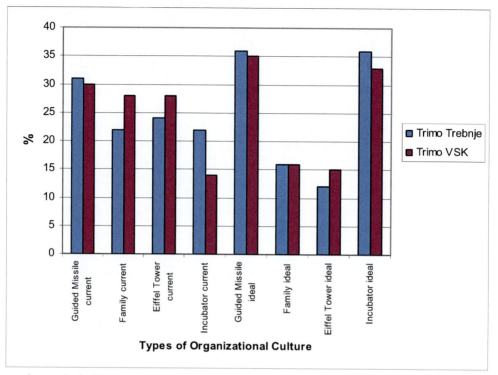

Source: Own calculations, THT Database.

Figure 17.2. Comparison of Organizational Cultures between Trimo Trebnje in Trimo VSK.

The other three types of organizational culture are represented almost equally in Trimo, i.e. the Eiffel Tower (manifested in an emphasis on precision and orderliness and usage of supervision with the help of rules and procedures in Trimo), the Family (high orientation towards people and mutual relationships in Trimo and a strong influence of the managing director) and the Incubator (orientation towards people, low level of centralization, great importance of teamwork, flat organizational structure in the form of process and molecular organizational structure, learning organization and high level of flexibility).

We have observed that Trimo has realized that a fast and open flow of information and ideas and effective problem solving are of key importance in monitoring events in the business environment and implementing changes. That is why they adapted their way of doing business and formed a team approach, which manifests itself in the way the company is managed as well as in the actual task implementation. In addition to transferring knowledge and information, teamwork also contributes to a better definition of problems and their faster resolution. This also includes the increase of responsibility at work (particularly responsibility for the quality of work and continuous improvement of work processes and products or services). In Trimo all employees are informed about the key goals of a financial year and long term strategic goals through various communication methods. Let us only mention the annual meeting for all employees when the management presents the results of the previous period and the future goals and values of the company, and the Trimo dialogs where leaders and coworkers discuss the achievements of individual employees as well as the individual's and company's goals for the future.

Considering the existing combination of types of culture we have observed that Trimo management has succeeded in making the employees aware of the goals and the mission of the company and accept them as their own. This directs the employees towards teamwork and motivates them to work for more than just their personal interest. By setting high standards for themselves and all employees and by consistently verifying the fulfillment of set goals, the management has acquired the respect and trust of the employees. The management team entirely accepts the vision and work values and transfers them to other employees by their own example. Trimo management has through training and communication with employees ensured that the employees sense the urgency for changes and at the same time feel the responsibility for quality work, not only as individuals but also as members of various teams and the whole company. Such a way of operating also manifests itself in yearly increases in revenue, profit and added value per employee.

Employees as an ideal culture see an equal combination of the Guided Missile and the Incubator – we could say they desire the Guided Incubator, but they would severely reduce the characteristics of the Family and the Eiffel Tower. This means that employees desire even more flexibility that allows a fast response to changes in the environment and adaptation to new customer demands. Here Trimo's belief that the main contributors to customer satisfaction should be the employees is evident, since they are the ones who with their knowledge and ideas continuously develop products and services and improve their quality. Considering the ideal culture we have noticed that people in Trimo are aware that it is one of the foundations for the fulfillment of Trimo's strategy (Peljhan, 2005; Zupan, 2000; Zupan and Rejc, 2005). By creating an ideal culture where orientation towards people is highly emphasized, the company would move even more towards achieving employee satisfaction, which Trimo already now believes to be one of the key factors for successful business. Trimo's ideal culture is in sync with Trimo's strategic orientation of the company's long term growth because it encourages creativity, which is necessary for the company's growth.

Considering the success of the mother company in Trebnje is primarily the result of implementing Trimo's way of work (Zupan and Rejc, 2005), the key challenge in internationalizing the company is how to transfer the Trimo way to other environments. When comparing the Russian and the Slovenian company we notice that the current organizational cultures differ. Although the Guided Missile is the prevailing culture in both companies, the culture in Trimo Trebnje includes more elements of the Incubator, while in Trimo VSK the Family and the Eiffel Tower are more prevalent. It is important for the mother company that it has already succeeded in transferring part of the values of innovativeness and performance orientation to Trimo VSK, since the ideal organizational cultures of the Russian and the Slovenian company are similar. Because the companies agree on the ideal organizational cultures, we do not anticipate much resistance in changing the current organizational cultures, especially not in Trimo VSK, where the current and ideal culture differ greatly. In the ideal culture of Trimo Trebnje, an orientation towards people and an emphasis on equality stand out, while Trimo VSK desires more elements of hierarchy compared to the Slovenian company. The reason for this is the more development focused nature of the work in Trimo Trebnje, the more manufacturing focused nature of work in Trimo VSK and the influence of Russian national culture, where status and power are recognized more on the basis of the position in the hierarchy, title, etc. (Figure 17.1 – Achievement Orientation).

To what extent the organizational culture in Trimo Trebnje should be transferred to Trimo VSK depends partially on the strategic development of the relationship between the two companies. If Trimo VSK is given more incentives to innovate, then the ideal culture in Trimo VSK should include more Incubator elements (learning organization, high level of flexibility, great importance of teamwork). If Trimo VSK stays a mere implementer of the technical developments from Slovenia, what is now seen as ideal culture in Trimo VSK should suffice to implement constant improvements in production and marketing. Such a strategy is also more in sync with the dimensions of national and organizational culture currently in place in Trimo VSK.

ANALYSIS OF CULTURE AT DEPARTMENTAL LEVEL

Within the framework of a company's organizational culture certain subcultures exist. A subculture is a culture formed within a company by a group that regularly communicates and cooperates, e.g. a department in a company, where culture is formed by individuals with a certain profession. According to research (Lok and Crawford, 1999), subcultures have an even bigger impact on the employees' dedication than the organizational culture. In Tables 17.2 and 17.3 we show the equality and deviation of groups (11 from the Slovenian and 3 from the Russian company) that participated in the research. Comparisons refer to the current and ideal culture in Trimo (see Figures 17.1 and 17.2).

In the research we have noticed that the manufacturing departments in Trimo Trebnje and Trimo VSK are relatively homogenous in the dimensions of national culture, since they only differ on the dimension of specificity, which refers to strict division between business and personal relationships at work. In Trimo Trebnje manufacturing workers know each other very well also in personal life since they are practically neighbors and the higher presence of a personal note at work is therefore expected. Homogeneity of the cultures of both manufacturing departments can be a consequence of a very similar nature of work (professional culture effect) or it can also be the result of very well communicated values and practices in the past. The effect of Russian national culture on the manufacturing workers in Trimo VSK can be seen in that the workers more strictly differentiate between business and personal relationships (they are more specific) and emphasize status over achievements. Although the current organizational cultures of the manufacturing departments differ (Table 17.3), the values of innovativeness and performance orientation have obviously been clearly articulated, since there are practically no differences between the ideal cultures.

Certain differences exist among managers in Trimo Trebnje and Trimo VSK. Managers in the Slovenian company are more performance- (achievement-) oriented and emphasize strict adherence to standardized rules and procedures (universalism) more than managers in Trimo VSK. On the other hand, managers in Russia emphasize a lower level of acceptance of expressing emotions (neutrality) more. It has to be pointed out that relatively high levels of individualism and specificity of managers in the Russian company can present a barrier to the implementation and increased usage of teamwork as well as knowledge transfer, both of which are Trimo values. Since in the ideal culture of Russian managers a higher presence of the Guided Missile is desired, individualism could be expressed by personal achievements in a team.

Table 17.2. Comparison between Groups Regarding Dimensions of National Culture

Dimension / Group	UN	IN	NE	SP	AO	SE	IC
Top Management		+		+	+	−	+
Middle Management		−			+		+
Low Management	+	+	+	+			+
Manufacturing			−	−	−	+	−
Development and Design		−	+	+	+	−	+
Procurement and Sales				+	+	−	+
Project Management	−	−		−	+	+	
Quality Assurance		+	+				+
Accounting and Finance	+	+	+	−			+
HRM and General Affairs	+		+	−		−	−
Organizational Development and IT	−	−		+		+	
Management Trimo VSK	−	+	+	+	−		+
Manufacturing Trimo VSK	−	−		+	−	+	
Other Trimo VSK	+			+			+

Key: UN – universalism; IN – individualism; NE – neutrality; SP – specificity; AO – achievement orientation; SE – sequentially; IC – internal control; +: the dimension is more prevalent than in the Trimo culture; −: the dimension is less prevalent than in the Trimo culture; a blank cell indicates the same level of the dimension as in the Trimo culture.

Source: Own calculations.

Table 17.3. Comparison of Groups Regarding Dimensions of Organizational Culture

Organizational culture / Group	GM C	GM Id	F C	F Id	ET C	ET Id	I C	I Id
Top Management	+	+	−		−	−	−	+
Middle Management					+	−	−	+
Low Management		−			+		−	
Manufacturing	−					+	−	
Development and Design					−	−	+	
Procurement and Sales	+				−	−	+	
Project Management						+	−	
Quality Assurance	−		−		+			
Accounting and Finance		+				−	+	
HRM and General Affairs	−	−	+	+				
Organizational Development and IT	+	+	+	−				−
Management Trimo VSK		+	+				−	−
Manufacturing Trimo VSK	−	−	+		+	+	−	−
Other Trimo VSK			+				−	

Key: GM – Guided Missile; F – Family; ET – Eiffel Tower; I – Incubator; C – Current; Id – ideal; +: the dimension is more prevalent than in the Trimo culture; −: the dimension is less prevalent than in the Trimo culture; a blank cell indicates the same level of the dimension as in the Trimo culture.

Source: Own calculations.

We still have to point out the fact that a high specific culture may create a divide between "them and us", i.e. Trimo VSK and Trimo Trebnje Management. Due to the existing gap between the stated Trimo values and the current characteristics of Trimo VSK Management particular attention needs to be devoted to this issue. Reconciliation of differing views among company managers should also support the strategy for the future relationship between Trimo Trebnje and Trimo VSK. The 360-degree evaluation of managers is thus taken into account, since strategic action and communication are emphasized simultaneously.

When analyzing subcultures in the company we have noticed that Trimo has a relatively homogenous organizational culture, undoubtedly a result of the multi-annual continuous education of all employees regarding the values, strategy, mission and goals of the company. In Trimo we can talk about a relatively strong organizational culture because it is visible that the important values are included in the mind map of the majority of the employees, i.e. are generally accepted.

CULTURE AND STRATEGY: PRACTICAL IMPLICATIONS FOR TRIMO

The relationship between culture and strategy is two-fold. On one hand, culture fosters the implementation of the desired strategy, while on the other hand, any strategy is influenced by the current organizational culture (Higgins and McAllaster, 2004). Each company has to develop, articulate and communicate its organizational culture (Schein, 1985). What type of culture will be created depends on the company's strategy but also, as in the studied case, on the culture of the mother company. Because Trimo VSK operates in a different national culture, its organizational culture will include at least some elements of Russian national culture.

The current Trimo's strategic orientation of employees being the primary source of the company's success is not yet completely in sync with the currently most prevalent Guided Missile culture, where task and project orientation are more important than orientation towards people. The existing Family and Incubator elements in Trimo's current culture and importance of the Incubator in the ideal culture show the existence of a dilemma that needs to be reconciled: fast completion of tasks has to be supplemented with an increased focus on people. For this goal to be achieved, learning and teamwork have to become the basis on which tasks are accomplished and employees compensated. For a faster transition towards the ideal culture that supports Trimo's strategy, more motivational factors such as bonuses for team performance that encourage employees to work together have to be included.[85] Educational and promotional opportunities have to remain a part of the non-monetary rewards that stimulate personal and professional growth on one hand and loyalty to the company on the other. Transfer of knowledge (existing as well as, for example, knowledge gained at seminars) needs to become a mandatory part of job descriptions.

The strategy of continuous improvements is supported by orientation towards control over environment and recognition of status and power based on competencies and achieved results, which show the proactive orientation of the employees. Improvements within the CIP

---

[85] Trimo currently uses compensation of team members in implementing improvements in the CIP and TQM projects.

project are also very important in the Manufacturing department where we noticed higher orientation towards the adaptation to the environment than towards the control over it in both the Russian and the Slovenian company. This means that currently there is a lack of initiative for improvement in the Manufacturing department and therefore the management has to encourage the employees even more to contribute suggestions. We suggest informal meetings between the manufacturing workers and their leaders, where the employees might suggest more improvements during a conversation than if they had to complete a formally prescribed form. Because the modern environment makes economic and timely achievement of goals increasingly important, the Guided Missile elements should be kept. A dilemma between innovation, which requires financial support and is time consuming, and cost-consciousness emerges. Learning and innovation should thus become a part of job descriptions but should be monetarily rewarded when innovation contributes to cost savings. The company is making positive strides in this area since it is creating competencies maps, which will in the future become the basis of the new compensation and promotion system.

Our research has shown that Trimo Trebnje has a high potential for innovation because of its employees, who are achievement-oriented and oriented towards control over the environment. In Trimo they are aware of changes in the environment and try to control them. Management has to pay particular attention to the fact that the employees put strict adherence to the standardized rules and procedures before a flexible approach to problem solving, which can be an obstacle in implementing changes because most of the time new challenges require new solutions that are not universal solutions to past problems. The company's orientation towards continuous improvements and innovative ideas represent a good framework to direct employees towards more flexible problem solving. According to our findings, the employees desire changes in culture and are willing to accept them; therefore we do not anticipate much resistance to their implementation but instead a gradual inclusion of the elements of the ideal culture into the current culture.

If Trimo wishes to surpass customer expectations, it has to give relatively more advantage to a flexible approach for solving problems compared to a strict adherence to standardized rules and procedures that often slow down decision making. This, however, by no means implies that they have to dispose of the certain level of universalism that dictates equal treatment of employees and strict implementation of the key values and norms.

REFERENCES

Bartlett, C.A., Ghoshal, S., and Birkinshaw, J. 2004. *"Transnational Management: Text, Cases and Readings in Cross-Border Management."* USA: McGraw Hill.

Briški, P. 2005. *"Pot do priznanja za odličnost."* (EFQM 2004). Forum SFPO 2005 in EFQM – Konferenca zmagovalcev, Ljubljana 2005. Ljubljana: GV Izobraževanje.

Dimovski, V., Penger, S., Škerlavaj, M., and Žnidaršič, J., 2005. *"Učeča se organizacija – Ustvarite podjetje znanja."* Ljubljana, Slovenia: GV Založba.

Dimovski, V., Škerlavaj, M., Hristovski, Z., Janežič, M., Székely, A., and Šmajdek, U. 2005a. "Strateška usklajenost podjetij Trimo Trebnje d.d. in Trimo VSK." In Prašnikar, J. and Cirman, A. (eds): *"Globalno gospodarstvo in kulturna različnost."* Ljubljana: Časnik Finance: 415–430.

Dimovski, V., and Škerlavaj, M. 2005. "Performance Effects of Organizational Learning in a Transitional Economy." *Problems and Perspectives in Management*, 3 (4): 56–67.

Finance. "Finance Top 101 Slovenian Companies 2005". Ljubljana. June 20, 2005.

Higgins, J., and McAllaster, C. 2004. "If You Want Strategic Change, Don't Forget to Change Your Cultural Artifacts." *Journal of Change Management* 4 (1): 63–72.

Johansson, J. K. 2004. "*Global Marketing.*" USA: McGraw Hill.

Kranjec, S. 2003. "Trimo želi postati vodilni v Evropi." *Finance (Priloga)* No. 208: 20. October 28, 2003.

Peljhan, D. 2005. "Management Control Systems for Organisational Performance Management: A Case of a Slovenian Company." PhD Thesis. Ljubljana: University of Ljubljana, Faculty of Economics.

Pre-fabricated Steel Buildings, [http://www.trimo.si/], 2005.

Schein, E. H. 1985. "*Organizational Culture and Leadership.*" San Francisco CA: Jossey-Bass.

SiOK. 2004. "Projekt primerjalnega raziskovanja organizacijske klime v slovenskih organizacijah." Slovenija: Gospodarska Zbornica.

Slovenian Biggest Exporters, [http://www.gvin.com/Lestvice/], 2005.

Tekavčič, M., and Peljhan, D. 2004. "Achieving Business Excellence Prize: The Case of Trimo Trebnje d.d." *International Business and Economics Research Journal* 3 (10): 49–63.

Tekavčič, M., Peljhan, D., Avramska, I., Drešar, M., Filipič, P., Lapajne, P., and Saich, A. 2005. "Analiza organizacijske kulture in kulturne usklajenosti: Primer Trimo Trebnje d.d. in Trimo VSK." In Prašnikar, J. and Cirman, A. (eds): "*Globalno gospodarstvo in kulturna različnost.*" Ljubljana: Časnik Finance: 431–444.

THT database. 2005. Trompenaars Hampden-Turner.

Trimo. 2002. Business Excellence Report.

Trimo. 2002a. Trimo Standards.

Trimo. 2003. Annual Report 2003.

Trimo. 2004. Annual Report 2004.

Trimo. 2004a. Interview with Manufacturing Director, March 2004.

Trimo. 2005. Business manual. Ninth Edition.

Trimo. 2005a. Interview with Trimo's managing director.

Trimo. 2005b. Managing director's presentation at the 2005 Strategic Conference.

Trimo. 2005c. Interview with Trimo's HR director.

Trimo. 2005d. Interview with Trimo's TQM coordinator.

Trompenaars, F. 1993. "Riding the Waves of Culture: Understanding Cultural Diversity in Business." London: The Economist Books.

Trompenaars, F. 1996. "Resolving International Conflict: Culture and Business Strategy." *Business Strategy Review* 7 (3): 51–68.

Trompenaars Hampden-Turner's web page, [http://www.7e-culture.nl], 2005.

Trompenaars, F., and Woolliams, P. 2003. "A New Framework for Managing Change Across Cultures." *Journal of Change Management* 3 (4): 361–375.

Trompenaars, F., and Wooliams, P. 2004. "Business Across Cultures." Chichester: Capstone Publishing Ltd.

Zagoršek, H. and Štembergar, M. 2007. "Culture and Its Influence on Business Performance." In this volume.

Zupan, N. 2000. "Kako vključiti zaposlene v uresničevanje vizije podjetja - primer Trimo, d.d. in internacionalizacija slovenskega podjetja." Ljubljana: Časnik Finance.

Zupan, N. and Rejc, A. 2005. "Growing Through the HRM Strategies – Trimo Trebnje." *Medium-Sized Firms and Economic Growth,* New York: Nova Science Publishers.

PART VI: DOING BUSINESS WITH CHINA

In: New Emerging Economies and Their Culture
Editors: J. Prašnikar, A. Cirman, pp. 271-282

ISBN: 978-1-60021-754-8
© 2007 Nova Science Publishers, Inc.

Chapter 18

GLOBALIZATION AND FDI: THE ROLE OF CHINA

Črt Kostevc and Tjaša Redek

INTRODUCTION

Globalization refers to the increasing integration of economies around the world, particularly through trade and financial flows. The process impacts broader cultural, political and environmental dimensions. The source of globalization lies in the development of technology. The costs of transport, travel, and above all the costs of communicating information have fallen dramatically in the post-war period, almost entirely because of the progress of technology (World Economic Outlook, 2005). The most striking consequences of globalization have been the advancement of trade, the surge in capital flows, technology transfer, production reallocation and the growing cooperation among world economies. The opinions on the long term effects of the process remain divided. Whereas the developed world is facing fears of unemployment among low-skilled workers, the developing economies seem to have benefited from exploiting the advantages of export-led growth (Krugman, 1999).

In theory, processes of economic growth, trade and foreign direct investment (FDI) are intertwined in an export-led model of growth (Todaro, 2000). Traditionally, FDI is viewed as an attempt to exploit firm-specific assets in a foreign market and at the same time allowing the investing firm to avoid bearing the transaction costs of arms-length trade (Markusen, 2002). Investing firms therefore manage to internalize their firm-specific advantages by establishing foreign-based production facilities rather than entering into contractual market mechanisms (such as franchising, licensing agreements, etc.) (Denekamp, 1995). The choice of location for FDI is based on the location advantages that maximize the value of firm-specific assets net of the set-up costs (Chen and Chen, 1998).[86] With respect to location, FDI can be motivated by either factor costs, the size of the available market or other advantages of the target location (a qualified labor force, availability of intermediate products, access to

---

[86] In fact, firm-specific or ownership advantages, location advantages and internalization advantages form the "basic ingredients" of the eclectic theory or OLI paradigm (Dunning, 1981). Currently (according to data on trade growth and FDI) India does not present a serious competitor to China, but due to its large labor force and increasing competitiveness of its labor cost compared to China, India might be the next emerging economy.

other markets, etc.). In turn, different types of FDI have various effects on trade flows; market seeking FDI will serve as a substitute to trade, while resource seeking FDI will likely boost trade flows (Brainard, 1997).

The process of globalization has significantly affected the FDI flows and trade through several channels. First of all, the steady decline of transport costs coupled with a faster (and cheaper) flow of information has led to an expansion of resource seeking FDI as well as trade (Hummels, 1999; 2001). Second, the fragmentation and standardization of individual phases of production have enabled firms to achieve the optimal geographical dispersion of their production process and therefore minimize the costs of production (as pointed out by Krugman and Venables, 1995). This, in turn, also stimulated trade in primary and especially in intermediate products. Third, developing countries have adopted a more open stance towards FDI, thereby adding further stimulus to their growth efforts (IMF, World Economic Outlook, 2005).

The purpose of this paper is to examine the impact of globalization (specifically FDI) on trade and economic growth in the world markets. We show that globalization enabled a surge in FDI, followed by a boost in trade, which benefited developing economies. In doing so, we will discuss their past performance and provide a future outlook. The focus will be primarily on the role of China as the country that has caused the biggest stir in the world markets.

RECENT TRENDS REFLECTING THE PROCESS OF GLOBALIZATION

Globalization has been characterized above all by an immense expansion of world trade and, since the 1980s, also by a massive surge in capital flows. On average, trade growth (1950 − 2004, approximately 6.5% annually) significantly surpassed production growth (1950 − 2004, approximately 4% average growth), especially in manufacturing (average growth of manufacturing trade was 8%, production of manufactured goods grew on average 5.5%) (WTO database, 2004). Developing economies have been strengthening their position in world trade and their role in the world economy with their share in world production growing rapidly.

The world has changed significantly due to globalization. China, Vietnam, Turkey, India and some of the transition economies are the emerging production powers of tomorrow. Twenty years ago the picture was completely different. The developed economies of North America (United States and Canada) and Europe were the largest exporters; North America had a 25% share in world exports and Western Europe had a 30% share (but intra-regional trade accounted for over 60% of EU trade). Today, this share has fallen to 13%. On the other hand, Asia gained ten percentage points.

Asian economies and transition economies are becoming world's biggest producers of manufactured goods due to their cheap labor force (the data for 2001 reveals that average labor cost per hour in China, Bulgaria, Romania, and India are below USD 1 per hour, in Slovakia, the Czech Republic and Turkey between USD 1 and 2, while in Germany they are USD 25 per hour (EIU, 2002)). Among developing economies, China is taking the lead. Its remarkable economic growth of 10% annually on average and a surge in exports with growth rates of even 40% has placed China on top. Its share in world exports has risen in only ten years (1993 to 2003) from 2.5 to 6%, while its share in world imports has risen from 2.8 to

5.5%. China has also been one of the main destinations for FDI, which is motivated mainly by low production costs and a huge domestic market. Also, with the fall of socialism, transition economies have attracted substantial FDI inflows (ITS, 2004).

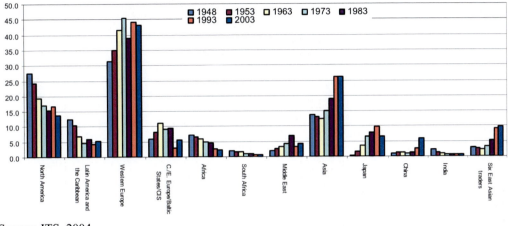

Source: ITS, 2004.

Figure 18.1. Shares of Economies in World Exports.

Clearly, the differences among the developing economies are substantial in several aspects: location, costs of labor, institutional arrangements, sizes of domestic markets, which will in turn have an impact on their performance as FDI recipients, and consequently also their economic structure. The interaction of globalization forces with the specific country characteristics will determine the development trajectory (and, in turn, their role in world markets). Especially China, the transition economies and Turkey have made the biggest progress in trade and have become among the most important destinations for FDI. Therefore, their main economic characteristics must be examined first so as to make a credible forecast of the future.

THE IMPACT OF GLOBALIZATION IN CHINA

In the past thirty years, South and South East Asia have been the fastest growing regions in the world, but the development of China has significantly surpassed the performance of other Asian economies. In the past thirty years, the average growth rate in China has been 9.3% per year. Chinese real GDP per capita in 2003 prices grew from USD 183 in 1979 to USD 1,090 in 2003 (Lau, 2004).

Two Growth Sources

The outstanding growth has been the result of mainly two factors: very high capital accumulation (both domestic accumulation and foreign capital inflow) and a boost in trade. Both have significantly contributed to the outstanding performance.

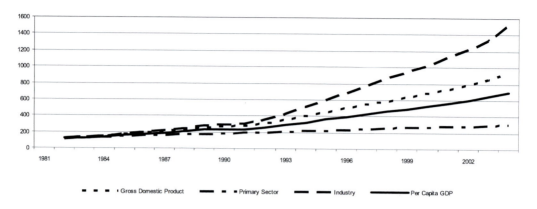

Source: National Bureau of Statistics of China, 2005.

Figure 18.2. Indices of National Production Aggregates, 1978=100.

Capital accumulation is the first major factor of economic growth. Despite the much talked about foreign investment to China, the Chinese economy actually has a very strong trend of domestic investment. In the first quarter of 2004, the growth rate of domestic investment was 43%. In the period from 1997 to 2004, the growth rate of domestic investment only fell below 10% (to around 9%) in the second half of 1999, otherwise it was on average between 15 and 20%. In 2003 it rose to between 25 and 35%. Actually, domestic investment represents about 89% off the total addition to capital in China (Lau, 2004).

Nonetheless, FDIs are also very important for the Chinese success story. They represent not only an addition to capital, but bring new technology, new knowledge, new skills, and open markets. And when Chinese firms penetrate foreign markets, these factors become very important. The history of FDI in China began in 1972 when FDI was first allowed. In 1979 "special economic zones" (SEZ)[87] were established, foreign firms were offered preferential tax and administrative treatment,[88] and completely foreign owned enterprises were permitted. In 1984, fourteen additional areas known as "open coastal cities" were given similar exemptions from taxes and administrative procedures in a bid to attract FDI.

In 1986, the implementation of the so-called "Twenty-Two Regulations", made foreign owned enterprises eligible for reduced business income tax rates regardless of location, and they were given increased managerial autonomy. Two categories of foreign investments were eligible for additional special benefits – "export-oriented" projects (defined as projects exporting 50% or more of their production value) and "technologically advanced" projects.[89] The special benefits clearly show a dedication of Chinese authorities to follow the Japanese model of development: growth will be export based and although at the time it was still labor intensive, even twenty years ago the Chinese were looking to attract higher value added

---

[87] It is important to recognize that none of the original special economic zones were in developed industrial centres in 1979. In fact, these zones were established outside the state's industrial centres to prevent the "contamination" of Chinese heavy industry by outside influences. These "experiments" in attracting foreign direct investment were successful (according to Branstetter and Feenstra (1999)).

[88] These zones charged a reduced tax of 15% on business income of foreign affiliated firms (as compared to 33% for domestic firms), but these taxes were not levied during the first two years of operation and charged at one-half of the full rate in the third through fifth year.

[89] Defined as projects which upgrade domestic production capacity through the use of "advanced" technology.

manufacturing. Figure 18.3 clearly demonstrates that foreign capital did indeed facilitate faster growth.

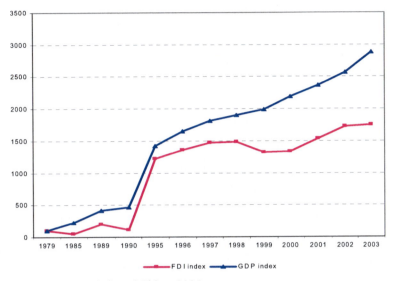

Source: National Bureau of Statistics of China, 2005.

Figure 18.3. FDI and Economic Growth in China.

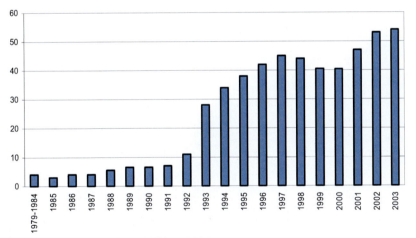

Source: National Bureau of Statistics of China, 2005.

Figure 18.4. FDI Flow to China in USD billions.

FDI inflows in the post-1990 era were much larger than those of the 1980s, both in absolute quantities and as a percentage of GDP (inward FDI reached a striking 35% of GDP; for comparison among transition economies, Slovakia and Azerbaijan stood out in 2002 with "only" 16.6 and 17% of GDP respectively (Transition Report, 2004)). In the late 1980s and 1990s, substantial FDI began to flow in significant quantities into the centers of China's (state-owned) heavy industry, manufacturing and financial industry.

Roughly 80% of FDI (the leading sources of capital are Hong Kong and Taiwan accounting for 48%, other Asian countries provide 26%, EU 15% and USA 10% of total capital inflows) is allocated to manufacturing, 50% of which is directed into labor intensive sectors, around 25% to technologically intensive and around 22% to capital intensive production (Davies, 2003). Multinational firms like Volkswagen, Nokia and Motorola earn about 15 – 20% of their total revenue in the Chinese market. But the majority of foreign firms earn less than 5% of their total revenue in the Chinese market (Sony, Siemens, General Motors) (Yin and Choi, 2005), which is an indicator that China is still interesting more as a world factory than as a world market. This is also confirmed by its *trade* patterns.

Chinese *exports growth* has been fastest in manufacturing, especially in labor intensive production. Whereas in 1995 China represented only 11% of Asian exports, its exports share grew to 23% in 2003 (mainly replacing Japanese exports whose share fell from 34 to 25%). Although the growing importance of Asian nations is further exemplified by the exporting achievements of India, the Philippines, and Vietnam, their share of exports (and imports) is dwarfed by China. In this process China has also firmly positioned itself as one of the major exporters to the United States, the EU and Japan as it has managed to increase its exports to these regions to 17, 13 and 9% respectively. Growth was particularly fast in semi-manufactures, machinery and transport equipment, telecommunications equipment, electrical appliances and furniture, average growth rate was between 15 – 24% in the 1995 – 2003 period (WTO database, 2004).

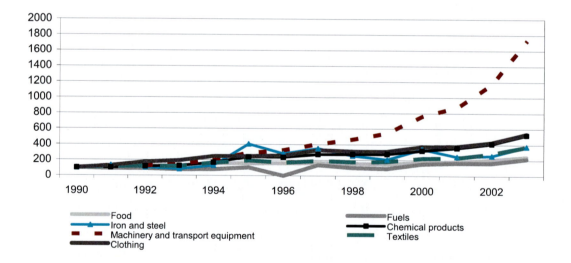

Source: WTO Database, 2004.

Figure 18.5. Chinese Exports Index (1990=100), Selected Product Groups.

Despite the widely discussed textiles export, China has actually recorded its fastest expansion in machinery and transport equipment, which has by far surpassed both textiles, clothing and chemicals, which have also been growing fast. China is the world's second largest exporter of office and telecommunications equipment.

It experienced a rapid rise from a market share of only 0.1% (1980) to 12% (2004). The expansion of Chinese influence came at the expense of the three leading economic entities (USA, EU, Japan), whose combined market share nearly halved (from 80 to 48%) in the same period.

Chinese expansion has been most notorious in the textile market. China has been outperforming even other low cost Asian and Eastern European economies and has more than tripled its share in the world textile markets (4.6% in 1980 to 15.9% in 2003, ITS, 2004). In the beginning of 2005 the quotas on textile imports were relaxed by the developed countries but the excess of cheap textiles soon forced a reintroduction of trade limitations. Along with China, other low cost producers of textiles and clothing (Turkey, Pakistan, India, Korea, Vietnam, Morocco) also came to the forefront, which serves as a manifestation of the changing geography of world production.

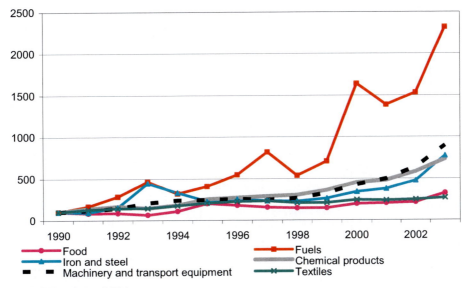

Source: WTO Database, 2004.

Figure 18.6. Chinese Imports Index (1990=100), Selected Product Groups.

On the other hand, China has been experiencing equally impressive *growth rates in terms of imports*. Predictably, in addition to its neighboring countries most of Chinese imports came from Japan, the United States and the EU, respectively. China is the second largest importer after the EU, with a market share of 11.4%.[90] In the past three years, the world has been most worried about the impact of China on oil and steel prices. In 1997 Chinese net imports of oil was 16 million tons, in 2003 it reached 132 million tons (WTO database, 2005). The average growth rate of iron and steel imports was 8% in the 1995 – 2000 period, but it rose sharply in 2002 and 2003 when the growth rate was 27 and 62%. Chemicals are also a crucial import product for China. Its share in world imports rose from 2% to 6% in the 1980 – 2003 period. On average its import rose by 12% each year between 1995 and 2000, while in 2002 and 2003 the growth rate of imports was 22 and 25%. China is one of the major importers of

---

[90] There has been a substantial increase in Chinese imports of steel since 1980: the Chinese share rose from 2% in the world steel market in 1980 to 11.4% today.

automotive products. It is a huge market for the car industry; a number of big companies are opening up plants to satisfy rising demand. Its imports grew by 8% on average (1995 – 2000), in 2002 and 2003 they grew by 42 and 84%.

China at the moment and possibly in the next few years will record faster growth of imports primarily due to its large domestic market. On the other hand, its abundant and cheap labor force, might soon make it Asia's biggest car exporter, ahead of Korea and Thailand.

China has been exhibiting very high growth rates since the beginning of reforms in 1979. The average growth has been above 9%. The two major motors of high economic growth keep exhibiting strong performance: both domestic accumulation and foreign capital inflow were high in 2004 and export performance is also strong. It is thus possible to expect that China will continue to be one of the major players in the world economic arena. Several factors speak in favor of that, although some worries have also arisen.

THE FUTURE? GLOBALIZATION, CHINA AND THE WORLD

Short-Term Economic Outlook for China

The Chinese economy is expected to grow at an annual rate of 8 % during the period of the 11th Five-Year Plan (2006 – 2010). That means China will achieve its goal of quadrupling its GDP from 2000 to 2020 ahead of schedule (China Daily, 2005). Macroeconomic developments do speak in favor of this scenario. In 2004 domestic investment grew by 43%, foreign capital inflow was high, imports and exports growth were also strong. In addition the domestic market has also been gradually developing: in 2004 domestic retail sales grew by 9%.

But many warn that the future of Chinese economic expansion will depend crucially upon its ability to tackle the internal and external limitations that are becoming more and more apparent. First of all, the financial system is often mentioned as one of the weaknesses of the Chinese economy. China's state-owned banks are saddled with an enormous load of bad debts. Banks are offering cheap consumer loans to a new middle class, so that some people carry monthly mortgage and other repayments that are bigger than their salaries. This also means that the famous Chinese frugality and the Chinese inclination to high saving (savings rate was 30% GDP), which has been one of the major engines in Chinese growth, is decreasing (Gunde, 2005).

China is facing some crucial demographic challenges. The Chinese economic miracle of the past decades depended on the duality between the industrial centers on the coast and the heavily rural inner China. The western and central regions that serve as a seemingly endless source of labor are likely to face additional migratory pressures as the regional disparities intensify. Unless a more balanced regional approach is adopted, these parts of the country will stagnate at best. In addition, the one family-one child policy will cause a demographic crunch with a high proportion of elderly population being supported by a comparatively small active labor force.

The development of infrastructure is mentioned often as a potential problem:[91] infrastructure development did not follow economic growth at the same pace. Specifically,

---

[91] Sebastian Edwards (UCLA) at The Third Wilbur K. Woo Conference

the past problems in electricity supply and several blackouts in the past were pointed out. If infrastructure is not modernized faster (China has devoted a great amount of resources to modernizing it, but still not enough by far), this might affect production.

Another major issue is the growing income disparities among regions, which are placing major development centers under huge migratory pressures with unforeseen consequences. Shanghai and Guandong have developed a business infrastructure, which is an important pull factor, leaving other regions behind (Yin and Choi, 2005).

A major internal issue is the political scene. Concerns have arisen about the problem of corruption, political stability in times of fast reforms and dealing with the politically sensitive issues of Taiwan. Political issues are not just an internal problem, it seems that they are going to be a major obstacle also from the outside. The Chinese external expansion is becoming an important political issue in the developed economies. China is viewed by some as a threat to social and economic stability in the developed world, which has been manifested by the EU trade restrictions (textiles) and recent objections by the United States to Chinese outward FDI (e.g. Unocal, IBM).

Another major external limiting factor is also trade dependency. The Chinese economy is heavily dependent on trade: China's trade dependency ratio is 60 or 70%, compared to 20% in the United States and 15% in Japan (Chua, 2005). Exports play a crucial role in spurring growth in China's economy. At the same time, China is becoming an important buyer in the world markets (oil, steel, and cement) and thus making its growth dependent on external supplies, which makes it vulnerable to market fluctuations and rising prices.

The continuation of Chinese exceptional growth will rely in large part on its ability to generate technological improvements. With the ever lessening gap the possibilities of technological transfer will become progressively smaller.

Long-Term Economic Outlook for China

In the longer run China is facing some major development challenges. China is one of the world's biggest economies. In 2003, its aggregate output was 8 times lower than US output, while in per capita terms, Chinese output was 38 times smaller than US per capita output. Analysts forecast that Chinese per capita output will remain low compared to G-7 countries for at least three more decades.

The prediction of the long term development path in China must take into consideration its short term limitations and long term development rules, applicable to any economy. Asian growth in the past has been mainly driven by tangible input accumulation, especially capital accumulation (Young, 1994). But at the same time it is important to know that in the long run technological progress is the most important source of growth, contributing more than 50% of total growth (Lau, 2004).

China has significant reserves in all major growth factors. Its long term growth will depend on a successful mix of domestic policies oriented towards infrastructural and institutional reforms and a reorientation of the economy towards higher value added production. As the economy grows, technological transfer, which was a very important side inflow of FDI, will become much smaller. The economy will have to focus on developing its own technology. R&D expenditure in China is still relatively low compared to the developed economies. In 1996 it was only around 0.5% of GDP, but then it rose sharply and in 2004 it reached about 1.3% of GDP. Also the proportion of the high tech sector in total industrial output rose from 10 to 20% in the period between 1993 and 2002 (Lau, 2004). But Chinese R&D expenditure is still well below the levels of the United States, Japan or Germany, which all spend about 2.5% of their GDP on R&D, indicating that China has significant reserves in this area. China is already focusing on accelerating the high-tech sector with tax benefits and by purchasing foreign high-tech companies (IBM).

A second very important resource, still highly underutilized, is the enormous Chinese human potential and dedication to learning. Today, human capital, measured in average years of schooling per person, is still low with an average of six years, even compared to the rest of Asian economies like South Korea, Hong Kong, where the average is eight years. Japan and other developed nations with twelve years are well ahead of China. Nonetheless, China is making significant progress in this field as well (Lau, 2004).

China is thus making progress in the field of technological development and human capital accumulation, which will help the economy refocus towards higher value added production. Additionally, China has a growing domestic market and also a huge world market. To continue stable long term growth, China has to focus especially on solving internal obstacles to growth. With successful solutions to these, China will remain a major player in the world economic arena and possibly become a member of the developed group towards the middle of the century.

LESSONS

Dynamic globalization processes that have been altering the world economic map and changing the nature of trade and capital flows demand swift action and adjustments from the affected economies if they hope to take advantage of the possible payoffs. Developing economies as the biggest FDI recipients are facing major shifts in their status. Their opening up to trade and foreign capital has stimulated economic growth via a boost in the growth of the target sectors for FDI and trade.

The benefits of globalization seem to be primarily on the side of the developing countries, which have been able to escape the poverty trap (also with the aid of foreign capital) by refocusing their production to match globalization needs. While there have been some adverse effects of these processes in both developing and developed nations, the populist view in developed nations fuels fears of rising unemployment and stagnation.

Fast economic growth is taking a toll on commodity markets. Rising demand and political uncertainties have stimulated an unprecedented rise, especially in oil markets. But sharp price increases have also been recorded in steel, concrete, soybean and other primary products.

Currently, China is considered to be the frontrunner among many nations to benefit from globalization. Although because of its size, China may not be representative as a case study for globalization success, it still offers many lessons for other countries. The transition economies of Eastern Europe have managed to cash in on their proximity to developed EU markets and relatively skilled and cheap labor. Notwithstanding their initial success, recent developments even among them have shown that capital is turning towards cheap labor, which indicates that economies will soon have to become investors themselves (some already are, i.e. Hungary, Slovenia).

It is apparent that relying on cheap and abundant labor and other natural resources is not a long term solution for fast development (even for China). Policymakers have to adopt measures to attract more capital intensive production, invest into their own R&D, educate their labor force, restructure their economies and refrain from selective opening up to foreign competition. Only this will ensure stable growth in the future.

REFERENCES

Boillot, J. J. 2002. *"Institutional Change and Economic Integration: The Way Around."* RECEP Conference, Moscow.

Brainard, L. S. 1997. "An Empirical Assessment of Proximity-Concentration Trade-Off Between Multinational Sales and Trade." *American Economic Review* 87 (4): 520–544.

Chen, H., in Chen, T. 1998. "Network Linkages and Location Choice in Foreign Direct Investment." *Journal of International Business Studies* 29: 445–467.

Chinese Ministry of Commerce 2005. [URL: http://english.mofcom.gov.cn/].

China Daily: China's Economy to Grow 8% Annually from 2006 to 2010, 2005. [URL: http://www.chinadaily.com.cn/english/doc/2005-03/21/content_426718.htm]

Davies, K. 2003. "FDI in China. Policy Development in Historical Perspective. Presentation." Washington: Centre for Strategic and International Policy.

Denekamp, J. 1995. "Intangible Assets, Internalization and Foreign Direct Investment in Manufacturing." *Journal of International Business Studies* 26: 493–504.

Dunning, J. H. 1980. "The Location Foreign Direct Investment Activity, Country Characteristics and Experience Effects." *Journal of International Business Studies* 11: 9–22.

Dunning, J. H. 1974. "Multinational Enterprise and Economic Analysis." Cambridge: Cambridge University Press.

Edwards, S., Chua, R., and Gunde, R. 2005. Panelists at the Third Wilbur K. Woo Conference on the Greater China Economy, UCLA. [URL: http://www.international.ucla.edu /asia/article.asp?parentid=21291].

Herald Tribune Online. 2005. *"China Oil Imports Up By 35%."* [URL: http://www.iht.com/ articles/2005/01/12/bloomberg/sxoil.php].

Hummels, D. 1999. *"Have International Trade Costs Declined."* Purdue University, Indiana: Mimeo. West Lafayette.

Hummels, D. 1999. *"Time as a Trade Barrier."* Purdue University, Indiana: Mimeo. West Lafayette.

International Monetary Fund. 2005. *"World Economic Outlook: Globalization and External Imbalances."* Washington: International Monetary Fund.

International Steel and Iron Institute: Steel Statistical Yearbook. 2006 [URL: http://www.worldsteel.org/pictures/publicationfiles/SSY%202005.pdf].

Krugman, P. 1999. *"The Accidental Theorist and Other Dispatches from the Dismal Science."* West Drayton: Penguin Books.

Krugman, P., and Venables, A. J. 1995. "Globalization and the Inequality of Nations." *Quarterly Journal of Economics* 110: 857–880.

Lall, R. 2004. "FDI in China." Presentation. [URL: http://www.scid.stanford.edu/events/China2004/Presentations/LallChinaFDIv12.ppt].

Lau, L. 2004. *"China in Global Economy."* Presentation. Stanford Graduate School of Business, Stanford University. [URL: http://www.stanford.edu/%7Eljlau/Presentations/Presentations/040503.pdf].

Markusen, J. R. 2002. "Multinational Firm and the Theory of International Trade." Cambridge, Massachusetts: MIT Press.

People's Daily Online. 2005. "Economists Predict 8 % Growth Rate." [URL: http://english.people.com.cn/other/archive.html].

Todaro, M. 2000. "Economic Development." Boston: Addison Wesley Longman Publishing.

Tulay, A. 1999. "Financial Markets and Globalization in Turkey." [URL: http://www.sba.luc.edu/orgs/meea/volume1/arin.html].

Vernon, R. 1966. "International Investment and International Trade in Product Cycle." *Quarterly Journal of Economics* 80 (2): 190–207.

Williamson, J. 2006 "Globalization: The Concept, Causes and Consequences." Keynote address to the Congress of the Sri Lankan Association for the Advancement of Science, World Bank. [URL: http://www.iie.com/publications/papers/paper.cfm?Research ID=330].

Young, A. 1994. "The Tyranny of Numbers: Confronting the Statistical Realities of the East Asian Growth Experience." *National Bureau of Economic Research Working Paper,* No. 4680.

Yin E., Choi C.J. 1995. "The Globalization Myth: The Case of China." *Management International Review* 45(1): 103–120.

In: New Emerging Economies and Their Culture   ISBN: 978-1-60021-754-8
Editors: J. Prašnikar, A. Cirman, pp. 283-306   © 2007 Nova Science Publishers, Inc.

Chapter 19

CHINESE BUSINESS CULTURE AND NEGOTIATING STYLE

Tony Fang

INTRODUCTION

The purpose of this chapter is to present a framework for understanding Chinese business culture and negotiating style. I have had opportunities to discuss this topic with a large number of foreign executives. Many of them said they loved to negotiate and work with the Chinese. They perceived Chinese businesspeople as sincere business "gentlemen" who worked at a high level of mutual trust and respect. However, many others gave a diametrically different picture; they hated to negotiate with the Chinese and they were fed up with the tricky Chinese style of negotiating. In their eyes, the Chinese are "immoral" businesspeople who can "cheat", "lie", or just do whatever is necessary to knock you off balance at the negotiation table.

I was struck by this contradictory image and was myself very much a part of this Chinese phenomenon some years ago when I was negotiating (as a Chinese negotiator) with foreign businesspeople: the Chinese negotiator is a both sincere and deceptive negotiator. This chapter aims to decode the paradox of Chinese negotiating style. I will start by discussing the philosophical foundation of Chinese culture. Next I will present a model of Chinese business culture. The chapter will conclude with managerial implications about how to do business effectively in China. A case study of Chinese negotiation behavior will be presented in the Appendix.

PHILOSOPHICAL FOUNDATION OF CHINESE BEHAVIOR

To understand the richness and complexity of Chinese business culture we need to start with the image of Yin Yang, a Chinese philosophical principle of dualism and a cosmic symbol of primordial unity and harmony. Yin Yang is illustrated in a circle being equally divided by a curved line forming the black and white areas. Yin represents female energies/elements such as the moon, night, water, weakness, darkness, mystery, softness, passivity, etc., while Yang stands for male energies/elements such as the sun, day, fire, strength, brightness, clearness, hardness, activity, etc. Yin and Yang are not two absolute opposing forces but rather the paired nature of everything in the universe (Picture 19.1).

Picture 19.1. The Yin Yang Principle.

In the image of Yin Yang we see a dot of black in the white and also a dot of white in the black. The Yin Yang principle suggests that there exists neither absolute black nor absolute white. Opposites contain within them the seeds of the other and together form a dynamic unity (Chen, 2001). Yin and Yang depend on each other, exist within each other, give birth to each other, and succeed each other at different points in time. In other words, every universal phenomenon embraces contradiction, paradox and change.

The Chinese thought has been molded by three different philosophical traditions: Confucianism, Taoism, and Buddhism. Briefly, Confucianism deals with how to handle human relationships, Taoism deals with life in harmony with nature, and Buddhism deals with one's immortal world.

Whereas Confucianism teaches you how to do things, Taoism guides you how to do nothing (Wu Wei – both literally and strategically). Whereas Confucianism and Taoism are practical-oriented this-worldly philosophies, Buddhism with its doctrine of "reincarnation" opens an immortal world to the Chinese mind which allows Chinese people to see life in terms of the relationship between one's pre-life, present-life and after-life.

To most Chinese Confucianism, Taoism, and Buddhism are philosophical teachings instead of religions. Although these teachings "compete" and "contradict" with each other in many respects, Chinese people follow all of them, instead of sticking to just one of them, to enrich various aspects of their life. This makes Chinese behavior intensely practical, paradoxical, and embracing. Given different philosophical influences, the Chinese are morally able to play different roles in different situations and contexts. This is key to understanding the paradoxical and intensely flexible Chinese style of behaving and negotiating.

CHINESE BUSINESS CULTURE

In *Chinese Business Negotiating Style* (Fang, 1999), I have constructed a model of Chinese business culture to understand Chinese business negotiating style (Picture 19.2). The model captures the paradox of Chinese business culture through holding together three different yet interrelated driving forces: the PRC condition, Confucianism, and Chinese stratagems.

The PRC Condition

The PRC condition (*Guoqing*) refers to the distinctive characteristics of contemporary social political system and conditions of the People's Republic of China (PRC). The PRC condition involves variables such as Chinese politics, China's socialist planned market economy, legal framework, technology development, great size, backwardness and uneven development and rapid change. The central theme under the PRC condition is Chinese bureaucracy, characterized by centralized decision making, internal bargaining, bureaucratic red tape but quick learning in the age of reform. Politics plays an important role in Chinese business life. China is a changing, dynamic, and competitive market with huge regional differences. Economic exchanges with foreign countries and utilization of new technology are at the core of Chinese development.

China is undergoing a dramatic transformation; the diversity and changing aspects of the PRC condition warrant serious attention such as the rise of non-state sectors, the emerging values (capitalism, individualism, material success, quality of life, and environmental concern) given the influence of globalization and foreign direct investment in China. Today some 500,000 foreign invested enterprises are operating on the Chinese soil and China is full of Western commercials. An increasing number of Chinese brands (e.g., Haier, Huawei, Lenovo, etc.) are also going global.

Source: Fang, 1999.

Picture 19.2. A Model of Chinese Business Culture.

Confucianism

Confucianism (*Rujia*) is a fundamental philosophical tradition that has shaped Chinese culture for 2,500 years. Confucius (551–479 BC), a native of Qufu, Shandong province, is the founder of Confucian philosophy. Confucianism is a form of moral ethic and a practical philosophy of human relationship and conduct. Six Confucian values can be singled out to study Chinese business culture: moral cultivation, importance of interpersonal relationships (concepts of trust, *guanxi, renqing,* and *li*), family orientation, respect for age and hierarchy, avoidance of conflict and need for harmony, and concept of face. Guanxi means personal contacts and connections. Guanxi and family are important given the scarcity of resources and the lack of well-functioning legal and social welfare systems. The Chinese often make great efforts to avoid face-losing situations.

Confucianism sees the human world through the lens of the Five Cardinal Relationships (*Wulun*), i.e. the relationship between the ruler and subject, father and son, husband and wife, elder and younger brothers, and between senior and junior friends. Confucianism never defines any interorganizational relationship but rather views all types of relationships in human society from the interpersonal relationship perspective. The upshot is that the Chinese often do business with you as individual persons, not as organizations, which implies that in Chinese eyes, interfirm adaptations are essentially interpersonal adaptations.

All the five relationships defined by Confucianism feature "reciprocity". Confucianism demands the junior's loyalty, filial piety, obedience, and respect. Yet the senior must be self-righteous, benevolent, charismatic, and loving to enable the junior to become loyal, filial, obedient, and respectful. If not, the junior can disobey and even rise up to choose a better senior. Mencius (in Chan, 1963), a great Confucian philosopher second only to Confucius, writes: "If a ruler regards his ministers as his hands and feet, then his ministers will regard him as their heart and mind. If a ruler regards his ministers as dogs and horses, his ministers will regard him as any other man. If a ruler regards his ministers as dirt and grass, his ministers will regard him as a bandit and an enemy."

Yang (1957) elaborates on the Confucian notion of reciprocity by looking at the Chinese word "bao" (or "pao" in his original text), which possesses a wide range of meanings such as "to report", "to respond", "to repay" and "to retaliate". The center of this area of meanings is "response" or "return", which has served as one basis for social relations in China. The Chinese believe that reciprocity of actions (favor and hatred, reward and punishment) between man and man, and indeed between men and supernatural beings, should be as certain as a cause-and-effect relationship, and, therefore, when a Chinese acts, he normally anticipates a response or return. Favors done for others are often considered what may be termed "social investments", for which handsome returns are expected.

In traditional Chinese culture, relationship is a reciprocal, situational, and context-related concept. It is also through the rule of reciprocity that we see how Chinese stratagems (see the next section) work in Chinese negotiation processes. Chinese business people can be both sincere and deceptive when dealing with their counterparts by following the principle of reciprocity. The case study "If you honor me a foot, I will honor you ten feet in return" (in Appendix) illustrates this way of doing business from the traditional Chinese cultural perspective.

Chinese Stratagem

The Chinese stratagem (*Ji*) is a strategic component in Chinese culture. A Chinese proverb "The marketplace is a battlefield" reflects a deep-seated Chinese belief that the wisdom that guides the general commander in the battlefield is the same one that applies to business (Chu, 1991). Sun Tzu's *Art of War* is the best introduction to the strategic Chinese thinking or Chinese stratagems. Another widely read text is *The Thirty–Six Stratagems* which has crystallized the Chinese nation's wisdom in dealing with enemies and overcoming difficult and dangerous situations. Inherent in all Chinese stratagems lies Sun Tzu's (1982) admonition: "To win one hundred victories in one hundred battles is not the acme of skill. To subdue the enemy without fighting is the acme of skill."

Chinese stratagems assert the superiority of using human wisdom and indirect means rather than resorting to direct pitched battle to cope with various situations and to gain advantages over the opponent. The Chinese negotiator will typically not force you into accepting the Chinese terms but rather signals that your competitors are waiting next door preparing to present a better offer. All Chinese stratagems used by the Chinese negotiator at the negotiation table (Table 19.1) find their philosophical origins in the Yin Yang and Wu Wei ("do nothing") principles.

Table 19.1. The Thirty–Six Chinese Stratagems (Ji's)

Ji 1	Cross the sea without Heaven's knowledge (*Man Tian Guo Hai*)
	Deceive the Emperor ("Heaven") into sailing across the sea by inviting him into a seaside city which is in reality a huge camouflaged ship. Hide the deepest secrets in the most obvious situations.
Ji 2	Besiege Wei to rescue Zhao (*Wei Wei Jiu Zhao*)
	Save the state of Zhao by besieging the state of Wei, whose troops are out attacking Zhao. Avoid the strong to attack the weak.
Ji 3	Kill with a borrowed knife (*Jie Dao Sha Ren*)
	Make use of external resources for one's own gain.
Ji 4	Await leisurely the exhausted enemy (*Yi Yi Dai Lao*)
	Relax and preserve your strength while watching the enemy exhaust himself.
Ji 5	Loot a burning house (*Chen Huo Da Jie*)
	Take advantage of the opponent's trouble or crisis.
Ji 6	Clamor in the east but attack in the west (*Sheng Dong Ji Xi*)
	Devise a feint eastward but launch an attack westward.
Ji 7	Create something out of nothing (*Wu Zhong Sheng You*)
	Make the unreal seem real. Gain advantage by conjuring illusion.
Ji 8	Openly repair the walkway but secretly march to Chen Cang *(An Du Chen Cang)*
	Play overt, predictable, and public maneuvers (the walkway) against covert, surprising, and secretive ones (Chen Cang).
Ji 9	Watch the fire burning from across the river (*Ge An Guan Huo*)
	Master the art of delay. Wait for favorable conditions to emerge.
Ji 10	Hide a knife in a smile (*Xiao Li Cang Dao*)
	Hide a strong will under a compliant appearance, win the opponent's trust and act only after his guard is down.

Table 19.1. The Thirty–Six Chinese Stratagems (Ji's) (Continued)

Ji 11   Let the plum tree wither in place of the peach tree (*Li Dai Tao Jiang*)
         Make a small sacrifice in order to gain a major profit.

Ji 12   Lead away a goat in passing (*Shun Shou Qian Yang*)
         Take advantage of opportunities when they appear.

Ji 13   Beat the grass to startle the snake (*Da Cao Jing She*)
         Use direct or indirect warning and agitation.

Ji 14   Borrow a corpse to return the soul (*Jie Shi Huan Hun*)
         According to a popular Chinese myth, the spirit of a deceased may finds
         reincarnation. Revive something "dead" by decorating or expressing it in a new
         face.

Ji 15   Lure the tiger to leave the mountains (*Diao Hu Li Shan*)
         Draw the opponent out of his natural environment from which his source of
         power comes to make him more vulnerable to attack.

Ji 16   In order to capture, first let it go (*Yu Qin Gu Zong*)
         The enemy should be given room to retreat so that he is not forced to act out of
         desperation.

Ji 17   Toss out a brick to attract a piece of jade (*Pao Zhuan Yin Yu*)
         Trade something of minor value for something of major value in exchange.

Ji 18   To capture bandits, first capture the ringleader (*Qin Zei Qin Wang*)
         Deal with the most important issues first.

Ji 19   Remove the firewood from under the cooking pot (*Fu Di Chou Xin*)
         Avoid confronting your opponent's strong points and remove the source of his
         strength.

Ji 20   Muddle the water to catch the fish (*Hun Shui Mo Yu*)
         Take advantage of the opponent's inability to resist when they are put in a
         difficult and complicated situation.

Ji 21   The golden cicada sheds its shell (*Jin Chan Tuo Qiao*)
         Create an illusion by appearing to present the original "shape" to the opponent
         while secretly withdrawing the real "body" from danger.

Ji 22   Shut the door to catch the thief (*Guan Men Zhuo Zei*)
         Create a favorable enveloping environment to encircle the opponent and close
         off all his escape routes.

Ji 23   Befriend the distant states while attacking the nearby ones (*Yuan Jiao Jin Gong*)
         Deal with the "enemies" one by one. After the neighboring state is conquered,
         one can then attack the distant state.

Ji 24   Borrow the road to conquer Guo (*Jia Dao Fa Guo*)
         Deal with the enemies one by one. Use the nearby state as a springboard to reach
         the distant state. Then remove the nearby state.

Ji 25   Steal the beams and change the pillars (*Tou Liang Huan Zhu*)
         In a broader sense the stratagem refers to the use of various replacement tactics
         to achieve one's masked purposes.

Ji 26   Point at the mulberry tree but curse the locust tree (*Zhi Sang Ma Huai*)
         Convey one's intention, opinions in an indirect way.

Ji 27   Play a sober-minded fool (*Jia Chi Bu Dian*)
         Hide one's ambition in order to win by total surprise.

Table 19.1. The Thirty–Six Chinese Stratagems (Ji's) (Continued)

Ji 28	Lure the enemy onto the roof, then take away the ladder (*Shang Wu Chou Ti*) Lure the enemy into a trap and then cut off his escape route.
Ji 29	Flowers bloom in the tree (*Shu Shang Kai Hua*) One can decorate a flowerless tree with lifelike yet artificial flowers attached to it, so that it looks like a tree capable of bearing flowers. One who lacks internal strength may resort to external forces to achieve his goal.
Ji 30	The guest becomes the host (*Fan Ke Wei Zhu*) Turn one's defensive and passive position to an offensive and active one.
Ji 31	The beautiful woman stratagem (*Mei Ren Ji*) Use women, temptation and espionage to overpower the enemy; attach importance to espionage, intelligence and information collecting.
Ji 32	The empty city stratagem (*Kong Cheng Ji*) If you have absolutely no means of defense for your city and you openly display this vulnerable situation to your suspicious enemy by just opening the city gate, he is likely to assume the opposite. A deliberate display of weakness can conceal the true vulnerability and thus confuse the enemy. The stratagem can also be used to mean something with a grand exterior but a void interior.
Ji 33	The counter-espionage stratagem (*Fan Jian Ji*) When the enemy's spy is detected, do not "beat the grass to startle the snake", but furnish him with false information to sow discord in his camp. Maintain high intelligence and alertness.
Ji 34	The self-torture stratagem (*Ku Rou Ji*) Display one's own suffering in order to win sympathy from others.
Ji 35	The stratagem of interrelated stratagems (*Lian Huan Ji*) A stratagem combining various stratagems into one interconnected arrangement. Deliberately planning a series of stratagems.
Ji 36	Running away is the best stratagem (*Zou Wei Shang Ji*) Run away, when all else fails. Put up with temporary disgrace and losses to win ultimate victory. Running away to gain more bargaining power.

Source: Own work.

Sun Tzu's strategic thinking "victory without fighting" is often reflected in Chinese negotiating tactics. A common Chinese "ploy" is to conduct parallel negotiations with competing firms to play them off against each other. As mentioned earlier, a typical Chinese negotiator would not corner you to adjust your price level but rather signal that you are in a race and your competitors are to come to offer a better proposal so that you know how to modify your proposal automatically. This is a typical "Kill with a borrowed knife" stratagem (No. 3 in the list of The Thirty-Six Stratagems).

At the negotiation table your Chinese negotiation counterpart may appear absent-minded, not listening to you or silent as if he/she does not understand you to stimulate you to speak and promise more ("Play a sober-minded fool"; No. 27 in the list of The Thirty-Six Stratagems). Chinese hospitality and friendliness can be a double-edged sword, which can make it difficult for you to feel too business-minded. Much of the Chinese negotiating style is based on building up a mental guilt feeling which you are expected to be paid back in various ways. This tactic is illustrated in "Hide a knife in a smile" (No. 10 in the list of The Thirty-Six Stratagems) or "The beautiful woman stratagem" (No. 31).

WHAT IS A CHINESE NEGOTIATING STYLE?

Given the impacts of different driving forces, a Chinese negotiator often plays paradoxical roles. The Chinese negotiator may be understood as a blend of "Maoist bureaucrat in learning", "Confucian gentleman"[92], and "Sun Tzu-like strategist".

"Maoist Bureaucrat in Learning"

As a Maoist bureaucrat, the Chinese negotiator follows his government's plans to do business. He gives first priority to China's national interest and never separates business from politics. He avoids taking initiatives, shuns responsibility, fears criticism, and has no final say. He lacked international business experience but is currently moving quickly upward on the steep learning curve. He is a shrewd negotiator because he is trained daily in Chinese bureaucracy in which bargaining is an integrated element. Given the changing PRC condition and the increasing impacts of foreign direct investment, the Chinese "communist" bureaucracy has started embracing the capitalist spirit. Entrepreneurial passion is often reflected in the behavior of Chinese negotiator even from a state-owned enterprise.

"Confucian Gentleman"

Being a Confucian gentleman, the Chinese negotiator behaves on the basis of mutual trust and benefit, seeking cooperation and "win-win" solutions. He shows a profound capacity to conclude business without negotiating. He simply does not like the word "negotiation"; he prefers to use the words "talk" or "discuss"(as a matter of fact, the Mandarin words for negotiation is *Tan Pan*, which literally translates as "Talk" and "Judge", respectively) because the Western notion of "negotiation" suggests somewhat disagreeable connotations of conflict, which must be avoided at all costs. He views contracting essentially as an ongoing relationship or problem-solving process rather than a one-off watertight legal package. He associates business with *guanxi*, friendship, and trust. He is group-oriented, self-restrained, conscious of face, age, hierarchy, and etiquette, and suspicious of "non-family" persons. He can be a daunting negotiator, for example, when he revisits old issues in the light of a changing market situation to seek mutual benefits and when he bargains toughly in the interests of his "family." His negotiation strategy is characterized basically by cooperation.

"Sun Tzu-Like Strategist"

As a Sun Tzu-like strategist, the Chinese negotiator views marketplace as a battlefield. He sets out to "win-lose" you. He is a skilful negotiator, endowed with a formidable variety of Chinese stratagems from his ancestors. At the heart of his bargaining technique lies Sun Tzu's secret: "To subdue the enemy without fighting." He seldom wages a physical war;

---

[92] In this article, the words "gentleman" and "he", etc. are used for the sake of simplicity; they refer, however, to both genders.

rather, he is keen on a psychological wrestling of wit to manipulate you into doing business his way. His actions tend to be deceitful and indirect. He often creates favorable situations to attain his objectives by utilizing external forces. His most favored negotiating tactic is "Kill with a borrowed knife" (Stratagem 3). He is always ready to withdraw from the bargaining table when all else fails, but this is only a Chinese stratagem for fighting back (Chiao, 1981). His negotiation strategy is characterized by competition. As such, Chinese negotiating style is intrinsically a paradox. For example, the Chinese negotiator values *face* when doing business as gentlemen. But the same person values "thick face and black heart" (suggesting "faceless", "merciless"; Chu, 1992) when doing business as a strategist.

As such, the Chinese negotiating style is flexible, situation-related and paradoxical in nature. The frequently heard Chinese phrase "Foreign guests first!" is not just a courtesy invitation but also a strategic consideration. The Chinese negotiator uses both the Confucian-style cooperation strategy and the Sun Tzu style competition strategy in negotiations – a strategic paradox which I call the "coop–comp" Chinese negotiation strategy. The term *coop–comp* suggests that Chinese negotiators negotiate both cooperatively and competitively, and both sincerely and deceptively because they are driven by cultural traits of both – cooperative and competitive qualities.

But when would the Chinese negotiator use a cooperation strategy and when would the same person use a competition strategy? It depends ultimately on *trust* between the negotiating parties.

When mutual trust is high, the Chinese negotiator negotiates as a Confucian gentleman; when mutual trust is low, the same person manipulates as a Sun Tzu-like strategist. Meeting you for the first time, even the Chinese themselves are not sure which roles they should play; all depends on how you act in your first moves. The Chinese negotiator routinely examines and evaluates the state of trust between the parties at the outset of negotiation, and then calibrates his negotiation strategies in dealing with the other party based on the Confucian principle of reciprocity.

THE CHANGING SUCCESS AND FAILURE FACTORS IN NEGOTIATIONS WITH THE PRC

A survey of Swedish firms was conducted in 2003 concerning the success and failure factors in business negotiations with China (Fang and Fann, 2003, see "This study" in Table 19.2, Table 19.3). The survey used a questionnaire which was adopted in two earlier studies, one in the 1980s and the other in the 1990s. Although the empirical bases of these three studies differ from each other (size of the firm, location, and industry), the general trend seems to be pointing to a more professional and competition-oriented business environment in Post–WTO China where technical competence plays an increasingly important role. At the same time, the impacts of some cultural factors cannot be underestimated (e.g. your sincerity in negotiation – an important step to building up trust in negotiations).

Table 19.2. Success Factors in Negotiating with the PRC – A Comparison Between Three Studies

Items	This study			Leung and Yeung (1995)			Stewart and Keown (1989)		
	Mean	SD	Ranking	Mean	SD	Ranking	Mean	SD	Ranking
Sincerity on the part of our team	6.26	1.00	1	3.68	1.72	18	5.78	X	8
Preparation by our team	5.94	0.91	2	4.46	1.54	11	5.72	X	10
Our firm's technical expertise	5.87	1.16	3	4.18	1.60	13	5.82	X	6
Patience on the part of our team	5.64	1.09	4	4.45	1.64	12	5.93	X	5
Our knowledge of PRC business practices	5.17	1.17	5	5.80	1.02	2	5.80	X	7
Good personal relationships	5.02	1.37	6	6.01	1.07	1	5.98	X	4
Our willingness to sell at a good price	4.70	1.41	7	4.82	1.32	9	5.69	X	11
Uniqueness of our product	4.68	1.14	8	5.11	1.39	6	6.81	X	1
Our ability to meet delivery requirements	4.49	1.40	9	3.98	1.54	14	5.31	X	13
PRC's need for our product	4.43	2.00	10	5.26	1.36	5	6.34	X	2
PRC's requirement being clear	4.13	1.57	11	5.31	1.24	3	5.73	X	9
Our familiarity with PRC social customs	4.04	1.16	12	3.94	1.51	15	5.05	X	15
Good interpreter on our side	3.81	2.17	13	2.80	1.37	20	3.85	X	18
Our knowledge of the PRC's political and economic situation	3.64	1.52	14	3.77	1.63	17	5.11	X	14
Our use of the "old friend" approach	3.30	1.78	15	5.29	1.64	4	4.57	X	16
Our firm's past reputation in selling to PRC	3.28	1.68	16	3.86	1.54	16	5.35	X	12
Our willingness to offer good financing	3.04	1.69	17	5.07	1.25	7	4.38	X	17
Our use of an intermediary/agent	2.96	1.69	18	3.29	1.50	19	3.21	X	20
PRC's foreign exchange availability	2.74	1.92	19	5.04	1.68	8	6.22	X	3
Gift and tour service	2.19	1.46	20	4.73	1.56	10	X	X	X
Our willingness to arrange counter trade (e.g. buyback)	1.42	1.01	21	2.75	1.25	21	3.42	X	19

Table 19.3. Failure Factors in Negotiating with the PRC: A Comparison Between the Three Studies

Items	This study			Leung and Yeung (1995)			Stewart and Keown (1989)		
	Mean	SD	Ranking	Mean	SD	Ranking	Mean	SD	Ranking
Our inability to lower price	6.18	1.67	1	3.80	1.39	13	5.21	X	8
Too many competitors offering the same product	5.68	1.07	2	3.68	1.41	15	5.64	X	5
Lack of preparation by our team	5.27	1.20	3	4.10	1.55	10	4.64	X	13
PRC insincerity	4.91	1.12	4	5.20	1.51	2	5.36	X	6
Disagreement on contractual terms	3.61	1.24	5	3.81	1.55	12	4.79	X	12
Our inability to meet delivery requirements	3.55	1.76	6	3.80	1.33	14	5.15	X	10
Different objectives	3.45	1.39	7	3.05	1.53	19	3.71	X	18
A breakdown in communication	3.25	1.57	8	4.77	1.72	4	5.93	X	3
Our unwillingness to meet financing demands	3.16	1.67	9	4.73	1.38	5	5.21	X	9
Difference in business practices	3.11	1.73	10	4.71	1.61	6	4.36	X	15
Lack of patience by our team	3.11	1.53	11	3.63	1.47	16	5.14	X	11
Not knowing any "old friends"	2.86	1.46	12	4.61	1.40	8	5.23	X	7
PRC did not really need our product	2.84	1.36	13	4.86	1.39	3	5.86	X	4
Differences in negotiation styles	2.82	1.04	14	3.20	1.64	18	4.31	X	16
Our firm's lack of good reputation in PRC	2.77	1.46	15	3.85	1.45	11	4.64	X	14
PRC's shortage of foreign exchange	2.68	1.55	16	4.34	1.50	9	6.93	X	1
PRC's lack of budget	2.66	1.48	17	5.34	1.18	1	6.14	X	2
Difference in social customs	2.64	1.16	18	2.48	1.25	20	3.71	X	17
Not using an intermediary/agent	2.32	1.22	19	3.32	1.49	17	3.64	X	19
Language problems	2.00	1.56	20	2.37	1.24	21	3.62	X	20
Cannot cope with "stress" created by the PRC team	1.86	0.85	21	4.63	1.52	7	X	X	X

MANAGERIAL IMPLICATIONS

(1) Send Your Best Team to China

China is a demanding marketplace to which you need to send your best team. Your team leader should be a person with charismatic charm, a patient personality, credibility, and sufficient authority to make key decisions. If you need to send a young professional to China, you need to show that this young person is not every man or woman but a key person in your company who can make important decisions on behalf of the company. Technical and financial specialists must always be included on your team to be able to answer technical and financial questions raised by the Chinese counterparts, who are technology- and price-sensitive. Your lawyer, if participating in face-to-face meetings, should be well versed not only in Western laws but also in Chinese law and government regulations.

(2) Show Political Support

In China, the Chinese government is often found to be "the biggest boss" in many business projects. The all-pervasive influence of Chinese politics on Chinese business would imply that the Chinese may simply doubt your company's stability, reliability, and credibility if your government does not support your company. It is of crucial importance to show political support and governmental backing behind your important China missions especially when negotiating large industrial high-risk projects in China. Large business contracts can be secured and potential problems resolved if leaders of your government and your business community work hand in hand in doing business with China.

(3) Identify Real Chinese Negotiators

The real Chinese negotiators or final decision makers are often absent from formal negotiation sessions. High-ranking officials, private business owners and key profiles of certain interest groups and even their private networks can all drive the process of negotiations. Never miss the chance, if any, to meet directly with Chinese political and business leaders. By identifying and negotiating with the real Chinese negotiators, you can, as a Chinese proverb states, "get twice the result with half the effort."

(4) Take a People-Oriented Approach

There is a growing awareness of legalism in today's China. However, the traditional Confucian aversion to law still exists and many Chinese associate law and lawyers with coercion, troubles, and failure of the relationship. A cooperative spirit and trust are at least equally valued as formal contracts as the Chinese seldom expect one-off legal agreements to bring about an exactly planned outcome. Chinese business negotiation is distinctively people-oriented, and the Chinese do business with you as a person and not as a company. Many foreign firms have killed their negotiations in China before the negotiations even got started, because they did not give importance to "pre-negotiation" and "social talks" which would otherwise help build up trust (*xinren*) to open the door to formal negotiation processes.

(5) Local Presence

In the traditional Chinese culture trust is often high inside the family and low outside the family. Chinese negotiators tend to haggle "ruthlessly" when negotiations are held between parties who are strangers. Your local Chinese employees will be able to help you penetrate into "the Chinese family" and establish a trusting relationship with your Chinese customers and suppliers more effectively than would be the case otherwise. Chinese loyalty is not a universal notion but a highly reciprocal business, depending on how fair and trustful you are perceived in the eyes of your Chinese partners. A Chinese is your "friend for life" and behaves as a gentleman when you behave as a gentleman; he employs tricks and ploys when you play games. How to motivate, train, and retain your local Chinese human resources to contribute actively to your China market development strategies is an issue of strategic importance if you want to secure a long-standing foothold in the Chinese market.

(6) Maintain a Consistent Team

Maintaining the same team throughout the negotiation process is an essential means of gaining trust from the Chinese side. Chinese tend to do business with you as a person not as a company; your successor does not automatically inherit your personal networks. Trust which often takes time to build up may be undermined overnight if you frequently rotate members of your team. Therefore, it is important to retain a consistent team as much as possible when negotiating with the Chinese, allowing the same persons to deal with each other as long as business continues.

(7) Pad Your Price Culturally

Bargaining is a Chinese way of life, both politically and culturally. If the Chinese are not familiar with your culture and corporate practices, they tend to believe automatically that any price you quote must have some huge "water content" (*shuifen*). Chinese negotiators often set out automatically to squeeze out the water content. By doing so, a Chinese can not only gain face but also show that he/she is the "winner" in front of superiors. Therefore, it is often necessary to pad your price to a culturally reasonable level that allows you to give away some margin to the Chinese to help them gain face and satisfy their bureaucratic needs and wants. Today, foreign firms are bringing in new practices and new business culture. For example, although IKEA does not allow bargaining and price haggling in IKEA stores in China, the Chinese have accepted IKEA. China is a paradox and China is changing!

(8) Help Your Chinese Counterpart

The Chinese way of doing business is reciprocal. Favor (as well as disfavor) needs to be returned. For example, behind your Chinese negotiating counterpart often lies a complicated internal Chinese negotiation game. Helping your Chinese negotiating counterpart to avoid would-be criticism and punishment within Chinese systems would eventually help your negotiations.

(9) Invite the Chinese to Negotiate Abroad

Much has been written about how Westerners should adapt to the Chinese. Western firms can influence the Chinese as well. The Chinese are learning fast. Inviting the Chinese to visit your country for some of the negotiating sessions is a rewarding strategy. Even if you pay for the trip, the payment would be well worth the cost. A visit to your country, for example, would expose the Chinese to your culture and business ambience. The Chinese negotiators who come from a tradition in which bargaining is a way of life would probably alter their bargaining strategies to adapt to you. Moreover, access to high-ranking Chinese officials is far easier in your own country than in China.

(10) Design "8-Numbered" Products for China

Chinese society is shaped by a set of norms, rules, habits, symbols, and moral obligations different from those of Western societies. For example, number "8" is adored (whereas number "4" is disfavored) in Chinese culture. A careless unintentional violation of the Chinese codes of etiquette may risk losing business opportunities. Therefore, I use "Design 8-numbered products for China" as a metaphor to enunciate the importance of respecting and learning Chinese sociocultural traits. Your products should avoid a "4-numbered" identity when entering and operating in the Chinese market.

(11) Be Patient

From the perspective of the PRC condition, China is such a large country that problems of various types are bound to crop up. The formidable Chinese bureaucracy often invites marathon negotiations. From the perspective of Confucianism, China is a familistic society in which it takes time to build trust between non-family members. "The Chinese distrust fast talkers who want to make quick deals" (Pye, 1982). Remember that "Kung Fu" means essentially "time", "efforts" and "hard work" in Chinese. From the vantage point of Chinese stratagems, you need patience to deal with Chinese stratagems and strategists. By being patient, tolerant, calm, persistent, and honest in dealing with the Chinese, you will eventually win the Chinese heart and trust.

(12) Explode the Myth of Face

The Chinese are face conscious; they can go to great lengths to avoid saying the word "No" (in China, there are at least 16 ways of saying "no", including "yes"). However, respecting Chinese face and never saying "no" to a Chinese is advisable only within the domain of business relations between Confucian gentlemen or in an ideal Confucian working domain. The Chinese negotiators can, paradoxically, be both Confucian gentlemen and Sun Tzu-like strategists. Therefore, the advice that you should never say "no" to a Chinese could be dangerous when it is practiced in front of a Sun Tzu-like Chinese strategist. For example, your reluctance to say "no" can be taken advantage of by the Chinese strategist to suggest that you have agreed with the Chinese demand. Therefore, it is strategically important not to be shattered by the Chinese face. You must dare to explode the myth of face.

(13) Approach China as the "United States of China"

With a vast land area of 9.6 million square kilometers, a huge population of 1.3 billion inhabitants, and enormous ethnic, linguistic and subculture variations, China is a huge continent and may be called a "United States of China". Today more than 70% of all public spending is actually decided at the regional level instead of at the central level. Chinese regions are significantly different in purchasing power, attitudes, lifestyles, media use, consumption patterns, and customs and traditions. One of the reasons why many Western companies have failed to establish a firm foothold in China is their lack of a "regional approach" to the Chinese market (Cui and Liu, 2000). While various regions in China share common Chinese characteristics we discussed above, they also possess their unique regional features. For example, business style in Beijing, Shanghai, and Guangdong may be called relational, professional, and entrepreneurial, respectively (Fang, 2004).

REFERENCES

Chen, M. J. 2001. "*Inside Chinese Business: A Guide for Managers Worldwide.*" Boston: Harvard Business School Press.

Chiao, C. 1981. "Chinese Strategic Behaviors: A Preliminary List." In *Proceedings of the International Conference on Sinology*, Taipei, August 15–17, 1980, Taipei, Academia Sinica, 429–440.

Chu, C. N. 1991. "*The Asian Mind Game.*" New York: Rawson Associates.

Chu, C. N. 1992. "*Thick Face Black Heart: The Path to Thriving, Winning and Succeeding.*" Beaverton: AMC Publishing.

Cui, G., and Liu, Q. 2000. "Regional Market Segments of China: Opportunities and Barriers in a Big Emerging Market." *Journal of Consumer Marketing*, 17(1): 55–72.

Fang, T. 1999. "*Chinese Business Negotiating Style.*" Thousand Oaks: Sage Publications.

Fang, T. 2004. "Chinese Business Style: A Regional Approach." In Macbean, A. and Brown, D. (eds): "*Challenges for China's Development: An Enterprise Perspective.*" London: Routledge, 156–172.

Fang, T., and Fann, T. T. 2003. "Changing Success and Failure Factors in Negotiating with the PRC." *Competitive paper presented at The Annual EAMSA Conference*, Stockholm, October 22–24.

Pye, L. W. 1982. *"Chinese Commercial Negotiating Style."* Cambridge, MA: Oelgeschlager, Gunn and Hain.

Sun Tzu. 1982. *"Sun Tzu: The Art of War."* Translated by Samuel B. Griffith. London: Oxford University Press.

Chan, W. T. 1963. *"A Source Book in Chinese Philosophy."* Princeton, NJ: Princeton University Press.

Yang, L. S. 1957. "The Concept of 'Pao' as a Basis for Social Relations in China." In Fairbank, J. K. (ed): *"Chinese Thought and Institutions."* Chicago: The University of Chicago Press, 291–309.

APPENDIX

If You Honor Me a Foot, I Will Honor You Ten Feet in Return 93

China is the world's third largest shipbuilding nation, after Korea and Japan. Scandinavian countries are among the world's leading shipping nations. The Chinese shipyard C brought home from Scandinavia three new building contracts to build chemical tankers of 8,300 to 13,600 deadweight tons (1 for N, 3 for D, and 1 for S), with the total contract value worth around USD 100 million. All the important negotiation sessions took place in Norway, Denmark, and Sweden. The first contract involving the construction of one chemical tanker was signed between C and N in June 1996. C won the contract in tough competition with the Japanese and the Koreans because of its more attractive ship design (an outsourced product from a leading Norwegian naval architecture consulting firm) and cheaper price. It was agreed that NOR classified the vessel.

The second contract, regarding three chemical tankers, was signed between C and D in August 1996. These three vessels were also of the Norwegian design that was outsourced by C. This time, whereas the design and price still remained a major competitive advantage for the Chinese in comparison with those of the Koreans and the Japanese, the positive word of mouth from N helped increase D's confidence in C's ability to build technology-intensive chemical tankers. These three Danish vessels were classified by LL instead of NOR.

The third contract the Chinese signed in their Scandinavian tour was that with the Swedish ship owner S in the autumn of 1996. The vessel was a sister vessel of the Norwegian vessel that the Chinese, at that time, already had started constructing in Shanghai. The negotiation between C and S was largely ceremonial — this was a result of the positive word of mouth from N and D, and almost exactly the same design as that of its Norwegian sister vessel. This time, it was agreed that the Swedish vessel would be constructed in conformity with the NOR's rules and regulations.

Picture 19.3 shows the actors in the scope of this case and their interactions. Shipbuilding is a complex and time-consuming process. For the ship owner, it usually takes five to six years to plan a new building project, negotiate the contract, supervise the construction processes, and finally take over the vessel from the shipyard and put it into operation. For the shipyard/shipbuilder, the shipbuilding negotiation involves not only negotiations of the contract and technical specifications with the ship owner but also those with the classification society, insurance company, and marine equipment suppliers from around the world who often are connected to one another in the whole shipbuilding project. A chemical tanker of the size discussed in this study would take two to three years to construct after the signing of the contract. After a classification standard (e.g., NOR, LL, or others) is selected by the shipyard, the selected classification society will send its site supervisors to the shipyard to approve the drawings and plans and supervise the whole construction processes. After the vessel has passed the final inspection, this classification society will issue a certificate to the ship owner to certify that the vessel is seaworthy and ready for delivery to the ship owner. The whole shipbuilding process suggests that the shipyard, ship owner, classification society, and other

---

[93] This case study was originally a part of the author's article "Culture as a Driving Force for Interfirm Adaptation: A Chinese Case", which was published in *Industrial Marketing Management*, 2001, Vol. 30.

actors have to interact with, and adapt to each other intensively throughout the contract negotiation and shipbuilding construction processes. Three major adaptations that the Chinese shipyard has adopted during its negotiations with D and NOR are described in detail as follows.

Adaptation 1: The Chinese shipyard C agreed to the Danish ship owner D's request to change the main engine from the medium-speed type to a low-speed alternative even though the change would involve a great amount of work of a technological and management nature for C.

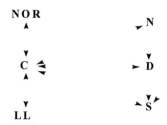

Picture 19.3. The Shipbuilding Case: Actors and Their Interactions.

Several months after C and D signed the shipbuilding contract (including the technical specification), D asked to modify the contract by changing the main engine from the agreed medium–speed type to a low–speed version (MAN/BandW 6S42MC). A more cost-effective vessel was the main reason behind D's desire to change the contract. The main engine of a vessel may be compared to the human heart. To change the main engine would cause a great amount of work of both a technological and management nature on the part of C. The Chinese negotiator, Mr. Q, detailed some of the major technical adjustments related to the change of the main engine. He said:

> "First, the weight of the vessel would be increased. Consider that the low-speed main engine body itself was heavier than the medium-speed main engine body by almost 50 tons. This means that the deadweight of the vessel would be decreased by 50 tons accordingly. Second, we would need to design some more daily fuel oil tanks if a low-speed main engine was adopted; this in turn would increase steel structures and space. Third, the low-speed main engine was greater in length. We would therefore need to calculate whether the engine room would be able to accommodate it [the new engine]. Fourth, a number of auxiliary systems were to be changed too. For example, the cooling system was to be expanded; oil heating equipment needed to be connected to the oil separating system, since heavy diesel oil would be used [for the proposed low-speed main engine]. Altogether, we had some 12 issues which needed to be discussed with the ship owner if it wanted to change [from the medium-speed main engine] to the low-speed main engine."

Despite all the foreseen and unforeseen difficulties, the Chinese agreed to D's request. When asked why they did so, Mr. Q replied:

> "This was, as we Chinese put it, 'If you honor me a foot, I will honor you ten feet in return.' Earlier I have said that M [D's vice president and technical director] had made a very good impression in our shipyard, P [D's sales and marketing director] too, in the whole of this project. In normal cases, a shipyard can refuse to accept such a request to change the type of

main engine, as suggested by the Danish ship owner, because the contract has already been signed. The shipyard may simply say 'No', and you can do nothing about it. If your ship owner insisted that I make the change, I would say, 'OK, 2 million US dollars.' There is nothing to be discussed, because the contract was signed and binding. But we did not do business in this way, *because* 'If you honor me a foot, I will honor you ten feet in return.'"

As such, the Chinese adapted positively to the demand of the Danish ship owner simply because the latter had earlier made a good impression on the Chinese and helped them to solve their problems. In Chinese terms, D had previously honored C "a foot" and it was now C's turn to honor D "ten feet in return." When asked "How did they honor you a foot?", Mr. Q answered:

"I always said that M was a very reasonable man. Take an example. By oversight, we had not discovered that the vessels' painting work, according to the specification, was a job that we would not be able to accomplish in reality. The specification prevented us from carrying out any welding work once the painting was finished. In other words, we were not permitted to paint the vessel before it had been completely constructed... Our shipyard lacked experience at that time; the person who was responsible for painting didn't realize this problem when proofreading the specification. I talked to M about my problem. Then, M said: 'OK, I agree to change to [the method of] sectional painting, without price adjustment.' His short answer had helped solve a big problem for our shipyard, a problem that could not be solved otherwise. Any ship owner has the right to refuse to accept a vessel that is not built exactly to the technical specifications. You simply can't pass the inspection, because your painting is not done in accordance with the contract. So, when M wanted us to change to a low-speed main engine, we responded to him in a very cooperative and active way."

According to the Chinese, C and D had established a high level of rapport and a strong "cooperation spirit". This was because C had got a very good impression of M, D's vice president and technical director, who had previously helped C to solve its painting dilemma. In other words, D had previously agreed to C's request to modify the contract to make it easier for the latter to do the painting work.

Mr. Q also mentioned that M had once helped him "personally" in the negotiation of the Danish project. The story started with the negotiation between C and NOR regarding the classification of the Norwegian vessel.

"It was in June last year [1996] when we were negotiating the Norwegian vessel. The vessel was to be classified by NOR. As a matter of fact, NOR was the only classification society that was endorsed in the specification. When we discussed the price, NOR [Shanghai] insisted 'USD 240,000' [for this vessel of 8,300 DWT]. Since then, I have had many discussions with the NOR Shanghai Office. I told them that the price was too high. They asked for my expectation. I said USD 200,000 to 220,000, about 1% of the price of the vessel. LL gave me a 'USD 210,000' offer, but unfortunately we couldn't talk further about it... NOR's trump card was: 'You had already signed the specification in which NOR was the only recommended classification society, you couldn't escape.'"

Mr. Q continued:

"Then, I went to the NOR Shanghai Office, together with five other people from our shipyard, for the final meeting... Now all other parts of the commercial negotiations were finalized except for the price. 'This is the first time I do business with NOR,' I said to the NOR Shanghai representative, a Hong Kong Chinese, and to his assistant, a Shanghainese, 'You all know our Chinese customs. Today, I would be heartily grateful to get even the slightest discount from you. I would see it as your giving me a *mianzi* ["face"].' Then, we were all sitting in silence, face-to-face, with the shipyard's six people on one side and NOR's two people on the other side of the table. About 30 minutes passed like this. Then, he [the Hong Kong Chinese] broke the silence: 'USD 240,000. Not a dollar's discount!' I took out my pen gently and put my signature on the contract. 'I agree with you, USD 240,000,' I said. After signing the contract, they invited us to stay to have a dinner together. 'No,' I replied, 'I do not have time. I must go.' But I also said, 'I don't know if my colleagues would like to stay. I can ask them.' Remember: I was the team leader; if I wanted to go, who else would dare to stay to eat? We all left ... As such, I declined the dinner. When leaving, I told them [NOR managers] clearly: 'Your price is too high. It seems that we will not be able to have any chance to serve you in the future.'"

The Chinese felt they had lost face badly in their encounter with the NOR managers. The last sentence by the Chinese signaled that they did not want to do business with NOR in the future. The story went on.

Adaptation 2: The Chinese shipyard C stood firm, not accepting NOR as the vessels' classification standard, even though NOR's price was eventually reduced to the level lower than that of its competitor LL.

Now the time came for the Chinese shipyard C to negotiate the new building project with the Danish ship owner D. Which classification standard was to be adopted, NOR, LL, or others, was an issue that had to be agreed upon between C and D. Because the Chinese felt that NOR's representative had, in the Norwegian project, made them lose face – a terrible shame in Chinese culture – they decided to use LL, not NOR, this time. But this had to be realized by a proviso in the shipbuilding contract that allowed the shipyard to make a choice among various classification societies. Mr. Q recalled:

"Then came the project of the three Danish new buildings in August last year [1996]. I was about to negotiate the shipbuilding contract with the Danish ship owner. NOR [Shanghai Office] got the news. The Shanghainese phoned me, asking if they could make an offer. 'Of course,' I said. And I described the general outline of the vessels. NOR said that because the ship owner was from Scandinavia, it was most likely that they would want to have their vessels classified by NOR. I asked them to make an offer first. In the meantime, I sent an inquiry to LL. Not long after, two offers arrived: NOR offered USD 380,000 and LL offered USD 210,000. This was the per vessel price for the three vessels. Then, [we] went to [Denmark to] negotiate with D. I talked to M about the vessels' classification issue. I told the story of NOR in [the negotiation of] Norwegian contract. I expressed my discontent with NOR. I said I had to modify the provision of the specification to the effect that a choice can be made [by the shipyard] between NOR, LL, or the equivalent, as the vessels' classification standard... Why was I so annoyed? Because NOR did not give me face. In other words, NOR utilized the fact that they were the only option in the specification to corner me into an indefensible position. This was not an issue of my own feeling but concerned my shipyard's feeling... I felt that NOR looked down upon the Chinese; they went too far. Lao M understood me very well. After I told the story, he said, 'No problem. NOR and LL mean the same to us. We can accept both.' As such, the specification was signed which allowed our shipyard to choose between NOR, LL, or the equivalent. Then, I sent a fax [to NOR]: 'Dear NOR, we have signed the agreement with the Danish ship owner. Now, it's high time to discuss one of the most important issues – classification. Your offer has already been received. Thank you very much. Would you please consider reducing your price because your price is higher than that of LL.'"

From the ship owner's point of view, NOR and LL meant pretty much the same. However, the shipbuilding contract between C and D, which allowed C "to choose between NOR, LL, or the equivalent" as a classification standard, provided C with an opportunity to take a handsome revenge upon NOR.

NOR managers approached the Chinese for the Danish project. But the Chinese had long set out to offend them. Mr. Q said:

"Now, the NOR Shanghai Office was managed by a Norwegian who once was NOR's regional manager in Dalian. This general manager and his assistant, the same Shanghainese as before, came to our shipyard one day at about 11 o'clock. I was sitting in a meeting. When I was informed that the general manager of NOR Shanghai Office was looking for me, I realized immediately what it was about. I wanted to show my discontent. But out of *limao* ["courtesy"], I asked my colleague to tell them to wait 15 minutes or so because I was in the middle of an important meeting. The two gentlemen were then left alone to cool their heels in the waiting room. In fact, I could have stayed away from the meeting, which was not as important as I told them. About 15 minutes later, I came out to meet the gentlemen. He [the Shanghainese] introduced his new boss to me and we exchanged a few courtesy words. They certainly felt I was fairly cold. They then asked me about the progress of the project, the agreement with the Danish ship owner, etc. I told them what was going on and said I was now handling four contracts, the first two of which were already concluded: the ship owner contract, the design contract, the ship classification contract, and the ship insurance contract. The last one, the ship insurance contract, was no panic; it was still not yet on the agenda. Then, the gentlemen said, 'How about going out to eat together?' I replied, 'Not necessary. If you talk business, we can do it right here.' 'Yes, we are here to talk business, but we can still eat and talk,' they persuaded me. Then I said, 'Let's do this way. You come to visit me; you are the guests and I am the host. Let me entertain you in our shipyard.'"

Mr. Q. continued:

"Then, I phoned the shipyard's general office, asking them to arrange three working luncheons for me. To be frank, I had never entertained my guests to a working luncheon before. Whenever I received guests, I always did it in decent restaurants, never in the works canteen ... This time, I would say, I intended to offend them. I placed them on a low-ranking shelf, and myself with them. We went to the works canteen. It was a canteen for site supervisors and service engineers from overseas. Many of them were dressed in rather oily working clothes. I was in casual clothes that day. But the two NOR gentlemen were both in suits. The working lunch standard was eight yuan per person: several dishes, a bowl of rice, a bowl of soup, and a bottle of Coke ... Looking around the pretty noisy and 'working clothes background,' the NOR general manager certainly realized that something was wrong. So did the Shanghainese assistant, who told me at once that NOR had not treated me well before, or something like that. To this, the Chinese did not say 'Forget it.' I said: 'Never mind.'"

He went on:

"Then, I told the Shanghainese: 'You are Chinese too. You know the Chinese seldom hate or love a person too much. What the Chinese do is *li shang wang lai* ["A gift needs to be reciprocated," "Courtesy demands reciprocity"]. You remember: *li shang wang lai*'. Here, the word *li* means not only "gift," but also something negative, an insulting action, disrespectful, or a blow from the opponent, to name a few examples. Then, they asked me about the price offered by LL. I said: 'Sorry, this is a commercial secret. You shouldn't ask such question and I am not in a position to answer this question either. I can let you know that the LL's price is on my office desk right now. You just do your best.' They whispered a while. Then, the Shanghainese said to me: 'USD 300,000,' looking straight into my eyes. I smiled. I said: 'What I need is not a verbal promise but a written one. You may say 300,000 today, but say "I forget it" tomorrow. To whom would I turn for help then? I must have your offer in writing.' ... After the lunch, we went to the shipyard's foreign guests' house to drink tea. I answered their questions one by one except for those about the LL's price. They certainly found me annoying. Finally, before leaving, the Shanghainese said: 'If USD 300,000 is still too high, would you give me a hint please. We can do USD 240,000.' I smiled without saying a word. I asked him to send me a written offer... That evening, he did send a fax to my home: USD 220,000 per vessel."

Now, NOR had substantially reduced its price from the previous USD 380,000 to USD 220,000 per vessel. This offer was very close to LL's USD 210,000. But the Chinese stood firm. Mr. Q recalled:

"Yes, very close. But I told him [NOR manager] that I have almost decided to use LL. Then, he asked me how much LL had offered. I said: 'I can tell you now, USD 210,000 per vessel.' Three days later, he sent a fax to me again, offering USD 210,000 for the first vessel, and USD 180,000 for each of the two sister vessels. They also invited me to their office. I went to the NOR office, this time together with almost the same group of people as the last time. Before going, I told my colleagues that I would not sign any contract with them [NOR] on that day. I asked them not to make any preparations, because I would use LL this time. At the NOR Shanghai Office, the NOR people told us that it would be best to use the NOR classification, since NOR was already used for an earlier [the Norwegian] vessel at our shipyard. This allowed them to be able to offer very cheap prices for the rest of the vessels. And this was also why the price for the Norwegian vessel was relatively high and those for the Danish vessels were relatively low. They had clearly prepared for the meeting and put forth many reasons. They also admitted that several paragraphs in the Norwegian contract were not very fair to the shipyard. For example, the shipyard had to pay extra salary for the NOR supervisors' overtime work at the shipyard... The general manager told me frankly that they knew they had made a big mistake [regarding the Norwegian vessel]. But the contract was signed, he had no mandate to adjust the price. The only thing he could do at this moment, however, was to cancel those two 'overtime salary' paragraphs. Then, he cancelled the paragraphs and we both initialed the contracts. The general manager said: 'This is the only compensation I am able to make.'"

Mr. Q continued:

"Now I felt the need to say a few words, in English, to the general manager. But I changed my mind, because few of my colleagues understood English. I told the Shanghainese: 'I will speak Chinese and you help translate.' I said: 'Indeed, our cooperation for the first vessel was very unpleasant. I had never met a person who treated me so poorly. I viewed the matter not from the perspective of my personal *mianzi*, but from the perspective of the shipyard's *mianzi*. My feeling was when NOR was in an overwhelming negotiation position, it could give an unmerciful blow to its counterpart. This was what I did not understand most. The Chinese attach great importance to the word *li*. But I had not experienced it from you. I can tell you definitely that I will use LL this time, even though your price is lower.' Then, the Shanghainese wondered why I decided to use LL instead of NOR and how I could justify my decision. I replied: 'I can say that your price is lower but your service is worse than that of LL... You may make a report to the shipyard director, complaining about me selecting LL even though its price is higher than yours. But I believe if you did so, you would lose our shipyard for good... This time, what I want is to give you a lesson about how to deal with Chinese shipyards, and how to deal with the Chinese. You [the Shanghainese] are a Chinese; you should help them [Western people] to deal with the Chinese, not just to make money on the Chinese. I hope you translate my words over [to the general manager].' He did the English translation word for word from my original words. [I knew] because I understood English. The general manager looked very awkward. He apologized again and again. He said: 'I am so sorry. Mr. KK [the former NOR representative in Shanghai] made an unforgivable mistake... I have lived in Dalian for three years and I know how to do business with the Chinese. Had I been the person to negotiate with you that day, I would never have done it that way... I would try to give you face.'"

Mr. Q went on:

"That evening, NOR invited us to dinner and we all attended. We ate although we did not reach any agreement with NOR. I did not make a secret of my point; the reason why I did not sign the contract this time was simply because you pushed me too hard the last time. I took revenge on you. This was *yi ya huan ya* ["a tooth for a tooth"]."

Interestingly, the last time, they reached the agreement (on the Norwegian project) at the negotiation table, but could not get together at the dinner table. By contrast, this time, they did not reach any agreement (for the Danish project) at the negotiation table, but they could get together at the dinner table. At this moment, the Chinese began to recognize and accept NOR's sincerity. Rapport and trust were beginning to be built. This was a welcome sign for the future cooperation between C and NOR.

Adaptation 3: The Chinese shipyard C chose to use NOR's classification standard and did not bargain over the price at all, even though it was likely to be lowered considerably.

Now, the Chinese shipyard C was going to sign the shipbuilding contract with the Swedish ship owner S. Mr. Q recalled how he decided to let NOR do this business in their third encounter. He said:

"Then the new building project for the Swedish ship owner started. First, this was a sister ship to the Norwegian vessel. Second, I did not want to go too far. If I insisted on the wording 'LL, NOR, or the equivalent' [but finally chose LL], I believed the Swedish ship owner would 100% agree with me. But, I did not act in this way. Before I went to visit Sweden, I phoned NOR. It was that Shanghainese who answered the phone. I said I was going to Sweden to sign the contract. The vessel was of the 8,300 DWT type [the Norwegian vessel type]. My feeling was to use NOR, not LL, this time. Because this was about a sister vessel. 'Would you please consider giving me an offer to increase my confidence in making this decision?' I asked. He understood my meaning immediately... I was to leave for Sweden in a week. I hoped to receive their fax before my departure. I told him that LL had contacted me a number of times. But I had not said OK yet. This time, I might also put LL on it [the specification] but I thought

I would use NOR anyway. Taking revenge should not go too far. Once you have let him know your strength, you should try to get along with him. What I tended to employ was *en wei bin shi* ["Apply the carrot and stick judiciously"], or in other words, [the tactic of] using the carrot plus the stick. One must never chase one's opponent to nowhere."

He continued:

"I received the offer from NOR before my departure: USD 180,000. I believed I could further reduce the price to the USD 160,000 level. A normal situation would allow a 60% discount for sister vessels. But if various kinds of costs were included, USD 120,000 for the second vessel would be reasonable. But consider this time, the ship owner was new, although the vessel was of the same type. So, the ship owner might regard the vessel as a new vessel anyway. That's why I said USD 160,000 would work. But I did not haggle over the price with NOR. I knew that if I used LL, the price would certainly be around USD 210,000, because this was a new vessel for LL. LL had to examine and approve all the drawings from the beginning. So, my method was to give you a *mianzi* and make you feel comfortable. I knew I couldn't give this business to LL anyway, and I did beat you too hard the last time. I must let you be comfortable in order to thaw our relationship. The bottom line was your Norwegian vessel was being built in our shipyard; if you really became too upset and made trouble for the shipyard in the supervision process, we would have an even harder time. So, whatever style was adopted, *en* ["carrot"] or *wei* ["stick"], the purpose was *he wei gui* ["peace and harmony"]. This was my ultimate purpose."

Finally, the dinner was arranged and the contract was signed between C and NOR in a harmonious atmosphere. The parties have since had a very good business relationship. Mr. Q said: "After I came back from Sweden, the NOR general manager and the Shanghainese invited me out to dinner to welcome me back. I informed them of the changes that would be made on the vessel, etc. The previous [Norwegian] contract could be used almost at once after the change of price to USD 180,000. 'OK,' I said, 'I will not counter your price. I believe I can lower your price by USD 20,000–30,000, but I won't do that. What I have wanted to do is to let you understand how to deal with the Chinese. What is the most important is *guanxi* ["relationship"], *xianghu zunzhong* ["mutual respect"], and *xianghu peihe* ["mutual collaboration"].' Finally, the contract was signed at the NOR Shanghai office. Our very good relationship has been maintained to date."

In: New Emerging Economies and Their Culture
Editors: J. Prašnikar, A. Cirman, pp. 307-318

ISBN: 978-1-60021-754-8
© 2007 Nova Science Publishers, Inc.

Chapter 20

CHINESE NEGOTIATING STYLE: SLOVENIAN MANAGERS' PERSPECTIVE

Aleksander Kuljaj and Maja Makovec Brenčič

INTRODUCTION

With a population of more than 1.3 billion people, China is a country that has been undergoing a major transformation in the last three decades and experiencing one of the highest average economic growth rates in the world – above 8% a year. Chinese companies and the Chinese economy as a whole are becoming increasingly more important, if not the most important player in world trade. This fact is being felt by the vast majority of industries and companies around the world on a daily basis, especially through enormous direct and indirect competitive pressure. Slovenian companies that are internationally active also face this growing intensity of Chinese competition. These facts strongly motivate us to analyze all possibilities of entering this enormous economically and culturally heterogeneous market.

The Chinese market still poses a mystery to the outside observer. Its geographical and cultural distance on one hand and its various resource availability on the other constantly amaze its European challengers. For this reason, doing business in the Chinese market demands thorough preparations and studies of the market's characteristics and particularities. In addition, certain special knowledge and approaches to Chinese business negotiations are needed and presented in this chapter.

International negotiations are significantly more complex than negotiations occurring within just one cultural framework and demand a more detailed analysis. When we add to this usually very low familiarity with the Chinese cultural characteristics that represent the backbone of the negotiating style and above all the views of Chinese negotiators, we can easily state that preparations for such negotiations are both extremely important and demanding. Therefore, the research's fundamental goal was to present the most important characteristics of the Chinese negotiating style from the points of view of major world researchers in the field and of Slovenian negotiators with experience in this interesting market.

RESEARCH ON THE CHINESE NEGOTIATING STYLE

Methodology and Research Framework

Secondary research into existing theoretical sources and a qualitative empirical part, carried out at the end of 2004 and consisting of four in-depth interviews with Slovenian managers from selected Slovenian companies, represent the methodological and research framework. We selected globally focused companies with substantial experience in negotiating with Chinese businesspeople. The in-depth interviews were based on a comprehensive questionnaire that had three parts: the Chinese negotiating framework; preparations and negotiations between Chinese and Slovenian businesspeople; and Slovenian companies in China. Questions were based on tested findings on negotiating styles and cultural characteristics from world literature (Gesteland, 2002; Hampden-Turner and Trompenaars, 2002; Hofstede, 2001; Fang, 1999; Solomon, 1985; Woo and Prud'homme 1999; Buttery and Wong, 1999 etc.) as well as on interviews with the former Yugoslavia's senior councilor for China, Vinko Trček.

All companies included in the research are active in inter-organizational markets, namely in the production of electrical equipment and components for the automotive industry, the production of electronics and the food-processing industry. Two businesspeople came from large companies (more than 1,000 employees) and the other two came from medium-sized companies (from 50 to 250 employees). All four companies are strongly export-oriented as exports represent at least 70% of their sales (from 70% to 98%). The participants from these companies occupy the following positions:

- 2 participants are regional sales managers
- 1 participant is a member of the board
- 1 participant is a company president

All the participants have experience, mainly in sales negotiations.

Fundamental Characteristics of the Chinese Negotiating Style

The Chinese negotiating style is not unique in itself. However, it encompasses a series of very specific elements that together form a distinct style that demands a thorough knowledge of its particularities (Solomon, 1999). The negotiating process in China takes place within a very specific framework. The most recognizable characteristic of this framework is unquestionably the tendency to building close interpersonal, even friendly, relations – "guanxi" (Solomon, 1985; Woo and Prud'homme, 1999; Buttery and Wong, 1999).

"Guanxi". We can explain "guanxi" as "connections and acquaintances", also well known in Slovenia. In China, this concept is even richer due to its presence in all spheres of everyday life as a typical Chinese cultural element. A series of business and negotiating processes is usually ineffective without appropriate connections and approaches (also information and guidance) (Seligman, 1999; Fang, 1999). For this reason, the divide between being inside and outside of the group is very strong in China, where society is based on

membership in selected (often exclusive) groups. The key reason for such an organization of society is the utmost importance of the family as a fundamental constituent of society. In the traditional family, in a narrower and wider sense, its members are always obliged to help each other (Fang, 1999). The next most significant cause of the importance of within-group connectivity and interpersonal connections lies in the weakness and rigidity of the legal system. The security needed for doing business is therefore formed on the basis of interpersonal connections and trust (Blackman, 1997) within and between the mentioned groups. Experts believe "guanxi" will gradually lose its importance as a condition for doing business mostly due to the growing economic liberalization, the strengthening rule of law and coming of a younger generation of managers (Arias, 1998).

The research participants confirmed the importance of "guanxi" for doing successful business in China. They quickly accepted this fact and adapted their approach accordingly. Each mentioned at least one such experience, for example: "At the beginning we had several problems with customs officials. These problems were quickly solved because our partners had "connections" there". Or: "Our partner is a true local man of importance because his father is an important director and member of Parliament. When we are accompanied by him, everybody bows before us." A third participant summed up his views as follows: "In every business it helps to know people who can advise and help you, especially in China, as you come there with little or no knowledge. It is important to have somebody to help you and open the relevant doors for you." A fourth participant similarly stated that, at least in sales negotiations, you need several meetings in order to enter the "guanxi" circle. He is certain that doing business in China is really difficult if not impossible without entering such a circle.

"Mianzi". This concept holds utmost importance in China. It relates to a person's reputation and the respect they enjoy from others. In the West we appreciate honesty and see freedom of expression as one of the basic values. The Chinese tradition is appreciably different in this regard. In this part of the world cautiousness in presenting personal opinions plays an important role, especially when criticizing someone. Children are taught to be obedient. The Chinese are very sensitive to words expressed publicly and highly appreciate comments of praise. "Mianzi" can quickly become an element of negotiations as Chinese negotiators often do not openly discuss sensitive topics. Such an approach can often lead to many misunderstandings. Good Western negotiators therefore know that problems during negotiations often arise on account of saving face and use this knowledge to suggest appropriate solutions to the opposite side (Blackman, 1997).

Chinese negotiators often avoid admitting that something cannot be done or fulfilled. For this reason they tend to confirm that the situation is under control, even when this is not the case. During and after negotiations Western negotiators need to make sure several times whether both sides have agreed to the same thing. One participant told us: "We have noticed several times that Chinese negotiators did not understand what was said but still answered our question with YES. For this reason, you always need to check whether your Chinese colleague really understood your message or was he just trying to be polite by nodding. When they say YES it does not mean much." This is the reason why firm control during the negotiations (and also later during such business activities as control over employees) is essential for doing successful business in China.

Protocol. Elements of protocol are of course not only limited to the initial phase of business interaction. However, they are probably most important exactly in that phase. The pre-negotiation phase is the most appropriate for building trust, without which it is really difficult to reach any agreement. This phase has a strong influence on the course and atmosphere of the negotiating process. The Chinese ascribe great importance to status and cultivate a high respect for hierarchy. Banquets hold a special place when doing business in China. They present an opportunity for strengthening friendly relations in an informal environment.

The three participants who already had a chance to participate in such an event asserted that sociability, bolstering of friendly relations and making acquaintances are the main purposes of these events. All these elements have an indirect yet strong influence on business relations and negotiations. Business talks might sometimes come up at such informal events but they are actually quite rare and, as a rule, very general with no precise agreements or business deals taking place. Many people gather on such occasions, usually the partner's bankers and other friends and acquaintances are also present. One of the research participants mentioned: "It has happened that I did not have time to attend such a banquet. The partners were very offended." In China, businesspeople often spend a lot of time at such events, which can sometimes last well into the night.

The Chinese Negotiating Process or the "Seven Commandments"

The in-depth interviews revealed both positive and negative experiences of our participants when negotiating with their Chinese colleagues. They were positively surprised mainly by the Chinese openness to foreigners, light discussions, being straightforward and direct. They also noted an avoidance of complications, a business-friendly environment, willingness to work hard, and simple and fast procedures for acquiring documents in special economic zones. Officials in special economic zones guide foreign businesspeople through the whole procedure because strong competition for foreign investment exists between different regions. One participant asserted that foreign companies can receive all the licenses needed for a business activity within one month. Yet it takes three months for a permit to export to China.

Agreement uncertainty definitely lies at the forefront of our participants' negative perceptions. Foreign businesspeople are often really puzzled whether they have reached an agreement with their Chinese colleagues or not. Other negative elements are: poor English language skills (even among higher management), impossible demands (regarding delivery dates etc.), the inability to trust Chinese co-workers and employees and, finally, doing business almost exclusively through connections.

The role of translators. Selection of a good interpreter is clearly one of the key decisions for doing successful business in China. All our participants use translators in China because they realize that English language skills are on average very poor, even among the top management of Chinese companies and other organizations. Differences start to emerge on the question of which translators companies should engage – Slovenian or Chinese. In addition, there is the question of whether to use your own translator or perhaps the translator of the opposite side. Most of the participants agreed it is best to use your own translator. The first participant said his company had hired a representative office manager in China who speaks Chinese and is learning more and more about the Chinese culture as well as about the nature of their business. The second respondent's company has a representative from Hong Kong who helps them during negotiations in China. This company also employed a translator with Slovenian origins, who is of great help to the president of their company in China. The third company seeks help during negotiations from their consultant who has his own company with some well-educated Chinese employees (who studied in London). "He is extremely communicative and he helped create twenty-five joint ventures with German companies seeking co-operation in China. When I checked four of them they told me there is no better person for doing business in China with than him." The fourth respondent previously mostly relied on translators from the opposite side. Lately, he has been using his own translators as well (hired in China). He explained that Slovenians with knowledge of the Chinese language are welcome, however, he believes Chinese translators are more efficient due to their language skills and greater familiarity with Chinese culture and habits. Mr. Trček (Interview, 2004) suggested learning at least a couple of basic phrases in Chinese, which is highly appreciated by the Chinese and can have an important influence on building a positive atmosphere during the negotiations.

Corruption. In a study on corruption (2002) Transparency International ranked China in 59th place among 102 countries (Backman and Butler, 2003). Cases of corruption are becoming increasingly common in China as ever more officials become tempted to earn something "on the side". The worsening problem of corruption is understandable as officials' salaries are very low, especially compared to the salaries of foreigners, Chinese who work abroad and even domestic entrepreneurs and company managers. Despite serious penalties or even the death penalty in extreme cases, corruption remains one of the major barriers to free trade and investment (Wright, Szeto and Lee, 2003). All participants are certain that corruption in one form or another exists in China. However, they disagree about its intensity. Two participants are sure that corruption exists in China but have not experienced it directly. The third respondent believes one can do business without turning to any traditional bribing in China. On the other hand, he acknowledged the need for some alternative approaches such as dinner invitations, various gifts etc. He adds: "Such services can be indirect – for example, one director has a niece who is learning English and he expects you to help in all sorts of ways, perhaps with some English courses abroad, etc." The fourth, quite experienced respondent, mentioned that one always needs to offer something in the phase of sales negotiations, if nothing else, at least one new acquaintance the partners can use later.

The stated answers are in line with the many evaluated cases of corruption in the literature (Lee, 1996; Gesteland, 2002) and with the opinion of Mr. Trček (Interview, 2004) that corruption is a real problem in China.

Initial lack of trust of foreigners. Only one participant told us that their partner trusted them from the beginning and still trusts them today. He added that he can probably attribute this high level of trust to the important influence of their Chinese consultant. All other participants believe that the Chinese are quite mistrustful when doing business or negotiating with foreigners. "The Chinese treat foreign negotiators with gloves. It is hard to get close to them because they have two faces – one never exactly knows what are they thinking. What you agree on today might not be relevant any more the next day." Or: "I would say they are mistrustful simply because we come from Europe. We need to understand that they are used to doing business locally. Above all, they focus on prices. Quality does not concern them much."

The respondents mentioned quite a few things about the initial Chinese mistrust of foreign negotiators that we can also find in the literature. Blackman (1997) mentioned the belief of many Chinese businesspeople that foreign negotiators simply wish to take advantage of them. She listed numerous historical reasons for such a belief, from Great Britain's attacks and the consequential opium wars to communistic anti-Western propaganda after the Second World War. Seligman (1999) also found that the Chinese do not like to do business with foreigners and he therefore recommended communication through a middleman, which can help build initial trust between both parties.

Box 1

Personal Credibility Is Important

Mr. Trček (Interview, 2004) has a very interesting opinion on this topic. His views are in complete accordance with Fang's thesis (1999) about the latent characteristics of the Chinese negotiating style. Fang believes that the influence of the previously discussed individual latent elements depends on the level of trust created between both negotiating sides. The Chinese negotiating style can be so complex and unpredictable exactly for this reason.

"Regarding Chinese negotiators we can talk about the so-called latent characteristics, which means that a foreign negotiator is able to bring some of these to the forefront while putting others to the back with the right argumentation and with the appropriate directing of the discussion. This finding is based on my own observations of the initial Chinese mistrust of foreigners. The more a foreign businessman is able to come close to their way of thinking, the more they will trust him and relate to him. This is not about plain flattering and empty phrases, it is about an honest manifestation of desire to come to a mutually acceptable agreement. The Chinese can rapidly distinguish between honesty and opportunistic flattering. Further, they might quickly start to underestimate their partner when he is unable to develop the conversation and adapt to certain views. The Chinese are well known for developing a high level of trust in their partner after he manages to win their affection. The process that leads to this phase is usually intellectually very demanding for foreign negotiators. It is interesting that once this connection exists it stays in their memory for a very long time and might come to the surface in certain encounters even years later. This means that it is critical to create some sort of personal credibility during discussions with Chinese partners. Personal credibility is on average more important and longer lasting in China than it is for most other cultures. During the whole period of their existence the Chinese were a very isolated civilization. For this reason, they highly appreciate a person who is able to demonstrate a knowledge of the basic characteristics of Chinese history and culture and who shows some interest, for example with a couple of Chinese phrases" (Trček, Interview, 2004).

Chinese negotiating strategies. The choice of negotiating strategy depends on several factors that extend beyond the cultural element itself, so this choice is complex. Our participants had no difficulties assessing the type of strategy used by their Chinese counterparts. Two of them believe the Chinese tend to use a "win-lose" negotiation strategy, while another two are certain that the Chinese are well aware of the importance of long-term co-operation and are therefore closer to a "win-win" strategy. One of the former participants explains: "Clearly they are focused on winning so the real question is whether you will win as well." The second participant said: "The Chinese negotiators do not only have their goals in mind. They see cooperation as a long-term process." This statement is in line with the long-term orientation of Chinese culture described by Hofstede (2001). All participants warned us about the well-known technology-copying problem in China. This fact needs to be taken into consideration already during the strategy developing phase. "It would be difficult to operate in China without our representatives. The existence of certain protection from such copying is crucial in China," said one participant. "Usually, they perceive us as rich foreigners so they wish to gain something from this. In my specific case I believe they wanted to help us since we were the first company from Eastern Europe in their region. It is good for their image to have another flag hanging there. I do not agree that they want to win the negotiations at any cost," continued another respondent.

The responses of our participants clearly show that negotiations in China are far from simple. We ran into two opposing theories in connection with the Chinese negotiating strategy. The first is that the Chinese tend to use a "win-lose" negotiating strategy. The second one asserts that they perceive negotiations more as long-term cooperation and are therefore using a "win-win" strategy. Which theory is closer to the truth? Obviously both of them have some validity. One possible explanation of this interesting issue is Fang's (1999) perception of the Chinese negotiating style as a blend of three different influences – the People's Republic of China, Confucianism and Chinese (battle) stratagems. The prevailing influence is dependent on the level of trust between the negotiators. This leads us to believe that the choice of strategy on the Chinese side also depends on the approach and conduct of the foreign negotiators.

Chinese negotiating tactics. We asked our research participants to further assess, on a scale from 1 (never) to 5 (very often), how often different negotiating tactics (Table 20.1) were used in interactions with their Chinese partners.

Table 20.1. Assessing Negotiating Tactics Used by Chinese Negotiators from the Slovenian Managers' Perspective

1. Our guest always speaks first	2. Repeating demands and "generosity" manifestations
3. Using friendship for one's own ends	4. High initial demands
5. Influences for losing control over negotiations	6. Insulting
7. Taking advantage of mistakes of the opposite side	8. Tactics of irrelevant demands
9. Lying and deceiving	10. Minimum point seeking
11. Threatening	12. Insisting on a fixed position
13. Simultaneous negotiations with several companies	14. Price focus
15. Good guy – bad guy	16. Shaming
17. Hiding of feelings and emotions	18. Time-pressure tactics
19. Additional demands after agreement reached	20. Market for technology trading

Sources: Solomon, 1999; Pye, 1992; Blackman, 1997; Seligman, 1999; Fang, 1999; Backman and Butler, 2003.

Our analysis shows that during negotiations with their Slovenian counterparts Chinese negotiators most often use "market for technology" tactics, followed by "price focus", "hiding of feelings and emotions" and "high initial demands". We need to mention that the participants were quite in agreement here as there were no substantial deviations between the answers. We can classify these tactics as semi-intense tactics, which means that they appertain to a distributive strategy framework, but not to an extreme distributive approach, which indicates an acceptance of compromise and cooperation.

The participants assessed that the tactic least used by their Chinese colleagues was "insulting", followed by "threatening", "shaming" and "our guest always speaks first". Based on these evaluations we can describe the Chinese negotiators' approach as "moderately distributive". However, we need a more in-depth analysis to make any other conclusions and a larger sample. Most authors have found that the fundamental strategy of Chinese negotiators is most often distributive in connection with a "win-lose" approach (Pye, 1992; Blackman, 1997), which is more or less in line with our findings due to the relatively high number of tactics used by Chinese negotiators as seen by Slovenian managers.

Copying technology and sharing information. Choices about the appropriate level of information sharing with the opposite side are important in any negotiation – in China, they are crucial for all companies active in interorganizational markets due to the high danger of technology being copied. Three participants told us that they carefully select the appropriate information and transmit this in the most general form possible.

Every company makes its selection of information in a special way. "We prepared ourselves well in advance. For example, we presented only drawings of our products with no dimensions or other details," explained one participant. The second told us: "The production manager of our joint venture will of course be familiar with technologies to a certain extent but he will not know all the important details."

This part of our research fully coincides with the findings of other researchers (Pye, 1992; Blackman, 1997). Answers from the participants show that Slovenian companies are well aware of the danger of technology copying and also have well-prepared plans regarding the selection of relevant products and technology information they can transmit to their Chinese partners. Such dilemmas take place every day as companies are constantly under pressure to attract new projects while trying to keep their know-how well concealed. One participant mentioned that the motivation for copying by his competitors has somewhat decreased since his company has offered their products in the Chinese market at lower prices.

Additional "post-negotiations" after the contract has been signed. Our participants told us that one should always expect additional negotiations or at least some explanations after the agreement has already been made or signed. One of them explains: "The biggest problem I see is when you agree with them on something and they simply do not respect it afterwards. For example, we ordered our partner to employ additional three engineers with good English language skills. After three months the situation was exactly the same as before. The Chinese prefer to work at the lowest possible costs but do not understand that quality can suffer because of this. You need to know that an engineer already costs quite a lot of money in China. The more you move towards the West, the harder it is to find someone who speaks English. In Shanghai you can find them easily but you had better prepare 2,000 to 3,000 dollars."

These answers are in line with the findings from other sources, which also report on the high frequency of additional negotiations being needed after an agreement has been signed (Blackman, 1997; Solomon, 1999). For the Chinese, signing a contract does not mean that the negotiations are over. In their eyes, it simply represents a more solid commitment to continuation of the business relationship. Their negotiators repeat throughout the negotiations that agreements are based on friendship and mutual goodwill, which diminishes the importance of the formal contract (Buttery and Leung, 1998; Pye, 1992). From the answers of our participants we may conclude that comprehension between both sides still represents a key difficulty during negotiations in China. Often one side simply does not understand the other. The solution only lies in more thorough illustrations and frequent verifications of the agreements made. We can therefore conclude that demands for additional talks after the agreement has been signed are one of the more important characteristics of the Chinese negotiating style.

Negotiators have two options when misunderstandings or even disputes arise. They can either try to clarify the issue among themselves or try to settle the dispute in court or through arbitration. The participants were unanimous that foreign businesspeople should avoid going to court in China at any cost. There are mixed reasons for such views. One participant explained: "Our lawyers are certain it makes no sense to try to seek justice in Chinese courts. That is because the Chinese government protects their producers and they also expect a similar "treatment" before the courts. I believe the state also helps them with different subsidies, otherwise they could not maintain such low prices on European markets." The second participant adds: "Chinese courts are not unbiased so the only solution is additional negotiation despite new demands for concessions. In this way we can still achieve better results than we would in court."

The respondent's answers were again completely in line with the findings of other sources (Blackman, 1997). The Chinese do not rely strongly on laws, above all due to the historical Confucian aversion to the legal system and laws (Fang, 1999). The assumption of one participant that even Chinese negotiators are themselves not too fond of court litigation is therefore quite accurate.

Research Contributions and its Evaluations

It is important to know that the findings of this research can also be found when researching negotiating styles in world literature. This assigns a positive meaning and a confirmation of the appropriateness of the research framework, together with the content directions of the research among Slovenian managers and it allows for a high rate of comparability with findings of earlier researches conducted by foreign authors. Here we must mention that other sources (Gesteland, 2002; Fang, 1999) stress some other characteristics of the Chinese negotiating style, to which no particular importance was ascribed by the Slovenian managers. One of these characteristics or particularities is the choice of place for negotiations. Some researches indicate the desire of Chinese negotiators to negotiate in their home country or company. Some Chinese authors explain that it is of course less complicated for domestic negotiators to have negotiations in China than abroad. However, traveling abroad is still quite exceptional and therefore very appreciated by Chinese businesspeople. Another such characteristic would be insisting on an agreement on general principles before moving to any concrete discussions. Our research participants did not experience such demands at all and asserted their Chinese colleagues are very concrete in their demands. The third characteristic not confirmed by our research is the size of Chinese negotiating teams and inscrutability of their members. Our participants said the Chinese side usually counted even fewer negotiators than their own, sometimes there was only one negotiator on the other side.

The stated unidentified or even contrary characteristics could result from the limitations of our research. On the other hand, this could also be the result of some stereotypical views of certain authors on the particularities of the Chinese negotiating style. It is a fact that modern China distinguishes itself from the China of a decade or two ago. Any deviation from the established and verified characteristics could result from the intensified globalization of the Chinese market.

Besides the mentioned discrepancies our research indicates some important common characteristics about Slovenian managers entering this market. We may conclude that Slovenian managers devote an insufficient amount of effort and time to negotiation preparations, although at the same time they realize that such preparations "are very important and can, together with ignorance of business customs, lead to a serious negotiation failure" (!). Our research clearly shows that the majority of Slovenian companies and their negotiators did not acquire the necessary knowledge of the Chinese market and negotiating style of its businesspeople before they set out to the "Central Kingdom". According to our participants the "lack of time" is supposed to be the main reason for this.

In addition, our research shows that our companies could act significantly quicker in the event of any complications with their partners in China if their managers were sufficiently prepared for such potential and frequent dangers. Among the more important findings we also need to mention the fact that all the participants have used an integrative (win-win) approach to the negotiations, something they believe is the only sensible approach to be used in successful negotiations in China.

Research Limitations

The research reveals some interesting results, especially the high rate of comparability between the findings of researchers on this topic in the world and in Slovenia. But we cannot treat the research results as being significant due to the limited number of participants (n = 4). For this reason any generalization could be dangerous. Notwithstanding, our participants established some important guidelines and significantly contributed to those entering this interesting market. This is why we can regard the results as providing solid foundations for further research including a larger group of participants. In addition, we can use the presented research framework as a verified framework for future research steps.

The next important research limitation is the selection of companies. We selected companies that were prepared to cooperate with us and have sufficient experience in dealing with their Chinese partners. As these companies are, without exception, only active in business-to-business markets, it would also be interesting to include some classical trading companies (e.g. sales agents) and other companies in Slovenian ownership or co-ownership that are already active in the Chinese market (final goods, production, sales units etc.). It would also be sensible to gather experience from Slovenian companies that have purchasing (and not only selling) experiences in China. Further, it would be reasonable to search for potential particularities of individual industries and sectors (services, etc.).

DOES CHINA (STILL) REPRESENT AN OPPORTUNITY FOR SLOVENIAN COMPANIES?

The Chinese market definitely still offers business opportunities as do all other world markets. This holds not only for the production of products and services but also for purchasing and other classical trading processes. Until now, the Chinese market was mainly entered by those Slovenian companies (mostly industrial) that followed their buyers that have moved some of their production to China. This fact has forced our companies to seriously think about their entering possibilities and entry modes. We cannot be sure if Slovenian companies would enter this enormous market without such huge pressure from their buyers and competitors. On the whole, we can assert that so far Slovenian companies have been quite shy about entering the Chinese market. There are plenty reasons for this. The research participants have above all pointed to the unsatisfactory administrative/governmental help, which is sometimes even seen as an impediment to our companies, particularly with the slow issuing of visas and inadequate awareness of all the opportunities of cooperating with China. Companies cannot rely (with the exception of the Slovenian Chamber of Commerce and Industry, based on the opinion of the participants) on the Slovenian government regarding the provision of important information and more detailed advice in connection with the Chinese market and are therefore left on their own.

Nevertheless, this deficiency cannot be the main reason for the "business bashfulness" of Slovenian companies – regardless of the target market. Our research indirectly indicates that a large part of the Slovenian economy lacks a global orientation and managerial proactive behavior. Amongst other key reasons for the weak presence of Slovenian companies in China we can point to poor knowledge about the country and its market by Slovenian managers who are, for this reason, incapable of assessing the present importance and potential of this market and its future opportunities for global business layers.

Also strongly present, no matter how unfounded, is the fear of the greatness and distance of markets like China and the costs related to this distance. The language barrier and poor knowledge of English by Chinese managers poses a special difficulty. However, this could be overcome by greater familiarity with the Chinese culture, hiring capable translators or even by learning Chinese.

We can therefore conclude that thorough knowledge of the market and its characteristics, systematic market research and a highly proactive approach are the most important preconditions for successful and efficient global activities of Slovenian companies. To decide on a new market entrance each company needs not only financial resources, technological and sales know-how but also more and more knowledge and information about market characteristics, among which the cultural component occupies a very important position. This component especially defines the processes of international business and negotiations. Due to geographical distance and other reasons this component is particularly relevant in China, which we have shown with our research into the Chinese negotiating style. Despite this awareness, Slovenian companies do not devote enough time and resources to acquiring such market knowledge. Due to a "lack of time" companies are not proactive enough. This is one reason for Slovenian companies' low level of boldly entering new "unusual" or "exotic" markets and their attainment of a relatively low global orientation.

REFERENCES

Arias, J. T. G. 1998. "A Relationship Marketing Approach To Guanxi." *European Journal of Marketing*: 145−156.

Backman, M., and Butler, C. 2003. *"Big in Asia - 25 Strategies for Business Success."* Hampshire: Palgrave Macmillan.

Blackman, C. 1997. *"Negotiating China."* Crows Nest: Allen and Unwin.

Buttery, E. A., and Leung, T. K. P. 1998. "The Difference Between Chinese and Western Negotiations." *European Journal of Marketing*: 374−389.

Buttery, E. A., and Wong, Y. H. 1999. "The Development of a Guanxi Framework." *Marketing Intelligence and Planning* 3: 147−154.

Fang, T. 1999. *"Chinese Business Negotiating Style."* Thousand Oaks: Sage.

Gesteland, R. R. 2002. "Cross-Cultural Business Behavior." Copenhagen: Copenhagen Business School Press.

Hampden-Turner, M. C. 2002. "Trompenaars Fons: Building Cross-Cultural Competence." Chichester: John Wiley and Sons.

Hofstede, G. 2001. "Culture's Consequences." Thousand Oaks: Sage Publications.

Interview with Mr. Vinko Trček. Sinologue. Ljubljana, September 25, 2004.

Interviews with selected Slovenian managers. 2004.

Lee, Kam-hon. 1996. "Moral Consideration and Strategic Management Moves: The Chinese Case." *Management Decision* 9: 65−70.

Lewicki, J. R., et al. 1994. "Negotiation." Burr Ridge: Richard D. Irwin.

Moise, E. E. 1994. "Modern China: A History." London: Longman.

Pye, W. L. 1992. "Chinese Negotiating Style." Westport: Quorum Books.

Rošker, J. 1992. "Zmajeva hiša: Oris kitajske kulture in civilizacije." Ljubljana: Cankarjeva založba.

Seligman, D. S. 1999. "Chinese Business Etiquette." New York: Warner Books.

Solomon, H. R. 1985. "Chinese Political Negotiating Behavior – A Briefing Analysis." Santa Monica: Rand Corporation.

Solomon, H. R. 1999. "Chinese Negotiating Behavior." Washington, D.C.: United States Institute of Peace Press.

Sun-Tzu. "Art of War." [URL: http://www.chinapage.com/sunzi-e.html].

Woo, H. S., and Prud'homme, C. 1999. "Cultural Characteristics Prevalent in the Chinese Negotiation Process." *European Business Review* 5: 313−322.

Wright, P. C., Szeto, W. F., and Lee, S. K. 2003. "Ethical Perceptions in China: The Reality of Business Ethics in an International Context." *Management Decision* 2: 180−189.

INDEX

H

Q

R

stereotypes, 241

stimulus, 272

stock, 6, 31, 109, 110, 128, 133, 137, 211, 231, 233, 238, 252

storage, 255

strain, 212

strategic management, 67

strategic planning, 62, 69

strategies, 7, 9, 15, 18, 26, 27, 31, 34, 46, 51, 53, 66, 69, 101, 147, 152, 162, 165, 196, 209, 224, 242, 255, 291, 295, 296, 312

strategy use, 312

stratification, 39

strength, 12, 132, 155, 156, 157, 158, 160, 161, 162, 163, 217, 224, 256, 284, 287, 288, 289, 306

stress, 9, 15, 80, 86, 167, 226, 236, 293, 315

strikes, 31

structural changes, 171

structural reforms, 14, 185, 188, 198, 235

structuring, 69

students, xi, 80, 88, 95, 174, 236, 243, 244, 246, 247, 250

subsidy, 41

substitutes, ix, 7, 34, 58, 156

substitution, 121, 123, 140

Sudan, 48

suffering, 133, 289

suicide, 52

summer, 149

Sun, 17, 287, 289, 290, 291, 297, 298, 318

superiority, 287

supernatural, 286

supervision, 61, 63, 64, 133, 260, 306

supervisors, 258, 299, 303

suppliers, 27, 51, 58, 142, 156, 157, 165, 167, 253, 295, 299

supply, ix, 4, 7, 8, 9, 23, 25, 26, 27, 28, 29, 30, 31, 32, 33, 34, 35, 51, 109, 163, 164, 165, 167, 185, 233, 279

supply chain, ix, 4, 7, 8, 9, 23, 25, 26, 27, 28, 29, 30, 31, 32, 33, 34, 35, 165, 233

suppression, 51

surplus, 233, 239

surprise, 288

surveillance, 12, 103, 115, 116

survival, 23, 26, 31

sustainability, 8, 14, 23, 31, 32, 33, 34, 43, 125, 184, 185, 253

sustainable development, 9, 18, 32

sustainable growth, 13, 17, 133, 207

Sweden, 82, 90, 109, 117, 162, 166, 247, 299, 305, 306

Switzerland, 90, 108, 110, 111, 162, 163, 250

symbols, 10, 59, 61, 74, 77, 149, 296

sympathy, 289

synergistic effect, 67, 216

systems, x, 11, 12, 24, 27, 29, 30, 34, 35, 46, 58, 69, 73, 75, 101, 102, 103, 104, 107, 108, 114, 116, 180, 202, 205, 213, 224, 242, 252, 255, 286, 296, 300

T

tactics, 17, 288, 289, 313, 314

Taiwan, 73, 77, 78, 81, 82, 276, 279

takeover, 96, 108, 109, 114, 115

talent, 20

tanks, 300

targets, 33, 101, 107, 113, 114, 116, 213

tariff, 202, 205

task performance, 158

tax collection, 198

tax evasion, 124

tax rates, 274

tax reform, 233

tax system, 197

taxation, 129

taxonomy, 12, 105

teachers, 80, 243, 244

team members, 264

technological advancement, 4

technological developments, 139

technological progress, 18, 279

technology, 4, 17, 18, 23, 25, 31, 33, 35, 59, 75, 125, 135, 140, 163, 214, 223, 224, 239, 249, 271, 274, 279, 285, 294, 299, 313, 314

technology transfer, 271

teenagers, 160

telecommunications, 276

television, 141, 145, 146, 147, 148, 149, 150

tension, 39, 42, 256

territory, 11, 85, 86, 196, 206

terrorism, 9, 31, 40, 41, 45, 46, 47, 48, 49, 52

terrorist acts, 52

terrorist groups, 52

terrorist organization, 52

textiles, 151, 276, 277, 279

Thailand, 73, 82, 278

theory, 25, 43, 67, 69, 115, 183, 243, 244, 249, 271, 313

thinking, 17, 18, 23, 24, 35, 46, 59, 61, 62, 80, 87, 222, 226, 287, 289, 311, 312

threat, 33, 101, 133, 156, 234, 253, 279

threats, 9, 13, 46, 47, 48, 53, 103, 132, 133, 162

time, ix, xi, 3, 15, 17, 18, 23, 24, 25, 28, 30, 33, 40, 42, 45, 47, 48, 50, 51, 57, 60, 62, 66, 69, 73, 75,

76, 78, 79, 80, 81, 85, 87, 92, 93, 94, 95, 96, 97,
98, 102, 109, 121, 123, 124, 127, 132, 133, 140,
146, 147, 158, 162, 167, 168, 172, 183, 185, 188,
202, 205, 210, 212, 213, 215, 216, 217, 218, 219,
224, 226, 231, 242, 243, 244, 246, 247, 248, 249,
256, 261, 265, 271, 274, 279, 284, 291, 295, 296,
299, 301, 302, 303, 304, 305, 306, 310, 312, 316,
317
timing, 189, 253
tobacco, 142, 143
top management, 35, 94, 98, 102, 218, 255, 310
torture, 52, 289
total factor productivity, 17
total revenue, 159, 160, 161, 252, 276
tourism, 136, 184
Toyota, 27
trade, ix, 4, 5, 6, 9, 16, 18, 33, 34, 125, 132, 133,
160, 172, 173, 183, 184, 185, 196, 199, 202, 203,
204, 205, 206, 213, 233, 271, 272, 273, 276, 277,
279, 280, 292, 307, 311
trade agreement, 172, 202, 206, 213
trade deficit, 183, 184, 199
trade liberalization, 185, 202, 206
trade policy, 173, 204
trade-off, 33, 34
trading, 186, 204, 206, 213, 313, 316, 317
tradition, 17, 63, 78, 79, 80, 160, 286, 296, 309
training, 11, 12, 69, 74, 75, 76, 82, 83, 103, 104, 167,
214, 225, 252, 256, 257, 261
training programs, 256
traits, 115, 291, 296
trajectory, 273
transaction costs, 4, 26, 271
transactions, 29, 121, 165, 184
transformation, 8, 24, 125, 147, 180, 185, 221, 242,
249, 285, 307
transformations, 13
transition, 9, 15, 81, 97, 179, 180, 183, 184, 185,
186, 190, 195, 196, 197, 199, 201, 202, 204, 205,
206, 236, 241, 242, 246, 249, 264, 272, 273, 275,
280
transition countries, 9, 205
transition economies, 183, 185, 199, 201, 206, 272,
273, 275, 280
transition period, 15, 81, 246
transitional countries, 11, 14, 85, 89, 181
transitional economies, 224
translation, 224, 305
transmission, 224
transmits, 149
transparency, 12, 30, 127, 129
transport, 4, 165, 271, 272, 276
transport costs, 272

transportation, 4, 32, 124, 142, 214
treaties, 41, 52
trend, 4, 7, 39, 40, 46, 114, 124, 127, 128, 132, 182,
198, 206, 209, 245, 249, 274, 291
trial, 52
tribes, 148
triggers, 3
Trimo Trebnje, vi, 16, 20, 21, 251, 258, 259, 260,
261, 262, 264, 265, 266, 267
trust, xi, 12, 18, 78, 81, 101, 116, 174, 192, 242, 245,
248, 261, 283, 286, 287, 290, 291, 294, 295, 296,
305, 309, 310, 311, 312, 313
Turkey, vi, ix, 9, 11, 12, 13, 83, 88, 90, 119, 121,
122, 123, 124, 126, 127, 132, 133, 134, 137, 139,
140, 141, 142, 143, 144, 146, 147, 150, 151, 152,
153, 160, 163, 171, 172, 173, 174, 175, 189, 190,
191, 196, 272, 273, 277, 282
turnover, 132, 211, 254

U

UK, 42, 153, 163
Ukraine, 160, 213, 235, 236
UN, 9, 39, 41, 42, 46, 47, 48, 49, 50, 51, 53, 196,
263
uncertainty, 7, 10, 58, 60, 75, 79, 80, 81, 82, 87, 88,
105, 114, 156, 179, 209, 218, 244, 247, 248, 310
undergraduate, 89, 243
unemployment, 14, 15, 81, 122, 145, 181, 186, 199,
231, 236, 271, 280
unemployment rate, 14, 145, 199, 236
uniform, 3, 86, 149, 186, 251
United Nations, 21, 48, 49, 53, 204, 207, 236
United States, 9, 23, 32, 49, 272, 276, 277, 279, 280,
297, 318
universe, 284
urban areas, 142
urban population, 141, 142, 143, 145
urbanization, 124, 142
users, 242

V

validity, 313
values, 10, 11, 12, 15, 16, 52, 59, 60, 61, 62, 63, 64,
69, 73, 74, 75, 77, 79, 80, 81, 82, 85, 87, 88, 89,
90, 91, 92, 93, 94, 95, 101, 102, 103, 104, 106,
115, 139, 141, 149, 157, 158, 166, 167, 168, 170,
216, 217, 219, 221, 223, 224, 225, 241, 242, 243,
244, 246, 247, 249, 251, 252, 255, 256, 257, 258,
260, 261, 262, 264, 265, 285, 286, 291, 309
variable, 27, 103, 104, 108, 113